PENTAGON PRESS

COMMITTED TO SERVE THE ARMED FORCES

PERSIAN GULF 2016-17

India's Relations with the Region

PERSIAN GULF 2016-17

India's Relations with the Region

Editors

P. R. Kumaraswamy

and

Meena Singh Roy

PENTAGON PRESS

Persian Gulf 2016-17: India's Relations with the Region

P. R. Kumaraswamy and Meena Singh Roy (Eds.)

First Published in 2018

ISBN 978-93-86618-19-1

Published by

PENTAGON PRESS
206, Peacock Lane, Shahpur Jat
New Delhi-110049
Phones: 011-64706243, 26491568
Telefax: 011-26490600
email: rajan@pentagonpress.in
website: www.pentagonpress.in

In association with
Institute for Defence Studies and Analyses
No. 1, Development Enclave,
New Delhi-110010
Phone: +91-11-26717983
Website: www.idsa.in

Printed at Avantika Printers Private Limited.

To

K. Subramanyam

With deep respects

CONTENTS

LIST OF TABLES AND FIGURES

1

INTRODUCTION

Since the election of Narendra Modi as Prime Minister in May 2014, the ever turbulent Middle East, especially the Persian Gulf region, has been receiving considerable political, diplomatic, strategic, economic, and hence media attention in the country. Since the days of Prime Minister Jawaharlal Nehru, foreign policy has been the domain and prerogative of the Prime Minister, and Narendra Modi has added his personal touch to it. Through his active role, often accompanied by popular engagements with the overseas Indian communities loosely termed as the Indian diaspora, he has brought new focus to India's approach towards the hydrocarbon-rich Persian Gulf region. Rather than seeing the large Indian expatriate community merely as workers earning their livelihoods abroad, the Modi government looks at them as a socio-cultural bridge between the Indian homeland and offshore. An effective use of this strategy should enable India to tap and expand its economic relations with the outside world and, in the process, secure political influence. At the same time, the Gulf region is undergoing far reaching changes and transformation which would continue to affect the direction and contours of Indo-Gulf relations during 2015 and 2016, the focus of this volume. For example, the nuclear deal, which was the crowning moment for the eight-year long Obama presidency, also rattled many Arab capitals who felt let down despite their long and unflinching support for Washington.

Strategic Scenario

Since 2013, the religious extremist and xenophobic Islamic State, popularly known as Daesh in the Arab world and Islamic State of Iraq and Syria (ISIS) by the international community, has emerged as the major challenge to the already fragile political order in the Middle East.[1] Far from being an ideological fringe, it has transformed into a territorial entity, controlling vast swathes of area across Iraq and Syria where the central authorities have been under attack and unable to govern. Angered over the sudden marginalisation in the wake of the post-Saddam political order in Iraq, Sunni extremists as well as former Ba'athist sympathizers galvanized towards the call by Abu Musab al-Zarqawi, and this took a concrete shape in October 2006 in the form of Islamic State of Iraq and eventually led to Abu Bakr al-Baghdadi declaring the formation of Islamic Caliphate in June 2014.[2] Before long, this transformed into a political entity capable of shouldering some of the basic functions of state such as administrative control, levying of taxes, preparation of budget, education, and other welfare measures.[3]

In the past, state failures have resulted in the emergence of Islamist non-state actors in the region who began shouldering social welfare activities. The ISIS is different in two aspects. Though territorial, it does not respect the Westphalian notion of state boundaries but is committed to the traditional Islamic notion of *ummah*, a community of Muslim believers living under one political rule. More importantly, the ISIS is far more radical and extremist than some of the Islamist groups that have emerged since the mid-20th century. With the exception of the Taliban in Afghanistan, even though these groups also adopted an extremist position towards the West and the non-Muslim "other" (for example, Syed Qutb termed the West as "backward", "rubbish heap", "hollow and worthless", called Jews "evil" and Christians "deviant")[4], they did not 'control' a state or territories, and hence their harmful effects were limited.

However, the limited territorial control of the ISIS in Iraq and Syria, does not limit its wider regional and international appeal. According to Hussein Solomon, in some form or another, the ISIS is present and active in as many as 17 countries in the Middle East, Europe, Asia, and Africa.[5] If one includes sympathizers of the cause espoused by the group, an estimated 80,000 persons, mostly youth, can be identified as its members. Since 2014, ISIS or its affiliates have claimed responsibility for a number of terror attacks in Belgium, Britain, France, Germany, Turkey, Saudi Arabia, Afghanistan, etc.

Writing within the Jordanian context, one study has observed that:

> ...many Jordanian fighters come from middle-class backgrounds. In 2013, a Jordanian Air Force captain from a well-known family defected to join [the] Nusra Front; he was later killed fighting for the Islamic

> State. Last fall, a Member of Parliament's son was killed driving an IS car bomb. Finally, ground zero for Salafist-jihadi recruitment is no longer the impoverished southern town of Ma'an, but instead northern cities like Irbid and Salt. These more modernized cities barely resemble the tribal backwaters assumed to embrace extremist ideologies. Their youths targeted by Salafist-jihadi recruiters often have private-sector jobs and have seldom faced real destitution.

However, these youths share something else in common—a sense of *desperation* permeating their lives. They have lost faith in the government's ability to fix the economy, provide services, and induce pride in citizenship. Their turn to religion is a deliberate one, motivated by a desire to find meaning and purpose. This is the resounding theme in interviews with jailed IS affiliates and other radical Islamists in Jordanian prisons.[6] This is equally valid for other countries in the region and beyond.

The ISIS phenomenon poses a new type of challenge to India. Since 2015, the media has been reporting that a small but growing number of Muslims, largely youths but in some cases young families as well, are being attracted towards the ISIS. Some have gone beyond sharing its ideology, and volunteered to fight for the Islamic State; a few have become recruiting agents through social media networks. In either case, the number is extremely small: a few dozens, in a country of over 150 million Muslims. The most disturbing aspect is the external-domestic linkage, especially the influence of ISIS upon the expatriate Indian community in the Gulf countries. Until recently, the non-political nature of the Indian community has often been hailed, and described as one of the reasons behind the continuous flow of Indians to the Gulf countries. This narrative has been dented by the arrest and extradition of Abdul Wahid Siddibapa by the UAE authorities in May 2016,[7] and the deportation of many others from UAE and other Gulf Cooperation Council (GCC) countries.[8] As will be discussed, this largely explains the inclusion of a number of security-related understandings in India's engagements with key countries along the Persian Gulf, especially the UAE and Saudi Arabia.

The common threats posed by the ISIS and its appeal among the youth of different countries have proved to be insufficient to bring about a collective response. On 17 December 2015, the UN Security Council unanimously adopted Resolution 2253 that called on states to work towards rooting out terrorism through asset freeze, travel ban, arms embargo, and enhanced vigilance.[9] This, however, did not lead to a collective international response. Due to conflicting national interests, there are three distinct international coalitions against the ISIS: a predominantly western coalition of nine countries headed by the US;[10] a counter coalition of four countries headed by Russia;[11] and an Islamic coalition of 34 countries headed by Saudi Arabia.[12] Interestingly, each of these coalitions includes and excludes key countries of the Middle East due to their different and differing national interests.

Two, for a long time, the succession question has dominated the future of some Gulf monarchies. The deteriorating health of Sultan Qaboos has caused anxieties in Oman over the future direction of the sultanate. Ever since seizing power from his father in a bloodless palace coup in 1970, the Sultan has navigated the country with dexterity, foresight, and politico-economic independence. Unlike much richer neighbours, Sultan Qaboos has religiously guarded his regional autonomy from Saudi Arabia by adopting independent positions on various issues affecting the region, such as Camp David Accords, Islamic Revolution, Iran-Iraq war, and the isolation of Iran over the nuclear controversy. Not having an heir or publicly declared successor, the fate of the Emirate continues to be a major concern, especially in the light of his long medical treatment in Germany during 2014–15, and his not appearing in public since November 2016.

However, the period under discussion in this volume, saw a relatively smooth transition in Saudi Arabia. Upon the death of King Abdullah, his half-brother and Crown Prince Salman ascended the throne in January 2015. Prince Muqrin, who was made Second Deputy Prime Minister by King Abdullah in March 2014 was quickly elevated as the new Crown Prince but this arrangement did not last long. Upon the 'resignation' of Muqrin in April 2015, King Salman named his son Mohammed as Second Deputy Prime Minister while making Mohammed bin-Nayef the Crown Prince. Thus, for the first time in the history of the Kingdom, the Crown Prince and his deputy belong to the third generation—that is, the grandsons— of the founder King Ibn Saud. Being the son of the King and Defence Minister, Mohammed bin-Salman has emerged more powerful than the Crown Prince since January 2015, and has been the architect of the new pace of economic reforms. Through his *Vision 2030*[13] unveiled in April 2016, the young prince seeks to reorient the tax-free cradle-to-grave social welfare arrangement by gradually levying taxes, first on the expatriate community and gradually upon the citizens. Through a host of measures, he seeks to end the oil component of the economy by 2020 and, in the process, limit Saudi dependence upon the foreign workforce.[14]

Three, the popular protests—which began in Tunisia in December 2010—continue to dominate the regional political landscape. However, with the exception of Yemen, the Arab states along the Persian Gulf have largely weathered the Arab Spring and its adverse effects. The Gulf monarchs settled for popular co-option through financial largesse to blunt the demands for political reforms. Since 2011, Saudi rulers have announced several rounds of financial benefits totalling more than US$ 100 billion. Upon becoming King, Salman announced financial bonuses,[15] and similar financial benefits were given earlier by Abdullah in February 2011.[16] However, the situation in Bahrain, continues to deteriorate, with a growing number of arrests, prosecution, public restrictions, and even the stripping of citizenship.

Four, regional upheavals have brought about internal tensions among the GCC member-states. The Qatari support for the Egyptian Islamists, especially towards the deposed President Mohammed Morsi, has angered al-Saud, and contributed to a temporary breach of diplomatic relations in 2014 when Saudi Arabia, Bahrain, and the UAE withdrew their Ambassadors from Doha.[17] While Oman did not join hands with this Saudi-led move, Kuwait sought to mediate. Even though the three ambassadors returned to Doha in December 2014, tensions continued.

The Saudi-led military offensive against Yemen, *Operation Decisive Storm* (March–April 2014) and *Operation Restoring Hope* (April 2015–present) also highlighted the differences within the GCC. While Saudi Arabia blamed Iran for the Yemeni crisis, Oman continued to maintain its neutrality, partly due to its traditional policy of regional autonomy and partly due to closer ties with Iran. Other GCC countries joined the Saudi-led military offensive that was launched on 26 March 2015. However, due to mounting military casualties, the UAE announced its withdrawal from the Yemeni operation and pulled out its soldiers in June 2016.

Furthermore, the Saudi-led military campaign in Yemen in support of the beleaguered President Abdrabbuh Mansur Hadi has proved to be costly and destructive. From March 2015 until December 2016, an estimated 10,000 Yemenis, mostly civilians, were killed; 40,000 were wounded; and 3 million were internally displaced.[18] A number of heritage sites recognised by the UNESCO were destroyed in the air campaign, and there were periodic popular protests in the country against the Saudi-led war, which was also supported by the US through technical assistance and air support.[19]

Five, the period under review also witnessed a continuing tension between the two regional rivals, Iran and Saudi Arabia. The nuclear deal concluded in Geneva in July 2015, only increased their mutual anxiety, distrust, and animosity. It intensified the sectarian tension in the form of increased violence in Iraq and Yemen and, to a lesser extent, in Syria. Perceived Iranian involvement in internal Arab affairs, especially in areas which Riyadh considers as its domain, namely Bahrain and Yemen, led to war of words between the two,[20] and was partly responsible for the prolonged violence in Yemen and the absence of a political solution in Bahrain.

At one level, the Joint Comprehensive Plan of Action (JCPOA) signed in Geneva in July 2015, between Iran and the P5+1 countries, closed a decade-long controversy over the Iranian nuclear programme. It put an end to periodic speculations about a possible military solution.[21] Though the agreement provides for a stringent verification mechanism, everyone was not happy, especially Israel and Saudi Arabia. Both felt that, in a hurry to reach a political settlement, President Barack Obama ignored their security concerns, and reoriented American policy in the Gulf. Driven by slow economic growth domestically and unpopularity in the region, the US was not in a position to be confrontationist vis-à-vis Iran, and hence some countries fear that Washington accommodated Iran at the cost of its traditional Arab allies.[22] The Saudi reservation vis-à-vis JCPOA manifested in two ways: low-level diplomatic contacts with Israel,[23] and overwhelming support for Donald Trump who was elected President in November 2016.[24] It was no accident that President Trump chose Riyadh as his maiden foreign visit in May 2017.

Six, the oil prices—which had reached US$ 60 per barrel in December 2014—continue to fall, and dropped to US$ 50 per barrel in December 2016 primarily due to slow growth of the global economy and energy alternatives. The emergence of the US as a net exporter of oil in November 2016 was accompanied by a greater American reluctance to ensure the energy security of its European allies without burden sharing, a prominent theme during President Trump's election campaign.[25] As a result, the Geneva agreement did not bring about a financial windfall that the Iranians were hoping for. The removal of some international sanctions in January 2016 and the unfreezing of some assets by the US brought some relief. The falling oil prices were compounded by increased Iraqi production, which reached the pre-2003 levels, and undermined the anticipated recovery of the Iranian economy.

Falling oil prices also affected the oil-rich Gulf Arab countries which faced huge budget deficits. For the first time in their history, all the GCC countries were forced to introduce, albeit on a limited scale, a small portion of taxes to meet budgetary deficits. Countries like Saudi Arabia have imposed certain limits on the overseas remittances by its expatriate workers,[26] and are seeking to reduce the share of oil in their economies through diversification and tax revenue.[27] With limited oil resources, Bahrain resorted to reducing subsidies on key issues such as water, electricity, and fuel.[28] Countries like Saudi Arabia and Kuwait were forced to dip into their sovereign wealth to bridge current account deficits.[29] As a result, oil-poor countries like Bahrain are becoming increasingly dependent upon the economic largesse of their richer neighbours. These are unchartered waters for the GCC countries whose citizens have been accustomed to subsidized welfare arrangements, especially since the early 1970s.

Thus, regional tensions, the sectarian divide, continuing civil war in Iraq and Yemen, Arab-Persian political rivalry and, above all, falling oil prices marked 2015 and 2016. How did India navigate these challenges? Before going into specifics, it is essential to look at some of the significant changes that are taking place at the political level.

Bridging the Gulf

It took Prime Minister Modi nearly 15 months to make his maiden visit to the Middle East when he chose the UAE as his first destination in August 2015. Coming days after Indian Independence Day, this visit signalled a new page in Indo-Gulf relations. Given the regional tensions, rivalries, and the sectarian divide, Abu Dhabi appeared to be the most neutral and hence least controversial port of call. Any other destination might have evoked unwanted criticism.

The visit also highlighted certain key features of India's new engagements with the region. First, the visit marked the end of prolonged Indian indifference towards the Middle East, including the Persian Gulf region. Periodic rhetoric of the Gulf being India's 'extended neighbourhood'[30] was accompanied by limited high-level political engagements, and the perpetuation of transactional relations without geostrategic contents. Indeed, since the outbreak of the popular protests in many Arab states, visits by Indian leaders to the wider Middle East have been minimal.

From December 2010 (when the Arab Spring broke out) until August 2015 (the visit of the Prime Minister to the UAE), India's political engagements were confined to the two non-Arab Islamic countries of the Middle East: namely, Iran and Turkey. Prime Minister Manmohan Singh's visit to Tehran for the 16th summit meeting of the Non-Aligned Movement in August 2012 was converted into a state visit. The other political contacts were the visit to Turkey by President Pranab Mukherjee in October 2013, and Vice-President Hamid Ansari's to Iran for the inauguration of the leadership of President Hasan Rouhani in August 2013. Indeed, the last state visit from India to the Arab Middle East was by President Pratibha Patil to the UAE as well as Syria in November 2010. This was literally days before the Jasmine Revolution broke out in Tunisia. During the same period, India hosted President Mahmoud Abbas of Palestine (September 2012), Crown Prince Salman bin Hamad al-Khalifa of Bahrain (May 2012), President Mohammed Morsi of Egypt (November 2013), King Hamad bin Isa al-Khalifa of Bahrain (February 2014), Crown Prince Salman of Saudi Arabia (February 2014), and Emir Tamim bin Hamad al-Thani of Qatar (March 2015).

In other words, from November 2010 onwards, there were no visits by Indian President, Vice-President, or Prime Minister to the entire Arab Middle East. Political engagements were confined to visits by External Affairs Ministers or Ministers of State in the MEA. Thus, the first state visit to any Arab country since November 2010 had to wait until August 2015 when Prime Minister Modi chose the UAE.

Secondly, even before his visit to the UAE, the Prime Minister set the tone for a reinvigorated engagement with the Gulf. Indeed, his second meeting with a foreign dignitary upon becoming Prime Minister was with Yusuf bin Alawi, the Minister Responsible for Foreign Affairs in Oman whom he met on 3 June 2014.[31] A few months later Modi met the then Crown Prince Salman of Saudi Arabia during the G-20 meeting in Brisbane in November, and had another meeting with Salman in the same forum in Antalya in Turkey in November 2015; but by then, Salman had taken over the reins of the Kingdom following the death of his half-brother Abdullah a few months earlier. Continuing with this trend, he met deputy Crown Prince Mohammed bin-Salman in the Hangzhou G-20 meeting in September 2016.

Thirdly, Modi's visit to the UAE was a stand-alone one—that is, he did not add any other country and make it into a regional tour, as has been the case for many visits in the past. Prime Minister Indira Gandhi, for example, visited Kuwait and the UAE in 1981; Prime Minister Manmohan Singh visited Qatar and Oman in November 2008; President Mukherjee visited Jordan, Palestine, and Israel in October 2015; and Vice-President Ansari visited Morocco and Tunisia in May–June 2016. At times, visits by External Affairs Ministers have become region engagements. S. M. Krishna, for example, visited Israel, Palestine, Jordan, and the UAE during his January 2012 visit to the region. Likewise, Salman Khurshid visited Morocco, Tunisia, and Sudan in January 2014. Visits to Israel by Jaswant Singh (July 2000) and Sushma Swaraj (January 2016) also included customary visits to Ramallah. These arrangements were primarily due to logistical constraints or compulsions of balancing India's ties with Israel and Palestine. At the same time, regional tours by senior Indian leaders tend to dilute the focus of the host country. Thus, since his visit to the UAE, all the visits undertaken by Prime Minister Modi to the region have been stand-alone visits. There are indications that this would be the case also for his much anticipated visit to Israel in mid-2017—that is, without the customary visit to Palestine.

Fourthly, if one excludes his visit to Turkey for the G-20 meeting in November 2014, all the Middle Eastern visits undertaken by the prime minister were to the Persian Gulf countries. In 2016, he undertook three visits to Gulf region: namely Saudi Arabia (April), Iran (May), and Qatar (June). In addition, he met the Saudi rulers during G-20 summits in Brisbane (November 2014), Anatalya (November 2015), and Hangzhou (September 2016).

Fifthly, unlike the past, security cooperation dominates India's engagements with the Persian Gulf states. All the official statements and communiqués issued at the end of Prime Minister Modi's visit to the region have a high emphasis on security cooperation, including counter-terrorism, cyber security, sea-lanes of communication, anti-piracy measures, terror financing, money laundering, periodic consultations between security establishments, intelligence sharing and combating terrorism, extremism, and radicalism. For example, the joint statement issued at the end of his UAE visit, identified 31 areas that both the leaders had agreed upon and, of these, as many as 17 were security related.[32] The same holds true for other countries: nine out of 36 agreed items with Saudi Arabia,[33] five out of 12 with Iran,[34] and 10 out of 38 with Qatar,[35] were security linked. The appointment of the then Mumbai Police Commissioner Ahmad Javed as ambassador to Saudi Arabia in December 2015[36] highlights the importance given to security cooperation with the Kingdom. India's ongoing engagements with the Kingdom of Bahrain also have a strong security dimension;[37] and the same holds true for the Hashemite Kingdom of Jordan.[38]

Six, in the past, military-security cooperation with the Middle Eastern countries was largely confined to Israel. New Delhi took more than four decades to normalise relations with the Jewish State; but since 1992, military-security cooperation has emerged as a major component of Indo-Israeli relations.[39] Under Modi, however, the canvas of security cooperation has expanded, and covers a number of Arab and Islamic countries, especially along the Persian Gulf, primarily due to the emergence of ISIS and its radicalizing impact both within and outside the region.

The roots of India's security-related cooperation with the Gulf countries dates back to the previous UPA government and, on a few occasions, both Saudi Arabia and the UAE deported persons wanted by India for various criminal offenses without much publicity.[40] However, the ISIS has brought about a new sense of urgency. A small number of Indian expatriates working in the Gulf, primarily in UAE, Saudi Arabia and Kuwait, were found to be attracted towards religious extremism propagated by the Islamic Caliphate through social media networks.[41] The cooperation of the Emirati authorities resulted in the nabbing of several persons in this connection. During 2015 and 2016, about 40 individuals in different parts of India—mostly from Kerala which sends the maximum number of migrant workers to the Gulf—were apprehended due to their sympathy for and connections with the ISIS.[42]

Seven, the attraction that some Indian expatriates feel for religious extremism is a dangerous trend. Though the size of such sympathizers and potential recruits is microscopic, one should not examine its lethality merely through the numbers. Only ten determined terrorists brought down the Twin Towers on 11 September 2001. Indeed, until recently, some Gulf countries and their wealthy citizens were providing politico-ideological, financial, logistical, and even military support to various radical groups and individuals in the Middle East and beyond. Like individuals, countries are also slow in learning from their past and, in the process, have created uncontrollable Frankenstein monsters. The emergence of the ISIS and its extreme xenophobia towards women, minorities, and sections of the Muslim population has forced these countries to fight religious extremism. Thus, for some of the countries in the Gulf, fighting terrorism has become more an existential necessity than a politico-ideological tool as was the case in the past. Therefore, it is reasonably accurate to argue that India's engagements with the Gulf countries would continue to be dominated by a strong security component in the years to come.

Economic Relations

India's economic engagements with the Persian Gulf countries during 2015 and 2016 were dominated by two challenges: continuing global economic slowdown, and falling oil prices. While the latter meant lesser hydrocarbon imports, the former meant a considerable drop in foreign trade. Indeed, since 2011–12, India's total trade has been declining: from being close to US$ 800 billion, it dropped to US$ 758 billion in 2014–15 and reached US$ 642 billion in 2015–16—that is, slightly more than in 2010–11 when its foreign trade stood at just over US$ 620 billion. In other words, between 2011–12 and 2015–16, its trade dropped over US$ 150 billion, or by a quarter. Likewise, oil prices also dropped from the peak of US$ 120 in 2012 to US$ 50 in December 2016.

The fall in trade as well as in oil prices were reflected in India's economic engagement with Persian Gulf countries. The UAE, which for a short period remained India's largest trading partner, has been losing its position since 2012–13 and became the third largest partner after China and the US (see Table 1.1), followed closely by Saudi Arabia. However, the gap between India's trade with the UAE and China has been widening and, during 2015–16, it was more than US$ 20 billion, with India's imports from China heavily titling in favour of the latter. With about US$ 49.7 billion in trade, the UAE accounts for 7.5 per cent of India's total foreign trade. Because of the domination of the energy trade, Persian Gulf countries continue to be among India's leading trade partners and, in 2015–16, five countries were among India's top 25 trade partners (see Table 1.2); Saudi Arabia was in the fourth slot; Iraq in the 17th; Qatar in the 19th, and Iran in the 21st. During the same period, Kuwait was pushed down to the 30th slot while lesser energy resource countries occupied far lower positions: Oman 40th; Bahrain 65th and Yemen 93rd.

Table 1.1: India's Five Largest Trading Partners in 2015–16 (US$ Million)

Country	Exports	Imports	Total Trade	Trade Balance
China	9,010.35	61,706.83	70,717.18	-52,696.48
United States	40,335.82	21,781.39	62,117.21	18,554.44
UAE	30,290.01	19,445.68	49,735.69	10,844.33
Saudi Arabia	6,394.23	20,321.33	26,715.56	-13,927.11
Switzerland	977.17	19,299.49	20,276.66	-18,322.32

Source: Director General of Foreign Trade, New Delhi, at http://commerce.nic.in/eidb/iecnttopn.asp

Figure 1.1: Exports and Imports with the Five Largest Trading Partners (2015–16)

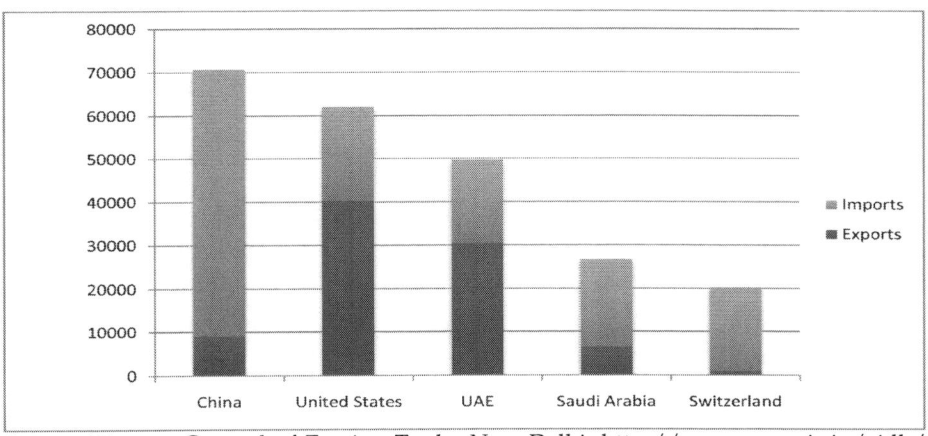

Source: Director General of Foreign Trade, New Delhi, http://commerce.nic.in/eidb/iecnttopn.asp

Table 1.2: Place of PG Countries among the top 25 Trading Partners of India during 2015–16

Country	Ranking	Imports from	Exports to	Total trade	Share (in per cent)
UAE	Three	19,445.68	30,290.01	49,735.69	7.73
Saudi Arabia	Four	20,321.33	6,394.23	26,715.56	4.15
Iraq	Seventeen	10,837.58	1,004.39	11,841.98	1.84
Qatar	Nineteen	9,022.16	902.04	9,924.20	1.54
Iran	Twenty One	6,278.75	2,781.51	9,060.26	1.41

Source: Adapted from Director-General of Foreign Trade, New Delhi, at www.dgft.gov.in

Figure 1.2: Exports, Imports, and Ranking of Persian Gulf Countries in India's Total Trade (2015–16)

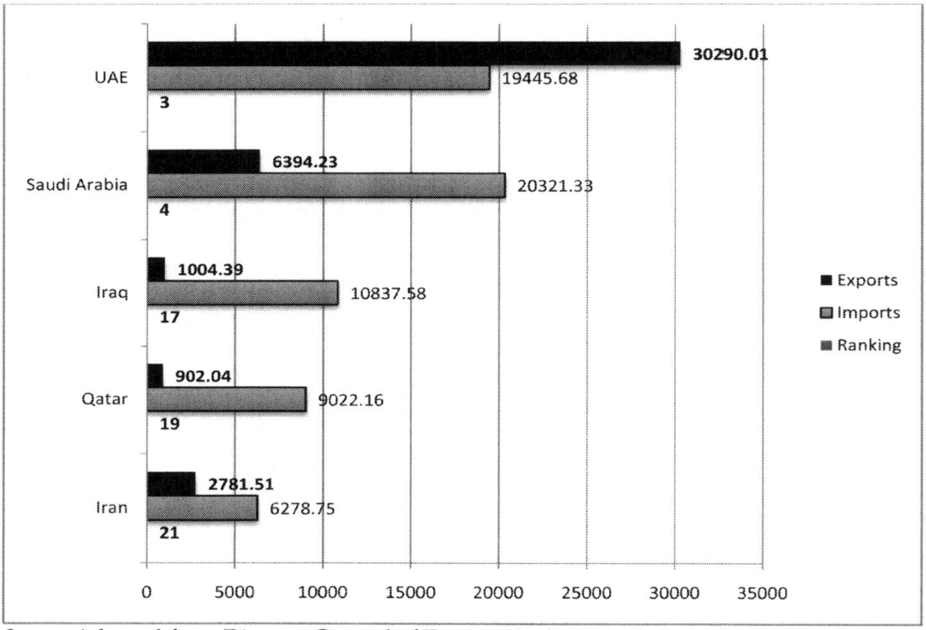

Source: Adapted from Director-General of Foreign Trade, New Delhi, www.dgft.gov.in

In terms of regional partners, the Persian Gulf countries continue to be India's largest trading partners; but, at the same time, the decline in foreign trade and falling oil prices have led to a slight drop in the share of the region in India's overall trade. Lower oil prices have contributed to a considerable fall in India's imports from the Persian Gulf. From the peak of 29.18 per cent during 2013–14, they dropped to 24.14 per cent in 2014–15, and to 19.13 per cent in 2015–16 (see Table 1.3). Indeed, this was the first time since the late 1990s that the share of the Persian Gulf countries in India's imports dropped to less than one-fifth. In other words, in 2011–12, India imported

US$ 133.8 billion worth of goods from the Persian Gulf countries, but this nearly halved to US$ 72.9 billion during 2015–16.

Table 1.3: Persian Gulf Share in India's Total Imports (in US$ million)

Year	Total Imports	Imports from Persian Gulf	Share per cent
1996-97	39,132.41	5,225.60	13.35
1997-98	41,484.49	5,182.19	12.49
1998-99	42,388.71	6,252.67	14.75
1999-2000	49,738.06	7,708.73	15.50
2000-01	50,536.45	1,914.12	3.79
2001-02	51,413.28	2,018.62	3.93
2002-03	61,412.14	2,189.82	3.57
2003-04	78,149.11	3,549.26	4.54
2004-05	111,517.43	7,505.67	6.73
2005-06	149,165.73	8,519.55	5.71
2006-07	185,735.24	46,131.24	24.84
2007-08	251,654.01	64,328.98	25.56
2008-09	303,696.31	80,292.24	26.44
2009-10	288,372.88	73,640.76	25.54
2010-11	369,769.13	96,595.68	26.12
2011-12	489,319.49	133,825.28	27.35
2012-13	490,736.65	139,892.75	28.51
2013-14	450,199.78	131,409.63	29.18
2014-15	448,033.40	108,176.01	24.14
2015-16	381,006.62	72,913.69	19.13

Source: Adapted from Director-General of Foreign Trade, New Delhi, at www.dgft.gov.in

Figure 1.3: Persian Gulf's Share in India's Total Imports

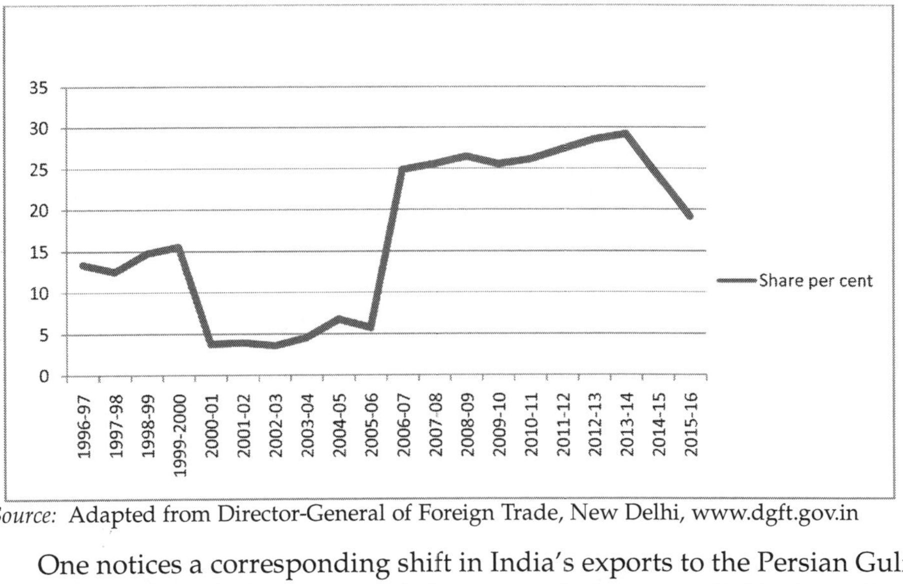

Source: Adapted from Director-General of Foreign Trade, New Delhi, www.dgft.gov.in

One notices a corresponding shift in India's exports to the Persian Gulf countries, although the margin of change is relatively small. During 2012–

13, it exported goods worth US$ 57.1 billion to the region; but these declined to US$ 55.2 in 2014–15 and to US$ 45.8 billion in 2015–16 (see Table 1.4). In other words, its exports dropped by over US$ 10 billion since 2012–13. At the same time, in terms of its share, the exports largely remained stable. During 2012–13, 19.03 per cent of its exports went to the Persian Gulf and this dropped to 17.48 per cent three years later. Despite these, both in terms of imports and exports, the Persian Gulf remains India's largest sub-regional trading partner.

Table 1.4: Persian Gulf Share in India's Total Exports (in US$ million)

Year	Total Exports	Exports to Persian Gulf	Share in per cent
1996-97	33,469.95	2,720.03	8.13
1997-98	34,784.98	2,952.81	8.49
1998-99	33,218.72	3,280.56	9.88
1999-2000	36,822.49	3,539.78	9.61
2000-01	44,560.29	4,376.42	9.82
2001-02	43,826.72	4,405.61	10.05
2002-03	52,719.43	5,946.79	11.28
2003-04	63,842.55	8,277.87	12.97
2004-05	83,535.94	11,423.92	13.68
2005-06	103,090.53	13,398.41	13.00
2006-07	126,414.05	19,209.10	15.20
2007-08	163,132.18	25,997.08	15.94
2008-09	185,295.36	35,104.98	18.95
2009-10	178,751.43	33,537.55	18.76
2010-11	251,136.19	50,076.90	19.94
2011-12	305,963.92	48,882.30	15.98
2012-13	300,400.68	57,160.12	19.03
2013-14	314,405.29	55,417.58	17.62
2014-15	310,338.48	55,292.31	17.81
2015-16	262,290.13	45,864.41	17.48

Source: Adapted from Director-General of Foreign Trade, New Delhi, www.dgft.gov.in

Figure 1.4: Persian Gulf's Share in India's Total Exports

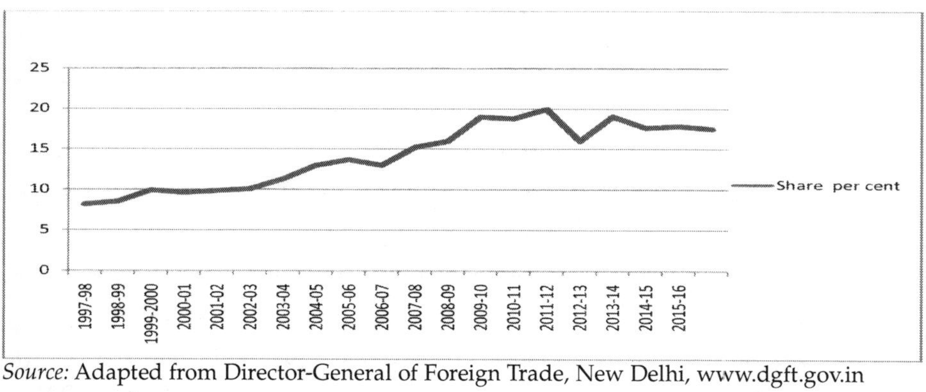

Source: Adapted from Director-General of Foreign Trade, New Delhi, www.dgft.gov.in

Today, bilateral trade continues to favour the Persian Gulf countries. During 2014–15 India imported US$ 108.1 billion worth of goods from the region, and its exports stood at US$ 55.2 billion. The corresponding figures for 2015–16 were US$ 72.9 billion and US$ 45.8 billion respectively. The drop in oil prices, and hence a corresponding decline in imports have had a positive impact on India's overall trade deficit. From the high of US$ 190.3 billion in 2012–13, it declined to US$ 137.6 billion in 2014–15 and further to US$ 118.7 billion in 2015–16 (see Table 1.5). Thus, for the first time since 2010–11, the share of energy imports to trade deficit dropped to less than 90 per cent.

Table 1.5: Trade Deficit-oil Import Linkages

Year	Total Exports	Total Imports	Trade Deficit	Energy Imports	Per cent of Oil Imports to Trade Deficit
1996-97	33,469.95	39,132.41	5,662.46	11,464.60	202.47
1997-98	34,784.98	41,484.49	6,669.51	10,067.75	150.95
1998-99	33,218.72	42,388.71	9,169.99	8,043.19	87.71
1999-2000	36,822.49	49,738.06	12,915.57	14,350.19	111.11
2000-01	44,560.29	50,536.45	5,976.16	17,545.14	293.59
2001-02	43,826.72	51,413.28	7,586.56	15,771.75	207.89
2002-03	52,719.43	61,412.14	8,692.71	19,680.60	226.40
2003-04	63,842.55	78,149.11	14,306.56	22,700.20	158.67
2004-05	83,535.94	111,517.43	27,981.49	34,818.66	124.43
2005-06	103,090.53	149,165.73	46,075.20	50,310.06	109.19
2006-07	126,414.05	185,735.24	59,323.19	61,778.90	104.14
2007-08	163,132.18	251,654.01	88,521.83	86,384.07	97.59
2008-09	185,295.36	303,696.31	118,397.95	103,933.81	87.78
2009-10	178,751.43	288,372.88	109,621.45	96,321.16	87.87
2010-11	251,136.19	369,769.13	118,633.24	115,929.02	97.72
2011-12	305,963.92	489,319.49	183,355.57	172,753.97	94.22
2012-13	300,400.68	490,736.65	190,335.97	181,344.67	95.28
2013-14	314,405.29	450,199.78	135,794.49	181,382.59	133.57
2014-15	310,338.48	448,033.40	137,694.92	156,400.01	113.58
2015-16	262,290.13	381,006.62	118,716.49	96,953.06	81.67

Source: Adapted from Director-General of Foreign Trade, New Delhi, at www.dgft.gov.in

Figure 1.5: India's Trade Deficit-Oil Import Linkages

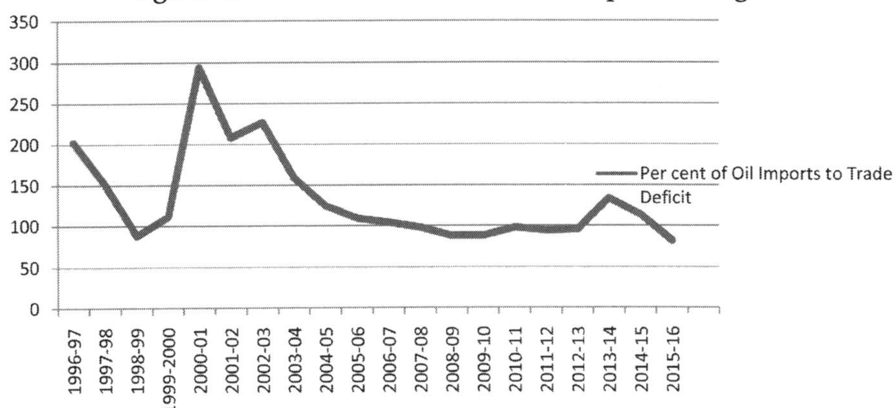

Source: Adapted from Director-General of Foreign Trade, New Delhi, at www.dgft.gov.in

During 2014–15 and 2015–16, India's trade deficit with the Persian Gulf stood at US$ 52.88 billion and US$ 27.05 billion respectively. During 2014–15 its imports were US$ 108.1 billion while exports stood at US$ 55.2 billion; the corresponding figure for 2015–16 were US$ 72.9 billion and US$ 45.9 billion, respectively. This gross asymmetry was primarily due to the large quantity of hydrocarbon imports from the region. India has been importing more oil and gas than in the past, and it imported 2.32 million metric tons of oil and gas during 2015–16 as against 2 million metric tons during 2012–13. This indicates that the imports have been partly aimed at shoring up strategic reserves that are currently being created by India. It plans to build a storage capacity for 10 days of supply, which would mean 36.87 million barrels of energy reserves.

Due to strategic considerations, India has been diversifying its energy imports. The share of the Persian Gulf countries in its overall energy imports has come down from about 63 per cent in 2007–08 to about 54.5 per cent in 2014–15 and to 52.59 per cent in 2015–16 (see Table 1.6). Depleting oil reserves have considerably reduced the share of Bahrain and Oman in India's energy imports while Saudi Arabia has been the largest supplier, followed by Iraq and Kuwait. Despite the nuclear deal and the return of Iran to the international oil market, payment difficulties continue to hamper Indo-Iranian oil trade, and hence there is a slight drop in its share.

Figure 1.6: India's Energy Imports from the Persian Gulf Region

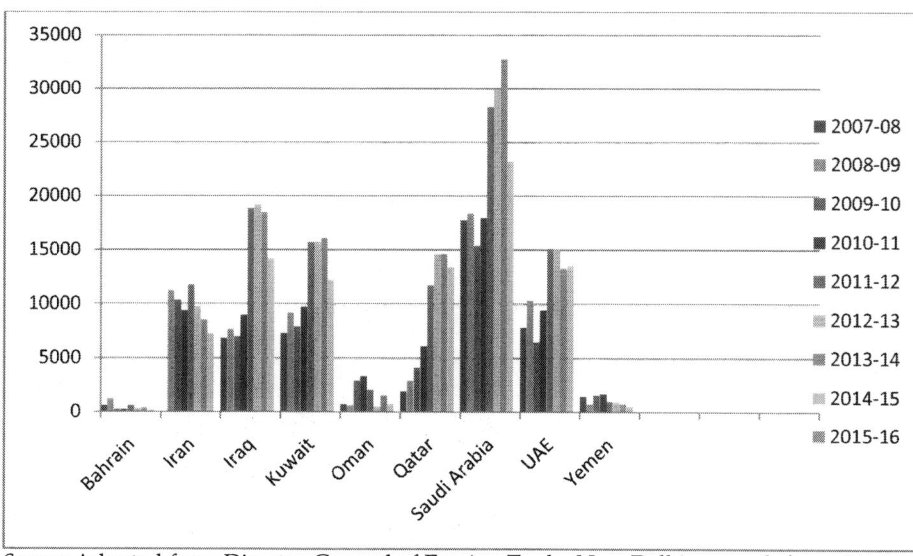

Source: Adapted from Director-General of Foreign Trade, New Delhi, www.dgft.gov.in

Table 1.6: India's Energy Imports from the Persian Gulf Region (in US$ million)

Country	2007-08	2008-09	2009-10	2010-11	2011-12	2012-13	2013-14	2014-15	2015-16
Bahrain	599.46	1,215.37	248.34	219.19	605.89	329.85	359.23	215.82	94.07
Iran	10,048,97	11,248.63	10,362.04	9,377.88	11,764.01	9,716.39	8,556.95	7,292.13	4,461.57
Iraq	6,834.57	7,660.78	6,981.32	8,954.66	18,826.19	19,166.06	18,450.33	14,177.22	10,759.19
Kuwait	7,289.51	9,193.78	7,909.80	9,729.09	15,718.33	15,737.46	16,121.78	12,228.71	4,059.61
Oman	688.68	624.70	2,904.41	3,293.14	2,083.84	507.88	1,514.11	732.51	584.67
Qatar	1,897.18	2,890.14	4,101.68	6,060.95	11,697.83	14,578.34	14,590.81	13,415.31	7,942.43
Saudi Arabia	17,755.00	18,386.52	15,390.04	17,932.31	28,302.37	29,896.53	32,781.57	23,212.88	15,177.91
UAE	7,806.25	10,317.90	6,443.36	9,398.23	15,102.54	14,984.68	13,263.35	13,509.04	7,912.80
Yemen	1,445.39	745.07	1,563.15	1,722.95	955.26	942.00	762.62	516.68	0.01
Total Persian Gulf	54,365.01	62,282.89	55,904.14	66,688.4	105,056.26	105,859.19	106,400.75	85,300.30	50,992.26
Total imports	86,384.04	103,933.77	96,321.16	115,929.06	172,753.97	181,344.67	181,382.56	156,399.98	96,953.02
Per cent Persian Gulf Imports to total Imports	62.93	59.93	58.04	57.53	60.81	58.37	58.66	54.54	52.59

Source: Adapted from Director-General of Foreign Trade, New Delhi, at www.dgft.gov.in

The drop in the overall share in India's energy imports does not reflect the role the Persian Gulf countries occupy in India's overall energy needs. Since the late 1990s when detailed data became widely available, the Persian Gulf countries have been among the top five energy suppliers of India (see Table 1.7). Notwithstanding the continuing internal violence, since 2011–12 Iraq has emerged as its second largest supplier after Saudi Arabia. Nigeria, indeed, is the only non-Gulf country among India's top five energy suppliers.

Table 1.7: Top Five Energy Suppliers

Year	First	Second	Third	Fourth	Fifth
1996-97	*Nigeria*	Saudi Arabia	UAE	Kuwait	*Australia*
1997-98	Saudi Arabia	*Nigeria*	*Australia*	Kuwait	UAE
1998-99	Saudi Arabia	Kuwait	*Nigeria*	UAE	*Australia*
1999-00	*Nigeria*	Saudi Arabia	UAE	Kuwait	Iran
2006-07	Saudi Arabia	*Nigeria*	Iran	Kuwait	Iraq
2007-08	Saudi Arabia	Iran	UAE	*Nigeria*	Kuwait
2008-09	Saudi Arabia	Iran	UAE	Kuwait	*Nigeria*
2009-10	Saudi Arabia	Iran	Kuwait	*Nigeria*	Iraq
2010-11	Saudi Arabia	*Nigeria*	Kuwait	UAE	Iran
2011-12	Saudi Arabia	Iraq	Kuwait	UAE	*Nigeria*
2012-13	Saudi Arabia	Iraq	Kuwait	UAE	Qatar
2013-14	Saudi Arabia	Iraq	Kuwait	Qatar	*Nigeria*
2014-15	Saudi Arabia	Iraq	*Nigeria*	UAE	Qatar
2015-16	Saudi Arabia	Iraq	*Nigeria*	Qatar	UAE

Source: Director-General of Foreign Trade, New Delhi, www.dgft.gov.in
Note: Non-Gulf suppliers are identified in italics.

A significant portion of India's energy imports are also export-oriented. In 2000–01, India exported US$ 1.9 billion worth of energy products and, since then, this has been gradually increasing. In 2007–08 this reached US$ 29 billion, and to US$ 64.6 billion in 2013–14. Due to the global economic slowdown, it dropped to US$ 57.6 billion in 2014–15 and to US$ 31.2 billion in 2015–16. Thus, its share dropped from 20.67 per cent in 2012–13 to 11.9 per cent during 2015–16 (see Table 1.8).

The overall decline in energy in India's imports as well as exports is reflected in the drop in the share of energy in India's overall foreign trade (see Table 1.9). During 2012–13, over 30 per cent of its trade was linked to energy, and this declined to 28.22 per cent in 2014–15 and to 19.96 per cent in 2015–16. Nevertheless, energy still makes up nearly a fifth of India's total imports and exports.

Table 1.8: Share of Oil-products in India's Exports (in US$ million)

Year	Total exports	Energy exports	Share in per cent
1996-97	33,469.95	516.43	1.54
1997-98	34,784.98	394.52	1.13
1998-99	33,218.72	141.08	0.42
1999-2000	36,822.49	90.87	0.25
2000-01	44,560.29	1,930.99	4.33
2001-02	43,826.72	2,182.94	4.98
2002-03	52,719.43	2,707.24	5.13
2003-04	63,842.55	3,734.32	5.85
2004-05	83,535.94	7,140.39	8.55
2005-06	103,090.53	11,866.60	11.51
2006-07	126,414.05	18,859.48	14.92
2007-08	163,132.18	29,085.48	17.83
2008-09	185,295.36	28,437.14	15.35
2009-10	178,751.43	29,036.29	16.24
2010-11	251,136.19	42,610.74	16.97
2011-12	305,963.92	57,391.93	18.76
2012-13	300,400.68	62,105.50	20.67
2013-14	314,405.30	64,685.27	20.57
2014-15	310,338.48	57,619.99	18.56
2015-16	262,290.13	31,231.49	11.9

Source: Adapted from Director-General of Foreign Trade, New Delhi, at www.dgft.gov.in

Figure 1.7: Share of Oil Products in India's Exports

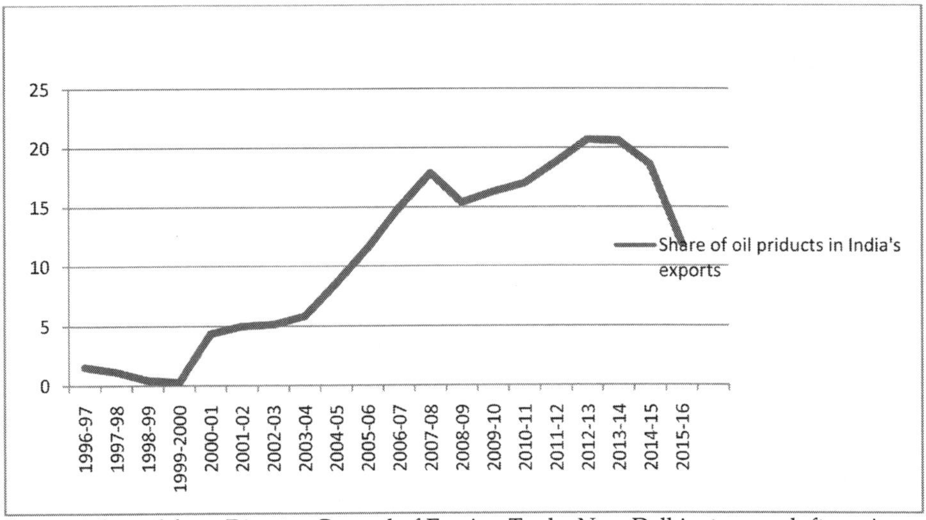

Source: Adapted from Director-General of Foreign Trade, New Delhi, at www.dgft.gov.in

Table 1.9: Share of Energy in India's Total Foreign Trade (in US$ million)

Year	Total trade	Energy exports	Energy imports	Total oil	Percentage of oil trade
1996-97	72,602.36	516.43	11,464.60	11,981.03	6.06
1997-98	76,269.47	394.52	10,067.75	10,462.27	13.74
1998-99	75,607.43	141.08	8,043.19	8,184.27	10.85
1999-2000	86,560.55	90.87	14,350.19	14,441.06	16.70
2000-01	95,096.74	1,930.99	17,545.14	19,476.13	20.50
2001-02	95,240.00	2,182.94	15,771.75	17,954.69	18.87
2002-03	114,131.57	2,707.24	19,680.60	22,387.84	19.63
2003-04	141,991.66	3,734.32	22,700.20	26,434.52	18.63
2004-05	195,053.37	7,140.39	34,818.66	41,959.05	22.00
2005-06	252,256.26	11,866.60	50,310.06	62,176.66	26.71
2006-07	312,149.29	18,859.48	61,778.90	80,638.38	25.83
2007-08	414,786.19	29,085.48	86,384.07	115,469.55	27.84
2008-09	488,991.67	28,437.14	103,933.81	132,370.95	27.07
2009-10	467,124.31	29,036.29	96,321.16	125,357.45	26.84
2010-11	620,905.32	42,610.74	115,929.02	158,419.95	25.51
2011-12	795,283.41	57,391.93	172,753.97	230,145.90	28.94
2012-13	791,137.33	62,105.50	181,344.67	243,450.17	30.77
2013-14	764,594.22	64,685.27	181,382.56	246,067.83	32.18
2014-15	758,301.08	57,619.99	156,399.98	214,019.97	28.22
2015-16	642,094.55	31,231.49	96,953.02	128,184.51	19.96

Source: Adapted from Director-General of Foreign Trade, New Delhi, at www.dgft.gov.in

Figure 1.8: Share of Energy in India's Total Foreign Trade

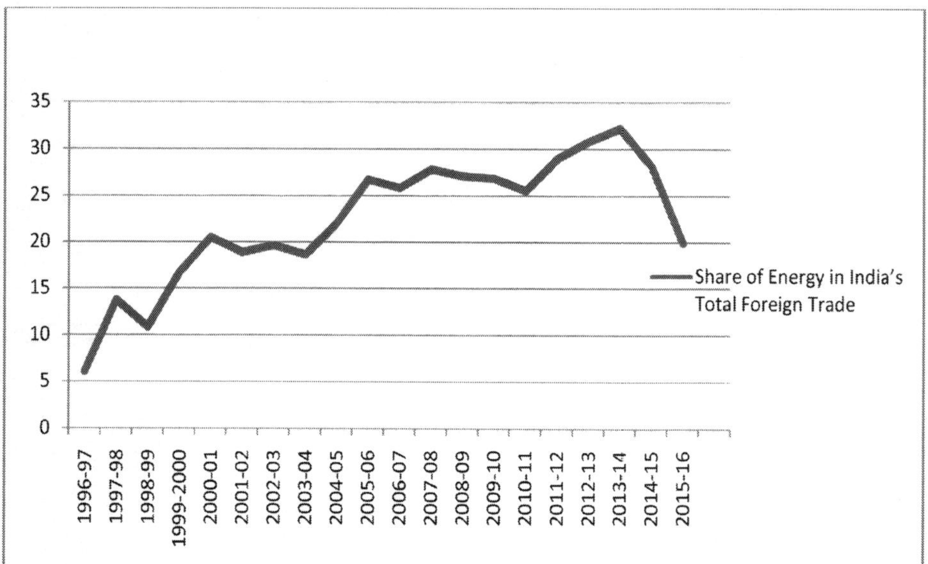

Source: Adapted from Director-General of Foreign Trade, New Delhi, at www.dgft.gov.in

The Persian Gulf countries account for a substantial portion of known oil (see Table 1.10) and natural gas (see Table 1.11) reserves in the world. Because of the low cost of production and logistical considerations, the region will continue to be of vital importance to India. Even if strategic considerations compel India to diversity its energy suppliers, India's growth story will remain intrinsically linked to the Persian Gulf region.

Table 1.10: Oil Reserves

Country	Thousand million barrels (at the end of 2015)	Share of global total %	R/P ratio
Iran	157.8	9.3	110.3
Iraq	143.1	8.4	97.2
Kuwait	101.5	6.0	89.8
Oman	5.3	0.3	15.3
Qatar	25.7	1.5	37.1
Saudi Arabia	266.6	15.7	60.8
UAE	97.8	5.8	68.7
Yemen	3.0	0.2	176.5

Source: BP Statistical Review of World Energy, June 2016.

Figure 1.9: Persian Gulf Share of Oil

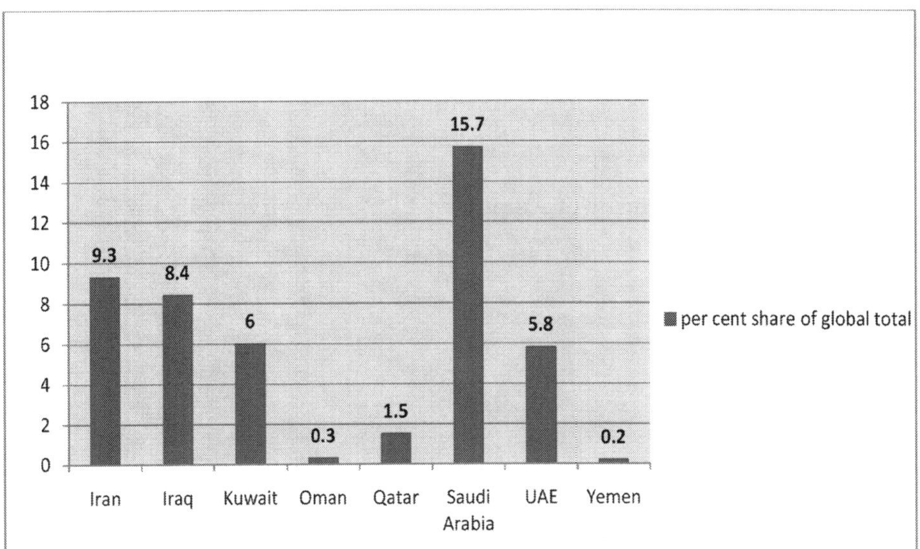

Source: BP Statistical Review of World Energy, June 2016.

Table 1.11: Natural Gas Reserves

Country	Trillion cubic metres (at the end of 2015)	Trillion cubic feet (at the end of 2015)	Share of global total %	R/P ratio
Bahrain	0.2	6.1	0.1	11.1
Iran	34.0	1,201.4	18.2	176.8
Iraq	3.7	130.5	2.0	More than 500 years
Kuwait	1.8	63.0	1.0	119.1
Oman	0.7	24.3	0.4	19.7
Qatar	24.5	866.2	13.1	135.2
Saudi Arabia	8.3	294.0	4.5	78.2
UAE	6.1	215.1	3.3	109.2
Yemen	0.3	9.4	0.1	100.0

Source: BP Statistical Review of World Energy, June 2016.

Energy supplies from the Persian Gulf are closely linked to the large Indian expatriate labour force working in the oil-rich Arab countries. The Middle Eastern region dominates Indian regulations concerning labour migration. As per the existing norm, the ECR is mandatory "only to those possessing educational qualification below Class-X", and this category of workers could be employed as unskilled or semi-skilled workers. Until 2006, ECR was required for labour migrants to 153 countries, but this was gradually pruned. Since August 2008, the ECR requirement applies only to 17 countries; of them, 13 are located in the Middle East, and include all the eight Arab countries of the Gulf. Only Iran is missing from the ECR category as it is not an attractive destination for Gulf migration from India (see Table 1.12).

Table 1.12: List of Countries Requiring ECR for Indian Migrant Labour

Global	Middle East Countries	Persian Gulf Countries
Afghanistan	Jordan	Bahrain
Indonesia	Lebanon	Iraq
Malaysia	Libya	Kuwait
Thailand	Sudan	Oman
	Syria	Qatar
		Saudi Arabia
		UAE
		Yemen

Source: Ministry of Overseas Indian Affairs, Annual Report 2014–15

As highlighted in Table 1.13, Saudi Arabia continues to be the most favoured destination for Indian workers; this is followed by the UAE,

Kuwait, and Qatar. The ECR data is available only until 2014 before the Indian government issued a travel advisory to Yemen. There are still a number of Indians currently working in that country, despite the civil war and after 4,741 persons were brought home in 2015 under *Operation Rahat*.[43]

Table 1.13: ECR Issued

Country	2008	2009	2010	2011	2012	2013	2014
Bahrain	31,924	17,541	15,101	14,323	20,150	17,269	14,220
Iraq	-	-	390	1,177	917	6,577	3,054
Kuwait	35,562	42,091	37,667	45,149	55,868	70,072	80,419
Oman	89,659	74,963	105,807	73,819	84,384	63,398	51,318
Qatar	82,937	46,292	45,752	41,710	63,096	78,367	75,935
Saudi Arabia	228,406	281,110	275,172	289,297	357,503	354,169	329,937
UAE	349,827	130,302	130,910	138,861	141,138	202,016	224,033
Yemen	492	421	208	29	0	3	4
Total Gulf	786,883	592,720	611,007	604,365	725,068	791,871	778,920
Gulf Share (%)	92.79	97.13	95.27	96.46	97.06	96.97	96.77
Total ECR	847,994	610,270	641,355	626,565	747,041	816,655	804,878

Source: Ministry of Overseas Indian Affairs, Annual Report 2014–15, p.50.

Figure 1.10: ECR Issued

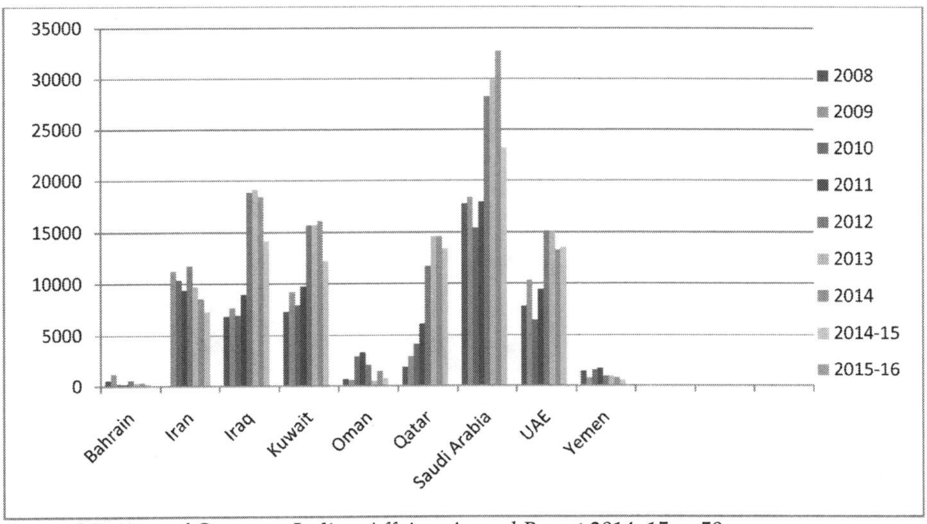

Source: Ministry of Overseas Indian Affairs, *Annual Report* 2014–15, p.50.

There are no accurate figures on the actual number of Indian workers in the Gulf Arab countries. Current estimates suggest that there are around 8.5 million Indians in the GCC countries, with over 3 million in Saudi Arabia—the largest Indian expatriate population in the world.[44] This is followed by the UAE, with about 2.8 million Indian workers.[45] There are about 923,000 in Kuwait, 316,000 in Bahrain, 600,000 in Qatar, and 796,000 in Oman.[46] Even war-torn Yemen has an estimated 10,000 Indians;[47] this is so despite the evacuation carried out by the government which brought home over 4,500 in March–April 2015.[48] According to a population study,

> Indian workers comprised the largest share of residency visas in Kuwait in 2011, while Indian expatriates currently constitute almost 50 percent of all foreign workers in the private sector in Oman. In 2014, Indian migrants had the largest share of migrants in the UAE, totalling nearly 3.1 million (excluding undocumented cases).[49]

Falling oil prices, domestic restiveness due to youth unemployment, the growing demand for women empowerment, and for jobs in the Gulf countries would have a long-term impact upon the size and composition of the Indian expatriate worker. For example, the Nitaqat policy introduced by Saudi Arabia in June 2011 resulted in the return of 141,301 Indian workers during 2012–13.[50] Similarly, there were 36,000 returnees from Kuwait in 2013. Due to the global economic slowdown, remittances to India also dropped. According to the World Bank, during 2015 and 2016, India received US$ 68.91 billion and US$ 62.75 billion respectively in the form of remittances from its overseas population, and the bulk of this came from the Gulf Arab countries.[51]

Challenges

Notwithstanding the growing importance given to the region since Narendra Modi became Prime Minister, it is possible to identity three broad issues which would undermine India's relations with the Persian Gulf countries. These are largely economic. One, during his visit to the UAE in August 2015, Prime Minister Modi and Emirati Crown Prince Muhammad bin Zayed al-Nahyan agreed, among other things, to work towards a US$ 75 billion India-UAE Infrastructure Investment Fund.[52] More than a year later, no progress seems to have been made; and when India hosted the Crown Prince in January 2017 as the Chief Guest of the Republic Day celebrations, there were no announcements regarding Emirati investments in India. This is primarily because Indian corporations, public or private, are not in position to absorb such a large investment. Their size and scale are still small, and are not commensurate to large investments.

Secondly, sovereign investors from the Gulf are not confident of, or are afraid of, the long gestation period needed in India. In recent years, some of Gulf investments have been overturned by the judiciary. For example, Etisalat invested US$ 750 million in the telecom industry, but was forced to pull out of India following the 2G scam and the overturning of the licenses by the Supreme Court in 2012.[53] Some of the large-scale highway projects are also in crisis after the judiciary cancelled agreements regarding toll-roads. Thus, infrastructure projects which can absorb heavy investments do not evoke the necessary confidence among Gulf Arab investors. The government has to evolve a credible, hurdle and hassle free roadmap if it is to attract a fraction of the US$ 75 billion visualized during Prime Minister Modi's meeting with the Emirati leadership.

Three, besides trade, energy, and expatriate components, the Gulf countries have become a major transportation hub for Indian travellers. Currently, there are about 300 weekly flights between India and Gulf Arab destinations. National carriers like *Qatar Air* and *Emirates* have expanded their presence in India, and *Etihad* has partnered with Jet Airways with 24 per cent equity.[54] *Qatar Air* is planning a domestic low-cost airliner for the Indian market.[55] In recent years, *Saudia* has overtaken *Air India*, and caters to a large portion of hajj-related travel. Due to severe competition from Gulf carriers, *Royal Jordanian* which in the past catered to Indians travelling to Europe and the US has ceased its operations in India since 2014. Global network, wide-ranging connectivity, and competitive costs have resulted in Arab carriers becoming attractive options for Indian travellers. No doubt this would further undermine the financial viability and hence long-term survival of *Air India*.

Looking Ahead

Until recently, the Persian Gulf region did not receive adequate attention within India. If Indian officials have given lip service to its importance, the academic and strategic community have avoided a sustained understanding of the region and its complexities. No doubt periodic cycles of violence and the plight of Indians in crisis situations drew media attention; however, otherwise this focus has largely been a passing cloud. South Asia continues to be a major preoccupation of the Indian intelligentsia that is not prepared to look at the challenges and opportunities available in the Persian Gulf region.

There is, however, some fresh air since Modi was elected; he is also not averse to using the internationally recognised and regionally accepted expression 'Middle East' to refer to this region. Even diplomats, who once served in the region, are no longer enamoured by the archaic expression 'West Asia' which evokes disapproval in the region.

With the purpose of generating a serious, nuanced, scholarly, and non-partisan understanding of the region and its complexities, the Middle East

Institute (MEI@ND) was founded in October 2010 as a private academic initiative. Since then, it has undertaken a number of academic and outreach activities, including *Contemporary Review of the Middle East* published by Sage (India).

The *Persian Gulf Series,* inaugurated in 2012, is another such endeavour. The primary Indian interest in the Middle East lies in the Gulf region and, given its political, strategic, economic, energy, cultural, and social importance, the MEI@ND has initiated this Series to closely follow, detail, and assess bilateral relations annually. The inaugural issue was published through Kindle;[56] *Sage* (India) published the subsequent *Persian Gulf 2013*[57] and *Persian Gulf 2014.*[58] The *Persian Gulf 2015* was published by Smashword.[59] The current volume "Persian Gulf 2016–17" deals with bilateral developments during 2015 and 2016. At the suggestion of our valued friend and well-wisher Commodore Uday Bhaskar, we have included exclusive chapters on the relations between China, Pakistan, Russia, and the US and the Persian Gulf region.

Regarding the nomenclatures, the MEI@ND prefers 'Persian Gulf' to other expressions merely because of its historic nature. If there can be a body of water called the Arabian Sea, none should object to the Persian Gulf; moreover, the term 'Persian Gulf' does not denote Iranian ownership of the said waters.

Three notes of caution. Trade figures put out by the Director General of Foreign Trade in India for a current year are often revised in the following year, and hence there could be a slight discrepancy. For example, the trade figures for 2012–13 would be different in *Persian Gulf 2014* and *Persian Gulf 2015*. Two, references to internet websites (URLs) were accurate at the time of writing; the authors or publisher are not responsible for URLs that may have expired or changed since the manuscript was finalized. And three, the key information at the beginning of country chapters are taken from data provided by following agencies: CIA, *The World Factbook,* at https://www.cia.gov/library/publications/the-world-factbook/; UN Human Development Report, *Statistics,* at http://hdr.undp.org/en/statistics/; United States Commission on Religious Freedom, US Department of State; *Annual Report 2015*; Briefs on Foreign Relations, Ministry of External Affairs, Government of India; and the BP Statistical Review of World Energy June 2016.

Like the previous volumes, *Persian Gulf 2016-17* is the result of a team of young researchers who are associated with or well-wishers of the MEI@ND. As the editor of this Series, the co-editor of this volume, and as the Honorary Director of the MEI@ND, I record my sincere gratitude to them. Special thanks are reserved for Md. Muddassir Quamar and Manjari Singh for their delicate skills in improving earlier drafts, and for Divya Malhotra who prepared the figures and diagrams. I am thankful to Preeti Singh for her meticulous editing.

All work for this volume would not be possible without the help and support of the IDSA, especially its Director General, Jayant Prasad, for his commitment to encouraging young scholars and for joining hands with the MEI in bringing out this volume.

With great personal gratitude, I am dedicating the fifth volume in the Series to the doyen of the strategic studies in the country, the late K. Subramanyam. All omissions and commissions are mine. And mine alone.

New Delhi **P. R. Kumaraswamy**

NOTES

1. Hussein Solomon, *Islamic State and the Coming Global Confrontation*, London: Palgrave Macmillan, 2016.
2. William McCants, *The ISIS Apocalypse: The History, Strategy, and Doomsday Vision of Islamic State*, New York: St. Martin's Press, 2015.
3. Solomon, *Islamic State*, op.cit.; McCants, *The ISIS Apocalypse*, op. cit.
4. Syed Qutb, *Milestones*, Delhi: Kazi Publications, 1981, p. 136–139.
5. Solomon, *Islamic State*, op. cit., p. 105.
6. Sean Yom and Katrina Sammour, "The Social Terrain of Islamic Radicalization: Insights from Jordan", *Lawfare*, 21 August 2016, at https://www.lawfareblog.com/social-terrain-islamist-radicalization-insights-jordan.
7. "List of Fugitives Extradited by Foreign Governments to India", Ministry of External Affairs (MEA), Government of India, December 2016, at http://www.mea.gov.in/toindia.htm.
8. Bharti Jain, "3 Indians with Islamic State Links Deported from a Gulf Country, Arrested", *The Times of India*, at http://timesofindia.indiatimes.com/india/3-Indians-with-Islamic-State-links-deported-from-a-Gulf-country-arrested/articleshow/50774325.cms.
9. "Unanimously Adopting Resolution 2253 (2015), Security Council Expands Sanctions Framework to Include Islamic State in Iraq and Levant", United Nations, 17 December 2015, at https://www.un.org/press/en/2015/sc12168.doc.htm
10. "The Global Coalition to Counter ISIS", US Department of State, 10 September 2014, at https://www.state.gov/s/seci/
11. "Russia, Iran, Iraq & Syria Setting Up 'Joint Information Centre' to Coordinate anti-ISIS Operations", *RT News*, 26 September 2015, at https://www.rt.com/news/316592-russia-syria-islamic-state/
12. "Saudi Arabia Announces 'Islamic Military Alliance' with 34 Nations to Counter Terrorism", *The Indian Express*, 16 December 2015, at http://indianexpress.com/article/world/world-news/saudi-arabia-forms-islamic-counterterrorism-coalition/.

13. The document can be accessed in full at: http://vision2030.gov.sa/en
14. *National Transformation Program 2020*, Kingdom of Saudi Arabia, at http://vision2030.gov.sa/sites/default/files/NTP_En.pdf
15. "King Abdullah Orders Social Benefits Package", Saudi-US Relations Information Service, 23 February 2013, at http://susris.com/2011/02/23/king-abdullah-orders-social-benefits-package/
16. "Saudi Big Firms to Pay Bonuses on Orders of New King", *The National*, 2 February 2015, at http://www.thenational.ae/world/middle-east/saudis-big-firms-to-pay-bonuses-on-orders-of-new-king
17. David Kirkpatrick, "3 Gulf Countries Pull Ambassadors from Qatar over its Support of Islamists", *The New York Times*, 5 March 2014, at https://www.nytimes.com/2014/03/06/world/middleeast/3-persian-gulf-states-pull-ambassadors-from-qatar.html?_r=0
18. Ahmed al-Haj, "Yemen Civil War: 10,000 Civilians Killed and 40,000 Injured in Conflict, UN Reveals", *The Independent*, 17 January 2017, at http://www.independent.co.uk/news/world/middle-east/yemen-civil-war-civilian-death-toll-10000-killed-40000-injured-conflcit-un-reveals-a7530836.html.
19. Jeremy M. Sharp, "Civil War and Regional Intervention", *CRS Report*, No. R43960, 21 March 2017, at https://fas.org/sgp/crs/mideast/R43960.pdf.
20. "Iran-Saudi War of Words Heats up ahead of Hajj", *The Indian Express*, 7 September 2016, at http://indianexpress.com/article/world/world-news/iran-saudi-war-of-words-heats-up-ahead-of-hajj-3018765/.
21. For a comprehensive analysis, see Special Issue of *Contemporary Review of the Middle East* on "Iran Nuclear Deal: The Joint Comprehensive Plan of Action", March 2016, Vol. 3, No. 1. It can be accessed at http://journals.sagepub.com/toc/cmea/3/1.
22. Dan Drollette Jr., "The Feud with Iran: A Saudi View", *Bulletin of the Atomic Scientists*, 5 January 2016, at http://thebulletin.org/feud-iran-saudi-view9033.
23. Md. Muddassir Quamar, "Saudi-Israel Rendezvous: Does it Indicate a Policy Change?" IDSA *Comment*, 29 July 2016, at http://www.idsa.in/idsacomments/saudi-israeli-rendezvous_mmquamar_290716.
24. Mohamad Bazzi, "Saudi Arabia has High Hope for Trump", *The Atlantic*, 20 May 2017, at https://www.theatlantic.com/international/archive/2017/05/saudi-arabia-trump-iran-riyadh-salman/527463/.
25. Chris Morris, "US Election 2016: Presidential Campaign Alarms Europeans", *BBC News*, 18 October 2016, at http://www.bbc.com/news/election-us-2016-37676976.
26. Ben Flanagan, "Saudi Cap on Remittances 'a deterrent' for Expats", *The National*, 20 November 2011, at http://www.thenational.ae/business/economy/saudi-cap-on-remittances-a-deterrent-for-expats.
27. Kingdom of Saudi Arabia, National Transformation Program 2020.
28. Ismael Naar, "Bahrain, Oman Cut Petrol Subsidies as Oil Hits 12-year Low", *Al-Arabiya*, 12 January 2016, at https://english.alarabiya.net/en/business/energy/2016/01/12/Bahrain-Oman-cut-petrol-subsidies-as-oil-hits-12-year-low.html.
29. Sarah Townsend, "The Gulf's Sovereign Dilemma," *arabianbusiness.com*, 9 April 2016, at http://www.arabianbusiness.com/the-gulf-s-sovereign-dilemma-627766.html.
30. For example, while addressing the Manama Dialogue in December 2013 External Affairs Minister Salman Khurshid said, "The Gulf region is India's extended

neighbourhood. It has historically been an important artery for the flow of goods and ideas and movement of peoples from and to India." See: Ministry of External Affairs, Government of India, "Address by Minister for External Affairs on 'International Interests in Middle East Security and Non-Proliferation' at IISS Manama Dialogue", 8 December 2013, at http://www.mea.gov.in/Speeches-Statements.htm?dtl/22592/Address_by_ Minister _for_ External_ Affairs_ on_ International_Interests_in_Middle_East_Security_and_NonProliferation_at_IISS_ Manama_Dialogue.

31. "Special Envoy of the Sultan of Oman Calls on PM", Press Information Bureau, Government of India, Prime Minister's Office, 3 June 2014, at http://pib.nic.in/newsite/PrintRelease.aspx?relid=105396
32. "Joint Statement between the United Arab Emirates and the Republic of India," MEA, Government of India, 17 August 2015, at http://www.mea.gov.in/bilateral-documents.htm?dtl/25733/Joint_Statement_between_the_United_Arab _Emirates_and_the_Republic_of_India.
33. "India-Saudi Arabia Joint Statement during the visit of Prime Minister to Saudi Arabia (April 03, 2016)," MEA, Government of India, 3 April 2016, at http://www.mea.gov.in/bilateraldocuments.htm?dtl/26595/IndiaSaudi_ Arabia _ Joint _Statement_during_the_visit_of_Prime_Minister_to_Saudi_Arabia_April_03_2016.
34. "India-Iran Joint Statement: 'Civilisational Connect, Contemporary Context' during the visit of Prime Minister to Iran," MEA, Government of India, 23 May 2016, at http://www.mea.gov.in/bilateral-documents.htm?dtl/26843/India__Iran_ Joint_ Statement_ quot_Civilisational_Connect_Contemporary_ Contextquot_during_ the_ visit_ of_ Prime_ Minister_to_Iran.
35. "India-Qatar Joint Statement during the visit of Prime Minister to Qatar," MEA, Government of India, 5 June 2016, at http://www.mea.gov.in/bilateral-documents.htm?dtl/26870/IndiaQatar_Joint_Statement_during_ the_ visit_ of_ Prime_Minister_to_Qatar.
36. "Mumbai Top Cop Ahmed Javed is New Indian Ambassador to Saudi Arabia," *Firstpost*, 11 December 2015, at http://www.firstpost.com/world/ahmed-javed-appointed-indian-envoy-to-saudi-arabia-2542670.html.
37. MEA, "India-Bahrain Relations", Government of India, August 2015, at https://www.mea.gov.in/Portal/ForeignRelation/Bahrain_2015_08_18.pdf.
38. Manjari Singh, "The Impending Visit of Jordan's King Abdullah", *IDSA Comment*, 20 March 2017, at http://www.idsa.in/idsacomments/the-impending-visit-of-jordan-king-abdullah_msingh_200317
39. Alvite Singh Ningthoujam, "India-Israel Defense Cooperation", BESA Center Perspectives Paper, No. 236, 27 January 2014, at https://besacenter.org/perspectives-papers/india-israel-defense-cooperation/.
40. "List of Fugitives Extradited by Foreign Governments to India", MEA, Government of India. http://www.mea.gov.in/toindia.htm
41. Sanjib Baruah and Rajnish Sharma, "ISIS Influence on Indians Abroad Rising", *The Asian Age*, 29 May 2016, at http://www.asianage.com/india/isis-influence-indians-abroad-rising-745.
42. Ibid.
43. "Recent Developments in the Republic of Yemen and Efforts Made for Safe Evacuation of Indian Nationals from There", Suo-Moto Statement by Minister of External Affairs and Overseas Indian Affairs in the Rajya Sabha, 27 April 2015,

MEA, Government of India, at http://www.mea.gov.in/Speeches-Statements.htm?dtl/25129/SuoMoto_Statement_by_Minister_of_External_ Affairs_and_Overseas_Indian_Affairs_in_Rajya_Sabha_on_Recent_ Developments _ in_the_ Republic_of_Yemen_and_Effor

44. "Population of Overseas Indians", MEA, Government of India, December 2016, at http://mea.gov.in/images/attach/NRIs-and-PIOs_1.pdf.
45. Ibid.
46. Ibid.
47. Ibid.
48. "Suo-Moto Statement..." MEA, Government of India, op. cit.
49. George Naufal et al., "Contemporary Indian Labour Migration in the GCC Region: Emerging Challenges and Opportunities", in S. Irudaya Rajan (ed.) *India Migration Report 2016: Gulf Migration*, New Delhi: Routledge, 2017, pp. 64–65
50. "Nitaqat in Saudi Arabia had no Major Impact on Indian Workers", *The Economic Times*, 11 December 2013, at http://economictimes.indiatimes.com/nri/visa-and-immigration/nitaqat-in-saudi-arabia-had-no-major-impact-on-indian-workers/articleshow/27220473.cms?intenttarget=no.
51. "Migration and Remittances Data", The World Bank, April 2017, at http://www.worldbank.org/en/topic/migrationremittancesdiasporaissues/brief/migration-remittances-data.
52. "Joint Statement between the United Arab Emirates and the Republic of India", MEA, Government of India, 17 August 2015, at http://www.mea.gov.in/bilateral-documents.htm?dtl/25733/Joint_Statement_between_the_United_ Arab_ Emirates_and_the_Republic_of_India.
53. John Sarkar and Sidhartha, "Resolve Etisalat Issues to Step up Infra Investment", *The Times of India*, 26 January 2017, at http://timesofindia.indiatimes.com/business/india-business/resolve-etisalat-issues-to-step-up-infra-investment/articleshow/56786673.cms.
54. Aneesh Phadnis, "All You Need to Know about Jet-Etihad Deal", *Business Standard*, 20 November 2013, at http://www.business-standard.com/article/companies/all-you-need-to-know-about-jet-etihad-deal-113112000302_1.html.
55. Aneesh Phadnis and Arindam Majumdar, "Flying Domestic: Qatar Airways is Planning a Fully-owned Airline in India", *Business Standard*, 9 March 2017, at http://www.business-standard.com/article/companies/flying-domestic-qatar-airway-planning-a-fully-owned-airline-in-india-117030801182_1.html.
56. *Persian Gulf, 2012*, at https://www.amazon.in/Persian-Gulf-2012-Indias-Relations-ebook/dp/B0099RZ6NG
57. *Persian Gulf 2013*, at https://us.sagepub.com/en-us/nam/persian-gulf-2013/book242306
58. *Persian Gulf 2014*, at https://us.sagepub.com/en-us/nam/persian-gulf-2014/book245036
59. *Persian Gulf 2015*, at https://www.smashwords.com/books/view/549471

2

BAHRAIN

Manjari Singh

Key Information

Ruling family: al-Khalifa; **Ruler:** King Hamad bin Isa al-Khalifa (since 6 March 1999); **Crown Prince:** Prince Salman bin Hamad bin Isa al-Khalifa (since 9 March 1999); **National Day:** 16 December; **Parliament**: 40-member Nominated Consultative Council and 40-member Elected Chamber of Deputies; **Last Parliamentary Election**: 22 November 2014; **Major group in Parliament**: Independents (Shia Opposition boycotted); **National Carrier**: Gulf Air.

Socio-Economic Indicators

Area: 760 sq km; **Population:** 1.37 million; **Native:** 46 per cent; **Expats:** 54 per cent; **Religious Groups:** Citizens (Muslims: 98–99 per cent (Shia 60–65 per cent and Sunni 30–35 per cent)); Resident (Muslim 70 per cent; Christian 14.5 per cent; Hindu 10 per cent; Buddhist 2.5 per cent; Jewish 0.5 per cent; and Others 2 per cent); **Youth:** 15.76 per cent; **Population growth rate:** 2.33 per cent; **Life expectancy at birth:** 78.9 years; **Major population groups**: Bahraini 46 per cent; Asian 45.5 per cent; other Arabs 4.7 per cent; African 1.6 per cent; European 1 per cent; Others 1.2 per cent (2010 est.); **Literacy rate:** 95.7 per cent; **National Currency**: Bahraini Dinar (BHD); **GDP:** US$ 31.82 billion (2015); **Foreign Trade:** US$ 20.06 billion; **Defence budget:** 4.2 per cent of GDP (2014); **Sovereign Wealth Fund:** US$ 10.6 billion; **External Debt**: US$ 21.16 billion; **Per capita income:** US$ 50,300; **Oil reserves:** 100

million bbl; **Gas reserves:** 92.03 billion m³; **HDI rank:** 45; **Infant Mortality Rate**: 9.2/1,000 live births; **UN Education Index:** 0.714; **Gender Inequality Index:** 0.265; **Labour Force:** 809,700; **Unemployment rate**: 4.1 per cent; **Total Urban Population**: 88.8 per cent; **Rate of Urbanization:** 1.71 per cent; **Last National Census**: 2010.

India Related

Indian Cultural Centre: None; **Number of Indians:** 350,000 (approximately); **Number of places of worship for Indians**: 1 Temple, 5 Churches and 6 Gurudwaras; **Indian Schools:** Seven; **Indian Banks**: State Bank of India (2), Bank of Baroda (1), Canara Bank (1), ICICI Bank (1) and HDFC Bank (1); **Currency exchange rate:** 1 BHD = INR 176.80 (Feb 2017); **Last visit to India by the ruler**: March 2014; **Last Indian Prime Minister to visit**: None since 1947.

* * *

The domestic situation in Bahrain continues to be tense due to the unrest among the Shia majority[1] starting 2011, and the subsequent government crackdown. Accusations of human rights violations and the prohibition of political opposition have led to the Freedom House retaining its characterisation of the country as "not free", with freedom rating of 6.5 on a scale of 10.[2] The demographic component of the country primarily involves two regional powers: namely, Iran and Saudi Arabia. With only limited oil reserves to its credit, the Kingdom is heavily dependent upon Saudi Arabia for political as well as economic support. In the light of the re-entry of Iran into the international oil market following the lifting of the nuclear controversy-related sanctions as well as falling oil prices, Bahrain faces an economic crisis. This, in turn, has pushed the country towards a desperate diversification drive in 2015 and 2016, when it decided to nurture the tourism sector as the major source of economy.[3]

Under these challenging circumstances, a study of India's relations with Bahrain during the period under review is important. Since 2014, under the NDA government, New Delhi has increased its politico-economic engagements with Manama.[4] What has been the reason behind this sudden change in New Delhi's attitude? Is trade with Bahrain not a feasible option for India? With a sizeable expatriate population in the Kingdom, what has been India's strategy during crises situations in Bahrain? Should the need arise, is India ready for the evacuation of a huge number of its citizens? This chapter tries to delve into these questions, and attempts to highlight the challenges and opportunities for India in Bahrain.

Domestic Developments

A constitutional monarchy, Bahrain is ruled by the Sunni al-Khalifa family. The al-Khalifa came to Bahrain in 1783, and were able to capture a Persian-controlled garrison in the island and have ruled the country since then. In 1830, Bahrain signed a treaty that made it a British Protectorate, and it gained full independence on 15 August 1971.[5] When it comes to domestic policies and issues, the ruling family is divided into two blocs. The reformist bloc comprises of King Hamad himself, Crown Prince Salman, the Deputy Prime Minister Muhammad, and Foreign Minister Khalid. The anti-reformist bloc comprises of Bahrain's Prime Minister and the King's uncle Khalifa bin Salman al-Khalifa, the Minister of the Royal Court Khalid bin Ahmad bin Salman, and his brother and Bahrain Defence Force (BDF) Commander Khalifa bin Ahmad bin al-Khalifa.[6] Together, the latter brothers are known as "Khawalids", and are opposed to any compromise with the Shia population. Moreover, they have allies, and exercise control over security, intelligence, and the judiciary—the major sectors of Bahrain. This internal division within the ruling family has become a major stumbling block in the way of reforms and that is why most of the reforms suggested by the King and Crown Prince since 2011[7] never took off. The Prime Minister is an octogenarian, but is still very active politically, and has a strong hold on Bahrain's internal dimensions. Thus, scholars are of the opinion that substantial reforms with respect to the Shias in the country can happen only after him.[8]

The Arab Spring protests sweeping the Middle East did not spare Bahrain, with protests and demonstrations against the ruling family and the government being held since February–March 2011. The regime responded with a massive crackdown with the help of Saudi Arabia and, since then, the situation has not improved. Periodically, the opposition takes to the streets, with commoners protesting and demanding equal rights, and in response, the regime resorts to crackdowns, detentions, persecutions, and occasional executions. The imprisonment of opposition leaders, clerics, and human rights activists has become routine. The failure in implementing most of the recommendations suggested in the Bahrain Independent Commission of Inquiry (BICI) of November 2011[9] has aggravated the tension between the regime and the majority population.[10] The parliamentary election, held in November 2014, was boycotted by major opposition blocs—such as the Al-Wefaq—owing to mistreatment, corruption charges, and the gerrymandering of constituencies to favour Sunni candidates. Thus, there are only six Shia law-makers in a parliament of 80 members.[11] Detention, the revocation of citizenship, and the mistreatment of detainees have intensified.[12]

A Human Rights Watch report noted that, in 2015, many cases of torture of political detainees came to light, with methods such as "electric shocks, prolonged suspension in painful positions, severe beatings, threats to rape and kill, forced standing, exposure to extreme cold, and abuse of sexual nature" were commonly practiced.[13] On 20 January 2015, a Bahraini court sentenced Nabeel Rajab, a human rights activist, to six months imprisonment for his social media comments made against the regime in 2014. He was imprisoned in April that year. On 16 June, the Al Wefaq leader Sheikh Ali Salman was given a four-year prison term. A few days later, after serving imprisonment for four years, activist and former leader of the secular opposition society Wa'ad, was released only to be rearrested on 12 July.[14]

Apart from the imprisonment of renowned voices from the opposition, activists and individuals associated with non-governmental bodies, a number of cases of the revocation of nationality also came to light. As per the amendments made in the citizenship law No. 21 made in July 2014, the interior ministry, along with cabinet approval, can revoke the citizenship of any person who, "helps or engages in the service of an enemy country" or who "causes damage to the interest of the Kingdom or has committed a disloyal action against the Kingdom."[15] Based on this law, on 31 January 2015, the authorities revoked the citizenship of 72 people, which included individuals such as former parliamentarians, doctors, politicians, human rights activists, and several individuals for allegedly joining the Islamic State of Iraq and Syria (ISIS).[16]

Owing to domestic unrest and a sharp decline in oil prices, the economy of Bahrain has been severely affected, and a visible fall has been evident since mid-2014. However, with the diversification of its economy, the country has been able to pay most of its bills to an extent. In 2016, Bahrain's economy grew by 3 per cent due to the "encouraging performance" by the non-oil sector.[17] Hydrocarbon exports still account for about 80 per cent of government revenues. Most of it consists of oil exports from the Abu Safa Field which the country shares with Saudi Arabia; the field has a production capacity of 300,000 barrels per day.[18] Bahrain's oil and gas reserves are the lowest among the Gulf Cooperation Council (GCC) states, and are estimated at 210 million barrels and 5.3 trillion cubic feet, respectively. Indeed, the fall in oil prices since 2014 has caused Bahrain to cut subsidies provided to its citizenry as part of a rentier state welfare system.[19] To address its fiscal deficits, subsidies have been cut for some fuels such as kerosene (regarded as poor person's fuel) and some food items primarily meat (which is comparatively cheaper in Arab countries compared to cereals and proteins, and hence consumed widely by the poorer sections of society). This move has primarily affected the Shias as well as the expatriate population in the country; it affects the relatively richer Sunnis less.

The financial crisis has further contributed to a lack of implementation of the government's initiative to provide low-income housing. In January 2016, because of a further drop in oil prices, the government cut subsidies on gasoline, thereby raising the price by 60 per cent.[20] The other items which saw the slashing of subsidies in 2016 are kerosene and diesel; natural gas for industrial users; food items; and water and electricity.[21] In 2014, the Food and Agricultural Organization (FAO) declared Bahrain the world's most "water poorest" country, and subsidy cuts on such a wide range of commodities directly affected the poorest of poor in a big way.[22]

Partly to overcome the situation, Bahrain is investing in the banking and financial sectors that together comprise 25.5 per cent of the GDP.[23] Based on the economic freedom index of the American think tank, the *Heritage Foundation*, the country is ranked at 44th in the world, its economic freedom score is 68.5, whereas world average stands at 60.9 and regional average is at 61.9. Bahrain is categorised as "moderately free" in its economy.[24] According to the *Heritage Foundation*, despite regional and domestic challenges, Bahrain continues to be a business and financial hub in the Middle East, and high levels of international trade and investment in the country are sustained by a competitive and efficient regulatory environment. In the regulatory efficiency section, Bahrain's Business, Labour, and Monetary freedom stands at 69.4, 78.7 and 80.7 per cent respectively, wherein business and labour freedom have declined over a period of time; in the Open market section, trade, investment, and financial freedom stands at 82.8, 75 and 80 per cent respectively, and all the categories are increasing over the period.[25]

In July 2015, Bahrain passed its budget for 2015 and 2016; it was described by the Bahrain's Minister of Finance, Sheikh Ahmed bin Mohammed al-Khalifa, as the "most difficult budget" in the past 12 years. He was quoted as saying that the more the country borrows, the more its currency gets lower; and thus, it should learn to live in whatever it has, and it should spend according to the country's capability. This may be a subtle hint suggesting more subsidy cuts in the future. It is also a reminder that since Bahrain does not have huge financial reserves, it has less room to manoeuvre.[26] The budget spending was calculated at US$ 9.47 billion for 2015 and US$ 9.86 billion for 2016; while the deficit was forecast at US$ 3.89 billion and US$ 4.13 billion for 2015 and 2016, respectively.[27]

However, contrary to this, according to data issued by Bahrain's major financial body, the Economic Development Board (EDB), in July 2016 the country's economy expanded by 4.5 per cent year-on-year, which is regarded as the best rate of increase since 2014. While the oil sectors contributed about 12.4 per cent of this growth, the non-oil sectors, mainly services and construction, drove the growth by 2.7 per cent. The social sectors—which include education and health—expanded by 8.4 per cent, and construction and financial services by 5.4 and 31 per cent, respectively. According to the Chief Executive of EDB, Khalid al-Rumaihi, these results underline that Bahrain would soon recover from its losses in these times of a challenging global economy, and that this is good news for the country. He pointed out that this would reflect the strength of the fundamental factors responsible for such growth, and would have a positive impact of infrastructure investment.[28]

The International Monetary Fund's (IMF) study has a different view. It reveals that the country's economy is expected to slow further from 2016 onwards, and is weighed down by weak investors and fiscal adjustments. According to the study, Bahrain's fiscal deficit would rise to 19.5 per cent of its GDP in 2016 despite the country's measures to ensure fiscal sustainability. The country's revenues were hit by falling oil prices, and its GDP dropped to 3.2 to 3.3 per cent in 2015–16.[29]

On religious freedom, Bahrain is more accommodative towards many faiths such as Christians, Hindus, Jews, and Baha'is. However, its sectarian treatment is not the same. When it comes to its Shia population, both the years 2015 and 2016 recorded targeted persecution. For example, in October 2015, experts and officials of the United States Commission on International Religious Freedom Report found that there was a "pattern" of cultural, educational, economic, and social discrimination against Shia Muslims.[30] It was apparent that there was excessive use of force and abuse targeting Shia clerics, and discrimination existed in the educational system, media, public sector employment, housing, and even in welfare programmes. For instance, as stated earlier, the provision of low-income housing projects was stopped in its infancy, and this has largely affected the Shias. They continue to be interrogated, detained, arrested, convicted, and sentenced to prison on a number of occasions.

Three such examples are the detention of Al Wefaq party leader Shaikh Salman, the human rights activist Nabeel Rajab, and the Shia Cleric and interfaith activist Maytham al-Salman.[31] Around 30 Shia mosques were destroyed in 2011 by the government to quell protests. However, after pressure from international players and agencies, the government promised to rebuild the destroyed mosques. While the government did not meet the deadline in October 2015, it later announced that 27 mosques have been rebuilt. Nevertheless, as of February 2016, some sources revealed that only 20 structures were built by the government, of which only 15 are fully functional, whereas it was the Shia community which had built the remaining seven mosques but have yet not been reimbursed.[32] Controversy does not end here: of these rebuilt mosques, one of the Shia mosques—the Mohamad Al Barbaghi mosque—is rebuilt 200 metres away from its original location. While the government cited security reasons for the shift in location, the Shia community insists on the sanctity of the original location, and felt that the mosque cannot, and should not, be shifted.[33]

Following these developments, in December 2015, the country's Shura council approved amendments to the law that governs political societies, and banned clerics from delivering sermons and practicing religious duties while also being politically active. Thus, in 2016, there were several detentions and the imprisonment of Shia clerics. Since June 2016, Bahraini authorities interrogated, charged, and/or sentenced about 80 Shia clerics, and imposed travel bans against many.[34] In October 2016, it was reported that the local authorities removed Ashura banners in some locations where commemorations were taking place and which had resulted in clashes.[35] Since public gatherings are not allowed, there have been instances when protesters have taken to the streets and gathered to discuss political developments even during funerals. One such example was Hassan Al Hayki's funeral procession during which the mourners confronted the authorities, and shouted anti-government slogans.[36]

Thus, the domestic situation in Bahrain is uncertain. It has been criticized time and again by the international community—and many a times even by the US—for human rights violation and the mistreatment of the majority Shia population.

Bilateral Relations

In spite of domestic unrests and protests in Bahrain, the slowing of its economy, and subsidy cuts, India's relation with the country has been described as "excellent" by the Indian Ministry of External Affairs (MEA) in its annual report for 2015–16.[37] It highlights a number of bilateral visits, and the various agendas that have been fruitful in terms of economic collaborations and trade. Added to these, cultural relations have also prospered.

Political Relations

A number of Indian official visits to Bahrain took place in 2015 and 2016. Beginning April 2015, there have been four Indian official visits to Bahrain, and as many as three from Bahrain to India. On 15–16 April 2015, a delegation from the Ministry of Overseas Indian Affairs (MOIA) visited Bahrain for the second Joint Committee meeting on Labour and Manpower development. As a goodwill gesture, two Indian naval ships—*INS Deepak* and *INS Talwar*—visited Bahrain from 9 to 12 September. On 1 November, a delegation led by Deputy National Security Advisor, Arvind Gupta, visited Bahrain to participate in the first institutionalised bilateral security dialogue. The delegation was also part of the Manama Dialogue taking place at the same time. On the sidelines of first India-Arab League Ministerial meeting in Bahrain (23–24 January 2016), an agreement between the two countries was signed regarding the transfer of 'sentenced persons.'

From Bahraini side, its Minister of Foreign Affairs, Sheikh Khalid Bin Ahmed Bin Mohamed al-Khalifa, visited India on 22 February 2015, and met External Affairs Minister Sushma Swaraj to discuss all the aspects of the bilateral relationship such as the expansion of cooperation in the fields of "education, trade, investment and commerce, security and defence cooperation, exchanges in media sectors and communication" as well as issues related to Indian expatriates.[38] The first Bahrain-India Joint Business Council meeting was held in New Delhi (28–30 September 2015) wherein the Bahraini delegation was headed by Khaled al-Amin who hails from the Bahrain Chamber of Commerce and Industry, and the Indian delegation by Nitin Joshi from the Federation of Indian Chamber of Commerce and Industry (FICCI).[39] The Bahraini Minister of Interior, Rashid bin Abdulla al-Khalifa, made an official visit to New Delhi (1–4 December 2015). During this meeting, several agreements on "cooperation in combating international terrorism, transnational organised crimes, and trafficking in illicit, drugs, narcotic and psychotropic substances and precursor chemicals" were discussed.[40]

Economic Relations

India-Bahrain bilateral trade was affected due to the domestic situation in Bahrain during 2015–16, though it did see a rise in India's exports to that country which was slightly more than the 2012–13 levels (See Table 2.1) Imports from Bahrain were the lowest in the four-year time period from 2011–12 being estimated at just US$ 356.90 million. The total bilateral trade was slightly higher. However, Bahrain's share in India's total trade is miniscule, and has remained static at 0.16 per cent levels since 2011-12 (See

Table 2.1). The major non-oil imports from Bahrain comprise materials made of "aluminium in chips, bars and raw form, materials and medical equipment made of plastic"; major non-oil exports from India to Bahrain are parts of machineries, centrifuges, pumps, storage units, and vehicles, machines, timber and textiles.[41]

Since much of India's oil needs are fulfilled by other countries in the Persian Gulf, Bahrain does not emerge as an important partner in that field and, owing to the slowing of its economy and the sharp decline in oil prices, trade in non-oil sectors would be more fruitful for that country.

Table 2.1: India-Bahrain Bilateral Trade (in US$ million)

	2011-12	2012-13	2013-14	2014-15	2015-16
India's Exports	439.99	603.47	639.36	472.98	654.14
India's Imports	905.98	664.66	563.24	446.25	356.90
Total bilateral Trade	1,345.97	1,268.93	1,202.60	919.23	1,011.04
Share in India's Total Trade	0.17	0.16	0.16	0.12	0.16

Source: Adapted from Director-General of Foreign Trade, New Delhi, at www.dgft.gov.in

Figure 2.1: India–Bahrain Bilateral Trade (in US$ million)

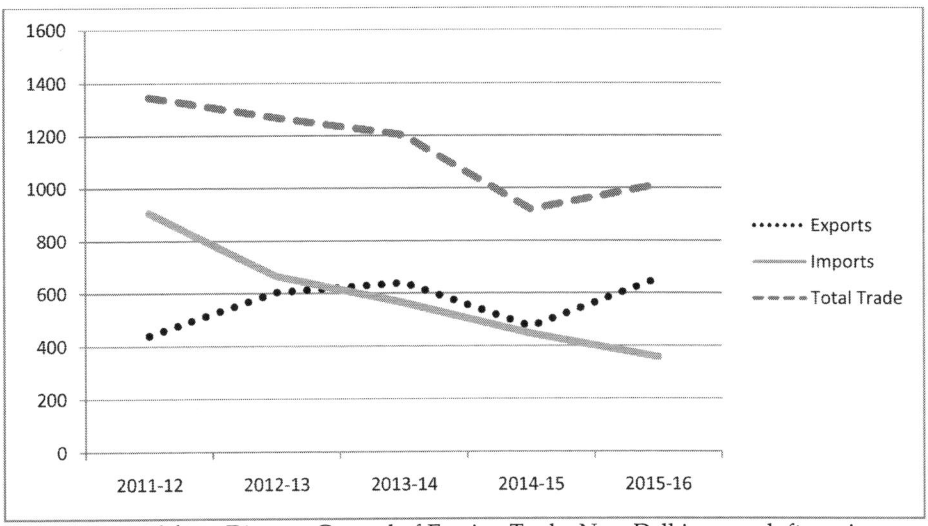

Source: Adapted from Director-General of Foreign Trade, New Delhi, www.dgft.gov.in

Energy Relations

In this context, the decline in oil prices have forced India and Bahrain to lower their oil related trade, and thus 2015-16 saw the lowest oil imports from Bahrain to India at US$ 94 million, which is nearly seven times lower than the 2011–12 levels. Nevertheless, India's total oil imports themselves have reduced from US$ 156,400 million in 2014–15 to US$ 96,953 million in 2015–16. This decrease is also reflected in the Bahraini share, and has affected the proportion of oil related imports from this country which stands at 26.36 per cent in 2015–16, almost half of the last level. Another interesting fact about the bilateral trade in 2015–16 is that the imports have decreased drastically from the 2011–12 levels when they were US$ 905 million, to US$ 356 million in 2015–16. The reason might be the internal crisis faced by Bahrain which has impacted its economy and, thus, like other countries in the world, India does not want to indulge much (see Table 2.2). Of India's total energy imports from the Persian Gulf, it is evident that Bahrain's share is one of the lowest; Saudi Arabia is the highest, followed by Iraq. In 2015–16, of its total imports from the Gulf Region, India imported only 0.18 per cent of its total energy requirements from Bahrain (see Table 2.3).

Table 2.2: Share of Oil in India's Imports from Bahrain (in US$ million)

Year	Oil Imports from Bahrain	Total Oil Imports	Share in Total Bahraini Oil Imports	Imports from Bahrain	Per cent of Oil in Imports from Bahrain
2011-12	605.89	172,753.97	0.35	905.98	67.53
2012-13	329.85	181,344.67	0.18	664.66	49.63
2013-14	359.23	181,382.59	0.20	563.24	63.78
2014-15	215.82	156,400.01	0.14	446.25	48.36
2015-16	94.07	96,953.06	0.10	356.90	26.36

Source: Adapted from Director-General of Foreign Trade, New Delhi, at www.dgft.gov.in

Figure 2.2: Share of Oil in India's Imports from Bahrain (in US$ million)

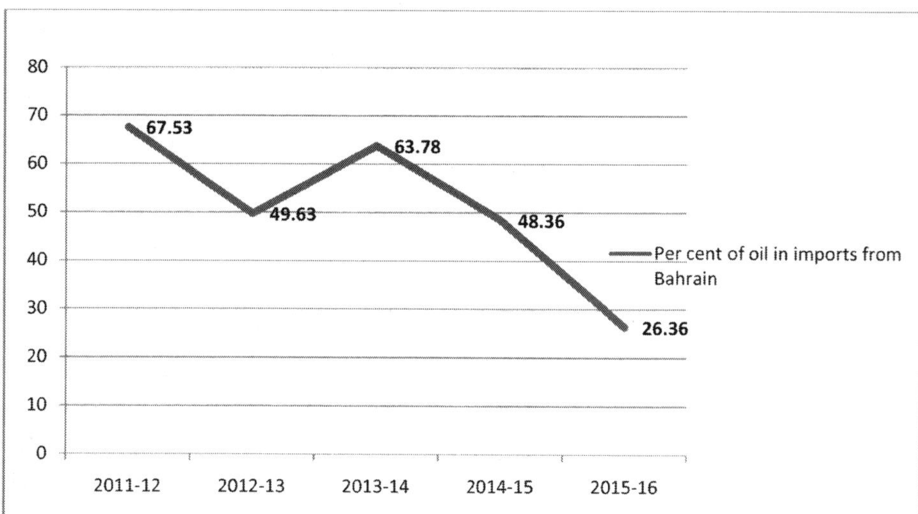

Source: Adapted from Director-General of Foreign Trade, New Delhi, at www.dgft.gov.in.

Table 2.3: India's Energy Imports from Bahrain (in US$ million)

	2011-12	2012-13	2013-14	2014-15	2015-16
Energy Imports from Bahrain	605.89	329.85	359.23	215.82	94.07
Total Energy Imports	172,753.97	181,344.67	181,382.59	156,400.01	96,953.06
Energy Imports from Persian Gulf	105,056.26	105,859.15	106,400.75	85,300.30	50,992.26
Share of Bahrain in Total Energy Imports	0.35	0.18	0.20	0.14	0.10
Share of Bahrain in Energy Imports from Persian Gulf	0.58	0.31	0.34	0.25	0.18

Source: Adapted from Director-General of Foreign Trade, New Delhi, at www.dgft.gov.in

Figure 2.3: Share of Bahrain in Energy Imports from the Persian Gulf

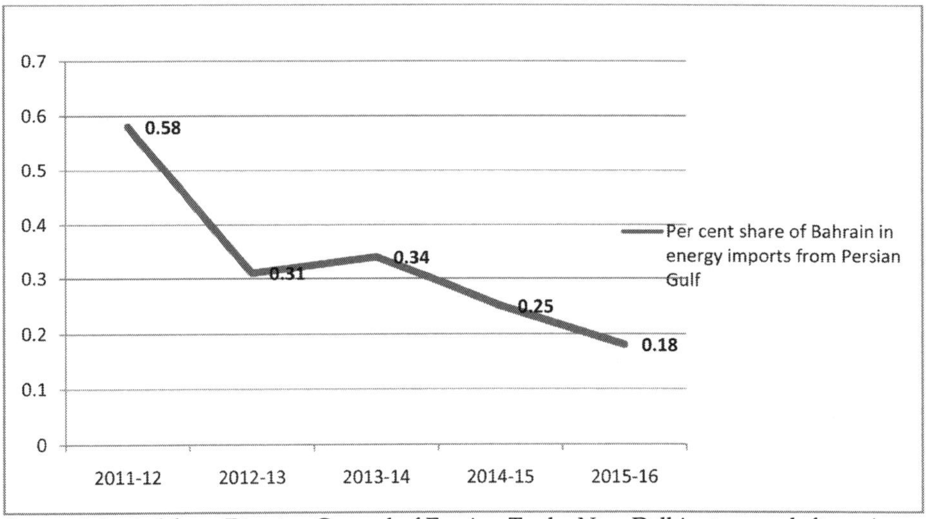

Source: Adapted from Director-General of Foreign Trade, New Delhi, at www.dgft.gov.in

Cultural Relations

With a 350,000 strong community in a country of about 1.2 million people, Indians constitute a substantial percentage of the resident population of Bahrain, and are thus seen as an important component of the country. This is so not just because they are apolitical but also because they are hard-working, and provide a support system to the rich Bahrainis. Probably this is reason why, on 19 December 2015, the "Little India in Bahrain" project was inaugurated to "celebrate and document" the contribution of Indians to the history and progress of Bahrain over the years. This project is also seen as a way to boost cultural tourism in the country. Situated in Manama, and initiated and supported by the Bahrain Authority for Culture and Antiquities (BACA), the project has beautified historical areas like the Manama Souq. The launch event was attended by the BACA President,

Shaikha Mai bint Mohammed al-Khalifa, the Bahraini Minister of Foreign Affairs Shaikh Khalid bin Ahmed bin Mohammed al-Khalifa, and Indian External Affairs Minister Sushma Swaraj, along with several Indian religious figures and Indian expatriates.[42]

The project incorporates three streets: the Bab Al Bahrain Avenue (gateway), the Al Tijjar Avenue (which implies traders), and the Al Hadrami Avenue (the temple road) in the city's old bazaar with an area of 5,000 square metres. Its aim is to preserve Bahraini houses, about 14 in number, constructed with Indian timber. It will also renovate a 200-year old Krishna temple in the city. The temple is known as the 'Shrinathji Temple', and is owned by the Hindu Bhatia community under the Thattai Hindu Mercantile Community Association. The inauguration date was deliberately chosen to coincide with Bahrain's National Day celebrations, and is also a part of Bahrain's declaration of 2015 as the year of heritage.[43] According to an official, it is a rare gesture on the part of the Minister of Foreign Affairs, a staunch Muslim, to have accompanied his Indian counterpart Sushma Swaraj to a temple. This shows that the relations between the two countries are congenial, and the "Little India in Bahrain" project reflects the Bahraini fondness for Indians.[44]

However, on this front, everything is not all hunky dory, and reports of human rights abuse and massive crackdown on its own population do not bode well for expatriate population and could pose a serious challenge in case violence spreads and force India to evacuate a large number of its citizens. Nevertheless, there has been no recorded violence against Indian expatriates in the country.

Opportunities and Challenges

In the given situation, Bahrain offers less opportunities and more challenges to India. The issues of counter-terrorism, increase in trade, and the problems of Indian expatriates only suggest a formal type of engagement from the Indian side. The lowering of oil prices has led to the decline in the oil trade between the two countries. Thus, there is need to explore non-conventional sectors in the relationship between the two countries. While defence ties and security collaboration are important, India can expand cooperation in the education and health sectors as also invest in R&D. Banking and commercial sectors are other areas in which the two countries could do well. With India's 'Make in India' project under Prime Minister Narendra Modi, Bahrain can harness a good deal. However, it would first have to address its domestic problems in order to have India collaborate in such projects which require considerable investment. Currently, given the declining economy of Bahrain, this seems to be a far-fetched idea.

Conclusion

2015 and 2016 have been marked as the year of tension, chaos, violence, detention, abuse, and the revocation of citizenship for Bahrain. Clearly, under such circumstances, development has become skewed, and this is well reflected in the falling economy of the country. Furthermore, Bahrain has been pressurised by various international players, including its ally the US and other international agencies, to implement all the 26 recommendations suggested by BICI. Given the domestic situation, falling oil prices, and regional tensions, India's engagement with Bahrain is rather pessimistic, with little political and economic interactions. While political and economic relations have not flourished at expected levels, cultural ties in the form of the "Little India in Bahrain" managed to light a little spark in the two country's bilateral ties.

NOTES

1. Andrew Hammond, "Bahrain holds vote to fill seats vacated during unrest," *Reuters*, 24 September 2011, at http://www.reuters.com/article/idINIndia-59524520110924
2. Freedom House (2016), "Bahrain", Freedom in the World, https://freedomhouse.org/report/freedom-world/2016/bahrain
3. Kenneth Katzman, "Bahrain: Reform, Security, and U.S. Policy", *Congressional Research Service*, 13 April 2017, https://fas.org/sgp/crs/mideast/95-1013.pdf
4. "India-Bahrain Relations", Ministry of External Affairs, Government of India, August 2015, at https://www.mea.gov.in/Portal/ForeignRelation/Bahrain_2015_08_18.pdf
5. Ibid.
6. Kenneth Katzman, "Bahrain: Reform, Security, and U.S. Policy", *Congressional Research Service*, 13 April 2017, at https://fas.org/sgp/crs/mideast/95-1013.pdf
7. Simeon Kerr, "Bahrain Crown Prince Given Political Role, *The Financial Times*, 11 March 2013, at https://www.ft.com/content/f2be4362-8a5d-11e2-bf79-00144feabdc0
8. Joost Hiltermann, "Pushing for Reform in Bahrain", *International Crisis Group*, 7 September 2011, at https://www.crisisgroup.org/middle-east-north-africa/gulf-and-arabian-peninsula/bahrain/pushing-reform-bahrain; see also, Geneive Abdo, "Talking About Reform in Bahrain", Brookings, 10 April 2013, at https://www.brookings.edu/opinions/talking-about-reform-in-bahrain/
9. Human Rights Watch (2016), Bahrain: Events of 2015", World Report, at https://www.hrw.org/world-report/2016/country-chapters/bahrain
10. "Bahrain's Reforms – No Backdown on Crackdown", *Human Rights First*, May 2012, at https://www.humanrightsfirst.org/wp-content/uploads/pdf/Bahrain_briefing_paper.pdf
11. Kenneth Katzman, "Bahrain: Reform, Security, and U.S. Policy", *Congressional Research Service*, 13 April 2017, at https://fas.org/sgp/crs/mideast/95-1013.pdf
12. "Bahrain: Events of 2015", *Human Rights Watch 2016*, World Report, at https://www.hrw.org/world-report/2016/country-chapters/bahrain; Human Rights

Watch 2017; "Bahrain: Events of 2016", World Report 2017, at https://www.hrw.org/world-report/2017/country-chapters/bahrain

13. "Bahrain: Events of 2015", *Human Rights Watch 2016*, World Report, at https://www.hrw.org/world-report/2016/country-chapters/bahrain
14. Ibid.
15. "Bahrain: Law No (21) for Year 2014 Amending Certain Provisions of the Bahraini Citizenship Act", National Authorities, Refworld, 24 July 2014, at http://www.refworld.org/docid/58dcfdae4.html
16. "Bahrain: Events of 2015", Human Rights Watch 2016, World Report, at https://www.hrw.org/world-report/2016/country-chapters/bahrain
17. "Bahrain Economic Outlook", *Focus Economics*, 9 May 2017, at http://www.focus-economics.com/countries/bahrain
18. Kenneth Katzman, "Bahrain: Reform, Security, and U.S. Policy", *Congressional Research Service*, 13 April 2017, at https://fas.org/sgp/crs/mideast/95-1013.pdf
19. Ibid.
20. Ismaeel Naar, "Bahrain, Oman Cut Petrol Subsidies as Oil Hits 12-year Low", *Al Arabiya*, 12 January 2016, at http://english.alarabiya.net/en/business/energy/2016/01/12/Bahrain-Oman-cut-petrol-subsidies-as-oil-hits-12-year-low.html;
21. "Bahrain", 2017 Index of Economic Freedom, Heritage Foundation, at http://www.heritage.org/index/country/bahrain
22. "Review of World Water Resources by Country", Food and Agricultural Organization (FAO), at http://www.fao.org/docrep/005/y4473e/y4473e08.htm
23. Kenneth Katzman, "Bahrain: Reform, Security, and U.S. Policy", *Congressional Research Service*, 13 April 2017, at https://fas.org/sgp/crs/mideast/95-1013.pdf
24. "Bahrain", 2017 Index of Economic Freedom, Heritage Foundation, at http://www.heritage.org/index/country/bahrain
25. Ibid.
26. "Bahrain Passes 2015–16 Budget after Parliament Forces Changes", *Reuters*, 6 July 2015, at http://www.reuters.com/article/bahrain-budget-idUSL8N0ZK07Y20150706
27. Ibid.
28. "Bahrain's Economy on the Rebound", Oxford Business Group, 28 August 2016, at https://www.oxfordbusinessgroup.com/news/bahrain%E2%80%99s-economy-rebound
29. Kuda Chikwanda, "Bahrain's Economy to Slow Further in 2016-17, IMF Says", *Gulf News*, 28 April 2016, at http://gulfnews.com/business/economy/bahrain-s-economy-to-slow-further-in-2016-17-imf-says-1.1813835
30. "2017 Annual Report", United States Commission on International Religious Freedom, at http://www.uscirf.gov/sites/default/files/2017.USCIRFAnnualReport.pdf
31. "Bahrain Chapter – 2016 Annual Report", United States Commission on International Religious Freedom, at http://www.uscirf.gov/sites/default/files/USCIRF_Monitored_Bahrain.pdf
32. "Bahrain Targets Shia Religious Sites", *Al-Jazeera*, 14 May 2011, at http://www.aljazeera.com/video/middleeast/2011/05/2011513112016389348.html
33. "Bahrain Chapter: 2016 Annual Report", United States Commission on International Religious Freedom, at http://www.uscirf.gov/sites/default/files/USCIRF_Monitored_Bahrain.pdf

34. "Bahrain Chapter: 2017 Annual Report", United States Commission on International Religious Freedom, at http://www.uscirf.gov/sites/default/files/Bahrain.2017.pdf
35. "Bahrain Chapter: 2016 Annual Report", op. cit.
36. Hamad Mohammed, "Mourners carry body of Hassan Al Hayki, who was detained by authorities more than a month ago and died on Sunday, during his funeral procession: File Photo", *Reuters*, 2 August 2016, at http://pictures.reuters.com/archive/BAHRAIN-POLITICS—S1BETTDONRAB.html
37. "Ministry of External Affairs: Annual Report 2015-16", Government of India, New Delhi, at https://www.mea.gov.in/Uploads/PublicationDocs/26525_26525_External_Affairs_English_AR_2015-16_Final_compressed.pdf
38. "India-Bahrain Relations", Ministry of External Affairs, Government of India, 18 August 2015, at https://www.mea.gov.in/Portal/ForeignRelation/Bahrain_2015_08_18.pdf
39. "Ministry of External Affairs: Annual Report 2015–16", Government of India, New Delhi, at https://www.mea.gov.in/Uploads/PublicationDocs/26525_26525_External_Affairs_English_AR_2015-16_Final_compressed.pdf
40. Ibid.
41. "Bahrain and India Economic Trade Relations", 2015, Bahrain Chamber of Commerce and Industry (BCCI), at https://www.bcci.bh/sites/default/files/library/Bahrain%20india%202015.pdf
42. "Little India in Bahrain", Bahrain Authority for Culture and Antiquities, 19 December 2015, at http://culture.gov.bh/en/theevents/current_events/Name,12640,en.html#.WSNbFeuGPIU
43. Anil D. Asarpota, "'Little India' Inaugurated in Bahrain's Historic Manama Souk", *The Times of India*, 22 December 2015, at http://timesofindia.indiatimes.com/nri/citizen-journalists/citizen-journalists-reports/anil-d-asarpota/Little-India-inaugurated-in-Bahrains-historic-Manama-Souk/articleshow/50280583.cms
44. "India, Bahrain to Strengthen Ties in Trade, Counter-Terror", *The Hindu*, 24 January 2016, at http://www.thehindu.com/news/India-Bahrain-to-strengthen-ties-in-trade-counter-terror/article14017624.ece

3

IRAN

Alvite Singh Ningthoujam

Key Information

Ruling Party: Combatant Clergy Association (*Jāme'e-ye Rowhāniyyat-e Mobārez*); **Supreme Leader (Wilayat-e-Faqih)**: Ali Khamenei (since 4 June 1989); **President**: Hassan Rouhani (since 15 June 2013); **National Day**: 1 April; **Parliament**: 290-member Majlis; **Last Parliamentary Election**: 26 February 2016; **Major Group in Parliament**: Reformists (coalition led by Mohammed Khatami; **National Carrier**: Iran Air.

Socio-Economic Indicators

Area: 1,648,195 sq km; **Population:** 82.8 million; **Native:** 100 per cent; **Expats:** NA; **Religious Groups:** Muslim 99.4 per cent (Shia 90–95 per cent; Sunni 5–10 per cent); Zoroastrian, Jewish and Christian 0.3 per cent (2011 est.); **Youth:** 16.57 per cent; **Population growth rate:** 1.18 per cent; **Life expectancy at birth:** 71.4 years; **Major population groups**: Persian 61 per cent; Azeri 16 per cent; Kurd 10 per cent; Lur 6 per cent; Baloch 2 per cent; Arab 2 Per cent; Turkmen and Turkic tribes 2 per cent; other 1 per cent; **Literacy rate:** 86.8 per cent; **National Currency**: Iranian Riyal (IRR); **GDP:** US$ 412.3 billion; **Foreign Trade:** US$ 159.64 billion; **Defence budget:** 4.1 per cent of GDP; **Sovereign Wealth Fund:** US$ 62 billion; **External Debt**: US$ 7.116 billion; **Per capita income:** US$ 18,100; **Oil reserves:** 157.8 billion bbl; **Gas reserves:** 34.02 trillion m^3; **HDI rank:** 69; **Infant Mortality Rate**: 37.1 deaths/ 1,000 live births; **UN Education Index:** 0.683; **Gender Inequality Index:** 0.515; **Labour Force:** 29.75 million; **Unemployment rate**: 10.7 per cent; **Urban**

Population: 73.4 per cent; **Rate of Urbanization:** 2.07 per cent; **Last National Census**: 2011.

India Related

Indian Cultural Centre: Tehran (inaugurated in 2013); **Number of Indians:** 700 (approximately); **Number of places of worship for Indians:** two Temples; and three Gurudwaras; **Indian Schools:** one; **Indian Banks:** State Bank of India; **Currency exchange rate:** IRR 1 = 0.0021 INR (Feb 2017); **Last visit to India by ruler**: President Mahmoud Ahmadinejad, 29 April 2008; **Last Indian Prime Minister to visit Iran**: Prime Minister Narendra Modi, May 2016.

* * *

After the signing of the Joint Comprehensive Plan of Action (JCPOA) between Iran and the P5+1 [the UK, China, France, Russia and the United States and Germany] in July 2015 and the lifting of some of the nuclear-related sanctions, it was expected that Indo-Iranian relations would regain lost momentum and develop faster. However, progress has been slow due to a variety of factors, including uncertainties about the economic situation amidst a global drop in international trade. More importantly, the glut in the international oil market has also ruined the chances of resurgence in the Iranian economy. This has been a major factor in the lack of serious economic engagement between India and Iran during 2015 and 2016. The signing of the trilateral Chabahar Port agreement during Prime Minister Narendra Modi's May 2016 visit was the highlight of the bilateral relations during 2015–16.

Domestic Developments

In 2015 and 2016, under the leadership of President Hassan Rouhani, the Iranian government made efforts to bring about domestic reforms in the country. However, major attention was paid to finalising a nuclear breakthrough with the P5+1. Due to this, many Iranians felt that the President had neglected basic and fundamental issues related to socio-economic and political reforms.[1] As a result, after the JCPOA was signed in July 2015, discussions began whether Rouhani would be able to deliver on the promises he had made, particularly to improve the Iranian economy. An analyst was of the view that while the Rouhani-led government showed a visible desire to "liberalize and privatize", the country's "moribund economy and the "possible loosen[ing of] the Islamic Revolutionary Guard Corps' (IRGC) chokehold on business", he became reticent with matters related to social and political reforms.[2] Although the popularity of the President increased after the breakthrough, other challenges were anticipated. One of them was the likely clash between the three centres of power in the Iranian political system—the Supreme Leader, the President, and the IRGC[3]—over domestic reforms and foreign policy approach.

Commenting on the reforms in February 2016, another Iranian analyst observed that the promises made by Iranian leaders remain largely unfulfilled.[4] After the sanctions were lifted in January 2016, President Rouhani urged the citizens to reduce their dependence on oil exports and, instead, focus on reforming the economy; but this in itself looked difficult, given the problems facing the economy and the reliance on oil.[5] This was primarily because in 2015, due to low oil prices and sanctions, Iran's revenue collected from oil exports fell to US$ 18 billion, and the country produced approximately 2.8 million barrels per day (bpd) in this year.[6] The hardliners still play an important role in the domestic, political and economic policies and, in late January, the Majlis passed a law promising guaranteed public trials for "political offences". This was considered a pragmatic step towards reform.[7]

A major highlight of 2016 was the parliamentary election held on 26 February. More than 12,000 candidates, including over 1,200 women, registered for 290 seats.[8] The reformists and moderates won over the hardliners by winning 42 per cent of the total seats, while the Independents won roughly 30 per cent.[9] A record number of 17 seats were won by women. Although this victory was not expected to bring a drastic change in overall policies, they were likely to push for further socio-economic reforms.

Matters relating to women's rights in Iran continued to dominate domestic developments. Although President Rouhani urged equal opportunities for male and female citizens, discrepancies still exist. In March 2015, a United Nations (UN) inspector blamed the Rouhani government for worsening the conditions of women, particularly limiting their economic and political opportunities.[10] The rate of executions has, reportedly, not decreased in recent times. On the contrary, Abdolhamid Ahmadi, Iran's Deputy Minister for Sports, talked about the approval given by the National Security Council to a government proposal that women should be allowed to watch outdoor games.[11] In the previous year, a woman was detained for trying to attend men's volleyball match. Hence, this was a breakthrough for a country known for subjugating women's rights despite their significant contribution in the 1979 revolution.

Economy

Since 2006, when the US-led sanctions were imposed over the nuclear controversy, the Iranian economy was crippled severely and thus, in 2015, there were high expectations as the country was heading towards a settlement of the longstanding negotiations over its nuclear programme. An immediate result which the Iranians anticipated was the unfreezing of an estimated US$ 100 billion in assets, and the economy reopening for the foreign investments.[12] The International Monetary Fund predicted that the economy would grow by 2 per cent in 2015.[13] The Iranians also expected to see an improvement in the quality of their lives. However, no economic benefits were visible. Some of the problems that remained during this year include stagnation in domestic production, low oil prices, and most importantly, a high rate of unemployment. For example, the unemployment rate for the age groups of 15–29 was estimated at 23 per cent, and was seen as a "worsening crisis".[14]

In October 2015, Iran announced a six-month package to revive the economy with the help of bigger investments and consumer spending.[15] Beyond this, the government, with the help of the banking sectors, agreed to provide credit cards at concessionary rates to enable the easy purchase of domestically-manufactured items; it also offered financial loans amounting up to 80 per cent of the value of cars, which could be repaid within seven years.[16] Inflation was down to 15 per cent in mid-2015 while it had been about 42 per cent in mid-2013. In 2015, the value of exports was US$ 77,974 million; the value of petroleum exports was US$ 27,308 million, crude oil exports were 1,1781 barrel per calendar day (bpcd); natural gas export was 8,541 million cubic meters, and the export of petroleum products was 514.3 barrels per day (bpd).[17]

The economy looked better in 2016, with sanctions lifted by Western powers. The IMF has forecast that Iran's Gross Domestic Product (GDP) is likely grow from 4 to 5.5 per cent for the fiscal year beginning from March.[18] The obstacles to the growth of the economy are the low oil prices. That said, by the end of 2016, Iran's oil revenue touched US$ 24.7 billion, and expected to reach US$ 41 billion in March 2017.[19] President Rouhani wound up the year by presenting the budget for the next financial year (beginning 21 March 2017), declared that the economy, "will exceed 10 quadrillion rials (US$ 328 billion at an exchange rate of 33,000 rials to the dollar) for the first time in Iran's history".[20]

Foreign Policy

The year 2015 was regarded as one of the most successful years for Iran, particularly for its foreign policy, as its leaders were making unrelenting efforts to engage with the international community by resolving the nuclear standoff.[21] Along with this, the fight against terrorism and extremism, especially with the rise of Islamic State of Iraq and Syria (ISIS), became an important agenda in forging closer ties with the outside world.[22]

During this year, another direct channel of communication was opened between the decades-old rivals. In February 2015, as a response to the diplomatic moves made by the US administration, Iran's Supreme Leader Ayatollah Ali Khamenei sent a letter to President Barack Obama. This was in reply to President Obama's letter to the Iranian leader in October 2014 in which the US President suggested a potential cooperation between the two countries in fighting the ISIS if a nuclear deal was reached.[23] A similar diplomatic effort was made by President Rouhani in late March 2015 by sending another letter to President Obama and other world leaders who, with the Iranian counterparts, were negotiating the deal.[24] This move by the Iranian president could be construed as his serious commitment to come to a mutually acceptable solution to the longstanding nuclear imbroglio. In September 2015, for the first time, President Obama mentioned that he would be willing to cooperate with Iran and Russia in bringing an end to the Syrian crisis. Simultaneously, Mohammad Nahavandian, the Chief of Staff of the President of Iran, put a pre-condition that this arrangement would be possible depending on how the US would fulfil its commitments to lift the sanctions. This gradual bonhomie led to the "historic handshake" between Obama and Iranian Foreign Minister Javad Zarif on 28 September at the UN.[25]

Following the signing of the nuclear deal in July 2015, Iran aspired to strengthen its relations with other countries in the region, and wanted to play its role in both regional and global crises, including in Syria, Iraq, Yemen and Afghanistan. President Rouhani gave importance to improving ties with the European Union (EU) countries, and visited Italy in January 2016 to improve economic cooperation and to combat terrorism and extremism. This was followed by a visit to France in the same month.[26] In December 2016, Iran and Airbus (of France) signed a landmark deal for the purchase of 100 French-made aircraft.[27] Further, weeks after the nuclear deal, the British Embassy in Tehran opened in August 2015, after a gap of four years.

Prior to these developments, Russian President Vladimir Putin went to Iran in November 2015 and vowed to cement bilateral ties, and to engage jointly in resolving the ongoing Syrian crisis. Besides enhancing political-economic ties, the two countries also decided to further their military cooperation, including arms trade.[28] Similar was the case with Sino-Iranian ties and both countries agreed to augment not only commercial and energy transactions but also defence ties. In November 2016, an agreement was signed between Iranian Defence Minister Hossein Dehgan and his Chinese counterpart, Chang Wanquan, regarding intensive military cooperation, particularly in training and counterterrorism.[29]

The 2016 US election was monitored closely by the Iranians. A major attention was given to the campaign rhetoric of Donald Trump who severely criticised and considered the 2015 nuclear deal as "suspicious."[30] Trump's victory reinforced the stand of the Iranian hardliners who remained opposed to the idea of bettering their country's ties with the West, particularly the US.[31] This even led to the debate whether the deal would collapse. Rouhani, with strong conviction, said that he would not let the deal to be torn apart by the new US president.[32] It is yet to be seen how the Iran-US relations will develop under the Trump presidency.

On the business front, in December 2016, Boeing signed a deal worth US$ 16.6 billion for the sale of 80 airplanes to Iran.[33] From the above developments, it seems clear that forging robust economic, military and political relations has become the top-most priority for Iran following the nuclear deal.

Military

Iran made progress in its military modernisation and missile development programmes during 2015–16. This was a trend similar to that which was prevalent during the years when sanctions were in place. In the budget ratified by the Majlis in April 2016, there was an increase in the military budget which stood at US$ 17.1 billion.[34]

On the missile front, in March 2015, Iran unveiled a domestically manufactured long-range and cruise missile called Soumar, with a range of 2,000 kilometres (km). Defence Minister Hussein Dehghan considered it a significant step towards enhancing Iran's defence and deterrence capabilities. Much to the dismay of the US, another medium-range ballistic missile (1,700 kms), Emad, was test-fired in October, and the system is very similar other missiles such as Qader, Shahab, and Sejjil.[35] Such tests were also conducted in 2016.[36] Finally, arms trade with its partners, namely China and Russia, are likely to grow as Russia delivered its S-300 missile systems to Iran in October even as this triggered a major concern within other Persian Gulf countries.

Bilateral Relations

Political Relations

Political relations between India and Iran during 2015 and 2016 witnessed noticeable improvement. This happened after the landslide victory of the Bharatiya Janata Party (BJP) in the May 2014 Lok Sabha elections. During these two years, there were several high-level official and ministerial visits. Chabahar port development, joint-efforts to bring stability in Afghanistan, counterterrorism cooperation, and the enhancement of energy and commercial relations were some of the important issues that dominated the political exchanges.

In 2015, one of the earliest visits was undertaken by the Minister for Shipping and Road Transport and Highways, Nitin Gadkari, on 5–7 May. This was considered an important visit as India was scaling up its relations with Iran, particularly to develop the Chabahar port to develop closer ties with Central Asian countries, especially after it sensed that a nuclear deal was on the horizon.[37] Despite strong caution by the US, Gadkari signed a Memorandum of Understanding (MoU) worth US$ 195 million to participate in the Chabahar port development project on 6 May. According to the official statement,

> With the signing of this MoU, Indian and Iranian commercial entities would now be in a position to commence negotiations towards finalization of a commercial contract under which Indian firms will lease two existing berths at the Port and operationalise them as container and multi-purpose cargo terminals.[38]

The port would give Afghanistan an alternate access to sea and also enhance its connectivity with regional and global markets.

Foreign Secretary S. Jaishankar visited Iran on 13-14 June 2015 as part of regular consultations. As bilateral relations remained hampered due to prolonged US-imposed sanctions, the visit focused heavily on cementing ties between the two countries as well as on issues such as port connectivity and the North-South Transportation Corridor.[39] The need to strengthen political ties with Iran was widely endorsed by many, including former diplomats and academicians.[40]

Some of the other high-level political engagements happened on the sidelines of important international events. On 9 July, marking the first ever highest political interaction, Prime Minister Narendra Modi met Rouhani in Ufa as both were attending the Brazil, Russia, India, China, and South Africa (BRICS) and Shanghai Cooperation Organisation (SCO) summits.

Amongst the host of issues (including trade, investment and connectivity) discussed, the rising threat of terrorism found focus as both have similar concerns about threats evolving from terror organisations such as ISIS. The deterioration of security order in Iraq and Afghanistan and in the wider region in the presence of "Takfiri terrorist groups" has been viewed as a major security challenge by Rouhani.[41] In June 2015, Ayatollah Ali Akbar Nategh Nouri, advisor to the Supreme Leader of Iran and also former Speaker of Iranian Parliament, was hosted by Chief Minister of Jammu and Kashmir, Mufti Mohammad Sayeed and discussed means of increasing cooperation in art and culture, sports, information and technology and technical education.[42]

From the Iranian side, its Foreign Minister Javad Zarif visited India during 2013–14 August. The focus of his conversation with Indian leaders was strengthening connectivity and increasing oil trade.[43] Possibilities to cooperate in railway projects, the development of the Farzad B gas field, and multilateral issues such as terrorism, ISIS, as well as the situation in Yemen, Syria, and Afghanistan were discussed. Notwithstanding this bonhomie, the Iranian ambassador cautioned that "India should take advantage of the time before the western countries start making their investments after the lifting of sanctions in the next 3–5 months."[44] However, in what could be considered as one impact of the growing political ties, the Indian government removed Iran from the list of countries which were put under the restricted visa category.[45] On 2 December, an approval for signing a "visa facilitation for Diplomatic, Official/Service and Ordinary passport holders" agreement approved given by the Indian cabinet.[46] These steps would not only ease the movement of high-ranking officials but would also facilitate enhanced people-to-people contacts.

The 18th India-Iran Joint Commission Meeting (JCM) was held in New Delhi in December 2015, and was co-chaired by External Affairs Minister Sushma Swawaj and Iran's Minister of Economic Affairs and Finance Ali Tayebnia. The Iranian side strongly suggested India's participation (in both public and private sectors) in the development of Chabahar Port, the Chabahar Free Trade Zone (FTZ), and in setting up industrial units in the FTZ.[47]

On a similar note, 2016 also witnessed a few landmark political developments between the two countries. As early as February, India's Foreign Secretary and Iranian Deputy Foreign Minister had foreign office consultations in New Delhi and cogitated on expanding the relations, particularly economic ties.[48] Following the July 2015 nuclear agreement, it was evident that both countries were keen on uplifting their energy and commercial cooperation. This was manifested in the several discussions and agreements that were signed pertaining to these areas. Amidst this, a major impetus to the political ties was given by the visit of Swaraj to Iran during 16–17 April. Apart from port connectivity and energy issues, she emphasized the importance of the trilateral agreement involving India, Iran, and Afghanistan on the Trade and Transit Corridor through the Chabahar port. During this visit, Iran also supported India's desire to join the Ashgabat Agreement.[49] This is a transport agreement started by Oman, Iran, Turkmenistan, and Uzbekistan as founding members, and its main objective is to facilitate the transportation of commodities and goods between Central Asian countries and the Persian Gulf. Other areas which were highlighted include the Double Taxation Avoidance Agreement, Bilateral Investment Protection and Promotion Agreement, and the launch of negotiations on the Preferential Trade Agreement.[50] Both sides also decided to resolve the longstanding payment imbroglio, and to intensify engagement between the National Security Council structures.

The biggest breakthrough happened when Modi visited Iran during 22–23 May 2016. Twelve MoUs or agreements pertaining to socio-cultural ties, foreign policy, science and technology, port development, maritime cooperation, transportation, cooperation between archives, and exports were signed.[51] The stand-alone nature of Modi's visit indicated the importance being given to this energy-rich country with which India had difficulties in exploiting maximum potential due to external pressures. Another major highlight was the signing of the Trilateral Transport and Transit Corridor agreement involving India, Iran, and Afghanistan which, according to Modi, "can alter the course of history of this region", and become a "foundation of convergence between our three nations."[52] In a bilateral pact with Iran, India agreed to invest US$ 500 million for port development and other infrastructure connected with it.[53] Although most of the discussions centred on matters related to commercial trade, connectivity, and infrastructural development, leaders acknowledged the security challenges deriving from non-state actors, and agreed to share intelligence and to combat terrorism robustly. To hasten the process of the trilateral agreements, ministers from the three countries met in New Delhi in late September 2016.

Economic Relations

Notwithstanding the US-led sanctions, economic relations have remained a salient feature of Indo-Iranian relations. Besides energy-related cooperation, both paid significant attention to non-oil trade. The volume of this trade has been fluctuating as is visible in Table 3.1. In 2012–13, the value of exports to Iran stood US$ 3.35 billion; it dropped to US$ 2.71 billion in

2015–16. A similar decline can be seen in India's imports which stood at US$ 11.59 billion in 2012–13 but came down to US$ 6.27 billion in 2015–16. As a result of this, the total volume of the bilateral trade also fell drastically in 2015–16 to US$ 9.0 billion.

Table 3.1: India-Iran Bilateral Trade (in US$ million)

	2011–12	2012–13	2013–14	2014–15	2015–16
India's Exports to Iran	2,411.33	3,351.07	4,971.35	4,175.06	2,718.51
India's Imports from Iran	13,790.16	11,594.46	10,307.16	8,955.02	6,278.75
Total bilateral Trade	16,201.48	14,945.53	15,278.51	13,130.08	9,060.26
Share of Iran in India's total trade	2.04	1.89	2.00	1.73	1.41

Source: Adapted from Director-General of Foreign Trade, New Delhi, and www.dgft.gov.in

Figure 3.1: India-Iran Bilateral Trade (in US$ million)

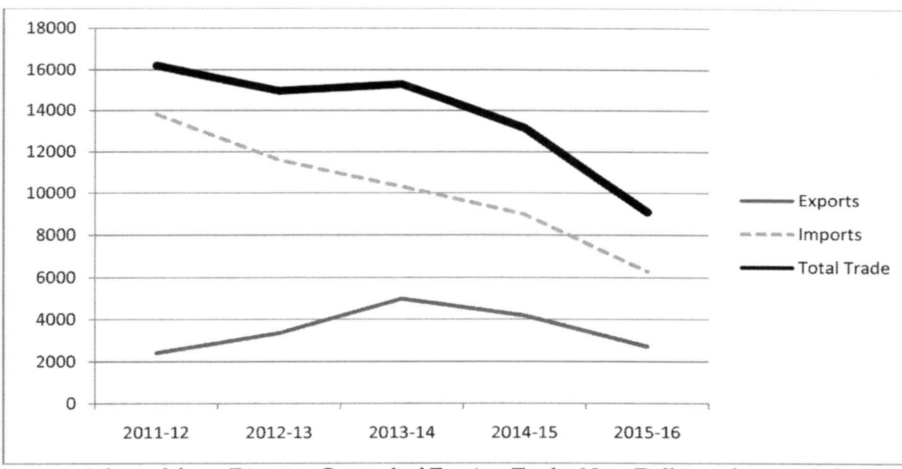

Source: Adapted from Director-General of Foreign Trade, New Delhi, and www.dgft.gov.in.

The major Indian exports include rice, tea, iron and steel, organic chemicals, metals, electrical machinery and drugs/pharmaceuticals.[54] Import items (excluding petroleum) include inorganic/organic chemicals, fertilizers, plastic and articles, edible fruit and nuts, glass and glassware, natural or cultured pearls, precious and semiprecious stones.

During 2015 and 2016, a heavy traffic of visits of Indians and Iranian officials from commercial establishments was witnessed between both countries. India engaged closely with attempting to increase export of commodities, such as rice, oilseeds, wheat, and medicines, and efforts were made to set up urea and uranium plants in this Persian Gulf country. In early 2015, reports of a possible resumption of Indian basmati rice exports to Iran began to surface from April onwards. Iran is one of the largest importers of this rice in recent years and it decided to relax the ban after its supply in the domestic market eased substantially. Moreover, with the easing of its economic sanctions, trade in this item looked promising, and in July 2015, both countries even agreed to establish referral labs in India to test rice consignments which are rejected by Tehran on the grounds of having high pesticide residue.[55] The Iranian government finally lifted the ban in November. In 2014–15, rice exports to Iran dropped 35 per cent to 935,567 tonnes; but in 2015–16, of the total export of Indian basmati of 4.05 million tonnes, one million tonnes went to Iran.[56]

Similarly, tea and medicines are other important trading items. In early April 2015, India's Commerce Secretary, Rajeev Kher, visited Tehran to augment trade in these two commodities. While there is an existing trade in this area, the value remains modest. Iran acknowledged the potential of Indian generic drugs, and wanted to increase imports.[57] In early December, an Iranian delegation from the Institute of Standards and Industrial Research of Iran (ISIRI) and the Health Ministry visited India, and toured a tea estate, a factory, and the Tocklai Tea Research Station in Jorhat—all in Assam.[58] Between January and September 2015, approximately 12.77 million kilogramme (kg) of tea was exported to Iran as compared to 13 million kg in 2014.[59] In February 2016, a 25-member Indian delegation led by Santosh Sarang, Chairman Tea Board of India, visited Iran to discuss similar issues as mentioned earlier.

Other important visits to Iran during 2015 include that of India's Finance Secretary Rajiv Mehrishi in July 2015; a nine-member delegation from the Tata Group in May-June 2015; ASSOCHAM-led 97 Indian companies to attend Iranian textile exhibition—Irantex—in Tehran in September 2016; and Federation of Indian Export Organisations (FIEO)-led delegation of 45 Indian companies to participate in the Tehran Internal Industry Exhibition in October 2015.[60]

With regard to fertiliser or urea, which remains an important trade item, in January 2015, the Indian government proposed fast tracking the setting up of a fertiliser plant in Iran. State-owned industries—Rashtriya Chemicals and Fertilisers (RCF), Gujarat Narmada Valley Fertiliser Corporation (GNFC), and Gujarat State Fertiliser Corporation (GSFC)—will be involved in setting up this plant.[61] This consortium appointed the SBI (State Bank of India) Capital to identify an Iranian local partner for the joint-venture (JV). Such a plant would help in meeting India's growing demand for urea which is estimated between 30 and 31 million tonnes, while the production capacity is around 22 million tonnes. Talks for this JV began in 2013, but unresolved issue for gas pricing have delayed the process. As a result, in late September,

India was offered natural gas at US$ 2.95 (about Rs. 195) per million British thermal units (mBtu) for the proposed plant at the Chabahar port.[62]

In May 2016, Iran's Bank Pasargad was selected as the local investor, and the plant is expected to produce 1.3 million tonne of urea annually.[63] During this month, delegations from the State Trading Corporation of India Ltd (STC) and the Federation of India Exporters Organisation (FIEO) visited Iran to explore economic cooperation in different areas. Indicating progress, in September 2016, the RCF formed a JV with GNFC and Iran's Faradast Energy Falat Company (FALAT) to construct the urea plant.[64] The rail sector is another potential area of cooperation between Iran and India and, in April 2016, the Managing Director of the Islamic Republic of Iran Railways (IRIR), Mohsen Pour-Seyyed Aqaei, talked about 250,000 tonnes of rails being purchased from India. As per an agreement, the IRIR would meet five per cent of the rail cost while the remaining 95 per cent would be provided by the Indian government.[65] This indicated India intensifying its export of steel to Iran as the latter is working towards connecting different corners—industrial centres, ports, and cities—through railway networks.

Energy Relations

Energy ties have remained one of the most important pillars of Indo-Iranian relations. For a prolonged period, the robustness of their cooperation was mostly identified by the volume of trade in oil and gas. However, for the last few years, there have been noticeable fluctuations, primarily due to US-led sanctions and the difficulties regarding payment mechanisms. India's oil imports from Iran dropped to US$ 4.46 billion in 2015–16 from US$ 7.29 billion in 2014–15 (see Tables 3.2 and 3.3). Throughout 2015 and 2016, several efforts were made to revive cooperation; but there is one sticking point that is likely to disrupt the purchase of oil and energy —the payment issue. This is still not completely resolved yet.

Table 3.2: Share of Oil in India's Imports from Iran (in US$ million)

Year	Oil Imports from Iran	Total Oil Imports	Iranian Share in Total Oil Imports	Imports from Iran	Per cent of Oil in Imports from Iran
2011-12	11,764.01	172,753.97	6.81	13,790.16	85.31
2012-13	9,716.39	181,344.67	5.36	11,594.46	83.80
2013-14	8,556.95	181,382.59	4.72	10,307.16	83.02
2014-15	7,292.13	156,400.01	4.66	8,955.02	81.43
2015-16	4,461.57	96,953.06	4.60	6,278.75	71.06

Source: Adapted from Director-General of Foreign Trade, New Delhi, at www.dgft.gov.in

Figure 3.2: Share of Oil in India's Imports from Iran

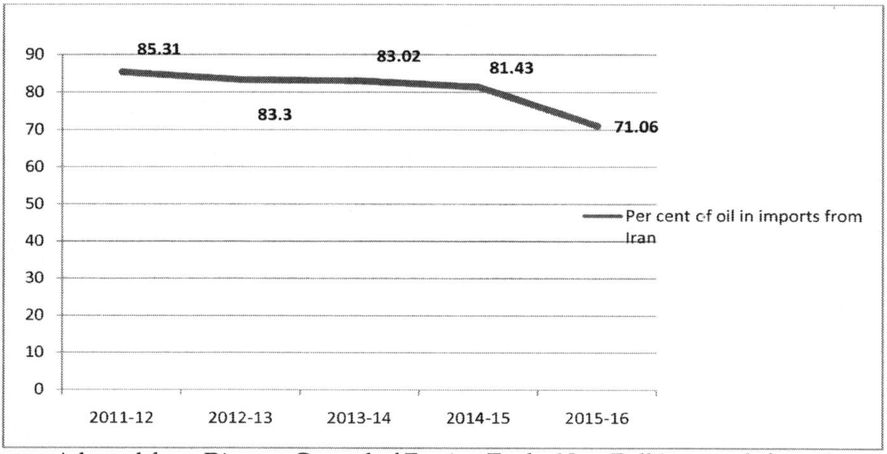

Source: Adapted from Director-General of Foreign Trade, New Delhi, www.dgft.gov.in

Table 3.3: India's Energy Imports from Iran (in US$ million)

	2011–12	2012–13	2013–14	2014–15	2015–16
Energy Imports from Iran	11,764.01	9,716.39	8,556.95	7,292.13	4,461.57
Total Energy Imports	172,753.97	181,344.67	181,382.59	156,400.01	96,953.06
Total Energy Imports from Persian Gulf	105,056.26	105,859.15	106,400.75	85,300.30	50,992.26
Share in Total Energy Imports (in per cent)	6.81	5.36	4.72	4.66	4.60
Share in Energy Imports from Persian Gulf (in per cent)	11.09	9.18	8.04	8.55	8.75

Source: Adapted from Director-General of Foreign Trade, New Delhi, at www.dgft.gov.in

Figure 3.3: Share of Iran in Energy Imports from the Persian Gulf

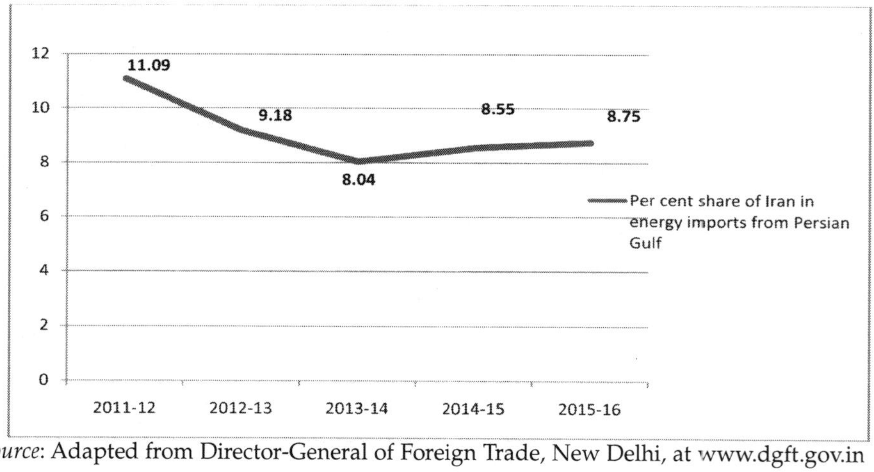

Source: Adapted from Director-General of Foreign Trade, New Delhi, at www.dgft.gov.in

The year 2015 did not begin on a positive note, and in February, India's major importers, such as Mangalore Refinery and Petrochemicals Ltd (MRPL), opted for Iraqi Basra oil replacing Iran's. This was done mainly to avoid pressure from external sources.[66] To avoid facing sanctions, IOC even rescheduled its shipment of oil to March and, the import of Iranian crude oil plummeted to 102,200 bpd, or a decline of 63 per cent from January.[67] The cut in imports was due to India wanting to maintain its import at 210,000–220,000 bpd, or about 11 million tonnes, so that it remains in consonance with one of the conditions of the nuclear deal which urged Iranian oil clients to retain import equivalent to the levels in 2013.[68] Other Asian buyers, including China, South Korea, and Japan, also cut their share of imports from Iran. Thus, Iranian crude exports to Asia fell by 23 per cent during January and February 2015.[69]

Until early 2015, India owed approximately US$ 8.8 billion for its oil imports from Iran. Refineries settled 45 per cent of the payments through deposits in Tehran's commercial bank account with UCO Bank, while withholding the remaining 55 per cent. In order to bridge the gap in trade, India allowed its exporters to opt for non-sanctioned or non-oil items. This arrangement has been in place since the last few years. Amidst this, the ONGC showed interest in involving itself in the construction of Farzad B gas field. This coincided with the efforts of the international powers to negotiate with Iran over the nuclear controversy. Iran, on the other hand, was not initially receptive to India's proposal as it wanted to auction the field, and doubted the latter's commitment to make investments.[70] As there was no breakthrough in this regard, negotiations continued in 2016 despite the April visit of India's Petroleum Minister Dharmendra Pradhan.[71] Iran appears to be unconvinced with India's "offer".[72]

During mid-2015, signs of progress in the energy trade could be seen as India's import of oil rose to its highest level in May when it shipped 367,900 bpd of crude—39 per cent more than that in April. The IOC received about a million barrels and 207,400 bpd by MRPL.[73] Moreover, with the nuclear deal, India wanted to push for, or revive, the Iran-Pakistan-India gas pipeline. However, the Associated Chambers of Commerce and Industry of India (ASSOCHAM) wanted India to bypass Pakistan, and even suggested signing a Preferential Trade Agreement (PTA) with Iran to increase merchandise trade.[74]

In July, the Reserve Bank of India (RBI) agreed to help the refiners clear the payment dues estimated at US$ 6.5 billion. In the following month, Iran asked India to pay these dues in three instalments within two months—partly in rupees and the remaining in either dollars or Euros.[75] As a follow up, the Indian Finance Secretary asked the refiners to pay US$ 1.4 billion in dues. Iran needed this to rebuild its economy which was crippled by the sanctions. The timing of the payment was unclear as India was waiting for an approval from the Office of Foreign Assets Control (OFAC) of the US Department of Treasury, and reports surfaced about the payment of US$ 700 million between September and October.[76] Despite these developments, fluctuation in Iranian oil imports remained towards the end of 2015; and by November, India's imports dropped to 138,100 bpd—a drop of 24 per cent from the previous month. Thus, from January to November 2015, the import went down to 206,000 bpd.[77] This was primarily due to the payment issue as both could not find a feasible solution even after the nuclear deal. Meanwhile, the possibilities of sealing an undersea gas pipeline with India—a project worth US$ 4.5 billion—was explored by Iran as part of the South Asian Gas Enterprise (SAGE) pipeline project.[78] This 1,400 km pipeline would enable India to receive gas from Iran through the Oman Sea and the Arabian Sea, with this infrastructure being utilised by major state-owned companies, including the Gas Authority of India Ltd (GAIL) and IOC.

During early 2016, officials of both countries gave considerable attention to streamlining the payment row. In January, they agreed to keep aside the dollar and, opted for rupee payment instead while settling all outstanding oil dues. This was seen as a move that would be applicable for future transactions. The option of the rupee did not last very long as Iran wanted Indian refineries to clear oil dues in Euros after sanctions were lifted. For this purpose, Iran was opening or re-activating its Euro accounts with some Indian banks; IDBI and SBI were approached, and settlements were to be carried out through the Asian Currency Union (ACU) with the consent of the RBI.[79] Unsettled payment mechanisms received adequate attention, particularly before Modi's visit in May and, as a "goodwill gesture", even agreed to the Iranian demand for 1.5 per cent interest rate on the US$ 6.5 billion oil dues, a situation arising due to differences in fluctuating foreign exchange rates.[80] This meant that "refiners will clear the past dues as per the exchange rate prevailing at the time of billing. This means refiners will pay the amount billed at the time of buying crude oil from Iran plus 1.5 per cent interest."[81] From June onwards, Indian refineries chose SBI and Germany's Europaeisch-Iranische Handelsbank AG (EIH) Bank to facilitate payment dues. Moreover, Indian refineries were informed that they were to arrange their own freight as Iran, after the easing of sanctions, ended the free shipping of crude oil.

Notwithstanding all these hardships, some headway in energy relations was made. This began with the plan of the National Iranian Gas Exports

Company (NIGEC) delivering gas to India by constructing the aforementioned undersea gas pipeline, or the "longest sea pipeline [which] would link Chabahar port and the state of Gujarat".[82] The estimated cost of this pipeline is US$ 4.5 billion. India plans to purchase six million barrels (four million barrels by Bharat Petroleum; two million barrels by MRPL) of crude from Iran for its "strategic oil reserves."[83] Overall, in 2016, India bought 473,000 bpd of Iranian oil as compared to 208,300 bpd in the previous year. Thus, Iran became the fourth largest supplier after Saudi Arabia, Iraq, and Venezuela.[84]

Military-Security Relations

The Indo-Iranian military-security cooperation is undergoing a gradual process of renewal but is likely to remain limited. In other words, the nature of the engagement is going to be concentrated more on naval exercises, the exchange of information and intelligence gathering, military training, anti-piracy, and counter-terrorism cooperation. For the first time after lifting the sanctions, both the navies conducted exercises in early June 2016 in the Strait of Hormuz.[85] In August 2015 also, an Indian naval delegation paid a five-day visit to Bandar Abbas port, and interacted with their Iranian counterparts.[86] In the previous month, the Deputy Secretary of the National Security Council of Iran, Ameer Saeed Iravan, visited India to discuss issues of bilateral and mutual interest, and met the Foreign Secretary, National Security Advisor Ajit Doval, and the Deputy National Security Advisor Arvind Gupta.[87]

For playing a constructive role in war-ravaged Afghanistan, enhancing security cooperation has become imperative. Likewise, the Chabahar port development programme requires considerable cooperation in security spheres so as to ensure a successful completion of the projects, and for the smooth conduct of trade and commercial transactions with the Central Asian Republics (CARs). Counterterrorism is another area where security cooperation is getting significant attention from both Iran and India. This is largely due to the ongoing politico-security crisis, particularly in the Middle East, Afghanistan, and South Asia, where terror groups such as ISIS have penetrated in different forms—physical and ideological. In almost all the high-level interactions between Iranian and Indian leadership, discussions on how to fight this global phenomenon remained on the top of the agendas.

Thus, counterterrorism is emerging as a salient feature of the ties between the two countries. During his May visit, Prime Minister Modi observed:

> We also have shared concerns at the spread of forces of instability, radicalism and terror in our region. We have agreed to consult closely and regularly on combating threats of terrorism, radicalism, drug trafficking and cyber crime. We have also agreed to enhance interaction between our defence and security institutions on regional and maritime security.[88]

Similarly, in August 2015, the Iranian Foreign Minister referred to threats in Afghanistan coming from ISIS, and sought India's cooperation in tackling the menace of extremism and terrorism in the wider region. The visit of the leader of Iranian Supreme National Security Council (SNSC), Ali Shamkhani (August 2016), could also be considered as a move to bolster security-related cooperation.[89]

Socio-Cultural Relations

India and Iran have immense pride in talking about their civilizational and historical linkages. This is one aspect of the ties which has remained unaffected for the last several decades. Significance placed on this was evident when a MoU between the Indian Council for Cultural Relations and the Islamic Culture and Relations Organisation of Iran was signed during Modi's visit and in his words:

> Our historical ties may have seen their share of ups and downs. But, throughout our partnership has remained a source of boundless strength for both of us. Time has come for us to regain the past glory of traditional ties and links.[90]

In April 2016, Indian Foreign Minister Sushma Swaraj began her Iran journey by first visiting a Gurudwara in Tehran where she assured the Indian community that their "problems and grievances" would be discussed with the Iranian authorities.[91] The important role played by the Indians and their contributions to Iran were acknowledged by her.

Music, art, and culture have also contributed significantly in cementing the ties between these two countries. In January 2015, renowned Indian musical maestro A. R. Rahman collaborated on a film by an Iranian director, Majid Majidi.[92] Despite a Fatwa issued by a Mumbai-based Sunni Muslim Organisation, Raza Academy, describing the film titled *Muhammad: the Messenger of God* as "blasphemous" and urging the government to impose a ban on it, the controversy died out quietly.[93]

For the last many years, cinema continues to remain a pivotal instrument that strengthens cultural and people-to-people cooperation. In 2016, Iranian films were screened in different film festivals held in India, and *Daughter*, directed by Reza Mirkarimi, won the Golden Peacock award at the 47th International Film Festival of India (IFFI) held in November.[94] In the previous month, Indian audiences watched several Iranian movies as both countries were commemorating the 60th year of signing their cultural agreements. The talent of Iranian filmmakers were also exposed during the *Dharamshala International Film Festival* (November 2016), and *Third Eye Film Festival* (December 2016) in Mumbai.

Conclusion

The nature of bilateral ties during 2015–16 was comprehensive. As was noticeable, leaders from both countries engaged intensively to strengthen cooperation in all the fields—economic, political, security, and socio-culture. Most of the dealings during these two years were largely concentrated on the development of the Chabahar port. The outcome of this project remains less than significant since there has been only limited progress on the ground. Executing all the agreements effectively and without further delays remains a major challenge for both countries. Despite some of the sanctions being lifted against Iran, payment issues still remain, leading to irregularities in the oil and energy trade; this leaves negative impact on the bilateral trade as well. Both countries need to streamline these issues at the earliest in the interest of strengthening the bilateral ties. Merely heralding civilisational links in public forums will be insufficient to improve relations in any meaningful way.

India cannot afford to have a lackadaisical attitude in its Iran policy as this would only give further leeway to other countries, including China, to secure its position in this Persian Gulf nation. India also needs to be mindful of the fact that the US is likely to emerge as a factor vis-à-vis Iran. Therefore, India needs to get its bilateral relations with Iran on the right track at the earliest—that is, much before overburdening itself with commitments and involvement in other multinational initiatives.

NOTES

1. Reza H. Akbari, "Rouhani ignores domestic political reforms", *Al-Monitor*, 23 April 2015, at http://www.al-monitor.com/pulse/originals/2015/04/iran-hassan-rouhani-interior-ministry-nuclear.html
2. Alireza Nader, "Post deal, can Rouhani deliver on promises of reform?", *Al-Monitor*, 24 July 2015, at http://www.al-monitor.com/pulse/originals/2015/07/rouhani-iran-reform-nuclear-deal.html
3. Alex Vatanka, "Pulling the Strings: How Khamenei Will Prevent Reform in Iran", *Foreign Affairs*, 25 November 2015, at https://www.foreignaffairs.com/articles/iran/2015-11-25/pulling-strings

4. Massoumeh Torfeh, "Iran 37 years later: Any hope for reforms?", *Al-Jazeera*, 12 February 2016, at http://www.aljazeera.com/indepth/opinion/2016/02/iran-37-years-hope-reforms-160210082641602.html
5. Amir Bagherpour, "Iran's hardliners will block economic reform", *The Guardian*, 18 January 2016, at https://www.theguardian.com/world/iran-blog/2016/jan/18/iran-economic-reform-blocked
6. "Iran's oil revenue falls to $18B in 2015", *Daily Sabah*, 21 October 2015, at https://www.dailysabah.com/energy/2015/10/22/irans-oil-revenue-falls-to-18b-in-2015
7. "Iran parliament defines 'political crimes' in apparent nod to reform", *Reuters*, 24 January 2016, at http://www.reuters.com/article/us-iran-politics-idUSKCN0V20P9
8. Garrett Nada, "Iran in 2016", *The Iran Primer*, 6 January 2016, at http://iranprimer.usip.org/blog/2016/jan/06/iran-2016
9. "Iran elections: Hardliners lose parliament to Rouhani allies", *BBC*, 30 April 2016, http://www.bbc.com/news/world-middle-east-36178276
10. Sangwon Yoon, "Iran's Oppression of Rights, Women Worse under Rouhani, UN Says", Bloomberg, 17 March 2015, at https://www.bloomberg.com/news/articles/2015-03-16/iran-s-oppression-of-rights-women-worse-under-rouhani-un-says
11. Saeed Kamali Dehghan, "Iran's deputy minister for sports: yes, women can go to watch big matches", *The Guardian*, 4 April 2015, at https://www.theguardian.com/world/2015/apr/04/iran-national-security-council-women-watch-big-sports-matches
12. For further analysis, see Cyrus Amir-Mokri and Hamid Biglari, "A Windfall for Iran?", *Foreign Affairs*, November/December 2015, at https://www.foreignaffairs.com/articles/iran/2015-10-20/windfall-iran
13. Masoud Movahed, "Nuclear deal could unleash Iran's economy", *Al-Jazeera*, 27 April 2015, at http://america.aljazeera.com/opinions/2015/4/nuclear-deal-could-unleash-irans-economy.html
14. "Iran: Unemployment crisis worsening", *Iran Focus*, 27 April 2016, at http://iranfocus.com/en/index.php?option=com_content&view=article&id=30448:iran-unemployment-crisis-worsening&catid=4:iran-general&Itemid=109
15. "Iran unveils stimulus package to lift economy", *Press TV*, 18 October 2015, at http://www.presstv.com/Detail/2015/10/18/433930/Iran-economy-government-stagnation-stimulus
16. Ibid.
17. *Iran Facts and Figures*, Annual Statistical Bulletin, Organisation of the Petroleum Exporting Countries (OPEC), 2016.
18. Garrett Nada, "Iran in 2016", op. cit. For a similar report, see "Iran's Economic Outlook-Spring 2016", The World Bank, at http://www.world bank.org/en/country/iran/publication/economic-outlook-spring-2016
19. "Oil revenues to top US$41bn", Mehr News Agency, 16 January 2017, at http://en.mehrnews.com/news/122755/Oil-revenues-to-top-41bn
20. Alireza Ramezani, "Rouhani's budget proposal reverses declining reliance on oil", *Al-Monitor*, 12 December 2016, at http://www.al-monitor.com/pulse/originals/2016/12/iran-rouhani-cabinet-budget-proposal-2017-1396-oil.html#ixzz4ePPww3DE

21. For further reading, see Arun Vishwanathan, "Iranian Nuclear Agreement: Understanding the Non-proliferation Paradigm", *Contemporary Review of the Middle East,* 2016, Vol.3, Issue1, pp. 3–22. Also, Ellie Geranmayeh, "Towards and Beyond a Final Nuclear Deal with Iran", *The International Spectator,* 2015, Vol. 50, Issue 2, pp. 1–7.
22. Behzad Khoshandam "Iran's Foreign Policy in 2015", *Iran Review,* 6 December 2015, at http://www.iranreview.org/content/Documents/Iran-s-Foreign-Policy-in-2015.htm
23. Jay Solomon and Carol E. Lee, "Obama Wrote Secret Letter to Iran's Khamenei About Fighting Islamic State", *The Wall Street Journal,* 6 November 2014, at https://www.wsj.com/articles/obama-wrote-secret-letter-to-irans-khamenei-about-fighting-islamic-state-1415295291
24. Laura Rozen, "Rouhani writes Obama as Iran talks enter endgame", *Al-Monitor,* 26 March 2015, at http://www.al-monitor.com/pulse/originals/2015/03/iran-nuclear-negotiations-obama-rouhani.html
25. "Obama engages Iranian foreign minister in historic handshake at UN", *The Guardian,* 27 September 2015, at https://www.theguardian.com/us-news/2015/sep/29/obama-iranian-foreign-minister-mohammad-javad-zarif-handshake
26. Michel Rose and John Irish, "Protesters march, France eyes business deals as Iran's Rouhani visits", *Reuters,* 28 January 2016, at http://www.reuters.com/article/us-iran-europe-rouhani-idUSKCN0V60TE
27. Tim Hepher, "Airbus seals deal with Iran for sale of 100 aircraft", *Reuters,* 22 December 2016, http://www.reuters.com/article/us-iran-aircraft-idUSKBN14B1H9
28. "Russia, Iran plan $10bn arms supply to Tehran", *RT,* 14 November 2015, at https://www.rt.com/news/366871-russia-iran-weapons-delivery/
29. Franz-Stefan Gady, "Iran, China Sign Military Cooperation Agreement", *The Diplomat,* 15 November 2016, at http://thediplomat.com/2016/11/iran-china-sign-military-cooperation-agreement/
30. Elliot Smilowitz, "Trump: Iran deal was so bad it's suspicious", *The Hill,* 2 January 2016, at http://thehill.com/blogs/ballot-box/gop-primaries/264598-trump-iran-deal-was-so-bad-its-suspicious
31. Parisa Hafezi, "Iranian hardliners see Trump's victory as a unique opportunity to claw back the power they lost under the Iran deal", *Business Insider,* 21 November 2016, at http://www.businessinsider.com/iranian-hardliners-see-trumps-victory-as-a-unique-opportunity-to-claw-back-power-2016-11?IR=T
32. Thomas Erdbrink, "Iran's President Says Donald Trump Can't Tear Up Nuclear Pact", *The New York Times,* 6 December 2016, at https://www.nytimes.com/2016/12/06/world/middleeast/hassan-rouhani-donald-trump-nuclear-agreement.html
33. Thomas Erdbrink, "Iran and Boeing Sign $16.6 Billion Deal on Sale of 80 Aircraft", *The New York Times,* 11 December 2016, at https://www.nytimes.com/2016/12/11/world/middleeast/iran-boeing-airplane-deal.html
34. "Rouhani's New Budget Increases Iran's Military Spending", Iran News Update, 25 April 2016, at http://irannewsupdate.com/news/economy/2715-rouhani-s-budget-for-persian-year-1395-offers-a-bleak-economic-outlook-with-an-increase-in-military-and-security-budgets.html
35. For a detailed report, see Abbas Qaidaari, "What's so special about Iran's latest missile?" *Al-Monitor,* 20 October 2015, at http://www.al-monitor.com/pulse/originals/2015/10/iran-missile-test.html

36. For additional information, see "Iran Missile Milestones: 1985-2016", *Iran Watch*, 13 July 2016, http://www.iranwatch.org/our-publications/weapon-program-background-report/iran-missile-milestones-1985-2016
37. Nidhi Verma and Manoj Kumar, "India to sign port deal with Iran, ignoring US warning against haste", *Reuters*, 5 May 2015, at http://www.reuters.com/article/india-iran-port-idUSL4N0XV16J20150505
38. "Inter-Governmental MoU between India and Iran", 6 May 2015, Ministry of External Affairs, Government of India, at http://www.mea.gov.in/pressreleases.htm?dtl/25185/InterGovernmental+MoU+between+ India+and+Iran
39. Dipanjan Roy Chaudhury, "India-Iran relations: Foreign Secretary S. Jaishankar to visit Iran this month; focus on Chabahar project", *The Economic Times*, 6 June 2015, at http://economictimes.indiatimes.com/news/politics-and-nation/india-iran-relations-foreign-secretary-s-jaishankar-to-visit-iran-this-month-focus-on-chabahar-port/articleshow/47564023.cms
40. Smriti Kak Ramachandran, "India moves to reset ties with Iran", *The Hindu*, 24 June 2015, at http://www.thehindu.com/news/national/india-moves-to-reset-ties-with-iran/article7347380.ece
41. "Iran, India must counter terrorism in region: Rouhani", Press TV, 9 July 2015, at http://www.presstv.com/Detail/2015/07/09/419479/Iran-President-Hassan-Rouhani-India-Prime-Minister-Narendra-Modi-Russia-Ufa-BRICS-SCO
42. Muhammad Raafi, "Ayatollah Nouri, Iranian Ambassador Call on CM Mufti", Kashmir Life, 3 June 2015, at http://www.kashmirlife.net/ayatollah-nouri-iranian-ambassador-call-on-cm-mufti-80200/
43. "Official Spokesperson's response to a question on the visit of the Iranian Foreign Minister", Ministry of External Affairs, Government of India, 14 August 2015, at http://www.mea.gov.in/incoming-visit-detail.htm?25727/Official+Spokespersons+ response+to+a+question+on+the+visit+of+the+Iranian+ Foreign +Minister
44. "Iranian Foreign Minister on India Visit From August 13", *NDTV*, 12 August 2015, at http://www.ndtv.com/world-news/iranian-foreign-minister-on-india-visit-from-august-13-1206351
45. Vijaita Singh, "Iran no longer on restricted visa list", *The Hindu*, 21 August 2015, at http://www.thehindu.com/news/national/in-sign-of-strengthening-ties-iran-no-longer-on-restricted-visa-list/article7562425.ece. According to this source, "The order means that Iranians can easily apply for visas at our consulate in Iran and each application will not have to be forwarded to [the] Intelligence Bureau and [the] Research and Analysis Wing here for verification".
46. "MoU between India and Iran on visa facilitation", Press Information Bureau, Government of India 2 December 2015, at http://pib.nic.in/newsite/PrintRelease.aspx?relid=132354
47. "18th India-Iran Joint Commission Meeting", Ministry of External Affairs, Government of India 28 December 2015, at http://mea.gov.in/press-releases.htm?dtl/26249/18th_IndiaIran_Joint_Commission_Meeting
48. *The Gulf and West Asia*, Annual Report 2015–2016, Ministry of External Affairs, New Delhi, p. 60.
49. "India to accede to the Ashgabat Agreement", Press Release, Press Information Bureau, New Delhi, 23 March 2016, at http://pib.nic.in/newsite/PrintRelease.aspx?relid=138309

50. "Visit of External Affairs Minister to Iran April 16–17, 2016)", Ministry of External Affairs, Government of India, 17 April 2016, at http://mea.gov.in/press-releases.htm?dtl/26630/Visit_of_External_Affairs_Minister_to_Iran_April_1617_2016
51. "List of Agreements/MOUs signed during the visit of Prime Minister to Iran, 23 May 2016", Ministry of External Affairs, Government of India, 23 May 2016, at http://mea.gov.in/outoging-visit-detail.htm?26841/List+of+Agreements MOUs + signed+during+the+visit+of+Prime+Minister+to+Iran+May+23+2016
52. "Remarks by Prime Minister at Chabahar Connectivity event, 23 May 2016", Ministry of External Affairs, government of India, 23 May 2016, at http://www.mea.gov.in/outoging-visit-detail.htm?26838/Remarks+by+Prime+ Minister + at+Chabahar+Connectivity+event+May+23+2016
53. "India to develop Iran's Chabahar port", *The Hindu,* 24 May 2016, http://www.thehindu.com/news/national/India-to-develop-Irans-Chabahar-port/article14336893.ece
54. "India-Iran Relations", *Foreign Relation,* Ministry of External Affairs, New Delhi, December 2016, at https://www.mea.gov.in/Portal/ForeignRelation/India-Iran_bilateral_December___2016.pdf
55. "Fillip to basmati exports from India likely", *Financial Express,* 15 July 2015, at http://www.financialexpress.com/economy/fillip-to-basmati-exports-from-india-likely/101094/
56. Madhvi Sally, "Basmati rice prices firm up as Iran lifts ban", *The Economic Times,* 11 January 2017, at http://economictimes.indiatimes.com/markets/commodities/news/basmati-rice-prices-firm-up-as-iran-lifts-ban/articleshow/56468470.cms
57. "Iran keen to increase tea, medicine imports from India: Commerce Secretary Rajeev Kher", *The Economic Times,* 14 April 2015, at http://economictimes.indiatimes.com/news/economy/foreign-trade/iran-keen-to-increase-tea-medicine-imports-from-india-commerce-secretary-rajeev-kher/articleshow/46919882.cms?intenttarget=no
58. Indrani Dutta, "Iranian team checks out Indian tea practices at farm and factory", *The Hindu,* 8 December 2015, at http://www.thehindu.com/business/Industry/iranian-team-checks-out-indian-tea-practices-at-farm-and-factory/article7958587.ece
59. Ibid.
60. "India-Iran Relations", Ministry of External Affairs, New Delhi, January 2016, at https://www.mea.gov.in/Portal/ForeignRelation/Iran_11_01_2016.pdf
61. "Govt to fast track talks with Iran for urea plant", *The Hindu Business Line,* 12 January 2015, at http://www.thehindubusinessline.com/economy/agri-business/govt-to-fast-track-talks-with-iran-for-urea-plant/article6781504.ece
62. "Iran has offered natural gas to India at $2.95 per unit for urea plant, says Gadkari", *Business Line,* 24 September 2015.
63. "Indian firms team up with Iranian investor for Chabahar plant", *Press TV,* 11 May 2016, http://www.presstv.ir/DetailFr/2016/05/11/465041/India-picks-Iran-bank-Chabahar-plant
64. Sanjay Jog, "Rashtriya Chemicals to set up 1.3-mt urea plant in Iran", *Business Standard,* 25 September 2016, at http://www.business-standard.com/article/companies/rashtriya-chemicals-to-set-up-1-3-mt-urea-plant-in-iran-116092500416_1.html. According to this source, "Both RCF and GSFC together

have proposed to hold 51 percent while the balance 49 per cent will be held by FALAT".

65. "Iran reports huge rail purchase from India", *Press TV*, 24 April 2016, at http://www.presstv.ir/Detail/2016/04/24/462332/Iran-reports-huge-rail-purchase-from-India
66. Nasir Ahmed, "India's MRPL buys Iraqi Basra oil to replace Iran oil", *Business Recorder*, 2 February 2015, at http://www.brecorder.com/2015/02/02/221418/
67. Nidhi Verma, "India's Feb Iran oil imports fall to lowest since July 2013", *Reuters*, 2 March 2015, at http://www.reuters.com/article/india-iran-imports-idUSL4N0W13Z620150302
68. Ibid.
69. Osamu Tsukimori, "Asian imports of Iran crude fall 25 pct, led by India, S. Korea", *Reuters*, 31 March 2015, at http://in.reuters.com/article/asia-iran-crude-idINKBN0MR0I320150331
70. Siddhartha P. Saikia, "India seeks field for OVL but Tehran talks tough", *Financial Express*, 29 April 2015,http://www.financialexpress.com/economy/india-seeks-field-for-ovl-but-tehran-talks-tough/67759/
71. Siddhartha P. Saikia, "India-Iran deal soon on Farzad-B project", *Financial Express*, 21 March 2016, http://www.financialexpress.com/economy/india-iran-deal-soon-on-farzad-b-project/227872/
72. Siddhartha P. Saikia, "ONGC Videsh Farzad B gas discovery: India-Iran gas deal delayed again", *Financial Express*, 27 October 2016, http://www.financialexpress.com/market/commodities/ongc-videsh-farzad-b-gas-discovery-india-iran-gas-deal-delayed-again/431374/
73. "India's May Iran oil imports hit highest since March 2014," *The Economic Times*, 2 June 2015, http://economictimes.indiatimes.com/industry/energy/oil-gas/indias-may-iran-oil-imports-hit-highest-since-march-2014/articleshow/47513620.cms
74. For a relevant report, see *News, ASSOCHAM*, "Time for Iran-India PTA as Iran-Pakistan pact becomes shallow: ASSOCHAM Paper", 4 October 2015, http://assocham.org/newsdetail.php?id=5243
75. "Iran asks India to clear $6.5 billion oil dues in 2 months", *The Economic Times*, 20 August 2015, http://economictimes.indiatimes.com/news/economy/foreign-trade/iran-asks-india-to-clear-6-5-billion-oil-dues-in-2-months/articleshow/48556130.cms. As per this source, "Essar Oil owes $3.34 million, MRPL ($.49 billion) and Indian Oil Corps ($581 million) to Iran. HPCL-Mittal Energy Ltd (HMEL) owes $97 million and Hindustan Petroleum Corp Ltd (HPCL) another $29 million. Besides, about Rs. 17,000 crore was lying in Iranian account with UCO Bank".
76. "India pays second tranche of $700 mln to Iran – sources", *Reuters*, 13 October 2015, at http://in.reuters.com/article/india-iran-payment-idINKCN0S71 FU 20151013 According to this source, "Essar Oil on Tuesday paid about $338 million, followed by about $299 million from Mangalore Refinery and Petrochemicals Ltd, the sources said, adding Indian Oil Corp paid about $60 million and Hindustan Petroleum Corp about $3 million".
77. "India's Iran oil import hit eight-month low", *The Economic Times*, 4 December 2015, at http://economictimes.indiatimes.com/news/economy/foreign-trade/indias-iran-oil-imports-hit-eight-month-low/articleshow/50040681.cms

78. "Iran may seal $4.5-bn undersea gas pipeline agreement with India", *Business Standard,* 8 December 2015, at http://www.business-standard.com/article/economy-policy/iran-may-seal-4-5-bn-undersea-gas-pipeline-agreement-with-india-115120700605_1.html
79. "Iran wants India to pay oil dues in Euros", *The Economic Times,* 7 February 2016, at http://economictimes.indiatimes.com/news/economy/foreign-trade/iran-wants-india-to-pay-oil-dues-in-euros/articleshow/50887318.cms
80. "As a 'goodwill gesture', India agrees to Iran's demand for 1.5% interest on $6.5-billion oil dues", *The Times of India,* 3 May 2016, at http://timesofindia.indiatimes.com/business/india-business/As-a-goodwill-gesture-India-agrees-to-Irans-demand-for-1-5-interest-on-6-5-billion-oil-dues/articleshow/52090364.cms
81. Ibid.
82. "Iranian gas to reach India via longest submarine pipeline", Mehr News Agency, 9 August 2016, at http://en.mehrnews.com/news/118767/Iranian-gas-to-reach-India-via-longest-submarine-pipeline
83. Nidhi Verma, "India set to buy Iran oil for emergency reserves: sources", *Reuters,* 20 September 2016, at http://www.reuters.com/article/us-india-iran-oil-idUSKCN11Q0P4
84. Nidhi Verma, "India's 2016 Iran oil imports hit record high – trade", *Reuters,* 1 February 2017, http://in.reuters.com/article/india-iran-oil-idINKBN15G3XR
85. "Iran, India hold first joint naval exercise since lifting of international sanctions", *Defence News* (India), 31 May 2016, at http://www.defencenews.in/article/Iran,-India-hold-first-joint-naval-exercise-since-lifting-of-international-sanctions-5564
86. "Two Indian Naval Ships Visit Iran", Press Information Bureau, Government of India, 28 August 2015, at http://pib.nic.in/newsite/PrintRelease.aspx?relid=126432
87. "Visit of Deputy Secretary of Supreme National Security Council of Iran", Press Information Bureau, Government of India, 24 July 2015, at http://pib.nic.in/newsite/PrintRelease.aspx?relid=123659
88. "Media Statement by Prime Minister during his visit to Iran (May 23, 2016)", Ministry of External Affairs, Government of India, 23 May 2016, at http://mea.gov.in/outoging-visit-detail.htm?26840/Media+Statement+by+Prime+Minister +during+his+visit+to+Iran+May+23+2016
89. "Top Iranian Security Official Due in India for Talks", *Tasnim News Agency,* 25 August 2016, https://www.tasnimnews.com/en/news/2016/08/25/1168133/top-iranian-security-official-due-in-india-for-talks
90. "Speech by Prime Minister on the occasion of inauguration of Conference on 'India and Iran, Two Great Civilizations: Retrospect and Prospects' and release of rare Persian manuscript (May 23, 2016)", Press Information Bureau, Government of India, 23 May 2016, http://pib.nic.in/newsite/PrintRelease.aspx?relid= 145578
91. "Grievances of Indian community to be taken up with Iran: Swaraj", *The Hindu,* 17 April 2016, http://www.thehindu.com/news/international/Grievances-of-Indian-community-to-be-taken-up-with-Iran-Swaraj/article14242344.ece
92. "A R Rahman composes music for Iranian filmmaker Majid Majidi", *The Indian Express,* 4 February 2015, http://indianexpress.com/article/entertainment/music/a-r-rahman-composes-music-for-iranian-filmmaker-majid-majidi/

93. Sankhayan Ghosh, "Ban film on Prophet with A R Rahman music: Sunni group to govt", *The Indian Express,* 7 September 2015, http://indianexpress.com/article/india/india-others/ban-film-on-prophet-with-rahman-music-sunni-group-to-govt/
94. "Iranian film 'Daughter' wins Golden Peacock Award at IFFI", *Deccan Herald,* 28 November 2016, http://www.deccanherald.com/content/583610/iranian-film-daughter-wins-golden.html

4

IRAQ

Premanand Mishra

Key Information

Ruling Party: Dawa Party; **President:** Fuad Masum (since 24 July 2014); **Prime Minister:** Haider al-Abadi (since 8 September 2014); **National Day:** 14 July; **Parliament**: 325-member Council of Representatives; **Last Parliamentary Election**: 30 April 2014; **Major group in Parliament**: State of Law Coalition; **National Carrier:** Iraqi Airways.

Socio-Economic Indicators

Area: 438,317 sq km; **Population:** 38.14 million; **Native:** NA**; Expats:** NA**; Religious Groups:** Muslim 99 per cent (Shia 60–65 per cent; Sunni 32–37 per cent); Christian 0.8 per cent; other 0.2 per cent; **Youth:** 19.07 per cent; **Population growth rate:** 2.87 per cent; **Life expectancy at birth:** 74.9 years; **Major population groups**: Arabs 75–80 per cent; Kurdish 15-20 per cent; Turkoman, Assyrian, or Other 5 per cent; **Literacy rate:** 79.7 per cent; **National Currency**: Iraqi Dinar (IQD); **GDP:** US$ 156.3 billion; **Foreign Trade:** US$ 87.94 billion; **Defence budget:** 8.7 per cent of GDP (2014); **Sovereign Wealth Fund:** US$ 44.15 billion; **External Debt**: US$ 68.01 billion; **Per capita income:** US$ 16,500; **Oil reserves:** 143 billion bbl; **Gas reserves:** 3.158 trillion m^3; **HDI rank:** 121; **Infant Mortality Rate**: 37.5 deaths/1,000 live birth; **UN Education Index:** 0.467; **Gender Inequality Index:** 0.539; **Labour Force:** 8.9 million (2010 est.); **Unemployment rate**: 16 per cent (2012 est.); **Urban Population:** 69.5 per cent; **Rate of Urbanization:** 3.01 per cent; **Last National Census**: 1997.

India Related

Indian Cultural Centre: NA; **Number of Indians:** 17,000 (approximately); **Number of places of worship for Indians**: NA; **Indian Schools:** NA; **Indian Banks:** NA; **Currency exchange rate:** 1 IQD = INR 0.057 (Feb 2017); **Last visit to India by the ruler**: Prime Minister Nouri al-Maliki, August 2013; **Last Indian Prime Minister to visit**: Indira Gandhi, January 1975.

* * *

Historically, India and Iraq have shared friendly relations and maintained strategic cooperation in several areas, most importantly in defence and security, since the 1980s. Even when Iraq faced serious external criticism for its invasion of Kuwait and human rights violations, Indian kept a neutral stance. The relationship underwent a transition after the US-invasion of that country in March 2003 that led to spiralling sectarian violence. After this, India has taken time to revive relations. Gradually, the situation has started to improve, but the rise of ISIS has again disrupted the ties. In the past two years, India has focussed on the revival of bilateral relations, and is keen on exploring possibilities for economic partnership as well as in the energy sector. The visit by the Indian Minister of State for External Affairs, M.J. Akbar, in August 2016 was an important development, signalling India's willingness to enhance bilateral relations.

Domestic Developments

Since the 2003 US-led invasion, the Republic of Iraq has been grappling with unprecedented crises, internally as well as externally. With the rise of the Islamic State, the impact of the Syrian civil war and the ensuing humanitarian crisis, the unresolved Kurdish question, the malice of sectarian identities and the uncertainty in foreign relations, Iraq is at a crossroads. The hope for a better Iraq after the 2005 elections—the first since 2003—withered after the withdrawal of US troops in 2011. Iraq's overdependence on oil revenue amidst falling prices brought major challenges. However, the biggest challenge for Iraq remains how to come back to normalcy amidst deepening uncertainties, especially the rise of the Islamic State (ISIS).[1]

Iraq has witnessed major political changes, primarily driven by existing sectarian divisions (Sunni versus Shia) that became wide open after the de-Ba'thification programme introduced during the American occupation.[2] Even before the rule of Saddam Hussein, Iraqi society was divided. The change in power dynamics after 2005 only accentuated sectarian and ethnical fault lines.[3] However, the current crisis due to the rise of the ISIS has impacted Iraq on an unimaginable scale. The ISIS was an outcome of continuous war and the persistent political instability in Iraq.

Patrick Cockburn has described the members of the monstrous organization ISIS as the 'children of war.'[4] Gyorgy Bustin from the UNHM (United Nations Head of Mission) explains how the ISIS benefitted due to the current political crisis in Iraq driven by existing political divisions and chaos.[5] The depleting oil prices and the cost of war against IS forces have brought forth major challenges regarding the maintenance of stability, especially in a state that is divided between three major groups: the Shias, the Sunnis, and the Kurds.[6]

According to the Iraqi Constitution adopted in October 2005 through a popular vote, the Kurdistan Regional Government (KRG) controls the federal Kurdistan region of Iraq. The KRG is significant for economic and security reasons, both for Iraq as well as for the stability of the region amidst the emergence of ISIS. Kurdistan lies in the oil-rich northern part of the country, and its security forces have played a key role against ISIS advances.[7] The KRG holds power in only three provinces of the state, but receives a disproportionate percentage of the national budget. The northern oil fields are another cause of tensions between the central Iraqi government and KRG.[8]

Economy

The current political crisis and the rise of extremism have augmented the bad situation of the economy. Declining oil prices in both 2015 and 2016, and the rise of the ISIS insurgency have contributed to a sharp deterioration of economic activity, and rapidly increased the fiscal and current account deficits. Considering Iraq's macroeconomic situation in the medium term, the economy also largely remained volatile due to price fluctuation in the oil market. Such challenges for the economy on multiple fronts have had a negative impact on economic growth, and have led to a further rise in poverty, vulnerability, and severe unemployment. Private consumption and investment remain subdued due to an unstable security and political situation, and a poor business environment.[9]

According to a World Bank report, in 2015 Iraqi economy saw a positive growth of 2.9 per cent, and a major contribution came from increase in oil production. This is significant as the major oil fields have remained out of the reach of the ISIS.[10] The non-oil sector witnessed a steep decline of 14 per cent in 2016, but was expected to recover due to an 11 per cent expected growth in the oil production. The uncertainty in the price in 2015 and 2016 undermined fiscal and external balances. The fiscal situation largely remained contested despite huge impetus in government expenditure and the negative growth of oil revenue. The security question, coupled with fluctuation in the economy caused a budget deficit at 13.5 per cent of GDP in 2015.[11] However, the year 2016 saw deterioration in the fiscal deficit, which reached 12 per cent of the GDP, largely contributed by low oil exports.

To check the volatility in the economy, in early 2016, Iraq received a sum of US$ 5.34 billion from international financial institutions. The World Bank gave support by introducing three instalments of financial assistance. In the first (December 2015) Iraq received US$ 1.2 billion; in the second (December 2016) it received US$ 1.44 billion; and the last is expected to be disbursed by December 2017. In the same year, the US also provided US$ 2.1 billion for 2016–18 in order to meet the challenges of the humanitarian crisis.[12]

In 2016, overall economic growth in Iraq is estimated to have reached 10 per cent due to strong oil production. The security and oil shocks forced the government to rapidly reduce expenditure which negatively affected private sector consumption and investment. The non-oil sectors contracted by 10 per cent in 2015 and 2016. Inflation averaged 0.4 per cent in 2016.[13]

In terms of oil reserves, Iraq has the third largest in the Middle East—after Saudi Arabia and Iran—and the fifth largest in the world. It is estimated to have 143 billion barrels.[14] Oil contributes close to 54 per cent of its economy as well as 99 per cent of its exports, thereby indicating both its excessive dependence on this commodity as well as a lack of diversity in the country's economy. Similarly, 93 per cent the Iraqi fiscal revenue comes from oil.[15] Between 2015 and 2016, the over dependence on oil amidst the rise of ISIS dented the production of oil. This had a huge impact on the economy. The limited diversification of the economy had devastating effects. The tension between Bagdad and KRG over the oil sharing agreement has damaged exports from northern oil fields. Oil exports in 2015 averaged 3 million barrels per day. Iraq's oil export needs further boost by oil processing, pipelines, and more export infrastructure to enable it to reach its economic potential.[16]

Oil production in Iraq in 2015—including in the oil fields under the KRG—was higher than in 2014. It reached almost 0.7 million barrel per day more oil in 2015, averaging almost 4 million bpd crude oil. In the same year, Iraq also became the second largest oil producer among Organisation of the Petroleum Exporting Countries (OPEC). Since the demand decreased domestically in Iraq, the level of export was augmented for the international market. The infrastructural changes in the oil production—especially pipelines, storage facilities, and the overall improvement in the quality of crude oil—contributed to the increase in production.

In June 2015, Iraq switched to producing heavy grade crude oil (known as Basra Heavy Grade) for marketing instead of the light crude oil which was the traditional source of crude oil production. Before this shift, Iraq had limited its production in those oil fields producing heavy oils in order to maintain the minimum standard for the light grade Basra crude oil.[17]

The Iraqi dilemma over paying dues to international oil companies (OICs) despite the huge level of production and growth in exports was largely due to its failure to keep up its share of payments. This eventually led to reduction in the investment in southern oil fields in 2016. In 2015, the export revenue of Iraq excluding the KRG dropped by US$ 35 billion as compared to the previous year. This resulted in economic apprehension since, according to the International Monetary Fund, crude oil export revenue in 2014 was over 90 per cent. EIA expects Iraq's production growth to remain slow in 2016 because of constraints arising from reduced export revenue.[18]

Due to the better export situation from KRG, Iraq received a windfall gain in 2015. The rapid advance of the self-proclaimed ISIS militants was the indirect catalyst for an upswing in volumes as the KRG took control of several fields around Kirkuk. An export deal was struck with the federal government under its new Prime Minister, Haider al-Abadi.[19] In the late 2016, Iraq exported nearly 4.1 million b/d of crude oil.

Besides oil, agriculture is an important component of the Iraqi economy as a potential driver for growth. Restoring agriculture should be a central component of reconstruction efforts. While the oil industry dominates Iraq's economy, agriculture may have recently employed up to one third of the population, and has the potential to drive future growth. Agriculture-driven growth also has the potential to improve food security, increase self-sufficiency in both rural and urban areas.[20]

Military and Security

Amidst the Syrian conflict and the brutalities perpetrated by the ISIS militia, Iraq has seen an unprecedented humanitarian crisis. The problems of human security in the wake of millions of displaced persons, civilian casualties, and crime against minorities and women are humongous. According to a report by the United Nations Assistance Mission in Iraq (UNAMI), in the twenty months period between January 2014 and October 2015, over 50,000 civilian causalities were recorded.[21] A *Human Rights Watch* report covering the events of 2016 stated that the war zone that erupted due to conflict with the rise of Islamic State further intensified when the clashes erupted over Ramadi and Fallujah, and later Mosul as well.[22] This whole operation throughout the year made for the displacement of almost 45,000 Iraqi people. According to the UNAMI, in 2016, almost 10,000 people lost their lives due to airstrikes, heavy explosions, open gunfire, and even suicide bombing. A 2016 International Federation of Journalists report deemed Iraq the deadliest country in the world for journalists, and a UNICEF report deemed it one of the deadliest for children.[23]

President Barack Obama was successful in ending the *Operation Iraqi Freedom*[24] that started during George Bush's presidency; but in the wake of threat from ISIS, the US was forced to send 3,000 American troops for assisting and training the Iraqi forces. After the commitment from the US, the international coalition also sent 15,000 additional troops. The air strikes against the ISIS militias were a significant response from the US. In early 2015, in an interview with *Al-Arabiya*, Stuart Jones (then the US Ambassador to Iraq) observed that more than 6,000 ISIS fighters had been killed in Syria and Iraq.[25] More Iraqi civilians were killed in 2015 than in 2010, 2011 and 2012 combined.[26] The affected areas were mainly Nineveh, Anbar, and Baghdad, followed by Salah al-Din and Diyala. These five provinces alone accounted for 90 per cent of civilians killed in Iraq in 2015 and 2016.[27]

Bilateral Relations

Traditionally India and Iraq have shared a long history of trade and commerce, largely comprising spices, textiles, food, and pearls which have contributed to the richness of the ancient market of Basra. Certain agricultural practices are common to both. The water buffalo—or what is better known as the breed of the Southern Iraqi *Jamus*—was imported to Iraq from India by the Abbasid emperor Harun al-Rashid. Similarly, under the British Rule, Indian soldiers and the railway workers have contributed to upholding security in the region. Apart from this, spiritual movements in India have been influenced by several spiritual leaders and Sufi saints from Iraq. Among the prominent leaders are Sheikh Behlul and Hasan al-Basri, both of whom had a tremendous impact in India. Similarly, thousands of Indians annually visit Karbala to pay homage to the shrines of Imam Hussein and Imam Abbas.[28]

Political Relations

India has been supportive of Iraq's post-war reconstruction programme under UN assistance. In 2003, the Indian Ministry of External Affairs committed US$ 20 million assistance to Iraq, and a further US$ 10 million for development programmes in Iraq under the International Reconstruction Fund Facility for Iraq (IRFFI). India has been supporting Iraq under the

Indian Technical and Economic Cooperation (ITEC) programme that is mainly planned to provide training to Iraqi officials.

After a long gap, in August 2016, the Minister of State for External Affairs, M. J. Akbar, visited Iraq. He met prominent political figures, including President Fuad Masum, Foreign Minister Ibrahim al-Eshaiqer al-Jaafari, the President of the Council of Representatives Salim al-Jabouri, and the National Security Advisor Faleh al-Fayyadh. Both countries share concerns on terrorism, and the meeting laid the platform for counter terrorism cooperation.[29] Akbar reiterated India's commitment and willingness to safeguard the territorial integrity and stability in Iraq, along with assuring India's support for the restructuring of the country. Akbar also visited Karbala and, apart from meeting the religious leader Nassif Jaseim Mohammed al-Khattabi, he interacted with several members of the Indian community.

In May 2016, the Indian Ambassador to Iraq, George Raju, visited Kurdistan with the proposal to open an Indian Consulate in Erbil. This received full support and appreciation from the KRG department of Foreign Relations. The Ambassador expressed India's desire to partner with both the people and the leadership in Kurdistan. The announcement was accepted by Minister Falah Mustafa. Both agreed that this would help in deeper bilateral co-operation.[30]

Economic Relations

Bilateral economic relations between India and Iraq were severely hampered in the aftermath of the 2003 US-led invasion of Iraq. The three largest suppliers of oil to India have been Saudi Arabia, Iraq, and Iran. Among the Indian companies, the single largest purchaser of Iraqi crude was the Indian Oil Corporation (IOC), followed by Hindustan Petroleum Corporation Limited (HPCL) and Bharat Petroleum Companies Ltd (BPCL). Beside crude oil, India also purchased raw wool and sulphur from Iraq. Bilateral trade between the two countries during 2015–16 was US$ 11.84 billion, of which Indian exports accounted for US$ 1.04 billion and imports for US$ 10.83 billion (see Table 4.1). Indian exports included cereals, iron and steel, meat products, pharma products, agro chemicals, cosmetics, gems, and jewellery. Dubai has emerged as the transit point for Indo-Iraqi trade. In 2015, the Diamond Power Infrastructure of India received a project from Iraq to supply 3,600 kilometres of aerial bunched cables. The deal—worth US$ 14.5 million—would help boost economic ties between the two countries.[31] In 2016, Iraq became India's most important crude oil supplier, toppling Saudi

Arabia; in 2014–15 and 2015–16, Saudi Arabia was largest exporter of crude oil to India; Iraq was second, followed by Nigeria.

Table 4.1: India-Iraq Bilateral Trade (in US$ million)

	2011–12	2012–13	2013–14	2014–15	2015–16
India's Exports to Iraq	763.97	1,278.13	918.03	892.32	1,004.39
India's Imports from Iraq	18,918.47	19,247.31	18,520.86	14,247.66	10,837.58
Total bilateral trade	19,682.44	20,525.44	19,438.89	15,076.98	11,841.98
Share of Iraq in India's total trade	2.47	2.59	2.54	1.99	1.84

Source: Adapted from, Government of India, Ministry of Commerce and Industry, Directorate General of Foreign Trade, at www.dgft.gov.in

Figure 4.1: India-Iraq Bilateral Trade (in US$ million)

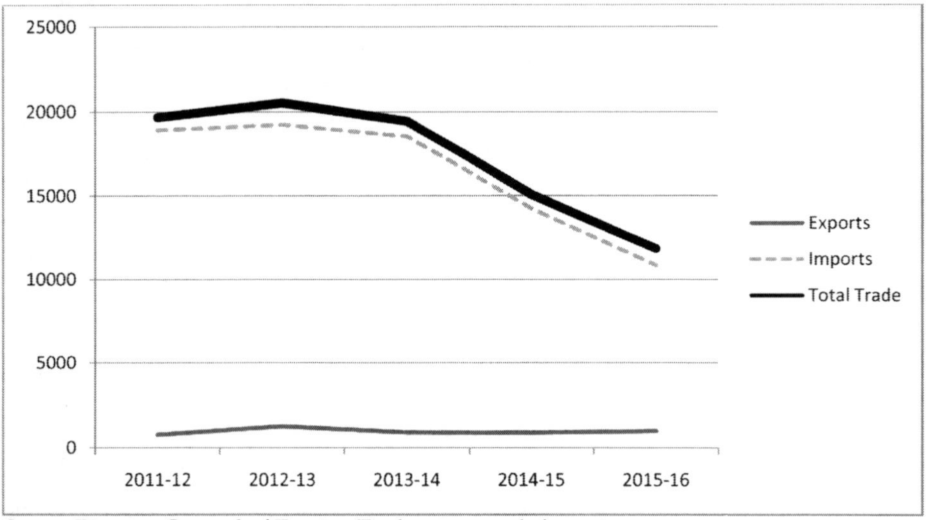

Source: Director General of Foreign Trade, at www.dgft.gov.in

Energy Cooperation

The decrease in crude oil prices, due to lesser demand amidst slowdown in Europe and other markets, has helped India's crude oil import bills. These reduced to nearly half at US$ 64 billion in 2015–16. The period saw India importing 202 million tonnes of crude oil compared to 189.4 million tonnes in 2014–15.[32] In March 2015, the Indian Ministry of Petroleum—foreseeing the difficult path ahead in managing oil trade—advised two Indian refiners, Indian Oil Corp and Hindustan Petroleum Corp to buy 8 million barrels of Basra crude oil from Iraq for India's Strategic Petroleum Reserves (SPRs).[33] In order to store the crude oil, the Indian Strategic Petroleum Reserves Limited built a rock cavern near Vishakhapatnam. Several talks have been held between the Indian refiners and Iraq's State Oil Marketing Organization to provide both light and heavy grades of Basra crude oil.[34] Similar deals have been made between Indian refiners and PERTAMINA, a state-owned energy company in Singapore. The tie up between this Energy Company and Indian refiners would enable the processing of one million barrels of crude oil from Iraq every month.[35]

Table 4.2: Share of Oil in India's Imports from Iraq (US$ Million)

Year	Oil imports from Iraq	Total oil imports	Iraqi share in oil total imports	Imports from Iraq	Per cent of oil in imports from Iraq
2011–12	18,826.19	172,753.92	10.90	18,918.47	99.51
2012–13	19,166.06	181,344.67	10.57	19,247.31	99.58
2013–14	18,450.33	181,382.59	10.17	18,520.86	99.62
2014–15	14,177.22	156,400.01	9.06	14,247.66	99.51
2015–16	10,759.19	96,953.06	11.10	10,837.58	99.28

Source: Adapted from Government of India, Ministry of Commerce and Industry, Directorate General of Foreign Trade New Delhi, at www.dgft.gov.in

Figure 4.2: Share of Oil in India's Imports from Iraq (US$ Million)

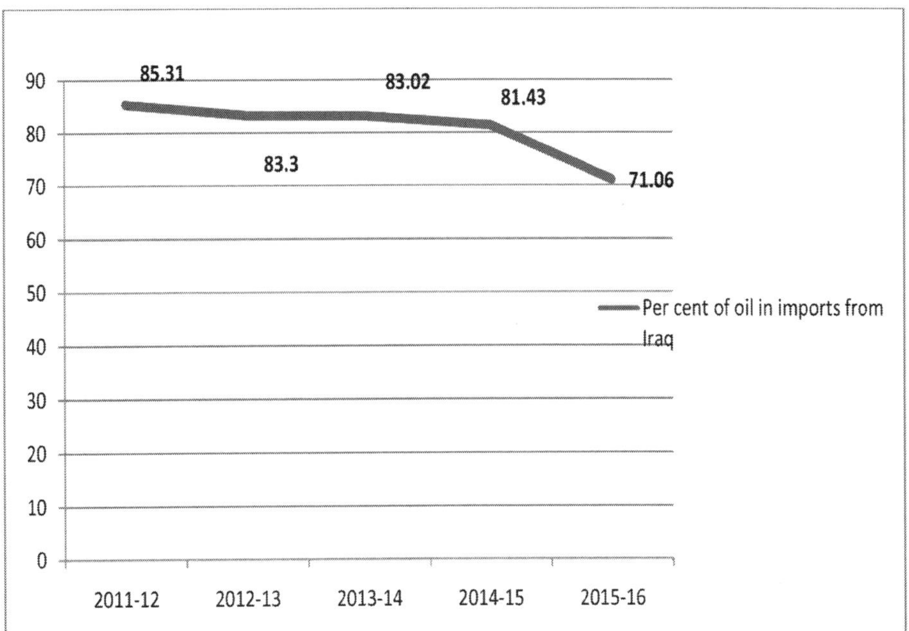

Source: Adapted from Director-General of Foreign Trade, New Delhi, at www.dgft.gov.in

Table 4.3: India's Energy Imports from Iraq (in US$ million)

	2011–12	2012–13	2013–14	2014–15	2015–16
India's Energy Imports from Iraq	18,826.19	19,166.06	18,450.33	14,177.22	10,759.19
India's Total Energy Imports	172,753.92	181,344.67	181,382.59	156,400.01	96,953.06
India's Total Energy Imports from Persian Gulf	105,056.26	105,859.15	106,400.75	85,300.30	50,992.26
Share of Iraq in Total Energy Imports (in per cent)	10.90	10.57	10.17	9.06	11.10
Share of Iraq in Imports from Persian Gulf (in per cent)	17.92	18.11	17.34	16.62	21.10

Source: Adapted from Government of India, Ministry of Commerce and Industry, Directorate General of Foreign Trade, New Delhi, at www.dgft.gov.in

Figure 4.3: Share of Iraq in Energy Imports from Persian Gulf

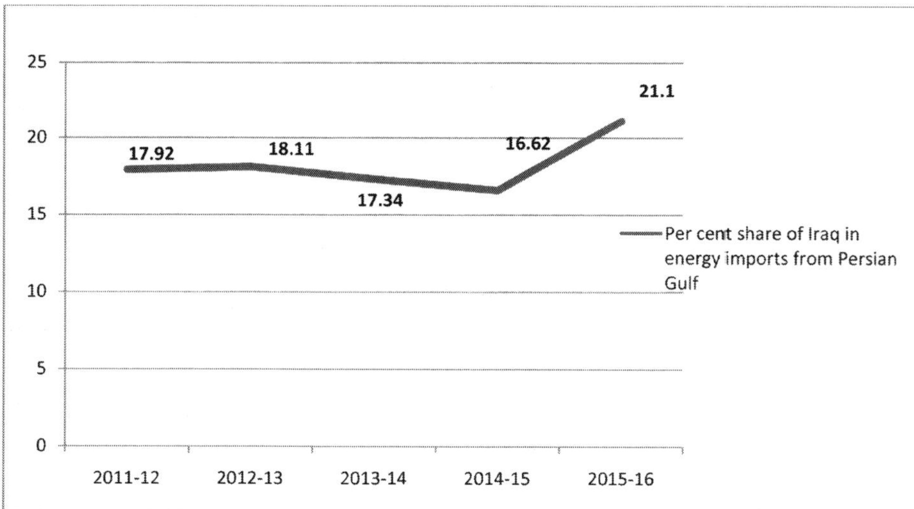

Source: Adapted from Director-General of Foreign Trade, New Delhi, at www.dgft.gov.in

Security Cooperation

The volatile situation, especially on the security front, has been an issue for the small number of Indian expatriates and companies operating in Iraq. They have faced huge challenges filled with uncertainties. The turmoil caused by the ISIS has compelled the India's BGR Energy System to cancel a contract made in 2013 in Nasiriya. The contract was about building a 500 mg watt turbine plant valued US$ 246 million. In spite of receiving a letter of credit, the company refused to continue with it, stating that it was not possible for the company to progress since the ISIS has captured and taken control over various parts of Iraq.[36]

A severe blow came with the abduction of 39 Indians in Iraq in 2014. Belonging to the state of Punjab, this triggered a panic situation domestically. The concern for their lives compelled External Affairs Minister, Sushma Swaraj, to meet the families in May 2015. The Indian government pursued diplomatic efforts through the Foreign Ministers of the GCC countries as well as other countries for securing the release of the expatriates from the ISIS. Sushma Swaraj met with the families several times, and briefed them about the efforts of the government.[37] In 2016, the Indian media reported that the workers abducted in 2014 are safe; however there has been no conclusive evidence and the issue continued to be unresolved even in mid-2017.[38]

In October 2016, *The Indian Express* reported that one Indian citizen, Subahani Haja Moideen, a resident of Tamil Nadu, was arrested by the National Investigating Agency (NIA) on his alleged association with the ISIS. Moideen, who left his home in 2015, was among the many that were influenced to join ISIS. This posed a major security challenge for Indian security agencies.[39]

Socio-Cultural Ties

India's success story was acknowledged worldwide when the UN celebrated International day of Yoga. In June 2016, Iraq also joined the UN programme. The prevailing political conditions in Iraq have evoked concerns for the Indian government regarding the welfare of Indians working in the region. The State Level Bankers Committee in Kerala has committed to the State Government to provide assistance to around 500 nurses who have returned from Libya and Iraq in 2014.[40]

Conclusion

The historical linkages between India and Iraq, based on mutual trust and respect, have travelled different trajectories in areas such as political, economic, the issue of sovereignty, the respecting of international laws, etc. For India, energy is a major component of its ties with the Persian Gulf in general, and Iraq in particular. Despite many constraints, Iraq has always been supportive of the Indian position. Similarly, India's refusal to accept US pressure to fight against Iraq, as well as its official position on the US invasion have cemented the ties between the two countries. However, in recent years, this situation has given rise to many issues. The rise of the ISIS and its global impact—mainly sectarianism and radicalization—is a cause of worry. Similarly, India's dependence on oil, and the safety of expatriates are common challenges.

The Indian official policy of non-intervention in the internal matters of other countries has maintained the trust factor in Iraq. The growing menace of the ISIS is not just restricted to Iraq but has ripple effects that can affect India's energy security as well as the safety of its expatriate workers. The two countries will benefit from close cooperation on these issues. Moreover, for Iraq, India's growing economy can be a huge help. The expertise of Indian companies in terms of infrastructure, and the engagement of Indian workers in the growth of the Iraqi economy can be important factors in facing the challenges of reconstruction and development. Indeed, both countries can benefit from future collaborations.

NOTES

1. Stansfield Gareth, "Explaining the Aims, Rise, and Impact of the Islamic State in Iraq and al-Sham", *The Middle East Journal,* Winter, 2016, Vol. 70, No. 1, pp. 146–151.
2. Alissa J. Rubin, "Ahmad Chalabi and the Legacy of De-Ba'athification in Iraq", *The New York Times,* 3 November 2015, at https://www.nytimes.com/2015/11/04/world/middleeast/ahmad-chalabi-and-the-legacy-of-de-baathification-in-iraq.html
3. Saad N. Jawad, "The Iraqi Constitution: Structural Flaws and Political Implications", LSE Middle East Centre Paper Series, November 2013, Series no. 1, at http://www.lse.ac.uk/middleEastCentre/publications/Paper-Series/SaadJawad.pdf
4. Cockburn Patrick, *The Rise of Islamic state: ISIS and the New Sunni Revolution,* New York: Verso Books, 2015.
5. Jason Dozier, "ISIS feeds on Iraq's political instability and oil", Global Risk Insights, 15 May 2016, at http://globalriskinsights.com/2016/05/iraq-political-instability/
6. According to the Central Intelligence Agency's *The World Fact Book,* of the total 38 million Iraqis (June 2016 est.), nearly 75–80 per cent are Arabs and 15–20 per cent are Kurds. Similarly, about 55–60 per cent are Shias and about 40 per cent are Sunnis. See also, "Middle East: Iraq", *The World Fact Book,* Central Intelligence Agency, 11 May 2017, at https://www.cia.gov/library/publications/the-world-factbook/geos/iz.html e two markets.e women activists fought for their causes against teh r from these two markets..
7. Jason Dozier, "ISIS feeds on Iraq's political instability and oil", op. cit.
8. James Cogan, "Relations Collapse between Iraqi Government and Kurdish Region", World Socialist Web site (WSWS), 12 July 2014, at https://www.wsws.org/en/articles/2014/07/12/iraq-j12.html.
9. "Iraq Overview", The World Bank, 1 April 2017, at http://www.worldbank.org/en/country/iraq/overview
10. Ibid.
11. Ibid.
12. Ibid.
13. "Iraq's Economic Outlook: April 2017", The World Bank, at http://www.worldbank.org/en/country/iraq/publication/economic-outlook-april-2017

14. Jason Dozier, "ISIS feeds on Iraq's political instability and oil", op. cit.
15. "Iraq, Overview", The World Bank, op. cit.
16. "Middle East: Iraq", CIA, op. cit.
17. "Iraq is second-leading contributor to global liquids supply growth in 2015", EIA, US Energy Information Administration, 29 Feb 2016, at https://www.eia.gov/todayinenergy/detail.php?id=25152
18. "Iraq is second-leading contributor to global liquids supply growth in 2015", US Energy Information Administration, 29 February 2016, at https://www.eia.gov/todayinenergy/detail.php?id=25152
19. Richard Mallinson, "Can Iraqi oil production surprise again on the upside?", The Oxford Institute for Energy Studies, October 2016, at https://www.oxfordenergy.org/wpcms/wp-content/uploads/2016/10/Can-Iraqi-oil-production-surprise-again-on-the-upside.pdf
20. "The Impact of ISIS on Iraq's Agricultural Sector", Relief Web, 15 December 2016, at http://reliefweb.int/report/iraq/impact-isis-iraq-s-agricultural-sector
21. "Report on the Protection of Civilians in Armed Conflict in Iraq: 1 May–31 October 2015", Office of the United Nations High Commission for Human Rights, United Nations Assistance Mission for Iraq (UNAMI), January 2016, at http://www.ohchr.org/Documents/Countries/IQ/UNAMIReport1May31October2015.pdf
22. "World Report 2017 (Iraq events of 2016)", Human Rights Watch, at https://www.hrw.org/world-report/2017/country-chapters/iraq
23. Ibid.
24. "Operation Iraqi Freedom", Frontline Documentary on The Invasion of Iraq, at http://www.pbs.org/wgbh/pages/frontline/shows/invasion/cron/
25. "Air strikes killed 6,000 ISIS fighters: U.S. ambassador", *Al-Arabiya* (English), 22 January 2015, at http://english.alarabiya.net/en/News/middle-east/2015/01/22/Air-strikes-killed-6-000-ISIS-fighters-U-S-ambassador.html
26. "Iraq 2015: A Catastrophic Normal", Iraq Body Count, 1 Jan 2016, at https://www.iraqbodycount.org/analysis/numbers/2015/
27. Ibid.
28. "India-Iraq Bilateral Relations", Embassy of India, Baghdad, Iraq, at http://indianembassybaghdad.in/eoi.php?id=Bilateral
29. "Official visit of Minister of State for External Affairs M.J. Akbar to Iraq (August 21–23, 2016)", Ministry Of External Affairs, Government of India, 22 August 2016, at http://www.mea.gov.in/press-releases.htm?dtl/27330/Official_visit_of_Minister_of_State_for_External_Affairs_MJ_Akbar_to_Iraq_August_2123_2016
30. John Lee, "India to Open Consulate in Erbil", *Iraq Business News*, 5 May 2016, at http://www.iraq-businessnews.com/2016/05/05/india-to-open-consulate-in-erbil/
31. John Lee, "Indian Firm Bags Power Cable Order", *Iraq Business News*, 10 July 2015, at http://www.iraq-businessnews.com/2015/07/10/indian-firm-bags-power-cable-order/
32. "India's Crude Oil import bill halves to $64 bn in 2015-16", *Financial Express*, 20 April 2016, at http://www.financialexpress.com/economy/indias-crude-oil-import-bill-halves-to-64-bn-in-2015-16/240446/
33. John Lee, "India Builds Oil Reserves with Basra crude", *Iraq Business News*, 22 March 2015, at http://www.iraq-businessnews.com/2015/03/22/india-builds-oil-reserves-with-basra-crude/

34. John Lee, "Indian Refiners in Talk with SOMO", *Iraq Business News*, 5 June 2015, at http://www.iraq-businessnews.com/2015/06/05/indian-refiners-in-talks-with-somo/
35. John Lee, "Pertamina looks to India to Process Iraqi Crude", Iraq Business News, 16 March 2016, at http://www.iraq-businessnews.com/2016/03/16/pertamina-looks-to-india-to-process-iraqi-crude/
36. John Lee, "BGR Abandons $246m Iraq Project", Iraq Business News, at http://www.iraq-businessnews.com/2016/06/02/bgr-abandons-246m-iraq-project/
37. " External Affair Minister meets families of Indian workers held captive in Iraq", Ministry of External Affairs, Government of India, 14 May 2015, at http://www.mea.gov.in/press-releases.htm?dtl/25237/External_Affairs_Minister_meets_families_of_Indian_Workers_held_captive_in_Iraq; See also, "All 39 Indian abducted by ISIS in Iraq alive: Swaraj", *India Today*, 14 May 2015, at http://indiatoday.intoday.in/story/indian-abducted-by-isis-in-iraq-alive-sushma-swaraj/1/438141.html
38. Praveen Swami, "40 Indians in ISIS custody 'safe'", *The Hindu*, 19 June 2014, at http://www.thehindu.com/news/national/40-indians-in-isis-custody-safe/article6127472.ece
39. Shaju Philip, "Tamil Nadu man who 'fought for IS in Iraq' held", *The Indian Express*, 7 October 2016, at http://indianexpress.com/article/india/india-news-india/kerala-indian-islamic-state-iraq-nia-3068865/)
40. John Lee, "Indian Banks to help Nurses Returning from Iraq", Iraq Business News, 8 November 2014, at http://www.iraq-businessnews.com/2014/11/08/indian-banks-to-help-nurses-returning-from-iraq/

5

KUWAIT

Hirak Jyoti Das

Key Information

Ruling family: al-Sabah; **Ruler:** Emir Sabah al-Ahmad al-Jaber al-Sabah (since 29 January 2006); **Crown Prince:** Prince Nawaf al-Ahmad al-Jaber al-Sabah (since 7 February 2006); **National Day:** 25 February; **Parliament**: 65-member (50 elected, 15 ex-officio cabinet) National Assembly; **Last Parliamentary Election**: 26 November 2016; **Major group in parliament**: Islamists (Salafi and Muslim Brotherhood); **National Carrier**: Kuwait Airways.

Socio-Economic Indicators

Area: 17,818 sq km; **Population:** 2.83 million; **Native:** 31 per cent; **Expats:** 69 per cent; **Religious Groups:** Citizen (Muslim 100 per cent); Resident population (Muslim 76.7 per cent; Christian 17.3 per cent; Other 5.9 per cent); **Youth:** 15.16 per cent; **Population growth rate:** 1.53 per cent; **Life expectancy at birth:** 78 years; **Major population groups**: Kuwaiti 31 per cent; Other Arab 28 per cent; Asian 37.8 per cent; African 1.9 per cent; Other 1.1 per cent; **Literacy rate:** 96.3 per cent; **National Currency**: Kuwaiti Dinar (KD); **GDP:** US$ 110.5 billion; **Foreign Trade:** US$ 72.16 billion; **Defence budget:** NA; **Sovereign Wealth Fund:** US$ 592 billion; **External Debt**: US$ 47.89 billion; **Per capita income:** US$ 71,300; **Oil reserves:** 104 billion bbl; **Gas reserves:** 1.784 trillion m^3; **HDI rank:** 48; **Infant Mortality Rate**: 7.1 deaths/ 1,000 live birth; **UN Education Index:** 0.646; **Gender Inequality Index:** 0.387; **Labour Force:** 2.546 million; **Unemployment rate**: 3 per cent; **Urban**

Population: 98.3 per cent; **Rate of Urbanization:** 3.63 per cent; **Last National Census**: 2005.

India Related

Indian Cultural Centre: India Study Centre (Faculty of Social Sciences, Kuwait University); **Number of Indians:** 900,000 (approx.); **Number of places of worship for Indians**: seven recognised Churches and a few non-recognised Christian worship facilities; **Indian Schools:** 20; **Indian Banks:** State Bank of India, Indian Overseas Bank, and HDFC Bank; **Currency exchange rate:** 1 KD = INR 218.14 (Feb 2017); **Last visit to India by the ruler**: Emir Sabah al-Ahmad al-Jaber al-Sabah, June 2006; **Last Indian Prime Minister to visit**: Indira Gandhi, May 1981.

* * *

Indo-Kuwait relations have covered a significant distance since 1991. Both countries have emerged as reliable partners with shared interests, extensive commercial relations, Indian expatriate presence, and cultural engagements. Bilateral relations remained stable during 2015 and 2016, although trade witnessed a drop. The growing focus on the Gulf region under Prime Minister Modi has created momentum, and the UAE along with Saudi Arabia have attained greater importance due to their economic advantages. This has led to lesser focus on Kuwait. Nevertheless, bilateral relations are smooth, with strong trade and commerce, growing cultural contacts, and increased mutual appreciation of threats emanating from terrorism.

Domestic Developments

Neighbouring Iraq and Saudi Arabia, Kuwait is ruled by the al-Sabah family, and has the oldest Constitution in the Persian Gulf region. It was adopted and ratified it on 11 November 1962 and, according to Article 4 of the Constitution, it is a hereditary emirate, with the Emir as the head of state.[1] It has a deep-rooted tradition of consensus through consultation, and cooperation among merchant families, tribal groups, and the ruling family, which has evolved into the present system.[2] It is a constitutional emirate in which the Emir is involved in the political process, and enjoys a wide array of powers. He shares executive powers with the Cabinet, presided over by the Prime Minister (Article 52), and is responsible for the appointment of the Prime Minister as the head of the government (Article 56). Judicial power rests with the courts which are exercised in the Emir's name, and he is responsible for the appointment of all judges. He serves as the Commander-in-Chief of the Kuwaiti armed forces.

In the Kuwaiti semi-parliamentary form of government, the Emir shares legislative authority with the *Majlis al-Umma* or the National Assembly (Article 51). The Assembly is unicameral, with members serving a four-year term.[3] The total composition of the assembly is 65, of which 50 are elected directly through multi-member constituencies, and 15 members are appointed by the Prime Minister. The voting age is 21 and, in the absence of political parties, blocs with distinct ideological and demographic characteristics compete for the assembly.[4] The assembly enjoys unique power in the region by being able to announce a vote of no-confidence against the cabinet ministers, excluding the Prime Minister (Articles 101 and 102). However, the Emir retains his preponderance over the legislative body through constitutional rights that allow him to propose, sanction and promulgate laws (Article 65). However, a two-third majority is required in the assembly to implement them.

In the wake of the Arab Spring protests and domestic political developments in the country, curbs on the political freedom of citizens have intensified, and the state has moved towards political and social de-liberalisation. The problem areas in the domestic context include restrictions on freedom of speech, assembly, and internet; political detentions; repressive legislations; curbs on the freedom of movement (especially of the Bedoon community and expatriate workers); and the lack of legal enforcement of laws to protect the rights of the expatriate workers resulting in arbitrary arrests and extrajudicial deportations.[5]

According to *Reporters without Borders*, Kuwait has been ranked 103 out of 180 countries on press freedom index in 2016.[6] Several media outlets have been shut down, and many journalists have faced harassment and jail terms. In January 2015, the government suspended the *Al-Watan* newspaper owned by former oil minister, Sheikh Khalifa al-Sabah, for publishing the transcript of a recording of an alleged plot to oust the present rulers, and the business and publishing licenses of the publishing house were revoked.[7] In June 2016, under the pretext of incurring financial loss, the licenses of television stations affiliated to the *Al-Watan* daily—*Al-Watan, Al-Watan Plus* and *Al-Watan Ghanawi*—and the business license of its publishing company, *Dar Al-Watan*, were withdrawn. The Court of Cassation upheld the government's decision to close down the news outlet. Under Kuwaiti Law, the licenses of companies that incur a loss of more than 75 per cent of their capital are withdrawn.[8] Earlier, in January 2016, the former Information Minister Saad bin Tefla who was in-charge of the website *Alaan News*, was detained and imprisoned for a week for writing an article in 2012 criticising Finance Minister Anas al-Saleh, and government spending.[9]

Legislative methods such as the new Telecommunications Law were approved by the National Assembly in 2014. It allows the government to censor, monitor, and block online material through a new body called the Commission for Mass Communications and Information Technology. In 2015, a few amendments were introduced to regulate the members' ties with the private sector, and grant the body more powers to pursue its objective.[10] The freedom of assembly and association is highly restricted in Kuwait although it is guaranteed by the Constitution. In 2012, a public gathering of more than 20 people was declared illegal. For his participation in protests in support of the rights of the Bedoon community, activist Abdullah al-Enezi was arrested in February 2014, and sentenced to five years imprisonment the following year. Enezi was also charged with criticizing the Emir which is considered a state security offence, with up to five years in prison. On 29 January 2015, six stateless activists were sentenced to pay a fine of US$ 700, or serve one year in prison for their 'illegal' activities.[11]

While overseeing a peaceful demonstration called by opposition groups demanding reforms in freedom of speech, release of political prisoners, withdrawal of citizenship for political reasons, Nawaf al-Hendal—the founder of the Kuwait Watch Organisation for Human Rights—was arrested in March 2015.[12] Earlier, in January 2015, Hendal had been arrested, along with Mohammed al-Ajmi and Musaid al-Musallam, on charges of slandering Saudi rulers on social media.[13]

Social media has been a prime target of political control, and the government has choked the freedom of dissent of opposition activists, bloggers, and citizen journalists for posting information that is critical of the government. In order to regulate the flow of online activities, the Cybercrime Law was passed in the National Assembly on 16 June 2015; it came to effect on 12 January 2016 and can further suppress online activism.[14] Opposition activist Saqr al-Hashash was arrested, and sentenced to 20 months in jail by the Court of Cassation for insulting the Emir on Twitter in January 2015. In April, he received a further sentence of 10 years for posting a diagram on how to make a petrol bomb on Twitter.[15] Saleh Othman al-Said, Abdulhamid Dashti, and Hamad al-Naqi were arrested for posting critical views on Saudi Arabia and Bahrain on internet and television in the same year.[16]

Politically motivated attacks on opposition politicians that are seen a threat to the government have continued during this period. Former parliamentarian, Musallam al-Barak, has been repeatedly arrested since 2012. Furthermore, on 22 June 2016, the National Assembly adopted an amendment to the election law that bars citizens from contesting or voting if convicted of hurting religious sentiments or criticising the Emir. This legislation is intended to prevent opposition members of the assembly to contest or influence future elections.[17]

The government has taken recourse to repressive legislations and actions towards stifling democracy, and sabotaged personal freedom. After the 26 June 2015 attack on a Shia Imam Sadiq Mosque in Kuwait city by the Islamic State in which 27 people died,[18] the Kuwaiti National Assembly passed the DNA testing law in order to create an integrated security database which is mandatory for both nationals and expatriates for the intended purpose of fighting crime and terrorism.[19] The gradual de-liberalizing trend in Kuwait has hampered state-citizen relations on the one hand, and legislative-executive relations on the other. In May 2015, the Kuwaiti Ministry of Social Affairs and Labour issued a decree to dissolve the international board of Transparency International Society, and replaced it with government appointed members on the pretext of monitoring NGOs supporting radical groups in the region. The government's actions are seen as vindictive, and are in response to the group's alleged political bias in showing the regime in a negative light, and exaggerating the level of corruption in the country.[20]

According to the 2015 *Corruption Perceptions Index*, Kuwait is ranked 55 out of 168 states. There is lack of transparency in government spending, and political corruption has seeped into government functioning. Corruption had caused political unrest in 2012. In March 2015, the government introduced regulations for the Public Anti-Corruption Authority (PACA), which was forwarded to the National Assembly by the cabinet. The Minister responsible for Electricity, Water, and Public Works, Ahmad al-Jassar, and 14 other state officials were sentenced to prison for two years in September 2015 for the secret acquisition of faulty electricity generators in 2007.[21]

In terms of expatriate domestic workers serving in Kuwaiti households and offices, there have been reports about numerous abuses, such as long working hours without holidays, late or non-payment of salary, physical and sexual assault, absence of grievance mechanisms, etc. A positive development in this regard was the passage of a new labour law by the National Assembly on 24 June 2015, which provides domestic workers enforceable labour rights, including a guaranteed day off every week, annual paid leave of up to 30 days, 12 hour working days with rest, and end of service benefits for one month at the end of the contract.[22] The minimum wage of domestic workers was fixed at US$ 200 (KD 60). The new law, however, falls short compared to the general labour law. The workforce in the private sector enjoys a 48 hour work week (that is, eight hours per day), an hour's break after five hours of work, and provisions of sick leave, etc.

Domestic workers are vulnerable due to the absence of enforcement mechanisms and the practise of *Kafala* (the visa sponsorship system) that restricts migrant domestic workers from finding another employer until the end of the original contract, or only with the owner's consent.[23]

The citizenship issue of the Bedoon community has remained in the limelight in the past two years. According to *Human Rights Watch*, in 2015 there were around 105,702 stateless Bedoons in Kuwait.[24] In the past few years, the emirate has been keen to send these Bedoons to Comoros, and offer money for accepting its citizenship. In May 2016, Comoros agreed to grant the Bedoons economic citizenship, thus regularising them as foreign citizens, and thereby making them liable for legal deportation from Kuwait.[25]

In national politics, on 16 November 2016, the Emir dissolved the Fourteenth National Assembly citing delicate regional circumstances, 'security challenges', and the 'lack of cooperation.'[26] The regional circumstances and security challenges refer to threats posed by the Islamic State of Iraq and Syria (ISIS) and the internal conflicts in Syria and Yemen which adversely affected the regional security situation. The issue of 'lack of cooperation' between the legislature and the executive has been a constant feature in Kuwaiti political history. The current context for the 'lack of cooperation' occurred due to differences among assembly members as well as against the cabinet over its decision to carry out austerity measures, including an 80 per cent hike in petrol prices.[27] The government intended to reduce dependence on the oil sector, and diversify the economy into non-oil sectors. In fact, due to the glut in international oil market and sharp slide in oil prices, oil revenue has dropped from 95 per cent to 60 per cent in two years.[28] In the 2015–16 financial year, Kuwait experienced a budget deficit of US$ 15 billion which has increased to a US$ 17 billion deficit in December 2016.[29]

A number of lawmakers have objected to the government's austerity measures expressing anxiety on their impact on social welfare such as free healthcare, education, subsidized basic products, free housing, interest-free loans, etc.[30] They have also demanded a cut in petrol prices, and have instead proposed a tax hike on the affluent class in order to accommodate the needs of low income groups. The election to the Fifth National Assembly was held on 26 November 2016 through multi-seat constituencies with a simple majority vote, and the result was announced the next day.[31] The number of registered voters was 439,911, and 70 per cent participated in the election. The opposition and its allies won 24 seats, and the pro-government members managed a fragile majority. In this election, only one woman, Safa al-Hashem, was elected to the National Assembly.[32]

In the regional sphere, Kuwait joined the Saudi-led efforts against the Houthis in Yemen. This began on 25 March 2015, and Kuwait participated in the war by supplying 15 fighter jets that were operated by the armed forces of Saudi Arabia, the UAE, and Jordan. On 28 March, the Emir reaffirmed his commitment against the regional threat posed by the Houthis.[33] Moreover, in order to solidify its unity with other Gulf States, Kuwait signed a GCC pact on 12 March 2015 that allows any Gulf government to extradite individuals engaged in political activities against—or threaten the security of—any other member state.[34] This decision has received widespread criticism domestically, and critics have accused the government of compromising the state's sovereignty which poses a threat to its democratic institutions.[35]

Bilateral Relations

This section examines the nature and depth of bilateral relations Kuwait enjoys with India in the areas of diplomacy, economy, energy, and cultural exchange. It also focuses on the dynamics of the Indian expatriate community living in Kuwait.

Political Relations

Political relations between India and Kuwait during 2015 and 2016 were limited, and there were no major political visits or contacts during the period under review. This is, however, compensated by the expansive trade, energy, and cultural ties that bind both countries. The scale of diplomacy was focussed on security and defence cooperation. From 13 to 16 September 2015, two Indian Naval Ships (INS), *INS Deepak*, a modern fleet tanker utilised as a fleet support ship[36] and *INS Tabar*, a frontline combatant in the western fleet, visited Kuwait's Al-Shuwaikh Port, and carried out interactions on sharing naval information pertaining to disaster management, combating maritime threats such as piracy and terrorism, greater sharing and understanding of each other's naval strength, joint sea exercises and sports events with the host navy.[37]

Economic Relations

India and Kuwait share robust economic relations, though the overall trade has witnessed a drop due to falling oil prices (see Table 5.1). The share of Kuwait in India's total trade has progressively shrunk from 2.22 per cent in 2011–12 to 1.92 per cent 2014–15 and 0.97 per cent in 2015–16 due to reduction in the bilateral trade from US$ 17.62 billion in 2011–12 to US$ 6.21 billion in 2015–16. While India's exports to Kuwait have remained more or less stable at US$ 1.18 billion in 2011–12 and US$ 1.24 billion in 2015–16, India's imports from Kuwait have drastically reduced (see Table 5.1). In 2011–12, India imported items worth US$ 16.43 billion from Kuwait which witnessed a minor decline in 2014–15 at US$ 13.38 billion. However, in 2015–16, India's imports from Kuwait fell to US$ 4.96 billion.

Table 5.1: India-Kuwait Bilateral Trade (in US$ million)

	2011–12	2012–13	2013–14	2014–15	2015–16
India's Exports to Kuwait	1,181.41	1,061.08	1,061.14	1,198.89	1,247.51
India's Imports from Kuwait	16,439.64	16,588.13	17,153.55	13,381.97	4,969.69
Total bilateral trade	17,621.05	17,649.21	18,214.69	14,580.85	6,217.20
Share of Kuwait in India's total trade	2.22	2.23	2.38	1.92	0.97

Source: Adapted from Director General of Foreign Trade, at www.dgft.gov.in

Figure 5.1: India-Kuwait Bilateral Trade

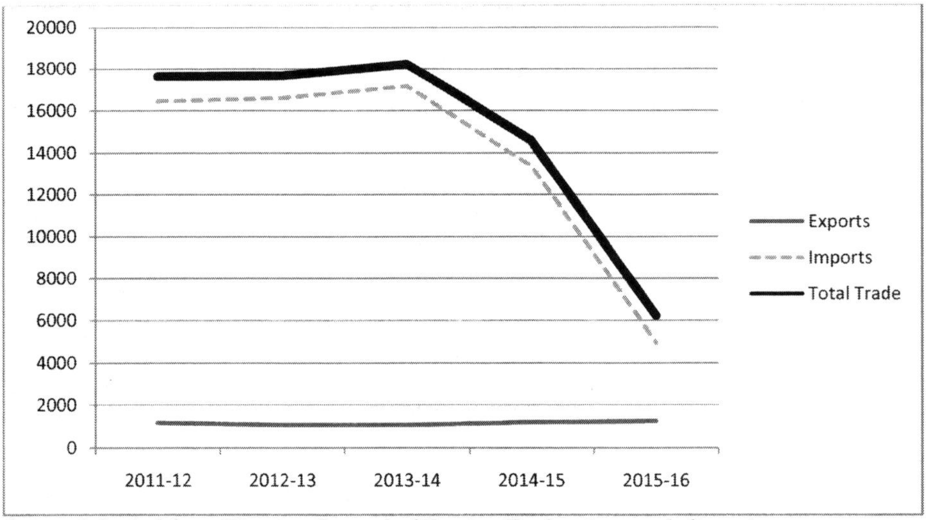

Source: Adapted from Director General of Foreign Trade, at www.dgft.gov.in

In the trade dimension over the last two years, conferences and workshops have been organised frequently to harness and innovate new areas of trade between both countries. Abdulmohsen Medeij al-Medeij, Kuwaiti Minister of Commerce and Industry, led a business delegation for a Partnership Summit held in Jaipur on 15–17 January 2015.[38] The Partnership summit organised jointly by the Confederation of Indian Industry (CII), the Department of Industrial Policy and Promotion (DIPP), the Ministry of Commerce and Industry, and the Government of Rajasthan was aimed at providing a global platform for dialogue and engagement in order to enhance understanding on forces that are shaping the world; to assess partnerships for global economic growth; to forge strong multi-country linkages and networks as well as address the challenges that require immediate attention.[39] In the plenary session themed "Defining Shared New Realities", Medeij stated that "the horizon of cooperation for shared growth and development is big and varied, and the opportunities of cooperation are many."[40] He stressed on orienting efforts to embolden the economic partnership on the principles of mutual interests and strong friendship.

In November 2015, the Indian Engineering, Procurement and Construction (EPC) companies secured contracts worth US$ 5 billion for development projects in Kuwait.[41] The EPC companies from India have acquired a niche status in providing cost-effective and efficient methods, and have been noticed by Kuwait. The companies have landed several projects in housing, hospitals, oil and gas sector, universities, power transmissions, etc. On 26 January 2015, Shapoorji Pallonji and Co. Ltd. signed US$ 150 million contract with Kuwait University (KU) for the construction, operation, and maintenance of buildings of the colleges of Law, Social Science, and Sharia and Islamic Studies in the Sabah Al-Salem University City.[42] Other Indian companies are involved in a number of development projects to modernise Kuwait's industrial infrastructure. In order to replace an old power substation at Al-Ahmadi refinery, Kuwait National Petroleum Corporation (KNPC) awarded a contract worth US$ 77 million to Larsen and Toubro in May 2015.[43] The Indian Embassy has been involved in promoting both Indian firms as well as initiatives such as *Make in India*.

Increased business interaction has expanded tourism and trade during this period, including in the civil aviation sector. Kuwait Airways has decided to connect with more Indian cities. With this objective, it has started direct flights to Ahmadabad and Bangalore three days a week from September 2015.[44] In order to bolster the inflow of Kuwaiti businessmen and tourists, India has regularly encouraged frequent visitors from Kuwait to apply through one and five year multi-entry Business Visas which are granted within 72 hours since August 2016.[45]

In the *Big 5 Kuwait*, an International Construction Technology & Building Materials Trade Exhibition held in September 2015 to tap Kuwait's booming construction market, 50 Indian companies participated to develop a platform for Indian bidders in the market and convene meetings with prospective customers. The "India Pavilion" was jointly organised by CII and Ministry of Commerce and Industry.[46] Moreover, 11 Indian companies participated in the Kuwait International Trade Fair in February 2016, displayed a variety of products, and provided further opportunity for business networking and involvement in development projects.[47]

Energy Relations

The share of Kuwaiti oil in India's total oil imports has reduced from 9.1 per cent in 2011–12 to 4.19 per cent in 2015–16 (see Table 5.2). Therefore, oil imports from Kuwait are at their lowest in five years, at US$ 4.05 billion in 2015–16.

Table 5.2: Share of Oil in India's Imports from Kuwait

Year	Imports	Total Oil Imports	Kuwaiti Share	Imports from Kuwait	Share of Oil in Imports from Kuwait
2011-12	15,718.33	172,753.92	9.10	16,439.64	95.61
2012-13	15,737.46	181,344.67	8.68	16,588.13	94.87
2013-14	16,121.78	181,382.59	8.89	17,153.55	93.99
2014-15	12,228.71	156,400.01	7.82	13,381.97	91.38
2015-16	4,059.61	96,953.06	4.19	4,969.69	81.69

Source: Adapted from Director General of Foreign Trade, at www.dgft.gov.in

Figure 5.2: Share of Oil in India's Imports from Kuwait (in US$ million)

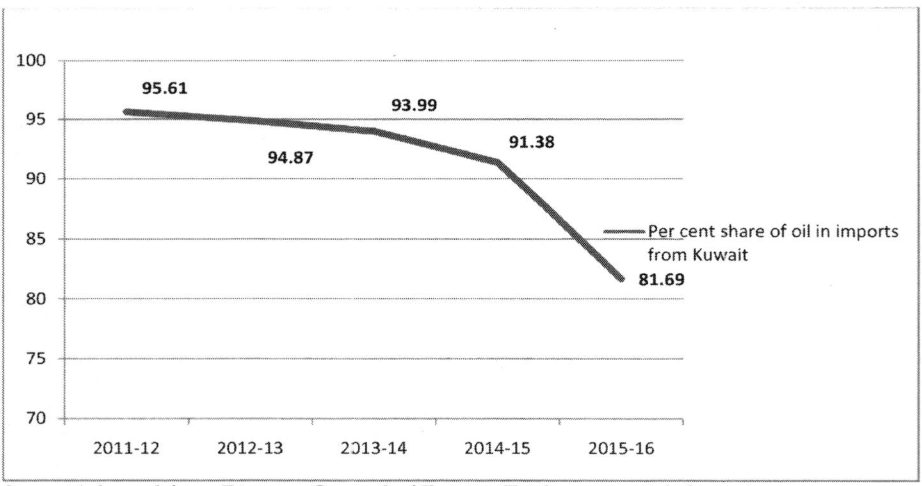

Source: Adapted from Director General of Foreign Trade, at www.dgft.gov.in

Table 5.3: India's Energy Imports from Kuwait (in US$ million)

	2011–12	2012–13	2013–14	2014–15	2015–16
Energy Imports from Kuwait	15,718.33	15,737.46	16,121.78	12,228.71	4,056.61
Total Energy Imports	172,753.92	181,344.67	181,382.59	156,400.01	96.953.06
Total Imports from Persian Gulf	105,056.26	105,859.15	106,400.75	85,300.30	50,992.26
Share in Total Energy Imports	9.10	8.68	8.89	7.82	4.19
Share in Energy Imports from Persian Gulf	14.96	14.87	15.15	14.34	7.96

Source: Adapted from Director General of Foreign Trade, at www.dgft.gov.in

Figure 5.3: Share of Kuwait in Energy Imports from Persian Gulf

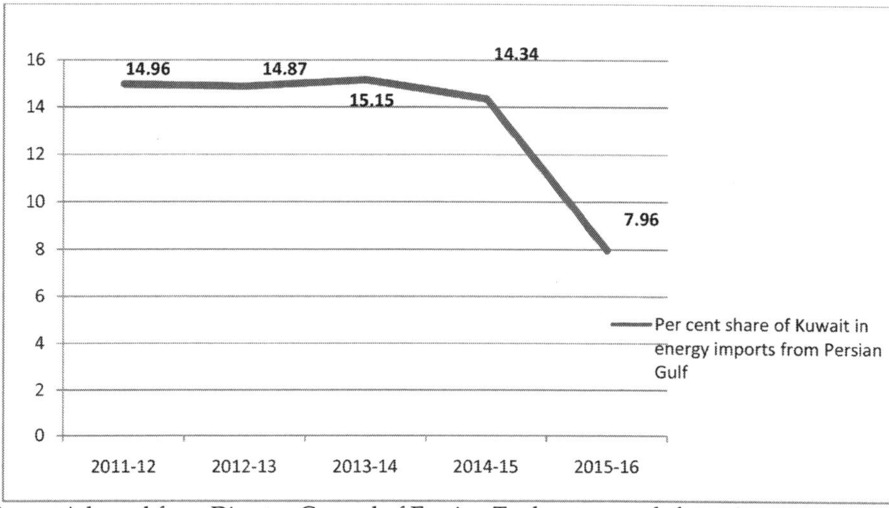

Source: Adapted from Director General of Foreign Trade, at www.dgft.gov.in

The engagement in the field of energy has been low key and marked by fewer engagements. In October 2015, Essar Projects Limited, along with Italian company Saipem, won a contract with Kuwait National Petroleum Company (KNPC) worth US$ 1.57 billion to set up Al-Zour Refinery Project (ZOR). It is the largest development project in Kuwait, with crude processing capacity of 615,000 barrels per day. Essar is responsible for building tanks, roads and bridges, civil works, etc.[48] Moreover, the Oil and Natural Gas Corporation (ONGC) participated in the Kuwait Oil and Gas Show (KOGS) 2015.

Cultural Relations

India through information and broadcasting has made serious efforts to deepen its cultural engagements with the Gulf States. On the occasion of Republic Day 2015, Doordarshan, India's state television broadcaster, launched a free-to-air mode television service in Kuwait and other Gulf states, and carried out live telecast of Republic Day parade and Beating Retreat.[49] The Indian embassy participated in the 15th Hala February Festival (HFF) through the "Incredible India" tourism campaign inaugurated on 15th January 2015; it lasted until 12 February to promote tourism. The programmes in the festival included art, sports, live carnival shows, entertainment events, and the showcasing of vintage cars and motorcycles.[50]

In March 2016, the Indian embassy organised Indian Food, Herbal and Handicrafts Exhibition to provide Kuwaitis different Indian flavours and other items such as ready-to-eat food, Indian snacks, spices, Indian tea, cosmetics as well as clothes, handicrafts and herbal products.[51] Moreover, Indian Handicrafts and Handloom Exhibitions have become a regular feature to promote the Indian textile industry.

Expatriates

Indians are the largest expatriate community in Kuwait, numbering around 900,000 and growing at 5–6 per cent per year, of which a significant majority (about 700,000) are men and approximately 200,000 are women.[52] A large section comprises domestic workers; there are also a substantial number of nurses, engineers, and other professionals. The Indian government has repeatedly raised concerns with the local government over issues of abuse and the inhumane treatment of its nationals in Kuwait who are at times forced to work against their. After an Indian national died working as a shepherd in a remote desert area due to dehydration (28 May 2015), the embassy has encouraged its citizens to report complaints in such instances.[53] In the 26 June ISIS attack on the Shia mosque in Kuwait city, two Indians, Rizwan Husain and Ibne Abbas, lost their lives. In accordance with the wishes of the family members, the Indian embassy undertook the responsibility of burying the deceased in Najaf, Iraq. It also advised the Indian community to take precautions from terrorist attacks.

In order to coordinate, engage, interact, and review labour and manpower cooperation related issues between both countries, the fifth session of India-Kuwait Joint Working Group on Labour, Employment, and Manpower Development was held in New Delhi on 14 December 2016. The Indian delegation was led by Manish Gupta, Joint Secretary (OIA-I Division), Ministry of External Affairs, Government of India, and the Kuwaiti delegation was led by Mobarak Al-Aazmi, Deputy Director General, Public Authority for Manpower, Sector of Planning and Professional Skill Levels Verification.[54]

To utilise the entrepreneurial skills of the Indian community living in Kuwait, a 19 member team of Indian businessmen residing in Kuwait, headed by S.K. Wadhawan participated in the 13th *Pravasi Bharatiya Divas* held in Gandhinagar on 7–9 January 2015. The summit aided in reasserting the need to strengthen ties with the diaspora, and provide a platform for networking and for recognising the contribution of the diaspora.[55]

Conclusion

While Indo-Kuwaiti relations have remained stable, political and energy ties have been minimal. However, the economic and cultural sphere has been dynamic and multi-faceted. Due to India's rapidly growing economy and enormous energy market, Kuwait has emerged as a stable energy partner. Kuwait is an important country, but is vulnerable to regional geopolitical and sectarian fault lines. Since India has vital interests in Kuwait, a proactive foreign policy towards Kuwait is required—with more political engagement and heightened security cooperation to address issues of common concern such as terrorism, maritime security, and energy security. At the same time, there is need to reduce the share of oil in the total trade and reorient it towards the non-oil sector. India can utilise its skilled population to further engage in Kuwait's development process. Moreover, on the issue of its nationals, India requires an effective framework and mechanism for accountability in order to reduce incidents of abuse in the country.

NOTES

1. "Kuwait's Constitution of 1962, Reinstated in 1992," 1992, Comparative Constitutions Project, at https://www.constituteproject.org/constitution/Kuwait_1992.pdf?lang=en
2. G. Alnajjar, "The Challenges facing Kuwaiti democracy," *Middle East Journal,* 2000, Vol. 54, No. 2, pp. 242– 258;
3. "Kuwait's Constitution of 1962, Reinstated in 1992", 1992, Comparative Constitutions Project, at https://www.constituteproject.org/constitution/Kuwait_1992.pdf?lang=en
4. M. Shalaby, "Women's political representation in Kuwait: An untold story", "Women's Rights in the Middle East Program," Baker Institute, 2015, at http://www.bakerinstitute.org/media/files/files/f812567d/WRME-pub-PoliRep Kuwait-091515.pdf; Also see D. Brumberg, "De-liberalization in Kuwait: The Limits of Power-Sharing in a Difficult Neighbourhood," Project on Middle East Democracy, June 2016, at http://pomed.org/wp-content/uploads/2016/06/POMED_Report_Brumberg_Final.pdf
5. K. Katzman, "Kuwait: Government, Security, and US Policy", Congressional Research Service, 1 December 2016, at https://fas.org/sgp/crs/mideast/RS21513.pdf
6. "2017 World Press Freedom Index", 2017, Reporters without Borders, https://rsf.org/en/ranking
7. "Kuwait takes three television channels off the air", *Gulf News,* 5 June 2015, at http://gulfnews.com/news/gulf/kuwait/kuwait-takes-three-television-channels-off-the-air-1.1530306
8. "Kuwait shuts down critical television channels", *The New Arab,* 8 June 2015, at https://www.alaraby.co.uk/english/news/2015/6/8/kuwait-shuts-down-critical-television-channels
9. "Former Kuwaiti minister jailed over news article," *Khaleej Times,* 11 January 2015, at http://www.khaleejtimes.com/article/20150111/ARTICLE/301119929/1016
10. "Kuwait 2016", Freedom House, accessed 13 March 2017, at https://freedomhouse.org/report/freedom-world/2016/kuwait
11. "Kuwait sentences stateless activist for insulting emir", *The National,* 1 February 2015, at http://www.thenational.ae/world/middle-east/kuwait-sentences-stateless-activist-for-insulting-emir

12. "Nawaf Al-Hendal arrested after speaking at 28th session of UN Human Rights Council", Gulf Centre for Human Rights, at http://www.gc4hr.org/news/view/960
13. "Release Nawaf Al Hendal and respect right to freedom of expression and assembly", International Service for Human Rights, 25 March 2015, http://www.ishr.ch/news/kuwait-release-nawaf-al-hendal-and-respect-right-freedom-expression-and-assembly
14. "Harsh penalties ... Cyber Crime Law effective Jan 12; Law reflects MOI efforts in fighting e-crimes," *Arab Times*, 6 January 2016, at http://www.arabtimesonline.com/news/harsh-penalties-cyber-crime-law-effective-jan-12-law-reflects-moi-efforts-in-fighting-e-crimes/
15. "Kuwaiti activist jailed 10 years for petrol bomb tweet", *Gulf News*, 28 April 2015, at http://gulfnews.com/news/gulf/kuwait/kuwaiti-activist-jailed-10-years-for-petrol-bomb-tweet-1.1500635
16. D. Brumberg, "De-liberalization in Kuwait: The Limits of Power-Sharing in a Difficult Neighbourhood", Project on Middle East Democracy, June 2016, at http://pomed.org/wp-content/uploads/2016/06/POMED_Report_Brumberg_Final.pdf
17. B. Izzak, "National Assembly approves amendment to election law—New election law bars those who insult God, prophets, Amir", *Kuwait Times*, 22 June 2016, at http://news.kuwaittimes.net/website/national-assembly-approves-amendment-election-law/
18. "Kuwait Shia mosque blast death toll 'rises to 27'", *BBC News*, 26 June 2015, at http://www.bbc.com/news/world-middle-east-33287136
19. Hanan Al-Saadoun, "Kuwait set to enforce DNA testing law on all – Officials reassure tests won't be used to determine genealogy", *Kuwait Times*, 23 January 2016, http://news.kuwaittimes.net/website/kuwait-to-enforce-dna-testing-law-on-citizens-expats-visitors-tests-wont-be-used-to-determine-genealogy-affect-freedoms/
20. "Authorities Dissolve Transparency Society: Accused of 'Meddling in Politics' by Reporting on Corruption", *Human Rights Watch*, 21 June 2015, at https://www.hrw.org/news/2015/06/21/kuwait-authorities-dissolve-transparency-society
21. "Kuwait 2016," Freedom House, at https://freedomhouse.org/report/freedom-world/2016/kuwait
22. "Analysis: Kuwait's new laws for domestic workers," *Kuwait Times*, 12 August 2015, at http://news.kuwaittimes.net/website/analysis-kuwaits-new-laws-for-domestic-workers/
23. "Rights group calls for end to Kuwait's kafala system", *Gulf Business*, 15 December 2016, at http://gulfbusiness.com/rights-group-calls-end-kuwaits-kafala-system/
24. "Kuwait: Events of 2016", *Human Rights Watch*, 2016, at https://www.hrw.org/world-report/2016/country-chapters/kuwait
25. "Kuwait courts Comoros to settle bidoon issue", *Kuwait Times*, 20 May 2016, at http://gulfnews.com/news/gulf/kuwait/kuwait-courts-comoros-to-settle-bidoon-issue-1.1831570
26. H. Toumi, "Kuwait parliament dissolved nine times in 54 years: Only six parliaments were able to run their election terms since 1962", *Gulf News*, 17 October 2016, at http://gulfnews.com/news/gulf/kuwait/kuwait-parliamentdissolved-nine-times-in-54-years-1.1913724

27. "Kuwait announces 'ultra' petrol price rise of 83%—to 55 cents a litre", *The Guardian*, 2 August 2016, at https://www.theguardian.com/world/2016/aug/02/kuwait-announces-petrol-price-hike-of-83-to-55-cents-a-litre
28. D. Bandow, "Kuwait needs economic reform, but opponents dominated National Assembly election," *Forbes*, 9 January–11 March 2017, at https://www.forbes.com/sites/dougbandow/2017/01/09/kuwait-needs-economic-reform-but-opponents-dominated-national-assembly-election/#d1233777c8df
29. "Kuwait records $17 bn budget deficit at end of 2016", *Gulf Business*, 26 January 2017, at http://gulfbusiness.com/kuwait-records-17bn-budget-deficit-end-2016/
30. "Polls close in Kuwait parliamentary elections", *Al-Jazeera*, 26 November 2016, at http://www.aljazeera.com/news/2016/11/polls-close-kuwait-parliamentary-elections-161126153654644.html
31. Ibid.
32. "Kuwait poll: Opposition wins nearly half of parliament" *Al-Jazeera*, 27 November 2016, at http://www.aljazeera.com/news/2016/11/kuwait-poll-opposition-wins-parliament-161127060822207.html
33. Justin Vela, "Kuwait role in Yemen a surprise, yet underlines frustrations with Tehran," *The National*, 11 April 2015, at http://www.thenational.ae/world/middle-east/kuwait-role-in-yemen-a-surprise-yet-underlines-frustrations-with-tehran
34. Madawi Al-Rasheed, "Kuwaiti activists targeted under GCC security pact", *Al-Monitor*, 20 March 2015, at http://www.al-monitor.com/pulse/originals/2015/03/saudi-gcc-security-dissident-activism-detention-opposition.html
35. "Kuwait MPs press for ratifying GCC security pact", *Gulf News*, 6 September 2015, at http://gulfnews.com/news/gulf/kuwait/kuwait-mps-press-for-ratifying-gcc-security-pact-1.1579211
36. Tejas Mehta, "Meet *INS Deepak*, Navy's new super-tanker", *NDTV*, 21 January 2011, at http://www.ndtv.com/india-news/meet-ins-deepak-navys-new-super-tanker-445644
37. "Visit of Indian Naval Ships (INS), INS Deepak and INS Tabar to Al-Shuwaikh Port", Embassy of India, Kuwait, 14 September 2015, at http://www.indembkwt.org/DispNews.aspx?ID=841
38. "India-Kuwait Relations", Ministry of External Affairs, Government of India, July 2016, at https://mea.gov.in/Portal/ForeignRelation/Kuwait_July_2016.pdf
39. Ibid.
40. "CII Media Releases: We need to make serious and devoted efforts to build economic partnership, says Deputy Prime Minister of Kuwait," Chamber of Indian Industries, 16 January 2015, at http://www.cii.in/Pressreleases Detail.aspx?enc =fdg0SQy3CsRkJ0zNGicyLwx GIXN35ANmz YQnt4ga ZYU=, accessed 27 March 2017.
41. "Indian EPC firms awarded projects worth over $5 billion in Kuwait", *The Economic Times*, 9 November 2015, at http://economictimes.indiatimes.com/news/industry/indl-goods/svs/engineering/indian-epc-firms-awarded-projects-worth-over-5-billion-in-kuwait/articleshow/49722856.cms
42. "Shapoorji Pallonji and Co. Ltd. finalized contract with Kuwait University" , *The Times*, 29 January 2015, http://www.timeskuwait.com/Times_Shapoorji-Pallonji-and-Co.-Ltd.-finalized-contract-with-Kuwait-University
43. "Indian EPC firms awarded projects worth over Rs 3,3185 crore in two years", *DNA*, 9 November 2015, at http://www.dnaindia.com/money/report-indian-epc-firms-awarded-projects-worth-over-rs-33185-crore-in-two-years-2143727

44. "Kuwait Airways flies direct to Ahmadabad and Bangalore", Embassy of India, Kuwait, 7 September 2015, at http://www.indembkwt.org/DispNews.aspx?ID=837
45. "Grant of 5-year and 1-year multi-entry Business Visa to visit India", Embassy of India, Kuwait, 3 August 2016, at http://www.indembkwt.org/DispNews.aspx?ID =970
46. "Indian Industry to showcase its mettle at Big 5 Kuwait", Embassy of India, Kuwait, 14 September 2015, at http://www.indembkwt.org/DispNews.aspx?ID =842
47. "Indian Exporters to showcase their mettle at 'The Kuwait International Trade Fair'," Embassy of India, Kuwait, 17 February 2016, at http://www.indembkwt.org/DispNews.aspx?ID=915
48. "KNPC awards contract worth USD 1.57 billion to Essar Projects Limited for Al-Zour Refinery Project, in Kuwait", Embassy of India, Kuwait, 28 October 2015, http://www.indembkwt.org/DispNews.aspx?ID=874
49. "Doordarshan India channel available in Free-to-Air mode in Kuwait", Embassy of India, Kuwait, 28 January 2015, http://www.indembkwt.org/DispNews.aspx?ID=718
50. "Indian Embassy participated in Hala February Festival", Embassy of India, Kuwait, 18 January 2015, http://www.indembkwt.org/DispNews.aspx?ID=713
51. "Indian Food, Herbal and Handicrafts Exhibition held", Embassy of India, Kuwait, 18 March 2015, http://www.indembkwt.org/DispNews.aspx?ID=756
52. "Statistics of Indian nationals in Kuwait" Embassy of India, Kuwait, 23 April 2015, http://www.indembkwt.org/DispNews.aspx?ID=774
53. "Advisory to stop taking up employment as shepherds", Embassy of India, Kuwait, 31 May 2015, at http://www.indembkwt.org/DispNews.aspx?ID=790
54. "Fifth session of India-Kuwait Joint Working Group on Labour, Employment and Manpower Development", Ministry of External Affairs, 16 December 2016, at http://www.mea.gov.in/press-releases.htm?dtl/27872/Fifth_session_of_IndiaKuwait_ Joint_Working_Group_on_Labour_Employment_and_ Manpower_Development
55. "Participation of an Indian delegation", Embassy of India, Kuwait, 1 January 2015, at http://www.indembkwt.org/DispNews.aspx?ID=699

6

OMAN

Jatin Kumar

Key Information

Ruling family: al-Said; **Ruler:** Sultan Qaboos bin Said al-Said (since 23 July 1970); **Crown Prince:** Not Nominated; **National Day:** 18 November; **Parliament**: 71-member nominated Majlis al-Dawla, 84-member elected Majlis al-Shoura; **Last Parliamentary Election**: 25 October 2015; **Major group in parliament:** NA; **National Carrier**: Oman Air.

Socio-Economic Indicators

Area: 309,500 sq km; **Population:** 3.35 million; **Native:** 60 per cent; **Expats:** 40 per cent; **Religious Groups:** Muslim 85.9 per cent (75 per cent Ibadhi Muslim; 25 per cent Shia and Sunni); Christian 6.5 per cent; Hindu 5.5 per cent; Buddhist 0.8 per cent; Other 1.3 per cent; **Youth:** 19.11 per cent; **Population growth rate:** 2.05 per cent; **Life expectancy at birth:** 75.5 years; **Major population groups**: Arab, Baluchi, South Asian, and African (distribution not available); **Literacy rate:** 91.1 per cent; **National Currency**: Omani Riyal (OMR); **GDP:** US$ 59.68 billion; **Foreign Trade:** US$ 56.17 billion; **Defence budget:** 12.75 per cent of GDP; **Sovereign Wealth Fund:** US$ 14.54 billion; **External Debt**: US$ 20.85 billion; **Per capita income:** US$ 43,700; **Oil reserves:** 5.3 billion bbl; **Gas reserves:** 688.1 billion m^3; **HDI rank:** 52; **Infant Mortality Rate**: 13.2 deaths/1,000 live birth; **UN Education Index:** 0.603; **Gender Inequality Index:** 0.275; **Labour Force:** 968,800; **Unemployment rate**: 15 per cent (2004 est.); **Urban Population:** 77.6 per cent; **Rate of Urbanization:** 8.54 per cent; **Last National Census**: 2010.

India Related

Indian Cultural Centre: NA; **Number of Indians:** 600,000 (2014 est.); **Number of places of worship for Indians**: Three temples, Five Gurudwaras, and Seven Churches; **Indian Schools:** 19; **Indian Banks:** State Bank of India (1), Indian Overseas Bank, Bank of Baroda (4) and HDFC Bank; **Currency exchange rate:** 1 OMR = INR 173.03 (February 2017); **Last visit to India by the ruler**: Sultan Qaboos al-Said, April 1997; **Last Indian Prime Minister to visit**: Manmohan Singh, November 2008.

* * *

Oman has been a key player in India's Gulf policy which is currently focussing on a greater synergy between India and the Persian Gulf countries. Oman's geographical location provides it a significant place in India's strategic calculations, especially with respect to maritime security. Besides its 1,200-mile coastline along the Indian Ocean, the Persian Gulf, the Arabian Sea, and the Gulf of Oman, it is also close to important maritime routes leading to Europe, Iran, Iraq, and other Gulf Cooperation Council (GCC) countries. While oil makes up the bulk of the country's revenues, it is also endowed with natural resources such as copper, petroleum, marble, limestone, asbestos, chromium, natural gas, gypsum. If Oman is important for India's Middle East policy, India is key ally for Oman in terms of food security as it supplies wheat, rice, sugar, and other food products.

India and Oman have enjoyed robust historical, economic, and political relations. It has been argued that, during ancient times, Oman was connected with the Indian land mass through ties of trade and sea based businesses since the Sumerian and Harappan civilizations.[1] India's commercial ties with Oman flourished in the 18th century when Haider Ali and Tipu Sultan established trade relations.[2] The beautiful aspect of this age-old relationship is that the maritime routes have played an important role in the flourishing of this relationship. These relations reached new heights when the Indian Prime Minister Manmohan Singh paid a visit to Oman in 2008 and, since then, these commercial relations have transformed into a strategic partnership.[3]

The credit of warm and cordial relations between the two countries goes back to the historical maritime trade relationship as well as to an estimated 700,000 strong Indian expatriate community which has played a vital role in the shaping of modern Oman.[4] In 2015, both countries celebrated the 60th anniversary of the establishment of diplomatic relations which have evolved from being mere diplomatic ties, to collaborations in defence and security, bilateral trade as well as expanding cultural, educational, and tourism sectors. The importance of Oman for India can be comprehended by the fact that, on regular intervals, the heads of Indian governments have visited Oman, including Rajiv Gandhi (1985), P. V. Narasimha Rao (1993), Atal Behari Vajpayee (1998), and Manmohan Singh (2008); and it is expected that Prime Minister Narendra Modi would undertake a visit in 2017.[5]

Domestic Developments

Oman was an isolated country until 1970. Currently, it is an active player in regional politics. It is has a traditional heritage and is the oldest sovereign nation in the Middle East.[6] The country is currently ruled by Sultan Qaboos bin Said al-Said, who seized power from his father, Sultan Said bin Taimur, in 1970. For the last few years, Sultan Qaboos has not been keeping well, restricting his public life and hampering government functioning. He returned to Muscat in April 2016, after receiving long medical treatment in Germany.

After taking over, Sultan Qaboos embarked on economic reforms, and "boosted spending on health, education and welfare."[7] He used oil revenues to start ambitious projects to modernise the country and improve health services and educational institutions. Unlike the other Gulf States, the mainstay of the Omani economy is not only oil but also a robust and fast developing agricultural market, alongside fishing. Though Oman has continued to take strides in modernizing its economy and advancing political changes, the society remains largely traditional. Women continue to face discrimination due to the dominant patrimonial social structure. As is the case in other Arab monarchies, men still rule the roost and are legal and moral heads of all units of Omani life, starting from the family.

For Omani authorities, the creation of jobs remains a significant challenge. A report released in 2015 by the National Centre for Statistics and Information (NCSI) underlined that 50 per cent "of all Omani young job seekers needed three and a half years to find a job."[8] The data also highlighted a huge gender disparity, "with males finding employment in less than two years, while females took up to four and a half years to get their first job."[9] According to Talib Al Dhabari, head of the media department at the Ministry of Manpower, the possible reason for the delay in receiving employment opportunities was that the unemployed youth wanted to join public sector jobs rather than joining private sector.

Since the 2010–11 uprisings in the region, the Omani authorities have intensified efforts to curb criticism of the government by arresting several human rights as well as political activists. During 2015–16, many human right activists were detained, including Mahmoud al-Fazari, Ali al-Muqbali,

Talib al-Saidi, Saleh al-Azri, and Mukhtar al-Hinai, all of whom were charged with undue criticism of the government on social media. On 8 November 2016, well known writer and cinema critic, Abdullah Habib, was arrested over views expressed on social media regarding human rights in Oman.[10] Furthermore, women continue to face discrimination in law and in practice.[11]

In January 2015, the Finance Ministry of Oman released the state budget for 2015 with a deficit of US$ 6.5 billion, equal to about 8 per cent of the GDP. The main reason for the deficit was the continuous fall in oil prices. In 2015, the total revenue stood at US$ 30.16 billion, a minor decline of 0.85 per cent in comparison to 2014. Significantly, oil and gas revenues constitute 78.97 per cent of the total revenues. It stood at US$ 23.81 billion, registered a decline of 5.08 per cent from US$ 25.09 billion in the 2014 budget. Non-oil and gas revenues of total revenue stood at 21.03 per cent, up by 19.02 per cent, year on year, at US$ 6.34 billion against US$ 6.18 billion in 2014. The government's expenditure in 2015 was estimated at US$ 36.6 billion; it saw an increase of 4.5 per cent (US$ 35.1 billion) in comparison to the 2014 budget.[12] As for 2015, according to the government of Oman, the planned growth rate was projected at 5 per cent. On the other hand, the growth rate of non-oil activities was projected to reach 5.5 per cent at constant prices (see Table 6.1).[13]

Table 6.1: Budget Comparison of 2015 and 2016 (in millions)

Revenues	**2015**		**2016**		**Change**
	Omani Riyal	**US Dollar**	**Omani Riyal**	**US Dollar**	
Oil and Gas	6,150	15,990	9,160	23,816	33
Taxes & fees	1,329	3,455.4	1,335	3,471	(0.4)
Others	1,111	2,888.6	1,105	2,873	0.5
Total non-Oil & Gas	2,440	6,344	2,440	6,334	0
Total revenues	8,600	22,360	11,600	30,160	(26)
Expenditure					
Defence and security	3,500	9,100	3,800	9,880	(8)
Civil ministries	4,600	11,960	5,166	13,431.6	(11)
Oil and Gas	490	1,274	560	1,456	13
Loan Interest	90	234	50	130	80
Investment expenditure	2,670	6,942	3,214	8,356.4	17
Other expenditure	550	1430	1,310	3406	58
Total expenditure	11,900	30,940	2,500	6,500	16
Deficit	3,300	8,580	2,500	6,500	32

Source: Ministry of Finance, Government of Oman; and Price Waterhouse Cooper

Note: The values in millions and billions are calculated from Omani Riyal to US$ at May 2017 conversion rate (1 Omani riyal = US$ 2.60)

Similarly, the 2016 budget was also affected by continuing low oil prices and, as a result, the government reduced spending and aimed to boost non-oil and gas revenues. In 2015 or 2016, the total public expenditure—expected to be about US$ 30.94 billion—saw a decline of US$ 3.9 billion, which is 11 per cent less than the actual spending in 2015.[14]

The oil and gas expenses were expected to be US$ 4.65 billion; this was 14 per cent less than the 2015 estimate. The expenditure on defence and security related issues was estimated US$ 9.1 billion, registering a decline of 12 per cent in comparison to previous year. The budget the deficit was estimated at US$ 8.58 billion, which was 13 per cent of GDP (see Table 6.1). The budget also highlighted the means to cover deficit, some of the proposed measures to reduce deficit were improve non-oil and gas revenues and rationalised spending.

In October 2015, Oman held its 8th Shura Council elections—"the second such election since the body was promised greater powers following the Arab Spring-inspired protests of 2011."[15] During the elections, 611,906 registered voters used their suffrage to elect 85 candidates from a total of 590 who were vying for seats in the Shura Council.[16] The candidates also included 20 women. In comparison to previous elections held in 2011, the number of candidates registered a sharp drop from 1,131 to 590. While highlighting the participation of voters, the Ministry of Interior said that 297,905 out of 525,785 registered voters participated in the polls; these represented 56.6 per cent, declining from 76 per cent of those voting in the 2011 elections (see Table 6.2). The significant drop in the voting was an indication of declining interest in the public in the electoral process.

Table 6.2: The Shura Council Elections Result 2011 and 2015

S. No.	Date of Election	Total Registered Voters	Numbers of Votes Polled	Turnout per cent	Numbers of Seats	Candidates
1.	2011	510,000	397,000	76	85	1300
2.	2015	525,785	297,905	56	85	590

Source: *Election guide Org*, 2003; Inter-Parliamentary Union, 2015 and Government of Oman, 2015

The Rapporteur of the Higher Committee for Majlis Al-Shura elections, Talal bin Ahmed al-Sa'adi, noted that,

> [T]he number of candidates in the elections stood at 590, including 12 holders of PhDs, 70 holders of the Masters degree, and 200 holders of the Bachelor degree, in addition to holders of higher education diploma post the general education. The number of voters stood at 525,785, including 237,918 females and 278,804 males.[17]

In December 2016, the Omanis queued up once again in polling stations across the country to cast their votes for the second municipal elections in the country. The number of voters stood at 623,224, including 333,733 men and 289,491 women, with an increase of 100,000 from the last elections (see Table 6.3).[18] The number of candidates who contested the election stood at 731, including 23 women, for 202 seats. According to the Ministry of Interior, seven women were elected to municipal councils. The election registered 39.85 per cent voting turnout, which included 63.2 per cent males and 36.8 per cent females.[19] In the first municipal council election held in 2012, the voter turnout was 50.3 per cent.[20]

Table 6.3: Municipal Election Results, 2016

Total Registered Voters	Turnout (per cent)	Numbers of Seats	Candidates
623,224	39.85	202	731

Source: *Gulf News* and *The News*

Bilateral Relations

In 2015, India and Oman celebrated the completion of 60 years of the establishment of diplomatic relations. External Affairs Minister, Sushma Swaraj, visited Oman during 17–18 February 2015 to kick-start the celebrations, thus also providing a new impetus to the bilateral relations. During the visit, she exchanged views on regional, bilateral, and other key issues of common interest. A special commemorative postal stamp was also issued by the Omani government.[21] It was the "first time when Oman Post had issued a special commemorative stamp to mark an important milestone in India's historical relations with Oman."[22]

Some of the other commemorative events which were held in 2015 were:

- In April An Indian Film Festival was organised in association with City Cinema and Yash Raj Films, in Muscat.
- A lecture on "India-Oman Relations in a Historical and Contemporary Perspective" by Talmiz Ahmed was organised on 14 May.
- Four Indian Naval Ships from the Western Fleet visited Muscat port on 19–22 September.
- A display of "Vastram: Splendid World of Indian Textiles", an Indian Council of Cultural Relations Collection, was held in Muscat from 15– 25 October.[23]

In last six decades, Oman has emerged as an important destination for tourism to and from India in the Middle East. During 2013, India received 62,252 visitors from Oman.[24] Both the countries have acknowledged the mutual benefits which can be achieved through tourism. Therefore, India and Oman created an institutional mechanism to enhance cooperation in this sector. In January 2015, the union cabinet chaired by Prime Minister Narendra Modi gave approval for a Memorandum of Understanding (MoU) for strengthening ties in the field of tourism between India and Oman.[25]

Political and Defence Relations

India and Oman have been collaborating on crime prevention and maritime security issues since 1970, when both the countries established defence ties. These ties have evolved over time as a good example of a crucial strategic partnership. In 1999, Oman became the first GCC country to sign a MoU on combating transnational crime and terrorism. A major milestone in furthering these relations was the visit of Prime Minister Manmohan Singh in 2008. This bond has been further enriched since Narendra Modi became the Prime Minister. There were a series of developments between the countries in 2015–16, starting with the visit of the External Affairs Minister, Sushma Swaraj, in February 2015.

In May 2015, the Indian Sail Training Ship *INS Tarangini* visited Salalah as a part of the commemorative events which were organised to celebrate the Diamond Jubilee of India-Oman diplomatic ties.[26] Soon after, the Chief of Air Staff of the Indian Air Force, Arup Raha, visited Muscat in August, and the Commander of Royal Navy of Oman visited India in September. These exchanges were complemented by other important events. In November "the Indian Navy Sail Training Ship *Tarangini* and Royal Navy of Oman Sail Training Ship *Shabab* set sail together to Kochi."[27] In February 2016, the Indian Coast Guard ship *Sankalp* undertook a goodwill visit to Muscat. In last three years, this was the third visit by an Indian Coast Guard ship to Oman. Prior to this, ICGS *Samundra Prahari* and *Vijit* had made friendly voyages to Muscat port in March 2013 and January 2015, respectively.[28]

On 10 February 2016, a three-member Indian delegation headed by the Indian Defence Secretary, G. Mohan Kumar, visited Oman to attend the 8th Meeting of the Joint Military Cooperation Committee which "reviewed the existing defence cooperation between the two countries, and identified further steps to strengthen it."[29] During the meeting, both the countries highlighted their determination to further expand their defence cooperation. The Defence Secretary also met the Chief of Staff of Sultan Armed Forces, Lieutenant General Ahmed bin Harith al-Nabhani, and the Secretary General of the National Security Council, Major General Ahmed Salman Khushoob.[30]

In May, the Defence Minister of India, Manohar Parrikar, paid a three day visit to Oman as the guest of Bader Bin Saud Bin Harib Al Busaidi, the Minister responsible for defence issues in Oman. During the visit, Parrikar also met Sayyid Fahd bin Mahmoud al-Said, Deputy Prime Minister for the Council of Ministers, and Lieutenant General Sultan bin Mohammed al-Nu'amani, Minister of the Royal Office. During the meetings, both sides talked about various aspects of defence cooperation and shared their points of view on regional developments of mutual interest.[31] During the meeting, Parrikar expressed his gratitude for Oman's constant support for the Operational Turnaround (OTR) of Indian naval ships for anti-piracy patrols as well as technical support for landing and over flight of Indian Air Force aircraft.[32] The Defence Minister also stopped over at the Military Technology College, and attended a reception to register the goodwill visit to Muscat of *INS Delhi, INS Deepak,* and *INS Tarkash* at Sultan Qaboos Port.

During this visit the four MOUs/agreements were signed, namely:

1. MOU on Defence Cooperation between the Ministry of Defence of Sultanate of Oman and Ministry of Defence of Republic of India;
2. MOU between the Royal Oman Police (Coast Guard) and the Indian Coast Guard in the field of Marine Crime Prevention at Sea;
3. MOU between India and Oman on Maritime Issues;
4. Protocol between the Government of the Sultanate of Oman represented by Royal Air Force of Oman and the Government of India represented by the Indian Air Force on Flight Safety Information Exchange.[33]

It was also decided that both countries would strengthen their bilateral defence ties.[34] Indian Naval Ships *INS Deepak, INS Tarkash* and *INS Delhi,* visited Muscat from 21–24 May 2016. A part of the Indian Navy's Western Naval Command, they were on a month-long deployment in the Gulf region to enhance bilateral ties with friendly regional Navies.

In the last few years, naval cooperation between the Indian and Omani Navies has progressed gradually, with increased visits and knowledge sharing. The biennial naval exercise *Naseem Al-Bahr* has played a key role in improving inter-operability and the successful accomplishment of this joint naval exercise (February 2016) strengthened the robust ties between the two Navies. The participation of Oman in the Indian Ocean Naval Symposium (IONS)—a co-operative initiative of 35 countries of the Indian Ocean Region—has also played a vital role in developing close chemistry between the two countries.

Economic Relations

The economic ties between India and Oman are an important pillar in the strategic partnership between the two. The mutual investment between the two has grown significantly in last few years, and stands around US$ 7.5 billion.[35] The first share of the India-Oman Joint Investment Fund has already been invested, which was around US$ 100 million; and talks are underway to finalize the second share of US$ 300 million.[36]

However, the bilateral trade has seen fluctuations in recent years. During 2011–12, India's exports to Oman stood at US$ 1.3 billion, which further increased to US$ 2.5 billion in 2012–13. In 2013-14, they stood at US$ 2.8 billion. However, after this it has been constantly declining. In 2014–15, India's exports decreased to US$ 2.3 billion, and dropped further to US$ 2.1 billion in 2015–16 (see Table 6.4). India's imports from Oman also saw a decline from US$ 5.7 billion (2013–14) to US$ 1.7 billion (2014–15) and US$ 1.6 billion (2015–16). Total trade declined in 2014–15 by 28 per cent to US$ 4.1 billion.

Table 6.4: India-Oman Bilateral Trade (in US$ million)

	2011–12	2012–13	2013–14	2014–15	2015–16
India's Exports to Oman	1,322.13	2,599.49	2,812.27	2,379.44	2,190.79
India's Imports from Oman	3,345.94	2,009.72	2,951.18	1,752.24	1,674.71
Total bilateral Trade	4,668.08	4,609.21	5,763.45	4,131.69	3,865.50
Share of Oman in total trade	0.59	0.58	0.75	0.54	0.60

Source: Adapted from Director-General of Foreign Trade, New Delhi, at www.dgft.gov.in

Figure 6.1: India-Oman Bilateral Trade (in US$ million)

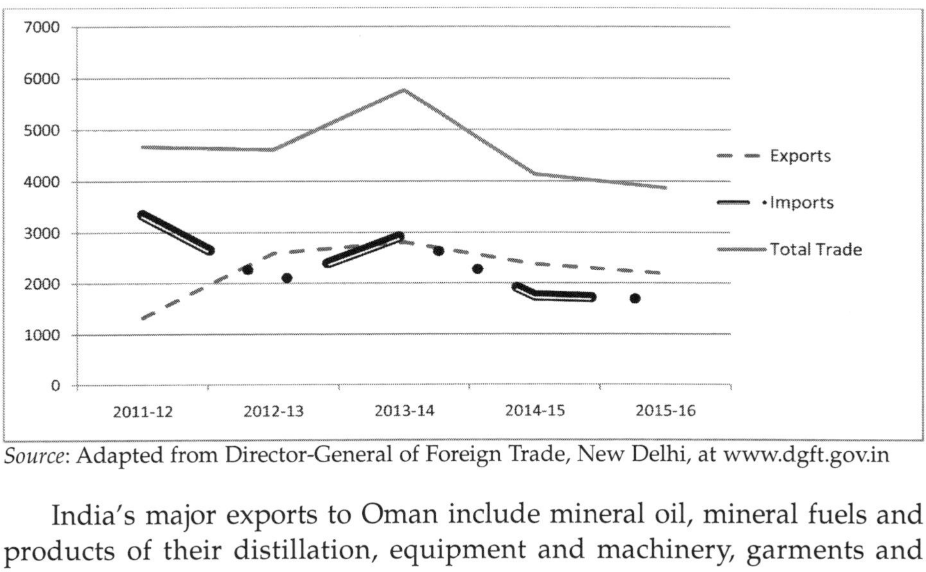

Source: Adapted from Director-General of Foreign Trade, New Delhi, at www.dgft.gov.in

India's major exports to Oman include mineral oil, mineral fuels and products of their distillation, equipment and machinery, garments and textiles, electronic items and electrical, chemicals, steel products, and iron.

Also included are customary things such as coffee, tea, spices, rice as well as meat products and seafood. The list of Indian imports includes LNG, urea, crude oil, polypropylene, lubricating oil, dates, and chromite ore.[37]

The economic and commercial relations between the countries have strengthened further by the vibrant presence of Indian private sector companies who are engaged in various projects in Oman.[38] According to Indian Ministry of External Affairs, among others, State Bank of India, HDFC Ltd., ICICI Securities, Life Insurance Corporation, New India Assurance Co., Engineering Projects India Limited (EPIL), and National Building Construction Company (NBCC) are present in Oman. An Indian-Omani joint venture—SebacicOman—will be constructing the SebacicDuqm Acid refinery which is worth around US$ 1,200 million. The foundation of this refinery was laid in October 2016.[39]

Oman plays an important role in increasing the agricultural productivity of India by providing fertilizer. Oman is one of the top five sources of fertilizers for India, and accounts for 5.26 per cent of India's fertilizer imports. India imports 8 Metric Tons (MT) of urea, 25 per cent of which is supplied by the Oman India Fertilizer Company (OMIFCO).[40] OMIFCO was established in 2006; since then it has played a key role in shaping bilateral cooperation in this sector. Additionally, in 2015–16, India's imports from Oman saw a steep drop; however, India's fertilizer imports from Oman grew by 39.3 per cent (see Table 6.5 below).

Table 6.5: India's Top Sources of Fertilizer Import (in US$ millions)

Country/Year	2014-2015	2015-2016	Share in total (Per cent)	Growth (Per cent)
China	3154.68	3268.09	46.21	3.59
Saudi Arabia	612.68	686.69	9.71	12.08
Russia	456.7	626.24	8.85	37.12
Iran	230.09	509.14	7.20	121.27
Oman	267.1	372.06	5.26	39.3
Total	6386.61	7072.88	-	10.75

Source: Export-Import Data Bank, Ministry of Commerce and Industry, Government of India

The Indian embassy in Oman has given high priority to discovering and utilizing available investment opportunities, and to boost the interaction with the entrepreneurs in Oman. To attract the Omani and Indian business community, it organised an 'Invest India' seminar on 20 January 2016, and in the following month, hosted a trade and investment promotion event in association with the Oman Chamber of Commerce & Industry (OCCI). The idea behind organizing this event was to highlight investment opportunities in Healthcare, Food Industry, Information Technology, Mining & Minerals, and the Construction & Infrastructure sectors.[41]

The Indian mission also organised a business-to-business meeting in association with the Oman Chamber of Commerce and Industry (OCCI) in September. This meeting was attended by over 180 Omani businessmen leading to Omani companies entering into business ties with a six-member Indian business delegation led by the Federation of Indian Export Organizations (FIEO).[42]

On 29 February, the Indian mission also organised the Indian Technical and Economic Cooperation Programme (ITEC) Day. Under the ITEC programme, India provides scholarships to Omanis, and these fellowships were increased from 50 (in 2011–12) and to 150 (in 2014–15 and 2015–16).[43]

From the Omani side, some important commercial visits were also made in 2015–16. In August 2015, the Chairman of Ithraa led a delegation of 14 Omani companies, including food processing, fertilizers, and the plastic sectors. In September 2016, the Omani Ministry of tourism organised a tourism road show in Hyderabad, Calcutta, Ahmadabad, and Pune.

Energy Relations

India greatly requires energy to speed up its economic growth. It does not have adequate energy resources to serve either its current or its future requirements. The increasing energy demand has enforced India to foster long term energy relations with Oman. However, "India does not get much oil from Oman, but the spot buying of oil is important in India's oil demand."[44] Oman is an interlocutor in the planned Middle East to India Deepwater Pipeline (MEIDP) (Iran-Oman-India pipeline), a big project to export Iranian natural gas to Oman and India via an undersea pipeline. The US$ 4.5 billion project plans to export Iranian natural gas to India (31.5 million cubic meters a day) via an undersea pipeline starting from Chabahar Port in south-eastern Iran, transiting through the Sea of Oman to Ras al-Jafan and the Arabian Sea, ending in Porbandar in South Gujarat, India.[45] Formal talks for the pipeline started in 2014 and, in August 2015, Sreekant Somany, the Chairman of the Confederation of India Industry's northern region, noted that the undersea project with Iran should be accomplished quickly.

According to media reports, the "Iranian Foreign Minister Mohammad Javad Zarif met with his Indian counterpart, Sushma Swaraj, at the Heart of the Asia Conference in Islamabad (December 2015). The two discussed the possibility of expanding their countries' mutual economic cooperation, particularly in regard to Iran exporting natural gas to India."[46]

Table 6.6: Share of Oil in India's Imports from Oman (in US$ million)

Year	Oil Imports from Oman	Total Oil Imports	Omani share in Total Oil Imports	Imports from Oman	Per cent of Oil in Imports from Oman
2011–12	2,083.84	172,753.92	1.21	3,345.94	62.28
2012–13	507.88	181,344.67	0.28	2,009.72	25.27
2013–14	1,514.11	181,382.59	0.83	2,951.18	51.31
2014–15	732.51	156,400.01	0.47	1,752.24	41.80
2015–16	584.67	96,953.06	0.60	1,674.71	34.91

Source: Adapted from Director-General of Foreign Trade, New Delhi, at www.dgft.gov.in

Figure 6.2: Share of Oil in India's Imports from Oman

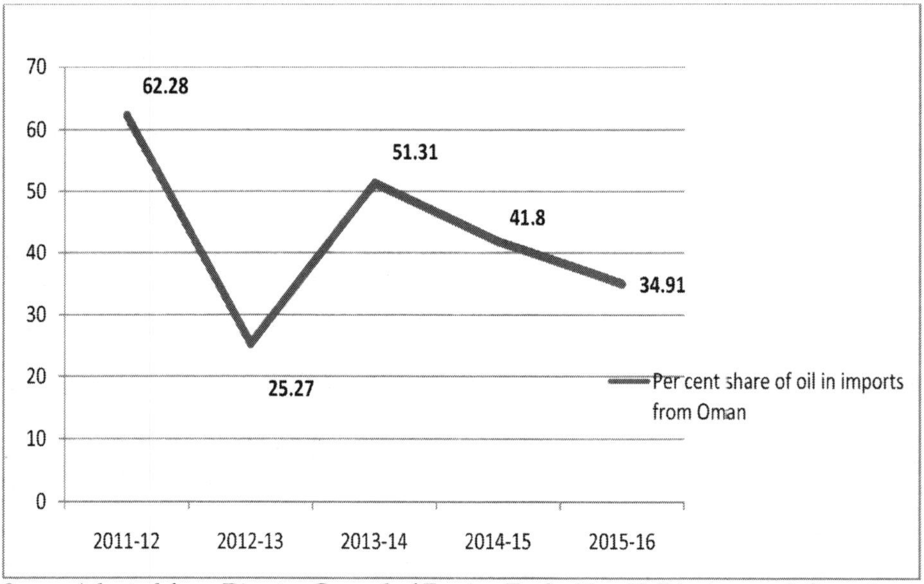

Source: Adapted from Director-General of Foreign Trade, New Delhi, at www.dgft.gov.in

Energy trends in previous years indicate that the total share of oil imports from Oman has witnessed a decline: from 1.21 per cent in 2011–12 it dropped to 0.6 per cent in 2015–16 (see Table 6.6). While there was a spike in oil imports in 2013–14 at US$ 1.5 billion, it dropped to US$ 584.67 million in 2015–16. Consequently, the share of oil imports from Oman has seen a drop from 62.28 per cent in 2011–12 to 34.91 per cent in 2015–16.

Table 6.7: India's Energy Imports from Oman (in US$ million)

	2011–12	2012–13	2013–14	2014–15	2015–16
India's Energy Imports from Oman	2,083.84	507.88	1,514.11	732.51	584.67
India's Total Energy Imports	172,753.92	181,344.67	181,382.59	156,400.01	96,953.06
Total Energy Imports from the Persian Gulf	105,056.26	105,859.15	106,400.75	85,300.30	50,992.26
Share in Total Energy Imports (in per cent)	1.21	0.28	0.83	0.47	0.60
Share in Energy Imports from Persian Gulf (in per cent)	1.98	0.48	1.42	0.86	1.15

Source: Adapted from Director-General of Foreign Trade, New Delhi, at www.dgft.gov.in

Figure 6.3: Share of Oman in Energy Imports from Persian Gulf

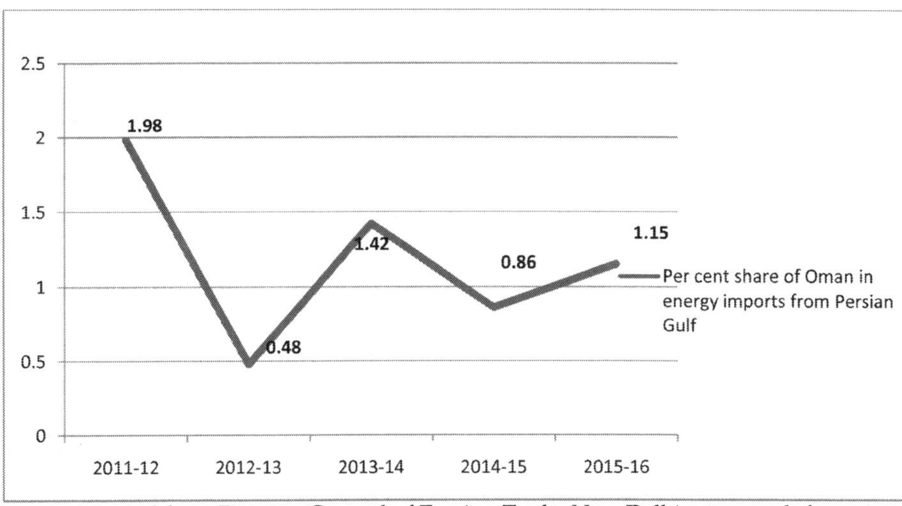

Source: Adapted from Director-General of Foreign Trade, New Delhi, at www.dgft.gov.in

Cultural Relations

The large Indian community in Oman has played a vital role in strengthening bilateral ties. A huge, diverse, and highly valued expatriate community has registered its presence in almost all spheres of Omani life in imparting skills as doctors, engineers, charted accountants, teachers, lecturers, nurses, etc. The contribution of Indians in shaping bilateral relations between the two countries has been acknowledged by the government of India through *Pravasi Bhartiya Samman*. As a part of the efforts to expand these ties, the Indian embassy in Muscat hosts various cultural programmes. It includes exhibitions, the screening of feature films, textile shows, folk and classical performances, musical performances, and theatre festivals. In June 2016, Oman celebrated the second International Yoga Day in which more than

3,000 thousand people from various part of the country performed yoga for the first time.[47] In November, for the first time the Festival of India was organised in collaboration with the Ministry of Culture in Oman. Apart from cultural activities many sports events were also organised to enhance bilateral ties.

Conclusion

India-Oman relations have moved further in the positive direction. No doubt cultural, political, and diplomatic relations have reached new heights; however, there is scope for further improvement. Domestic developments in Oman have opened opportunities for India. In Oman, a steady decline in its oil prices has forced the government to diversify the economy. This diversification process will generate several business opportunities for India, especially in the health care, information technology, agriculture, and mining sectors. Because of Oman's strategic location, it can be used by Indian firms as a manufacturing hub for export to other Gulf countries. If India does not grasp these available opportunities, no doubt other countries will be quick to do so. Recently, Oman and Chinese investors have signed a project to develop a new US$ 10.7 billion industrial city near the port of Duqm. If India is able to reach a similar agreement, the port would allow India to spread out its economic presence in the hydrocarbon rich Persian Gulf, and allow Indian Navy to play a greater role in the region.[48]

Pakistan is also interested in expanding its reach in Oman. Recently, Pakistan and Oman agreed to start a ferry service between Gawadar, Karachi and Muscat (Oman). Once implemented, this would have a great geostrategic impact on India's interests in the region. It would link not only Oman but the entire Gulf region to the China-Pakistan Economic Corridor (CPEC).[49]

NOTES

1. A.K. Pasha (eds.), *India and Oman: History, State, Economy, and Foreign Policy*, Delhi: Gyan Sagar Publications, 1999.
2. Irfan Habib (ed.), *Confronting Colonialism: Resistance and Modernisation under Haider Ali and Tipu Sultan*, Delhi: Tulika, 1999.
3. Marimuthu Ulaganathan, "Oman", in P. R. Kumaraswamy (ed.) *Persian Gulf 2013*, New Delhi: Sage, 2013, pp.143–165.
4. "Special Envoy of the Sultan of Oman meets PM Narendra Modi", 3 June 2014, at http://www.narendramodi.in/special-envoy-of-the-sultan-of-oman-meets-pm-narendra-modi-626.
5. Kallol Bhattacherjee, "Modi to Fast-track his Visit to Oman", *The Hindu*, 21 March 2017, at http://www.thehindu.com/news/national/modi-to-fast-track-his-visit-to-oman/article17547632.ece.

6. "Oman Country Profile" *BBC News*, 28 September 2016, http://www.bbc.com/news/world-middle-east-14654150
7. "Oman—Country Profile", *BBC News*, 17 November 2015, http://www.bbc.com/news/world-middle-east-14654261
8. Hasan Shaban Al Lawati, "3.5-year wait for job for young Omanis", *Times of Oman*, 9 February 2016, at http://timesofoman.com/article/77188/Oman/Government/An-Omani-job-seeker-needs-three-and-a-half-years-to-find-a-job
9. Ibid.
10. Rori Donaghy, "Oman arrests leading writer over government criticism: Rights group", *Middle East Eye*, 19 April 2016, at http://www.middleeasteye.net/news/oman-arrests-leading-intellectual-and-activist-rights-group-964650127.
11. "Amnesty International Report 2015/16: Oman", Amnesty International, 24 February 2016, at http://www.refworld.org/docid/56d05b28c.html
12. "2016 Oman State Budget—austerity measures and focus on non-oil and gas revenues", Price Waterhouse Cooper (PWC), January 2016, at https://www.pwc.com/m1/en/tax/documents/2016/oman-2016-budget-newsalert.pdf
13. "On the Draft budget of State for Fiscal Year 2015", Ministry of Finance, Government of Oman, at https://mof.gov.om/FileUpload/English/NewsAttachment/Ministry%20of%20Finance%20Press%20release.pdf
14. "Ministry of Finance issues statement on budget; proposes cost cutting measures", *Muscat Daily*, 3 January 2016, at http://www.muscatdaily.com/Archive/Oman/Ministry-of-Finance-issues-statement-on-budget-proposes-cost-cutting-measures-4iv5#ixzz4dSwWk1C1
15. Jatin Kumar, "Majlis al-Shura Elections in Oman, 2015", *Contemporary Review of the Middle East*, 2015, Vol. 3, No.4, pp. 455–462.
16. "Report on Majlis A'Shura 8th term", *Oman New Agency*, 3 November 2015, at http://omannews.gov.om/ona_en/description.jsp?newsId=257494.
17. Ibid.
18. Fahad Al Mukrashi, "High turnout for Oman municipal elections", *Gulf News*, 25 December 2016 at http://gulfnews.com/news/gulf/oman/high-turn-out-for-oman-municipal-elections-1.1951491
19. "Women win new seats on Oman municipal councils", *The News International*, 26 December 2016, at https://www.thenews.com.pk/latest/174592-Women-win-new-seats-on-Oman-municipal-councils
20. "Four women win elections, make history", *Times of Oman* 23 December 2012, at http://www.opemam.org/node/412
21. "Special stamp issued to mark 60 years of Oman-India diplomatic ties", *Muscat Daily*, 7 April 2016, at http://www.muscatdaily.com/Archive/Oman/Special-stamp-issued-to-mark-60-years-of-Oman-India-diplomatic-ties-4o5a.
22. "Oman Post Issues Special Postal Stamps to Mark the 60th Anniversary of establishment of Diplomatic Relations with India in 1955", Embassy of India, Muscat, 6 April 2016, http://www.indemb-oman.org/inner.aspx?type=All Speeches&id=0
23. Ibid.
24. "Signing of MoU between India and Oman in the field of tourism", Press Information Bureau, Government of India, 28 January 2015, http://pib.nic.in/newsite/PrintRelease.aspx?relid=115023
25. Ibid.,

26. "Visit of Indian Sail Training Ship to Port of Salalah", Press Release, Embassy of India, Muscat, 13 May 2015, at http://www.indemb-oman.org/inner.aspx?type=AllPressRelease&id=0.
27. "Joint Sail Voyage by Indian Navy Sail Training Ship *Tarangini* and Royal Navy of Oman Sail Training Ship *ShababOman* from Muscat to Kochi", Press Information Bureau, Government of India, 24 November 2015, at http://pib.nic.in/newsite/PrintRelease.aspx?relid=131854
28. "India-Oman Relations", Ministry of External Affairs, Government of India, at https://www.mea.gov.in/Portal/ForeignRelation/Oman.pdf
29. "Defence Secretary of India, H.E. G. Mohan Kumar, accompanied by a three-member delegation visited Oman", Press Release, Embassy of India, Muscat, 10 February 2016, at http://indemb-oman.org/inner.aspx?type=AllPressRelease&id=0.
30. Ibid.
31. "Defence Minister Manohar Parrikar Visits Oman", Press Information Bureau, Government of India, 22 May 2016, at http://pib.nic.in/newsite/PrintRelease.aspx?relid=145533
32. Ibid.
33. Ibid.
34. Ibid.
35. "Indian Embassy Hosts Business Event on 30 March 2016", Press Release, Embassy of India, Muscat, 23 March 2016, at http://www.indemb-oman.org/inner.aspx?type=AllPressRelease&id=0.
36. "India-Oman Relations", Ministry of External Affairs, at https://www.mea.gov.in/Portal/ForeignRelation/Oman.pdf.
37. Ibid.
38. The list of these companies includes, Wipro, Larson & Toubro, Shapoorji Pallonji, Jindal, Aditya Birla Group, Nagarjuna Construction Company, Simplex, and KEC.
39. "India-Oman Relations", Ministry of External Affairs, New Delhi.
40. Faisal Ahmed and Anurag Soni, "Enhancing India-Oman Economic Engagement: Four Promising Initiatives", 28 March 2017, Middle East Institute, at http://www.mei.edu/content/map/enhancing-india-oman-economic-engagement-four-promising-initiatives.
41. "The Embassy of India Muscat will be organizing a trade and investment promotion event", Press Release, Embassy of India, Muscat, 29 February 2016, at http://www.indemb-oman.org/inner.aspx?type=AllPressRelease&id=0
42. "FIEO and PHD CCI lead Indian Business Delegation to Oman", Press Release, Embassy of India, Muscat, 22 September 2016, at http://www.indemb-oman.org/inner.aspx?type=AllPressRelease&id=0
43. "Muscat is organizing the annual 'ITEC Day'", Press Release, Embassy of India, Muscat, 24 February 2016, at http://www.indemb-oman.org/inner.aspx?type=AllPressRelease&id=0
44. Seema Baidya, "Energy Security and India's Foreign Policy: the Persian Gulf Region", in Girijesh Pant (ed.), *India's Emerging Energy Relations: Issues and Challenges*, New York: Springer, 2015, pp. 83–102.
45. Reza Yeganehshakib, "Iran-India energy cooperation opens new horizons", *Al-Monitor*, 14 January 2016, at http://www.al-monitor.com/pulse/originals/2016/01/iran-india-oman-gas-pipeline-meidp-vs-tapi.html

46. Ibid.
47. Ibid.
48. Dipanjan Roy Chaudhury, "India eyes role for itself at Oman's strategic Duqm port", *The Economic Times*, 30 June 2016, at http://economictimes.indiatimes.com/articleshow/52981689.cms?utm_source=contentofinterest&utm_medium=text&utm_campaign=cppst
49. Anish Mishra, "Pakistan's Relations with Oman: An Important Gateway to the Gulf", *Insights*, Institute of South Asian Studies, No. 383, 24 January 2017, at https://www.isas.nus.edu.sg/ISAS%20Reports/ISAS20Insights%20No.%20383%%20-%20Pakistan's%20Relations%20with%20Oman%20-%20An%20Important%20 Gateway%20to%20the%20Gulf.pdf

7

QATAR

Priyanka Mittal

Key Information

Ruling family: al-Thani; **Ruler:** Tamim bin Hamad bin Khalifa al-Thani (since 25 June 2013); **Crown Prince:** Abdullah bin Hamad bin Khalifa al-Thani (since 11 November 2014); **National Day:** 18 December; **Parliament:** 35-member nominated Majlis al-Shura; **Last Parliamentary Election**: NA; **Major group in parliament:** NA; **National Carrier**: Qatar Airways.

Socio-Economic Indicators

Area: 11,586 sq km; **Population:** 2.25 Million; **Natives:** less than 40 per cent; **Expats:** more than 60 per cent; **Religious Groups:** Citizen (Sunni 90–95 per cent; Shia 5–10 per cent); **Residents** (Muslim 77.5 per cent; Hindu 14 per cent; Christian 8.5 per cent); **Youth:** 12.62 per cent; **Population growth rate:** 2.64 per cent; **Life expectancy at birth:** 78.7 years; **Major population groups**: Arab 40 per cent; Indian 18 per cent; Pakistani 18 per cent; Iranian 10 per cent; Other 14 per cent; **Literacy Rate:** 97.3 per cent; **National Currency**: Qatari Riyal (QAR); **GDP:** US$ 156.6 billion; **Foreign Trade:** US$ 98.45 billion; **Defence budget:** NA; **Sovereign Wealth Fund:** US$ 335 billion; **External Debt**: US$ 159.2 billion; **Per capita income:** US$ 129,700; **Oil reserves:** 25 billion bbl; **Gas reserves:** 24.53 trillion m^3; **HDI rank:** 32; **Infant Mortality Rate**: 6.2 deaths/1,000 live birth; **UN Education Index:** 0.686; **Gender Inequality Index:** 0.524; **Labour Force:** 1.691 million; **Unemployment rate**: 0.7 per cent; **Urban Population:** 99.2 per cent; **Rate of Urbanization:** 6.02 per cent; **Last National Census**: 2010.

India Related

Indian Cultural Centre: Doha (Inaugurated in 2000); **Number of Indians:** 600,000 (approximately); **Number of places of worship for Indians**: Catholic Church (opened in 2008); **Indian Schools:** 8; **Indian Banks:** State Bank of India (1); ICICI Bank (1); HDFC Bank; Indian Overseas Bank; **Currency exchange rate:** 1 QAR = INR 18.30 (Feb 2017); **Last visit to India by the ruler**: Emir Tamim bin Hamad al-Thani, March 2015; **Last Indian Prime Minister to visit**: Narendra Modi, June 2016.

* * *

Since taking over as Head of State in June 2013, Emir Tamim bin Hamad al-Thani has focused on giving a new momentum to Indo-Qatari relations. Bilateral ties are based on historical linkages, traditional friendship, mutually benefitting commercial ties, and people-to-people contact. India sees Qatari gas reserves and sovereign wealth funds as potential areas for trade and investment. In 2015, Emir Tamim said that his government "trusts" the Indian economy, thus underlining the potential for investment.[1] The Indian population in Qatar currently stands at around 600,000[2]—about 23 per cent of the total resident population—and hence labour migrants and trade form an integral part of the bilateral relations. Moreover, Doha is emerging as an overseas cultural destination for the Indian entertainment industry, and film awards and entertainment shows form a significant part of Qatari media and offer avenues for Indian investments.

Domestic Developments

Qatar is an absolute monarchy, with the Emir as the head of state and government. Sharia is the main source of legislation. A constitutional referendum held in April 2003 envisaged Qatar as a constitutional monarchy; but progress has been slow because of the reluctance of the ruling family. It is evident from the fact that, in July 2016, the monarchy postponed elections for the Advisory Council until at least 2019.[3] The lack of political reforms has led to citizens losing confidence in the existing institutions; this was evident from the low rate of registration for the 2015 municipal council elections.[4] In Qatar, no laws can be enacted without them being discussed by the Advisory Council.

Like other GCC countries, Qatar has, in the past, attracted criticism over its labour laws that favour local employers, particularly the *kafala* or sponsorship system that requires foreign workers to obtain their employer's consent to travel abroad or switch jobs. Partly to assuage this criticism, Qatar introduced a new labour law in December 2016 which aims to bring "tangible benefits" to expatriate workers who can change or resign from their jobs easily.[5] The reforms seeks to create state-run "grievance committees" to which foreign workers can appeal if employers deny them permission.[6] However, areas like press freedom, women's rights, and civil rights are yet to achieve desirable reforms.

Qatar has been balancing its foreign policy moves to align with its domestic requirements. With the change in leadership in the US, Qatar has signalled its support to President Donald Trump and his Middle East policies without side-lining its own interests with Russia. Qatar realises Russia's cardinal support to Syria, and sees Moscow's presence in the region as a counter to US influence in the Middle East and Israel. Qatar also understands the pragmatism in being involved with Russia which is a permanent member of United Nations Security Council, and so it is massively investing in Russia's economy. It bought 19.5 per cent stake in the Russian Rosneft Oil Company and, through this deal, it gets indirect access to Egypt's Zohr gas fields. Russia and Qatar remain tied together as world's leading energy producers and exporters, and as leading members of the Gas Exporting Countries Forum (GECF).[7]

Despite the reluctance of other countries of the Gulf Cooperation Council (GCC), Qatar has been pushing for monetary union along the lines of the European Union. It has been committed to developing GCC-EU efforts to expand region-to-region cooperation in the energy security realm.[8] As regards Europe, Qatar intends to develop a three-level multifaceted bilateral approach: first with the European Union collectively; secondly with individual states of Europe; and lastly with the non-EU European states. Qatar's interaction with Europe is based on its traditional areas of cooperation in trade and energy relations, technology transfer, sustainable diversification, human capital development, and investments.[9] It has major arms deals with the United Kingdom and France; these balance its security and strategic dependence solely on and against the US. It signed a major security cooperation agreement with the UK in 2014 and in May 2015, and it also decided to buy 24 Rafale fighter jets from the French manufacturer Dassault Aviation for US$ 7.1 billion as well as to employ the French Air Force to train dozens of its pilots and maintenance mechanics.[10] These mark an important step in Qatar's decision to diversify its security and go beyond the US protectionism.[11]

The Sino-Qatari interdependence is also growing, especially in the energy, infrastructure, and investment realms. China is now Qatar's fifth largest natural gas customer, accounting for 6.4 per cent of its natural gas and LNG exports.[12] Qatar's gas prices are quite competitive for Asia as against in Europe or in Japan. With Australian gas pipelines emerging by 2018, surpassing Qatar's capacity—that is, 85 mtpa as against Qatar's 77 mtpa—there could be a challenge to Qatar's pricing of gas in the world market.[13] Therefore, realizing the trends in the world energy market, Qatar plans to capture Asian markets with competitive pricing. Qatar aligning its foreign policy interests along with other GCC nations would not change anything much in regional politics.

However, despite being a small nation, Qatar remains the game-changer. How it would pursue its regional ambitions with the support of many regional powers emerging in the Persian Gulf needs to be watched. It has utilised its oil and gas income to develop its economy, and capitalized on various avenues to create soft power to invest in international diplomacy. It has projected itself as a regional mediator to broker peace—as in the Palestinian conflict, Afghanistan, Libya, Yemen, Sudan, etc.—but has largely failed to establish itself as a neutral mediator.[14] Qatari support for the Islamists in various countries has put it at odds with its neighbours, and has undermined its regional standing. However, since taking over as the ruler, Emir Tamim has steered Qatari foreign policy towards pragmatism by improving relations with countries such as Saudi Arabia and the UAE. Doha supports the rebels fighting against Bashar al-Assad in Syria,[15] and has welcomed US President Donald Trump's suggestions for safe zones in Syria. It works alongside Saudi Arabia, Turkey, and the US and offers arms and military training to moderate rebel forces that are overseen by the Central Intelligence Agency.[16]

Economic diversification and resource utilization have made Qatar one of the richest countries in the world in terms of per capita income, of US$ 105,000. It has also been scoring high on the UNDP's Human Development Index with a score of 0.856, and is ranked at 33.[17] The country is one of the dominant oil suppliers, and has the third highest natural gas reserves, after Russia and Iran. Petro-dollars largely funds its heavily subsided welfare state structure. The Arab Spring made a moderate impact in Qatar, and the strong assertive nature of its foreign policy took a back seat in 2015–16 due to domestic challenges arising out of low oil and gas prices as well as low public spending.

Under the new Emir, Qatar plans to diversify its economy and resource utilisation which would benefit the country in times of low oil prices. The diversification of the economy into tourism, education, infrastructure development, airways, and industrial creation has broadened its resource and income generation base. Qatar is moving out of its shell as a regional power, and is building relations with peripheral neighbours like Turkey as well as Israel.[18] Its pragmatic foreign policy is driving its interest towards building relations with Israel based on security ties.[19] Qatar has approved Ankara's establishment of its first military base in the Gulf and the Middle East, in which 3,000 soldiers would be stationed.[20] With low political risk and with a pan-Arab political move, Qatar aims to develop newer relations with neighbours as well as distant countries without hampering old ties. The Gulf monarchies are now introducing young generations into their administrations in order to counter the challenges of employment, human rights, and the generation gap. Qatar's new Emir is 36 years old, and this is pertinent to assess how he conducts his foreign policy in the region as well as with great powers.

Bilateral Relations

Formal relations between India and Qatar were established in 1973, and ever since then, both countries have maintained good ties revolving around trade, investment, and defence cooperation. Diversification is now the key to bilateral cooperation in various sectors of investment: education, labour, and energy. Indian nationals comprise the largest expatriate community in the emirate, and are engaged in a wide spectrum of professional activities, including medicine, engineering, education, finance, banking, business, media, and labour. This labour force is highly regarded for their hard work, qualifications, and their contribution to the development and progress of Qatar. The Joint Working Group on Labour and Manpower Development held its third meeting in Doha in August 2015.[21]

Political Relations

The Emir of Qatar, Hamd bin Khalifa al-Thani, made state visits to India in April 1999, May 2005, and April 2012. When the results of the Lok Sabha elections were announced on 16 May 2014, Sheikh Abdullah bin Nasser al-Thani, the Prime Minister and Minister of Interior of Qatar, made a congratulatory phone call to Prime Minister-elect Narendra Modi; the latter thanked the Qatari leadership, and tweeted: "We will take India-Qatar ties to newer heights."[22] Emir Tamim Bin Hamad al-Thani visited India in March 2015, imparting fresh impetus to bilateral ties.[23] The visit was significant as this was his first visit to India; it was also the first visit of a Head of State of an Arab country after Narendra Modi became prime minister.[24]

Both sides enthusiastically discussed ways and means of enhancing a forward looking partnership by expanding and deepening the areas of engagement in energy, power, petrochemicals, investment, infrastructure, development, project exports, education, culture, health, human resource, media, and information technology. During the Emir's visit, six MoUs entailing co-operation in several fields were signed, including an important agreement on prisoner repatriation. According to the agreement, citizens of India or Qatar who are convicted and sentenced for a crime can be extradited to their native country to spend the remaining years of their prison sentence.[25]

Both sides also signed six agreements or Memorandum of Understandings regarding mutual cooperation between India's Foreign Service Institute, and the Qatar's Diplomatic Institute; cooperation in information and communication technology; and exchange of news and mutual cooperation between the Qatar News Agency and the United New Agency. Prime Minister Modi paid a return visit to Qatar on 4–5 June 2016 during which both sides signed seven agreements, and Modi interacted with the Indian community in Doha. The focus of the visit was primarily on improving relations in the hydrocarbon sector as well as labour issues.

Prime Minister Modi had a fruitful interaction with top Qatari investors and businessmen. He, along with the Qatari Minister of Economy and Commerce of Qatar, Sheikh Ahmed bin Jassim al-Thani (the Vice Chairman of Qatar's Sovereign Wealth Fund and the Qatar Investment Authority [QIA]), co-chaired the meeting. During the ceremonial lunch organised by the Emir, the two leaders exchanged views on bilateral, regional, and multilateral issues of common interest, and agreed to constitute an inter-ministerial High Level Joint Committee to regularly review all bilateral matters, including regional and global issues of mutual interest. As a special gesture, the Emir pardoned and released 23 Indian prisoners on the first day of the holy month of Ramadan on 6 June.[26]

In a follow-up visit, India's MoS for External Affairs, V. K. Singh, visited Qatar on 5 September and met his Qatari counterpart to discuss issues of mutual interest. In December, the Qatari Prime Minister, Abdullah Bin Nasser al-Thani, came to India. Accompanied by a large business delegation, he discussed issues such as bilateral investments and regional developments. Further, the two sides announced the establishment of a Qatar-India Business Council. High level discussion on progress in areas such as energy, infrastructure, investment, trade, and security took place during the visit. Discussions on developing a framework provided by the Agreement on Defence Cooperation in the fields of specialized training, exchange of information, and the joint production of defence equipment were also held. They also exchanged mutual concerns regarding the political and security situation in the Middle East and South Asia, and discussed formats to work closely in combating terrorism, radicalization, and sectarianism.[27]

Economic Relations

Trade and commerce form a distinguishable part of the relations between Qatar and India. Earlier, in 2008, Qatar agreed to invest US$ 5 billion in India's energy sector. A deep-sea gas pipeline to India through Oman was also proposed. India is the third largest export destination for Qatar (after Japan and South Korea), and is its tenth largest imports source. Since 2014, India has made serious reforms in the investment and trade sector to ease foreign investment. During his visit to Qatar, Prime Minister Modi urged business leaders to invest in India, taking advantage of reformed business rules and procedures, and the removal of economic bottlenecks. A MoU for investment in India's National Investment and Infrastructure Fund (NIIF) was signed with the Qatar Investment Authority in 2016.[28]

Qatari participation in Indian business and investment events has been exemplary. Since 2014, Qatar has been actively participating in various events, including the Vibrant Gujarat Summit in Gandhinagar (11–13 January 2015); the Partnership Summit 2015 in Jaipur (15–17 January 2015); Black Rock India Investor Summit in New Delhi (3 February 2015)—in which the former Qatari Prime Minister, Sheikh Hamad bin Jassim bin Jaber Al Thani, was among the attendees—and Aero India in Bengaluru (18–22 February 2015).[29]

A 20-member NASSCOM delegation visited Doha on 18–19 March 2015.[30] A multi-sectoral delegation from the Confederation of Indian Industry (CII) led by its President-designate visited Doha on 20–21 October 2015.[31] The largest ever number (65) Indian companies participated in the Project Qatar Exhibition in May 2015.[32] There was high-level participation from Qatar at the Indian Investment Summit in New Delhi on 4–5 February 2016.[33] More than 50 Indian companies, under the banner of ASSOCHAM, participated in Project Qatar 2016 organised from 9–12 May 2016 at the Doha Exhibition & Convention Centre (DECC), in which a total of over 1,800 companies participated, with nearly 1,100 exhibitors.[34] The Qatar Chambers of Commerce and Industry and the Embassy of India organised an event to promote the participation of Qatari businessmen and investors at the 'Make in India' Week in Mumbai from 13–18 February 2016.[35]

A nine-member delegation from Gujarat (led by Rajiv Kumar Gupta, Principal Secretary, Government of Gujarat), visited Doha on 10–11 October 2016 to promote the 7th Vibrant Gujarat Global Summit held in Gandhinagar in January 2017.[36] This delegation participated in the networking event organised by IBPN, held a round table meeting with the members of Qatar Chamber of Commerce and Industry (QCCI), met the CEO and executives of the Qatar Development Bank (QDB), the senior representatives of the

Qatar Investment Authority (QIA), as well as "Muntajat", the Qatari PSU that markets petrochemical products.[37]

Qatar's FDI in India is modest; but its Sovereign Wealth Fund held by the Qatar Investment Authority (QIA) and other State-owned entities as well as the wealth held by private investors in the country are attractive investment propositions for India's growing market.[38] Qatar has several large-scale investments in India, including a more than US$ 1 billion stake in the telecommunications company Bharti Airtel.[39] Qatar Airways has expressed interest in expanding its routes to India, and in buying a stake in the Indian budget airline IndiGo.[40] Qatar Airways (QA) now has total of 102 weekly passenger flights across 13 key cities in India.

The Indian government wants Qatar to invest in the 'Make in India' initiative. Indian Business & Professional Network (IBPN), functioning under the aegis of the Indian Embassy, promotes trade and investment on both sides. The recent setting up of an India-Qatar Business Forum, comprising senior representatives of a number of Indian companies and Qatari businessmen nominated by Qatar Chamber of Commerce and Industry, is another positive development.[41]

India's corporate sector—particularly construction/infrastructure and IT sectors—has many operations in Qatar. These include Larsen & Toubro, Punj Lloyd, Shapoorji Pallonji, Voltas, TCS, Wipro, Mahindra Tech, HCL, etc. SBI, ICICI, and other Indian banks have limited operations under the Qatar Financial Centre or private exchange houses.[42] Indian investors are looking for constructing luxury housing, apartments, and hospitals.[43] Larsen & Toubro (L&T) has extended its infrastructural operations by constructing the Gold Line Metro and the Wakra Bypass highway.[44] On 7 June 2016, the Supreme Committee for Delivery & Legacy (SCDL) announced that a Qatari company, Al Balagh Trading & Contracting and L&T had been appointed as the main contractors to build the 40,000 seat capacity Al Rayyan Stadium for football in time for the World Cup matches scheduled for 2022.[45]

On 29 August 2016, the Qatar National Bank (QNB) (Qatar's largest bank) received RBI approval for retail operations and to open a branch providing comprehensive banking services. QNB (India) had hitherto provided investment and finance consultancy and advisory services only for Middle East companies establishing businesses and investing in India.[46]

India's precarious import-export situation stays lop-sided in Qatar's favour, but India is trying to solve the problem. Therefore, India's exports to Qatar have stabilized around US$ 900–1,000 million. Major items of Indian export are machinery and equipment, transport equipment, articles of iron or steel, plastic, construction material, electrical and electronic items, textiles and garments, chemicals, precious stones, rubber, spices, mineral fuel, and cereals.

There has been a substantial growth in India's exports, amounting to nearly US$ 1 billion out of two-way trade of nearly US$ 17 billion in 2013–14, registering an export growth of 45 per cent over the export figure (US$ 687 million) in 2012–13. In 2014–15, India's exports exceeded US$ 1 billion (about US$ 1,055 million). However, bilateral trade came down due to the decline in Qatar's exports to India from US$ 15.66 billion in 2014–15 to US$ 9.9 billion in 2015–16. As indicated in Table 7.1, the trade figures show a sharp drop over the last two years, attributed mainly to lower oil prices and slowdown in international trade.

Table 7.1: India-Qatar Bilateral Trade (in US$ million)

	2011–12	2012–13	2013–14	2014–15	2015–16
Exports	807.95	687.18	969.06	1,054.98	902.04
Imports	12,916.35	15,693.08	15,707.99	14,604.71	9,022.16
Total Trade	13,724.30	16,380.26	16,677.04	15,659.69	9,924.20
Share	1.73	2.07	2.18	2.06	1.54

Source: Adapted from Director-General of Foreign Trade, New Delhi, at www.dgft.gov.in

Figure 7.1: India-Qatar Bilateral Trade

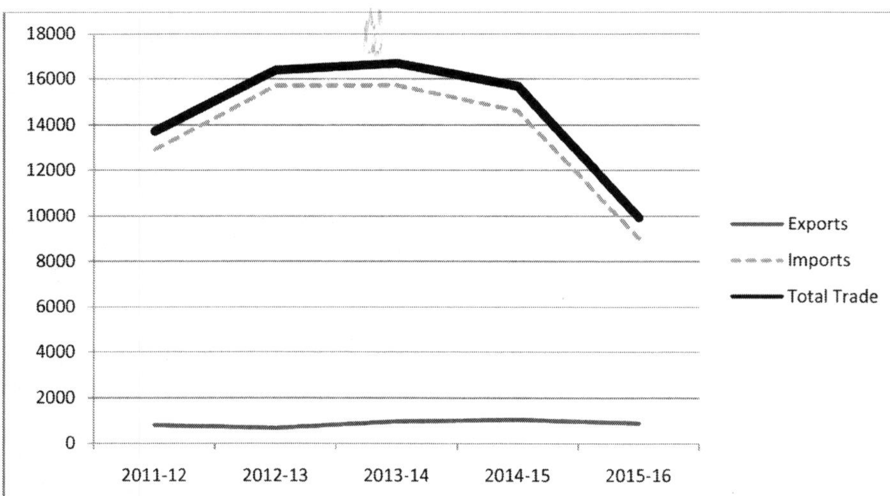

Source: Adapted from Director-General of Foreign Trade, New Delhi, at www.dgft.gov.in

Qatari imports from India amounted to US$ 1.2 billion or 3.8 per cent of its overall imports in 2014. At a value of US$ 215.3 million, cereals were India's top exported commodity. Machinery came second, at US$ 108.6

million. The export value for electronic equipment was US$ 93.2 million, making it the third most significant export to Qatar.[47]

Qatari exports to India totalled US$ 16.8 billion or 12.7 per cent of its overall exports in 2014. The highest valued export commodity is oil, of which US$ 14.9 billion worth has been exported to India. Vying for second place is plastics, which recorded a worth of US$ 700.8 million. The third highest valued Qatari export to India is organic chemicals, accounting for a total of US$ 554 million.

Table 7.2: Share of Oil in India's Imports from Qatar (in US$ million)

Year	Oil Imports from Qatar	Total Oil Imports	Qatar's Share in Total Oil Imports	Imports from Qatar	Per cent of Oil in Imports from Qatar
2011–12	11,697.83	172,753.92	6.77	12,916.35	90.57
2012–13	14,578.34	181,344.67	8.04	16,380.26	89.00
2013–14	14,590.81	181,382.59	8.04	15,707.99	92.89
2014–15	13,415.31	156,400.01	8.58	14,604.71	91.86
2015–16	7,942.43	96,953.06	8.19	9,022.16	88.03

Source: Adapted from Director-General of Foreign Trade, New Delhi, at www.dgft.gov.in

Figure 7.2: Share of Oil in India's Imports from Qatar

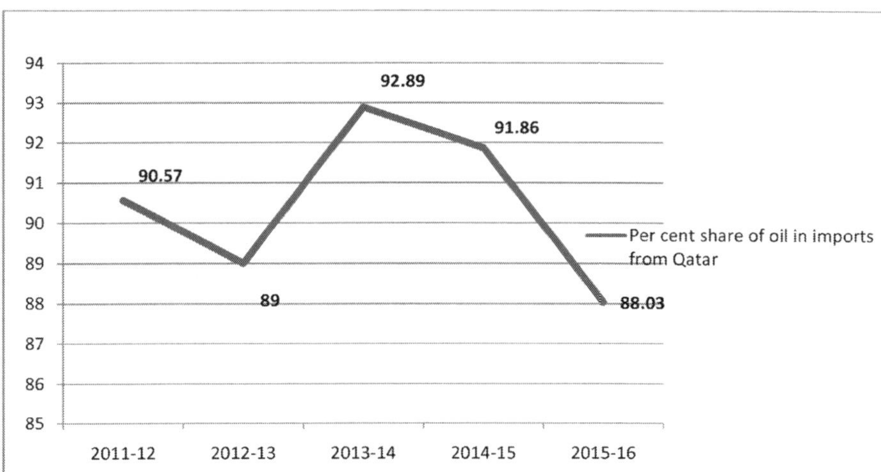

Source: Adapted from Director-General of Foreign Trade, New Delhi, at www.dgft.gov.in

Despite the competitive pricing of oil from Qatar, the share of Qatar imports declined, both in terms of monetary value and volume. As is clear in Table 7.2, Qatar's oil export to India reduced to almost half; so did the total oil imports, which include oil and oil-based products. It is significant that Qatar's export of oil to India is on the decline since 2011–12.

Qatar is the largest supplier of LNG to India, accounting for over 65 per cent of its global imports and 15 per cent of Qatar's export of LNG. Petronet of India and RasGas of Qatar signed a Sale Purchase Agreement (SPA) for the additional annual supply of one million metric tons of LNG by RasGas in New Delhi on 31 December 2015; this is in addition to the existing long term contract for supply of 7.5 million metric tonnes of LNG per annum.[48] The share of oil imports has been declining since the last five years. India also imports ethylene, propylene, ammonia, urea, and polyethylene from Qatar. Hence, the balance of trade always remains in Qatar's favour.

Table 7.3: India's Energy Imports from Qatar (in US$ million)

	2011–12	2012–13	2013–14	2014–15	2015–16
India's Energy Imports from Qatar	11,697.83	14,578.34	14,590.81	13,415.31	7,942.43
India's Total Energy Imports	172,753.97	181,344.67	181,382.59	156,400.01	96,953.06
Total Energy Imports from the Persian Gulf	103,915.24	105,809.19	106,400.75	85,300.30	50,992.26
Share in Total Energy Imports (in per cent)	6.77	8.04	8.04	8.58	8.19
Share in Energy Imports from Persian Gulf (in per cent)	11.26	13.78	13.71	15.73	15.58

Source: Adapted from Director-General of Foreign Trade, New Delhi, at www.dgft.gov.in

Figure 7.3: Share of Qatar in Energy Imports from Persian Gulf

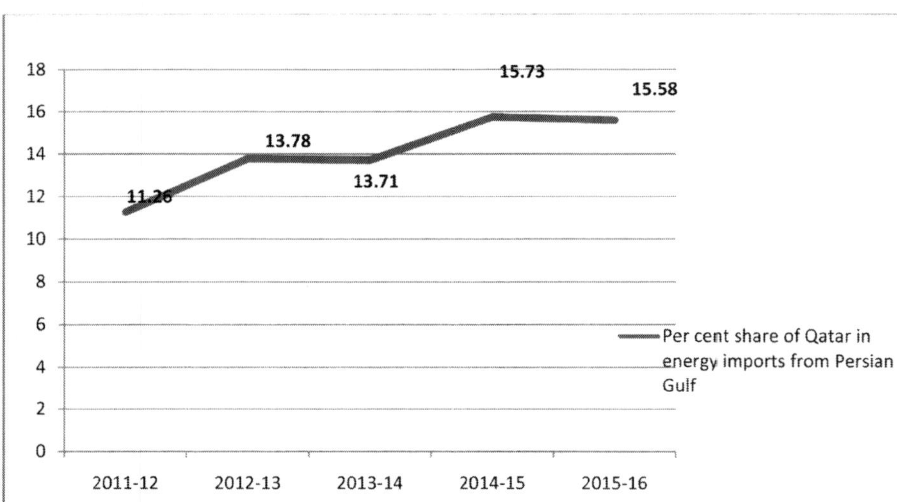

Source: Adapted from Director-General of Foreign Trade, New Delhi, at www.dgft.gov.in

In January 2016, Qatar agreed to decrease the selling price of gas to India from US$ 12 to13 per unit to US$ 6 to 7 per unit. This deal came as a result of the global reduction in gas prices and the surplus in gas supply worldwide. In addition to reducing the price, Qatar also agreed to exempt India of the US$ 1.8 billion fee that India owed due to its noncompliance in importing gas shipments which was previously agreed upon in 2015.[49] Prime Minister Modi's active energy diplomacy in the region has benefitted India in gaining reduced comparative gas pricing from the region.

Indian imports from Qatar in terms of monetary value have declined in the last one or two years due to a decrease in international oil and gas prices. Bilateral trade touched a high of US$ 16.68 billion in 2013–14 and dropped to US$ 9.93 billion in last fiscal 2015–16. To study the cumulative record of India-Qatar's energy trade, it is important to understand that declining oil prices in the world market were the deciding factor for the trade imbalance in the Persian Gulf. Notably, Qatar's share in India's energy imports from the Persian Gulf has increased—from 11 per cent in 2011–12 to 15 per cent in 2015–16.

Cultural Relations

Cultural ties between the two countries are deep rooted, and both had signed an Agreement on Cultural Cooperation in 2012. The Qatari side has proposed to celebrate the India-Qatar Year of Culture in 2019. The Indian Cultural Centre (ICC), the apex body of associations of the Indian community functioning under the aegis of the Indian Embassy, is generally responsible for organising events. Indian artists have been performing regularly at events managed by community organisations affiliated to the ICC and private sponsors.[50] The ICC has been organizing a large-scale Community Festival on *A Passage to India* in November 2013, March 2015, and April 2016, which presents India's rich cultural diversity and achievements in different spheres. In the education sector, Indians benefit from affiliated-foreign universities operating in the Emirate. There are about 14 Indian schools which offer the CBSE curriculum to over 30,000 students, and most of whom are children of Indian nationals working in the country.

Since Qatar has been actively attracting global games and sports events, Indian tourism has been successful in organising several events and tournaments in sports, such as athletics, boxing, volleyball, and wrestling. Hassan al-Thawadi, Secretary General of Qatar's Supreme Committee of Delivery and Legacy for FIFA 2022, along with other senior officials, participated in the Asian Football Confederation function in Gurgaon on 29 November 2015.

The *Fath Al Khair* (meaning 'the Victory of the Good') Dhow undertook a voyage from Doha to Mumbai via Oman, between 5 October and 17 November, 2015. It was received in a welcome ceremony presided over by Governor of Maharashtra, Chennamaneni Vidyasagar Rao. This event was launched by Emir Hamad al-Thani in 2013, and marks the commemoration of the historical pearl trade route that existed between the two countries in the past.

Yoga is the new area of cooperation, and Qatar came out with strong support of India's initiative of the International Yoga Day, and India deeply appreciated this gesture. Qatar was among the record number of 177 co-sponsors for the UN General Assembly Resolution 69/131 (unanimously adopted on 11 December 2014) declaring 21 June as the International Day of Yoga (IDY), and for various activities to celebrate the first IDY in Qatar. Qatar Post also released a commemorative stamp to mark the first IDY day in 2015. A public event was organised to celebrate 2nd International Day of Yoga at the Al Gharafa Sports Club in 2016.

Healthy bilateral relations are based on the large and diverse Indian community comprising a wide spectrum of professionals in medicine, engineering, education, finance, banking, business, and media. Volunteers from the Indian community are helping Indian workers mainly through the Indian Community Benevolent Forum (ICBF), functioning under the aegis of the Indian Embassy. An official delegation led by Qatar Ambassador in New Delhi attended the 5th Pravasiya Bhartiya Divas Panel Discussion, 'Managing Migration to ECR Countries', on 28 June 2016 in New Delhi. There is a Joint Working Group on Labour and Manpower Development between the two countries, and its fourth meeting was held in New Delhi on 24–25 November 2016.

Defence Relations

It was under the United Progressive Alliance (UPA) government headed by Prime Minister Manmohan Singh that defence relations between India and Qatar took a leap. The India-Qatar Defence Cooperation Agreement was signed during Prime Minister Singh's visit to Qatar in November 2008, and was extended until 2018. It is implemented through the Joint Defence Cooperation Committee (JDCC), which had its fourth meeting in New Delhi on 6–7 January 2015. Both sides inked a maritime defence agreement which would focus upon mutual maritime defence training, and facilitate mutual visits. The visit also resulted in an agreement pertaining to law enforcement and national security which focused on exchanging classified information to assist in suppressing threats posed by extremist elements. Continuing the cooperation on JDCC, meets were hosted in Doha in 2008; in New Delhi in 2011; Doha in 2013; and in New Delhi in January 2015.[51]

As a follow up of the 4th JDCC, two high-level delegations visited India from Ministry of Transportation, and the Qatar Emiri Air Forces at the AERO INDIA EXPO 2015, held at Bengaluru during 19–23 February 2015.[52] A three-member delegation from Joaan Bin Jassim Joint Command and Staff College visited India during 13–18 April 2015. This team, led by its Commandant, visited the National Defence College (NDC), Institute for Defence Studies and Analyses (IDSA), National Maritime Foundation (NMF), and Defence Services Staff College (DSSC, Wellington).[53] A Brigadier rank officer of the Qatar Armed Forces joined the 56th NDC course in January 2016.[54] The fourth edition of Exercise Ferocious Falcon 2015, a biennial multi-national crisis management exercise organised by the Qatar Armed Forces, was held during 10–26 May 2015.[55] A two-member delegation from HQIDS participated as observers during the Field Training Exercise (FTX) phase from 18–21 May 2015. Indian Naval ships *INS Delhi* and *INS Trishul* as part of Western Fleet's Overseas Deployment Programme (OSD) to the Gulf, paid a goodwill visit to the port of Doha from 14–17 September 2015.[56]

The Indian Coast Guard Ship *ICGS Sankalp* visited Doha Port from 24–28 January 2016 to mark India's 67th Republic Day celebrations. For the first time, the 34-member ceremonial band of the Qatar Armed Forces played the National Anthems of the two countries at the reception hosted by the Indian embassy to celebrate Republic Day in 2016.[57]

A delegation from Qatar Emiri Naval Forces (QENF) attended the International Fleet Review 2016 (IFR 2016) at Visakhapatnam from 4–8 February 2016. A high level delegation from the Qatar Emiri Land Forces participated at the Ninth International Land, Naval, Internal Homeland Security and Defence System Exposition (DEFEXPO INDIA-2016), held in Goa from 28–31 March 2016.[58] A high level delegation from India participated in the Doha International Maritime Defence Exhibition and Conference (DIMDEX 2016) held in Doha from 29–31 March 2016. The delegation was led by Vice Admiral Sunil Lanba, Flag Officer Commanding in Chief, Western Naval Command of the Indian Navy (later the Chief of the Naval Staff), and included two senior officers of the Indian Coast Guard. The Indian Naval Ship *INS Beas* visited Doha port from 28 March to 1 April 2016 to participate in DIMDEX 2016.[59] A three member delegation of the Qatar Emiri Naval Forces (QENF), led by Brigadier Tariq Khaled Al Obaidly, Director of Education and Courses, visited the Southern Naval Command, Kochi; Indian Naval Academy (INA), Ezhimala; and INS Hamla, Mumbai, from 18–22 April 2016.[60]

Conclusion

Indians consist a large segment of the migrant population in Qatar. The labour reforms undertaken by Qatar government might improve the conditions of Indian workers. India-Qatar relations are gaining momentum, especially when India's Gulf policy is acquiring a new vibrancy. Indian private sector investors are looking forward to attractive investment options in the infrastructure sector in Qatar—like the upcoming Al Houl Special Economic Zone. Similar momentum has been exhibited by Qatar's private investors who are looking to invest in infrastructure and other sectors in India. As India is revisiting its foreign policy with the Gulf countries under Prime Minister Modi, Qatar emerges as a major partner because of energy and investments.

NOTES

1. Indrani Bagchi, "Qatar has Big Investment Plans for India", *The Times of India*, 25 March 2015, at http://timesofindia.indiatimes.com/india/Qatar-has-big-investment-plans-for-India/articleshow/46682401.cms
2. "Population (Estimate/Assumed) of Overseas Indians: Country Wise", Ministry of External Affairs, Government of India, January 2015, at http://www.mea.gov.in/images/pdf/3-population-overseas-indian.pdf.
3. Shabina K. Khatri , "Legislative Elections in Qatar Postponed Until At Least 2019", *Doha News*, 17 June 2016, at https://dohanews.co/legislative-elections-in-qatar-postponed-until-at-least-2019/.
4. "Qatar: Freedom in the World 2016", Freedom House, at https://freedomhouse.org/report/freedom-world/2016/qatar.
5. "Qatar Introduces Changes to Labour Law", *Al-Jazeera*, 14 December 2016, at http://www.aljazeera.com/news/2016/12/qatar-introduces-labour-law-161213073333258.html.
6. Ibid.
7. Aurangzeb Qureshi, "The Qatar-Russia energy deal that might lead the way to peace in Syria", *Middle East Eye*, 21 December 2016, at http://www.middleeasteye.net/columns/can-qatar-russia-energy-ties-translate-peace-syria-1234735369
8. Rory Miller, and Khalid Al-Mansouri, "Qatar's Foreign Policy Engagement with the European Union: Evolving Priorities of a Small State in the Contemporary Era", *Camillas Journal of International Relations*, 2016, Vol. 5, pp. 46–64.
9. Federica Mastroforti, "Qatar's priorities and interests in the EU countries", *Mediterranean Affairs*, 21 September, 2016, at http://mediterraneanaffairs.com/qatar-s-priorities-and-interests-in-the-eu-countries/
10. Peter Kovessy, "UK Official push for multibillion dollar weapons deals with Qatar", 30 March 2016, at https://dohanews.co/uk-officials-push-for-multibillion-dollar-weapons-deals-with-qatar/
11. Rory Miller, and Khalid Al-Mansouri, "Qatar's Foreign Policy Engagement with the European Union", op. cit..
12. Chaoling Feng, *Embracing Interdependence: The Dynamics of China and the Middle East*, Brooking Institutions, 2015.

13. Tim Daiss, "LNG shake-up ahead as China pushes to renegotiate Pricing on Qatar Gas", Forbes.com, 11 March 2016, at https://www.forbes.com/sites/timdaiss/2016/03/11/china-national-petroleum-corp-wants-to-renegotiate-price-of-qatari-gas/#4ddc2b5760f8
14. Ruslan Minich, "Conflict Mediation: Qatar Experience", *Historia Polityka*, 2015, Vol. 14 (21), pp. 121–133.
15. Peter Kovessy, "Qatar Raises Stake in Syrian Conflict with Talk of Military Intervention", *Doha News*, 22 October 2015, at https://dohanews.co/qatar-raises-stake-in-syrian-conflict-with-talk-of-military-intervention/
16. "Qatar Welcomes Trump's Call for Syria Safe Zones", *Reuters*, 26 January 2017, at http://www.reuters.com/article/us-mideast-crisis-trump-qatar-idUSKBN15A1JB?il=0.
17. "Human Development Report 2016: Qatar", United Nations Development Program [UNDP], http://hdr.undp.org/sites/all/themes/hdr_theme/country-notes/QAT.pdf.
18. Samuel Ramani, "Israel is Strengthening its Ties with the Gulf Monarchies", *The Huffington Post*, 12 September 2016 at http://www.huffingtonpost.com/samuel-ramani/why-israel-is-strengthening_b_11946660.html.
19. "Qatar and Israel: A Strategic but Complicated Alliance", *Chronicle of Middle East and North Africa*, 27 April 2013, at https://chronicle.fanack.com/qatar/history-past-to-present/qatar-and-israel-a-strategic-but-complicated-alliance/
20. "Qatar and the Arab Spring: Transforming Regional Relations, Deepening Concerns", OrtadoðuStratejikAraþtýrmalarMerkezi (The Center for Middle Eastern Strategic Studies, ORSAM), 12 July 2016, at http://www.orsam.org.tr/index.php/Content/Analiz/4731?s=orsam%7Cenglish.
21. "3rd Meeting of India-Qatar Joint Working Group on Labour and Manpower Development", Press Information Bureau, Government of India, Ministry of Overseas Indian Affairs, 18 August 2015, at http://pib.nic.in/newsite/PrintRelease.aspx?relid=126141.
22. "India-Qatar bilateral Relations", Embassy of India, Doha, 12 June 2016, at http://indianembassyqatar.gov.in/pages/bilateralrelations.php
23. "Joint Statement During the State Visit Of the Emir Of The State Of Qatar To India, 24–25 March 2015", Ministry of External Affairs, Government of India, 26 March 2015, at http://www.mea.gov.in/Speeches-Statements.htm?dtl/25012/Joint+Statement+during+the+State+Visit+of+the+Emir+of+the+State+of+Qatar+to+India+March+2425+2015
24. "India-Qatar Relations", Ministry of External Affairs, Government of India, May 2016, at https://mea.gov.in/Portal/ForeignRelation/Qatar_May_2016.pdf
25. "PM Modi in Doha: India, Qatar inks seven agreements to bolster ties", *Zee News*, 5 June 2016, at http://zeenews.india.com/news/india/pm-modi-in-doha-india-qatar-inks-seven-agreements-to-bolster-ties_1891976.html
26. Asmita Sarkar, "23 Indians Pardoned by Qatar Emir for Ramadan to Return Home", *International Business Times*, 7 June 2016, at http://www.ibtimes.co.in/23-indians-pardoned-by-qatar-emir-ramadan-return-home-681664
27. Ibid.
28. "NIIF, Qatar Investment Authority sign MoU to boost infra investments", *The Times of India*, 9 June 2016, at http://timesofindia.indiatimes.com/city/delhi/NIIF-Qatar-Investment-Authority-sign-MoU-to-boost-infra-investments/articleshow/52673623.cms

29. "India-Qatar Relations" op. cit.
30. "NASSCOM Delegation to Middle East (Bahrain and Qatar)", NASSCOM, at http://www.nasscom.in/nasscom-delegation-middle-east-bahrain-and-qatar
31. "India-Qatar Relations", op. cit.
32. "India-Qatar Bilateral Relations", op. cit.
33. "India-Qatar Relations", op. cit.
34. At https://www.thepeninsulaqatar.com/uploads/2016/08/10/pdf/IndiaIndependenceDay2016.pdf
35. "Make in India Week", Qatar Chamber, at http://qatarchamber.com/4528
36. The delegation also visited Kuwait and Saudi Arabia.
37. "Delegation from the Indian State of Gujarat to Meet Leading Companies and Senior Government Officials in Saudi Arabia, Kuwait and Qatar", *The Business Wire India*, 3 October 2016, at http://businesswireindia.com/news/news-details/delegation-from-indian-state-gujarat-meet-leading-companies-senior-government-officials-saudi-arabia-kuwait-qatar/50408
38. Shabana Hussain and Debojyoti Ghosh, "RMZ to raise Rs 1000 cr funding from Qatar Investment Authority", *Forbes India*, 2 April 2015, at http://www.forbesindia.com/article/special/rmz-to-raise-rs-1000-cr-funding-from-qatar-investment-authority/39959/1
39. "Qatar-India trade at USD 133 bn", *BQ Magazine*, 6 December 2015, at http://www.bq-magazine.com/energy/oil-energy/2015/12/qatar-india-trade-at-usd-133-bn
40. "India, Qatar sign seven agreement to strengthen ties", *Dawn*, 5 June 2016, at https://www.dawn.com/news/1262917
41. "India-Qatar Relations" op. cit.
42. Ibid.
43. "Medanta to set up super speciality hospital in Qatar", *Business Standard*, 1 April 2015, at http://www.business-standard.com/article/pti-stories/medanta-to-set-up-super-speciality-hospital-in-qatar-115040100525_1.html
44. "Most Admired Companies-Larsen and Toubro", *Construction World*, August 2014, at http://constructionworld.in/News.aspx?nId=X6baboZMIq9OplVbmQlg0A
45. "Main Contractor for Al-Rayyan Stadium announced as Qatari-Indian Joint Venture", Supreme Committee for Delivery and Legacy, 5 June 2016, at http://www.sc.qa/en/news/al-rayyan-stadium-qatari-indian-joint-venture
46. "QNB gets go-ahead to open branch in India", *The Gulf Times*, 28 August 2016, http://www.gulf-times.com/story/509822/QNB-gets-go-ahead-to-open-branch-in-India
47. "India-Qatar Relations" op. cit.
48. Ibid.,
49. "Qatar halves gas price, waives India's Rs 12,000 cr liability", *The Times of India*, 1 January 2016. At http://timesofindia.indiatimes.com/india/Qatar-halves-gas-price-waives-Indias-Rs-12000cr-liability/articleshow/50401540.cms
50. Embassy of India, Indian Cultural Centre, Doha, at http://www.iccqatar.com/about-icc/
51. "Qatar and India Continue To Strengthen Military Ties", Future Directions International, 2 October 2013, at http://www.futuredirections.org.au/publication/qatar-and-india-continue-to-strengthen-military-ties/
52. "Shri Nitin Gadkari Releases E-Books of Ministries of Road Transport and

Highways and Shipping", Press Information Bureau, Government of India, Ministry of Road Transport & Highways, 24 December 2014, at http://pib.nic.in/newsite/PrintRelease.aspx?relid=114065

53. "HE Foreign Minister Visits Joaan Bin Jassim Joint Command and Staff College", Qatar News Agency, 23 January 2016, at http://www.qna.org.qahttp://pib.nic.in/newsite/PrintRelease.aspx?relid=114065 /en-us/News/16012311000011/HE-Foreign-Minister-Visits-Joaan-Bin-Jassim-Joint-Command-and-Staff-College
54. "India-Qatar Bilateral Relations", op. cit.
55. "'Ferocious Falcon 4' Military Drill Concludes in Qatar", *Qatar News Agency*, 27 May 2015, http://militaryedge.org/articles/ferocious-falcon-4-military-drill-concludes-qatar/
56. "India-Qatar Relations", op. cit.
57. "Republic Day Celebration at Embassy of India-Doha", *Gulf Times*, 26 January 2017, at http://www.gulf-times.com/story/530499/Republic-Day-Ce',lebration-at-Embassy-of-India-Doha
58. "India-Qatar Relations", op. cit.
59. "Indian Naval Ship To Take Part in Dimex 2016", *Gulf Times*, 26 March 2016, at http://www.gulf-times.com/story/486063/Indian-naval-ship-to-take-part-in-Dimdex-2016
60. "India-Qatar Relations", op. cit.

8

SAUDI ARABIA

Prasanta Kumar Pradhan

Key Information

Ruling family: al-Saud; **Ruler:** King Salman bin Abdulaziz al-Saud (since 23 January 2015); **Crown Prince:** Muhammad bin Salman al-Saud (since 21 June 2017); **National Day:** 23 September; **Parliament**: 150-member nominated Majlis al-Shura; **Last Parliamentary Election**: NA; **Major group in parliament:** NA; **National Carrier**: Saudi Arabian Airlines.

Socio-Economic Indicators

Area: 2,149,690 sq km; **Population:** 28.16 million; **Native:** 70 per cent; **Expats:** 30 per cent; **Religious Groups:** Citizens (Sunni 85–90 per cent; Shia 10–15 per cent); **Youth:** 18.85 per cent; **Population growth rate:** 1.46 per cent; **Life expectancy at birth:** 75.3 years; **Major population groups**: Arab less than 90 per cent; Asian and African more than 10 per cent; **Literacy rate:** 94.7 per cent; **National Currency**: Saudi Riyal (SAR); **GDP:** US$ 637.8 billion; **Foreign Trade:** US$ 363 billion; **Defence budget:** 12.6 per cent of GDP (2015); **Sovereign Wealth Fund:** US$ 576 billion; **External Debt**: US$ 200.9 billion; **Per capita income:** US$ 54,100; **Oil reserves:** 269 billion bbl; **Gas reserves:** 8.489 trillion m^3; **HDI rank:** 39; **Infant Mortality Rate**: 13.6 deaths/1,000 live birth; **UN Education Index:** 0.723; **Gender Inequality Index:** 0.284; **Labour Force:** 12.02 million; **Unemployment rate**: 11.2 per cent; **Urban Population:** 83.1 per cent; **Rate of Urbanization:** 2.1 per cent; **Last National Census**: 2011.

India Related

Indian Cultural Centre: NA; **Number of Indians:** 2.8 million (approximately); **Number of places of worship for Indians:** None; **Indian Schools:** 40; **Indian Banks:** State Bank of India (1); **Currency exchange rate:** 1 SAR = INR 17.77 (Feb 2016); **Last visit to India by the ruler:** King Abdullah, January 2006; **Last Indian Prime Minister to visit**: Narendra Modi, April 2016.

* * *

The beginning of the protests in the Arab world brought a number of political, security, economic and strategic challenges for the Kingdom of Saudi Arabia. Amidst unprecedented changes taking place throughout the region, Saudi Arabia was able to contain unrest in its Eastern Province and, at the same time, played a key role in trying to change the geopolitics of the region. It has faced strong internal security challenges emanating from terrorism and severe economic downturn following the fall of global oil prices. To protect its interests in the immediate neighbourhood, it has made military interventions in neighbouring Bahrain and Yemen. While the military intervention in Bahrain was relatively lower, in Yemen it has been intense and prolonged. Saudi Arabia has also stakes in other regional conflicts, such as Syria and Iraq. Amid all these domestic and external challenges, there has been a change of guard following the death of King Abdullah in January 2015. The new King Salman and his two Crown Princes have domestic and foreign policy challenges facing them. During the period under review, a number of ambitious projects have been launched, and measures were adopted to deal with the situation. Their outcomes, whether successful or not, would reflect in the next few years; but at present the Kingdom is certainly passing through a phase of huge uncertainty.

India's relationship with Saudi Arabia has remained unaffected by the internal changes in the Kingdom and the continuing regional turmoil. Bilateral trade continues to grow steadily, and Saudi Arabia remains the top supplier of oil for India. At the same time, both countries are looking to enhance ties in the political, security, and defence arenas, and to build a comprehensive strategic partnership. While for several decades, trade and energy ties remained the mainstay of the relationship, in recent years, the security and strategic aspects have received a boost due to regional environment and common threat perceptions. The exchange of high level bilateral visits and the signing of agreements on wide-ranging issues, indicate seriousness on both sides for a sustained political engagement.

Domestic Developments

The Royal Succession

Early 2015 witnessed a change of guard in the Kingdom, and following the death of King Abdullah, Crown Prince Salman became King on 23 January 2015. In April 2015, King Salman appointed his nephew Muhammad bin Nayef as the Crown Prince, and his son Mohammed bin Salman as the Deputy Crown Prince. The appointment of Prince Muhammad bin Nayef means that the reign would eventually be passed on to the next generation of royals—that is, the grandsons of Ibn Saud.[1]

King Salman appointed his son Prince Mohammed as Deputy Crown Prince, Minister of Defence, and Chairman of the newly established Council for Economic and Development Affairs. Since his elevation, Prince Mohammed Bin-Salman has emerged as the most influential leader, and a major force in the royal court. He has been instrumental in taking key decisions, including the unfolding of *Vision 2030*[2] as well as the Saudi-led military intervention in Yemen.[3]

Terrorism

The emergence of the Islamic State of Iraq and Syria (ISIS) has created a security challenge for the Kingdom. Since its declaration of a caliphate, the ISIS has launched a number of attacks within Saudi Arabia, including a bombing outside Prophet's Mosque in Medina in July 2016. The attacks witnessed an increase after Abu Bakr al-Baghdadi's speech (delivered in November 2014) urged his followers to launch attacks on the Kingdom.[4] The ISIS is trying to create sectarian strife in the Kingdom by deliberately targeting Shia mosques, particularly in the Shia-dominated Eastern Province. Saudi authorities also claim to have foiled several planned attacks by the ISIS. In July 2015, the authorities arrested 431 people linked to the ISIS, and accused them of planning to carry out attacks inside the Kingdom.[5] Earlier, in March 2014, Saudi Arabia designated the ISIS as a terrorist organisation.

In December 2015, Saudi Arabia announced a coalition of 34 Islamic countries to fight terrorism in the region. As a number of Islamic countries are fighting terrorism individually, this initiative is aimed at coordinating their actions. In January 2017, former Chief of Army Staff of Pakistan, General Raheel Sharif, was appointed the head of this coalition.[6] Deputy Crown Prince Muhammad Bin-Salman stated that, "The formation of the Islamic military alliance emanates from the Islamic world's keenness to fight terrorism and be a partner of the world in the fight against this scourge."[7] He also stated that the coalition would not focus on any one particular group (such as the ISIS) but on terrorist groups across the globe, and that the alliance would operate under the UN and OIC counterterrorism provisions.[8] This is a major Saudi initiative to build an alliance against terrorism by inviting Islamic countries from Middle East, Africa, and South Asia.[9]

The Economy

The economy of the Kingdom has been severely hit as a result of the sharp fall in international oil prices. The average price of the Arabian Light oil fell from US$ 110.22 in 2012 to US$ 49.85 in 2015.[10] As a result, oil revenues witnessed a sharp decline—from US$ 305.26 billion in 2012 to US$ 119 billion in 2015.[11] This led to a drastic increase in the budget deficit: from 3.4 per cent of GDP in 2014 to 16.3 per cent in 2015.[12] To deal with the situation, Saudi Arabia continued to increase its oil production through 2015 and 2016. This was intended mainly to dominate the supply market in the face of competition being faced from other big suppliers. It was also partly aimed at dealing with the low oil prices and the increase in Shale oil production by the US. In 2015, Saudi Arabia produced an average 10.2 million barrels per day (bpd), which was an increase from 9.71 million bpd in 2014 and 9.64 million bpd in 2013.[13]

Actual expenditures of the government also went down by 11.9 per cent in 2015; and the government was forced to adopt austerity measures. In December 2015, it announced a revision of prices of energy, water, and electricity "gradually over the next five years."[14] In September 2016, King Salman announced 20 per cent cuts in the salaries of ministers; 15 per cent reduction in the annual subsidy granted to Shura Council members for housing; and a 15 per cent cut from their car maintenance and fuel cost for four years.[15] The economy grew at the rate of 3.5 per cent in 2015, and the budget registered a deficit of US$ 96.58 billion in 2015.[16]

The Kingdom is planning to give a boost to non-oil revenues in order to diversify its economy and expand its tax base. For generating further revenue, the government has decided to impose five per cent value added tax (VAT), beginning 2018. This would be in accordance with the decision taken by the Gulf Cooperation Council (GCC) to impose a uniform VAT in all member countries. According to an IMF estimate, at the rate of 3 to 5 per cent of VAT, Saudi Arabia would be able to generate additional tax revenue of 1 to 1.6 per cent of its GDP.[17] The government has also decided to remove 50 per cent subsidy on seven items: port services, passport fees, car driving license fees, car transfer fees, traffic fines, and the renewal of residence permits for domestic workers.[18] To augment additional resources, the government increased visa fees in August 2016. Earlier, in November 2015, the Saudi Council of Ministers proposed to impose a 2.5 per cent White Land tax,[19] which was approved the following June.[20] The government believes that the imposition of such taxes would help address the increasing housing challenge due to the rapidly growing urban population in the Kingdom.

Saudi Vision 2030

On 25 April 2016, Deputy Crown Prince Mohammad bin Salman announced the *Saudi Vision 2030* which envisages making the Kingdom the heart of the Arab and Islamic worlds by turning it into an investment powerhouse, and the hub connecting the three continents of Asia, Europe, and Africa.[21] He has described the vision as "ambitious yet achievable blueprint"[22] for establishing the long term goals of a vibrant society, a thriving economy, and an ambitious nation.[23]

In June 2016, Saudi Cabinet approved the National Transformation Programme 2020 (NTP), with the objective of building the institutional capability to meet the aspirations of *Vision 2030*. The NTP identifies the strategic objectives of the Kingdom in different fields, and the initiatives necessary to meet the themes of the *Vision 2030*. The strategic targets of the NTP included, inter alia, an increase in non-oil governmental revenue from US$ 43.46 billion to US$ 141.32 billion; raising non-oil export commodities from US$ 49.33 billion to US$ 87.99 billion; and increasing foreign direct investment (FDI) from US$ 8 billion to US$ 18.66 billion by 2020.[24]

After the fall of oil prices during the last few years, the Saudi economy has been severely affected. This has been reflected in *Vision 2030*, which calls for diversification of the economy, generation of new job opportunities, attracting investments, supporting entrepreneurship and privatizing some government services. The targets mentioned in the vision document for the next 15 years look ambitious for a heavily oil-dependent centralised economy.

Foreign Policy

The developments in neighbouring Yemen remain a major cause of concern for Saudi Arabia. In the aftermath of the protests, Saudi Arabia played a key role in signing the 'GCC Initiative' in November 2011, which paved the way for the transition of power from Ali Abdullah Saleh to Abdrabbuh Mansur Hadi. Dissatisfied with the outcomes of the National Dialogue Conference (NDC), in early 2014, the Houthis started their forward march from Saada to the capital city Sana'a. They forced the Hadi government out and captured Sana'a in September 2014, and subsequently, announced the formation of their own government by dismissing the parliament. Saudi

Arabia decided to intervene militarily to push the Houthis out of the capital Sana'a, and started its military campaign (known as *Operation Decisive Storm*) on 26 March 2015—a military coalition enjoying the support of neighbouring countries such as Bahrain, Kuwait, Qatar, and the UAE. Other Arab countries, including Egypt, Jordan, Senegal, Sudan, and Somalia, also joined the coalition while the US agreed to provide intelligence support. The Saudi-led military has been able to achieve only limited success. On 21 April 2015, the coalition officially declared the end of *Operation Decisive Storm*, and began *Operation Restoring Hope* with the objective of protecting citizens, continuing to combat terrorism, and engaging in political negotiations to restore peace and stability in the country. However, despite officially announcing the end of the *Operation Decisive Storm*, military operations never ceased, and continue till date.

Saudi Arabia is continuing its political and diplomatic efforts for the removal of the Bashar al-Assad regime in Syria. Since November 2012, Saudi Arabia, along with the other members of the GCC, recognised the opposition National Coalition of Syria as the 'legitimate representative' of the Syrian people.[25] Riyadh believes that the opposition should be militarily strengthened as several political and diplomatic efforts by the international community to protect the Syrian people have failed. For Saudi Arabia, the Assad regime needs to be removed for any credible political transition and, in February 2016, the Saudi Foreign Minister Adel al-Jubeir stated that Assad would be removed if not by a political process then by the use of force.[26] In December 2015, Riyadh hosted a meeting of the Syrian opposition forces representing the armed revolutionary factions and various other groups. The participants stressed on the removal of Assad, the establishment of a transitional government with full powers as per Geneva Communiqué of June 2012, and their commitment towards democracy, pluralism, and sovereignty. After deliberations, the participants agreed to form a High Negotiations Committee (HNC) with its office in Riyadh, to negotiate with the Assad regime on behalf of the participants.[27]

In July 2015, Iran and the P5+1 (China, France, Germany, Russia, the UK, the US and the EU) agreed to sign the Joint Comprehensive Plan of Action (JCPOA) and end the prolonged controversy surrounding the Iranian nuclear programme. From the beginning, Saudi Arabia had expressed its reservations about the negotiations with Iran, preferring the opposite—that is, for the continuation and intensification of harsher sanctions against Iran. Though it formally welcomed the deal, Saudi Arabia remained wary of Iranian intentions and its ability to acquire nuclear weapons.[28] The Iranian nuclear talks have always raised doubts in the minds of GCC leaders, including

Saudi Arabia, about the commitment of the US towards Gulf security.[29] For its part, the US has tried to allay such apprehensions of the GCC leaders, and assured them of its continued security cooperation with them.[30]

As friction in US-Saudi relations began in the immediate aftermath of the Iranian nuclear deal, China has come forward to expand its relationship with Saudi Arabia by looking beyond trade and energy. Both China and the Kingdom have been looking to deepen their ties, and increase the scope of their engagements. This has been evident in the high-level bilateral visits and agreements between the two countries. Chinese President Xi Jinping visited Riyadh in January 2016, during which he and King Salman inaugurated the operation of the Yasref oil refinery, a joint venture between the two countries. Both sides decided to restart the China-GCC free trade agreement (FTA) talks, and agreed to enter into a 'comprehensive strategic partnership' for bilateral cooperation in several fields, including support for the Chinese Belt and Road Initiative.[31] Deputy Crown Prince Mohammed Bin-Salman visited China in August 2016, and discussed a number of mutual bilateral issues, including trade and investment, 'Belt and Road', Saudi *Vision 2030*, and a host of other regional issues. In November, Meng Jianzhu, a special envoy of President Xi Jinping, met King Salman, and both the countries discussed joint cooperation on counter-terrorism, among other issues.

Both the countries signed a five-year cooperation plan for security training.[32] In October 2016, China and Saudi Arabia conducted the joint military exercise *Exploration 2016* in the Chinese city of Chengdu, where Special Forces of the Royal Saudi Land Forces participated with their Chinese counterparts.[33] Growing Saudi-China ties got a further boost with the visit of King Salman to China in March 2017.

Bilateral Relations

Political Relations

India-Saudi Arabia relations continue to grow stronger, and the Kingdom remains a key partner of India in the Gulf region. Political, economic, and security ties have received a further boost with increased engagements and interaction at various levels. In the recent past, the bilateral relationship has touched new heights. The visit of King Abdullah to New Delhi in 2006 as the chief guest for the Republic Day celebrations was an important milestone, when both the countries signed the 'Delhi Declaration' in which they committed to strengthen their partnership further along an entire gamut of economic, political, and security issues.[34] The relationship got a further boost with the visit of Prime Minister Manmohan Singh to Riyadh in 2010, and the signing of the 'Riyadh Declaration'.[35] Both countries reiterated their commitment to the Delhi Declaration of 2006, and agreed to take the relationship to a strategic level by moving beyond the traditional buyer-seller relationship. Through the Riyadh Declaration, they reiterated their commitment to strengthening the relationship, and raising it to a strategic partnership covering political, economic, security, and defence areas. It also called for a strategic energy partnership based on complementarity and interdependence.

After coming to power in 2014, the Prime Minister Narendra Modi-led National Democratic Alliance (NDA) government has expressed India's keen interest to engage with Riyadh. As a result, a number of high level bilateral visits and meetings have taken place between India and Saudi Arabia since then. Undoubtedly, Prime Minister Modi inherited strong India-Saudi Arabia relations, and the government has identified a number of crucial areas of engagement, including trade, energy, investments, security, and defence cooperation.

A number of high-level bilateral visits have taken place during the last two years. The most important and visible of these was the visit of Prime Minister Narendra Modi in April 2016. His visit provided an impetus to the bilateral relationship, building further upon the Delhi Declaration of 2006 and Riyadh Declaration of 2010. During his visit, Prime Minister Modi articulated India's seriousness about deepening ties with the Kingdom even further, and laid emphasis on enhancing bilateral trade, investment, security, and strategic cooperation between the two countries. Presently, the Kingdom is India's fourth largest trading partner, and Prime Minister Modi has urged the further broadening of the scope of trade as well as inviting investments from the Kingdom. Similarly, security cooperation, especially on terrorism and piracy, has also been given high priority by India. During the visit, King Salman honoured Prime Minister Modi with the Order of King Abdulaziz, the highest Saudi civilian award.

Even before his visit to Riyadh, Prime Minister Modi had the opportunity to meet the top leadership of Saudi Arabia at other international forums which helped him strike a friendly chord. In November 2015, he met King Salman on the sidelines of the G-20 summit at Antalya, Turkey. Earlier, in November 2014, both the leaders met at Brisbane during the G-20 summit, when Salman bin Abdulaziz al-Saud was still the Crown Prince. Saudi Foreign Minister Adel al-Jubeir visited India in March 2016, and during this visit he met senior Indian leaders and discussed a range of bilateral issues, including political, economic, and security cooperation. He also stated that

Saudi Arabia accords high priority to its ties with India. When asked about Saudi position towards India and Pakistan in an interview, Jubeir famously stated that while India is a 'strategic partner', Pakistan is an 'historic ally', and clarified that Saudi relations with India are independent of Pakistan.[36]

Trade, Investment and Energy

During his visit, Modi reiterated that furthering bilateral trade and investment is a key area of importance for his government. India's bilateral trade with the Kingdom is on an upward trajectory, and Saudi Arabia is the fourth largest trading partner of India, with the total bilateral trade of US$ 26.71 billion in 2015–16. However, despite flourishing trade, there has been a sharp fall in the value of the trade from US$ 48 billion in 2013–14 to US$ 39 billion in 2014–15 and US$ 26 billion in 2015–16. The decline in the value of the total trade is primarily because of lower international oil prices. India intends to broaden the scope of the trade, especially in the non-oil sector, and this was emphasised by Modi during his discussions with the Saudi leaders.

Table 8.1: India-Saudi Arabia Bilateral Trade (in USS million)

	2011–12	2012–13	2013–14	2014–15	2015–16
Exports	5,683.29	9,785.78	12,218.95	11,161.43	6,394.23
Imports	31,817.70	33,998.11	36,403.65	28,107.56	20,321.33
Total Trade	37,500.99	43,783.89	48,622.60	39,268.98	26,715.56
Per cent of Total Trade	4.72	5.53	6.63	5.18	4.15

Source: Adapted from Director-General of Foreign Trade, New Delhi, at www.dgft.gov.in

Figure 8.1: India-Saudi Arabia Bilateral Trade

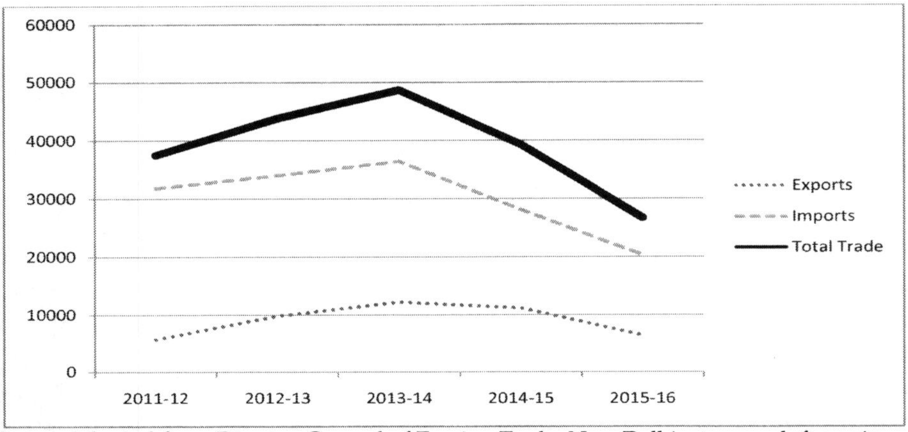

Source: Adapted from Director-General of Foreign Trade, New Delhi, at www.dgft.gov.in

Besides trade, India intends to draw more Saudi investments into its economy. Investment was accorded high priority in the joint statement issued during the visit of Prime Minister Modi who invited more Saudi investments. India tried to instil confidence in Saudi investors by highlighting the government's initiatives in the easing of foreign direct investment rules. Modi invited big Saudi companies—like Saudi ARAMCO and Saudi Basic Industries Corporation (SABIC), among others—to invest. During meetings, Saudi companies have also expressed interest in investing in the infrastructure sector, like railways, ports, and roads. India intends to draw investment from the huge Saudi sovereign wealth fund (SWF). According to the Sovereign Wealth Fund Institute, Saudi Arabia has the fifth largest SWF, with US$ 514 billion holdings at present.[37] Though it is an important trading partner, Saudi investments in India remains far below potential and, during the last 15 years, it has totalled only US$ 53.37 million.[38] To further promote cooperation on investment, both sides signed the 'Framework for Investment Promotion Cooperation' between Invest India and the Saudi Arabian General Investment Authority (SAGIA). The 11th India-Saudi Joint Commission meeting held in New Delhi in May 2015 also discussed exploring investment opportunities on both the sides.

While bilateral trade between the two countries continues to grow and both countries are also exploring future potential in the investment sector, oil still remains the most important component in the trade basket. For India, Saudi Arabia is the largest supplier of oil, exporting worth US$ 15.17 billion in 2015–16. There has been a drastic fall in the value of oil imported compared to 2013–14 when India imported around US$ 32.78 billion worth of oil from the Kingdom. This amounts to 15.65 per cent of India's total energy imports worldwide, and has also witnessed a fall from 18 per cent in 2013–14 (see Table 8.2). India believes that partnership with the Kingdom would meet the increasing energy demands of its growing economy. On the other hand, India seems to be a huge and assured market for its oil in the long term for Saudi Arabia.

India intends to build a Strategic Petroleum Reserve of five million metric tons to meet any future exigencies, keeping in mind the political and security volatility in some of the oil producing countries. In this regard, a strategic energy partnership with Saudi Arabia would address future energy security issues. A 'comprehensive energy partnership' with Saudi Arabia was proposed by Prime Minister Manmohan Singh during his visit to the kingdom in 2010. The strategic energy partnership suggested involvement and joint ventures in the production and technology involved in the oil business, thus moving beyond the simple buyer-seller relationship. Prime Minister Modi's visit has further accelerated this as both countries agreed to establish joint ventures and investments in the petrochemical sector in Saudi Arabia. In order to take their energy engagements to the next level, both have agreed to cooperate in the fields of training and human resource development; they have also decided to set up the 'India-Saudi Arabia Ministerial Energy Dialogue'. These are some significant steps in the direction of building a strategic energy partnership with Saudi Arabia.

Table 8.2: Share of Energy in India's Imports from Saudi Arabia (in US$ million)

Year	Oil Imports from Saudi Arabia	Total Oil Imports	Saudi Share in Total Oil Imports (in per cent)	Imports from Saudi Arabia	Per cent of Oil in Imports from Saudi Arabia
2011-12	28,302.37	172,753.97	16.38	31,060.10	91.12
2012-13	29,896.53	181,344.67	16.49	33,998.11	87.94
2013-14	32,781.57	181,382.59	18.07	36,403.65	90.05
2014-15	23,212.88	156,400.01	14.84	28,107.56	82.59
2015-16	15,177.91	96,953.06	15.65	20,321.33	74.69

Source: Adapted from Director-General of Foreign Trade, New Delhi, at www.dgft.gov.in

Figure 8.2: Share of Energy in India's Imports from Saudi Arabia

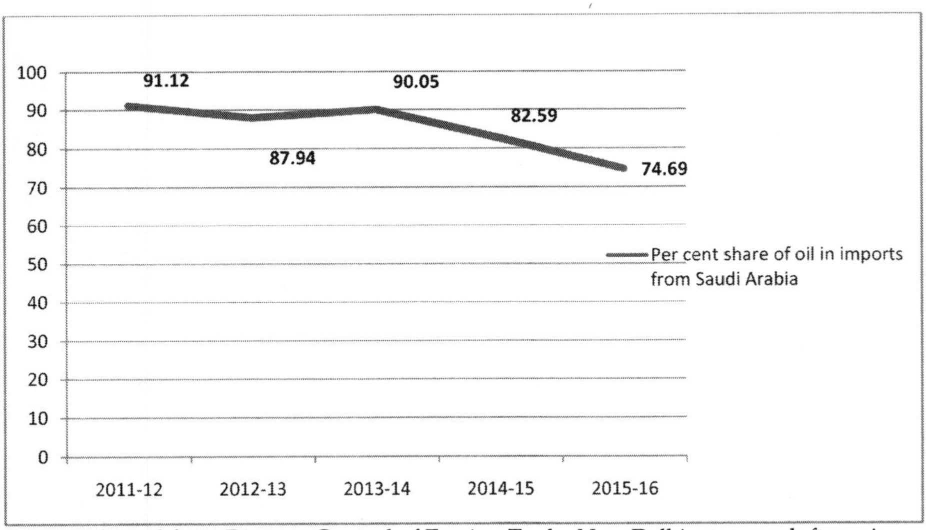

Source: Adapted from Director-General of Foreign Trade, New Delhi, at www.dgft.gov.in

Saudi energy supplies to India constitute around 30 per cent of its total imports from the Persian Gulf region, thus keeping itself ahead of other oil exporting countries of the region (see Table 8.3). Despite the fall in oil prices, Saudi Arabia has been consistent in its supply of oil to India. In order to follow up the discussions during Modi's visit, the Minister for Petroleum and Natural Gas, Dharmendra Pradhan, visited Saudi Arabia from 13–14 April 2016, and held bilateral meetings with the Chairman of Aramco, Khalid al-Falih, and the Saudi Vice-Minister for Petroleum, Prince Abdulaziz bin Salman, and discussed "various investment proposals in areas like oil, gas, petrochemicals, exploration, and production."[39]

Table 8.3: India's Energy Imports from Saudi Arabia (in US$ million)

	2011–12	2012–13	2013–14	2014–15	2015–16
Energy Import from Saudi Arabia	28,302.37	29,896.53	32,781.57	23,212.88	15,177.91
Total Energy Import	172,753.97	181,344.67	181,382.59	156,400.01	96,953.06
Total Import from Persian Gulf	95,915.24	105,859.19	106,400.75	85,300.30	50,992.26
Share in Total Imports	16.38%	16.49%	18.07%	14.84%	15.65%
Share in Imports from Persian Gulf	29.13%	28.26%	30.81%	27.21%	29.77%

Source: Adapted from Director-General of Foreign Trade, New Delhi, at www.dgft.gov.in

Figure 8.3: Share of Saudi Arabia in Energy Imports from Persian Gulf

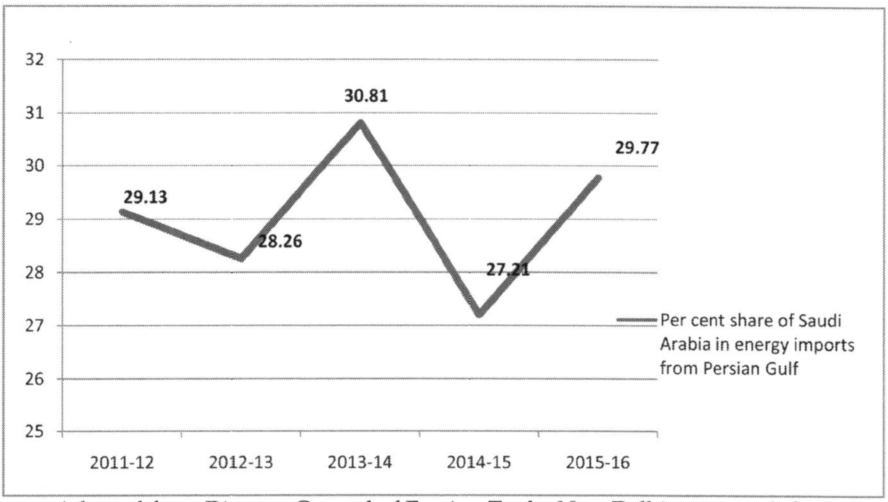

Source: Adapted from Director-General of Foreign Trade, New Delhi, at www.dgft.gov.in

Security Cooperation

Security cooperation is an emerging area of engagement between India and Saudi Arabia. It was a key focus during Prime Minister Modi's visit to Saudi Arabia. The joint statement issued at the end of his visit condemned terrorism in all its forms and manifestations, and emphasised the need for cooperation in combating extremism and terrorism. Both countries agreed to deepen their engagement over counter-terrorism operations as well as tackle the challenges of money laundering, drug-peddling, and other transnational crimes.[40] During Modi's visit, an agreement was signed between the Financial Intelligence Units of both the countries to exchange intelligence pertaining to terror financing and money laundering. While the rapid spread of the terror networks across the region and India seems to be a major reason behind such an agreement, it also reflects the desire of both countries to cooperate on combating terror.

Both countries have been facing the menace of terrorism, particularly from the ISIS, in recent years. The ISIS has launched terrorist strikes on Saudi Arabia, and several of their modules have been busted in the kingdom.[41] There are also reports of around two dozen Indians who have joined the organisation, and the extremist outfit is trying to radicalise and draw more Indian youths toward its ideology. Thus, the growing security challenges and the benefits of mutual cooperation in countering terror have been a key driver behind the need for both to cooperate on this issue. By emphasising security cooperation, India intends to further strengthen the relationship which has been consolidated in recent times, and establish a broad based strategic partnership with the Kingdom. Earlier, in 2014, India and Saudi Arabia also signed a defence cooperation agreement.[42]

Altogether, India is on the path of engaging with Saudi Arabia, and to forge a strategic partnership moving beyond the traditional buyer-seller relationship. Safety of the Sea Lines of Communications (SLOCs) is crucial for both the countries as they heavily depend on the maritime route for their international trade. Maritime piracy has emerged as a threat to the safety of the SLOCs. In the past, both have been victims of the piracy in the Gulf of Aden and the Indian Ocean. There is a commonality of interest from both the sides, and they have agreed to fight maritime piracy in the Gulf and Indian Ocean.[43]

The Indian Expatriate Community

There are around three million Indian nationals living and working in the Kingdom.[44] In July 2016, there were reports of several Indians facing hardships due to delays in salary payment, and a large number of Indians lost their jobs due to either closure or downsizing by some companies. Many Saudi companies suffered heavy losses because of the economic downturn in the Kingdom, and two major companies—Saudi Oger and Saad Group—failed to pay salaries to their employees. Over 10,000 Indians were affected by the layoffs by these two companies, and there were reports of Indian workers facing food crisis.[45] The Government of India intervened, and facilitated the return of a large number of workers.[46] On his part, King

Salman directed the Saudi authorities to resolve the issue, and to ensure that their legal and financial rights were protected. The Saudi government also agreed to provide free passage to those who intended to return to India, and also facilitated the transfers of sponsorship and payment of dues.[47] In April 2016, India signed an agreement with the Saudi Ministry of Labour for the protection of the general category of workers[48] from India.[49]

Conclusion

India has been successful in effectively engaging with the new team of Saudi leadership, building upon the progresses made during the reign of King Abdullah. The visit of Prime Minister Modi to the Kingdom is a sign of the growing mutual trust in the bilateral relationship. India's efforts to strengthen ties and initiatives in different fields have been reciprocated by Saudi Arabia. Both countries are moving in the direction of strengthening the recently built strategic partnership, and moving beyond the dominant trade and energy sectors. The political, security, and strategic aspects of the relationship are accorded high priority which was not witnessed in the past several decades. Common concerns over the rise and spread of terrorism, growing radicalisation, and religious extremism in the aftermath of the popular protests in the Arab world, maritime piracy, money laundering, etc. have necessitated greater cooperation between the two countries. While a strong foundation in the relationship has been laid, it depends upon the leadership and vision of both countries to explore further opportunities for cooperation.

NOTES

1. In a sudden move on June 21, 2017 Nayef 'stepped down' as crown prince and was replaced by King's son Mohammed bin-Salman.
2. The text of the document can be accessed at http://vision2030.gov.sa/en/foreword.
3. "Young Prince in a Hurry", *The Economist*, 9 January 2016, at http://www.economist.com/news/briefing/21685467-muhammad-bin-salman-gambles-intervention-abroad-and-radical-economic-change-home.
4. "Islamic State Leader Urges Attacks in Saudi Arabia: Speech", *Reuters*, 13 November 2014, at http://www.reuters.com/article/us-mideast-crisis-baghdadi-idUSKCN0IX1Y120141114.
5. Nasser Al-Haqbani, "Saudi Arabia foils ISIS terror plots, arrests 431 suspects: Officials", *Asharq Al Awsat*, 19 July 2015, at http://english.aawsat.com/n-alhaqbani/news-middle-east/saudi-arabia-foils-isis-terror-plots-arrests-431-suspects-officials.
6. Jon Boone, "Former Pakistan Army Chief Raheel Sharif to Lead 'Muslim Nato'", *The Guardian*, 8 January 2017, at https://www.theguardian.com/world/2017/jan/08/former-pakistan-army-chief-raheel-sharif-lead-muslim-nato.

7. "KSA forms 34-country Islamic military alliance against terror", *Saudi Gazette*, 16 December 2015, at http://saudigazette.com.sa/saudi-arabia/ksa-forms-34-country-islamic-military-alliance-against-terror/.
8. "Led by KSA, 34-nation alliance to wipe out terror", *Arab News*, 15 December 2015, at http://www.arabnews.com/featured/news/850596.
9. The members of the coalition are Bahrain, Bangladesh, Benin, Chad, Comoros, Djibouti, Egypt, Gabon, Guinea, Ivory Coast, Jordan, Kuwait, Lebanon, Libya, Malaysia, Maldives, Mali, Mauritania, Morocco, Niger, Nigeria, Pakistan, Palestine, Qatar, Saudi Arabia, Senegal, Sierra Leone, Somalia, Sudan, Togo, Tunisia, Turkey, UAE and Yemen.
10. "Fifty Second Annual Report 1437H, 2016", Saudi Arabian Monetary Agency, Kingdom of Saudi Arabia (SAMA, KSA), p. 24, at http://www.sama.gov.sa/en-US/EconomicReports/AnnualReport/Fifty%20Second%20Annual%20Report.pdf,
11. Ibid.
12. Thomas Grennes and Andris Strazds, "The Saudi Arabia Oil Shock: Crisis and Opportunity for Economic Reform", *Economonitor*, 15 June 2016, at http://www.economonitor.com/blog/2016/06/the-saudi-arabia-oil-shock-crisis-and-opportunity-for-economic-reform/, accessed on 3 March 2017.
13. "Fifty First Annual Report 1436H, 2015" (SAMA, KSA), p. 23, at http://www.sama. gov.sa/en-US/EconomicReports/AnnualReport/5600_R_Annual_En_ 51_ Apx.pdf.
14. Simeon Kerr, "Saudis unveil radical austerity programme", *Financial Times*, 28 December 2015, at https://www.ft.com/content/a5f89f36-ad7e-11e5-b955-1a1d298b6250,
15. "Ministers' pay cut by 20%", *Arab News*, 27 September 2016, at http://www.arabnews.com/node/990401/saudi-arabia, accessed on 11 February 2017.
16. "Fifty Second Annual Report 1437H, 2016", op. cit., p. 23,
17. Saad Alshahrani, "Value Added Tax: Its Implementation and Implications", SAMA Quarterly Workshop, 2016, at http://www.sama.gov.sa/ar-sa/Economic Research/Quarterly%20Workshops/الربع%20الأول_2016_العرض%20الثاني.pdf.
18. "Saudi Arabia to remove subsidies for 7 services", *Arabian Business*, 18 September 2016, at http://www.arabianbusiness.com/saudi-arabia-remove-subsidies-for-7-services-645613.html,
19. White Land tax is imposed on the large vacant plots in the urban areas. The tax is imposed on the owners of such plots to discourage holding lands for years without building it for personal, commercial, or housing purposes.
20. "White land tax law to spur KSA real estate market: JLL", *Arab News*, 16 June 2016, at http://www.arabnews.com/node/940051/economy,
21. See "Foreword", *Vision 2030*, Kingdom of Saudi Arabia, at http://vision2030.gov.sa/en/foreword
22. Ibid.
23. Ibid.
24. "National Transformation Program 2020", *Vision 2030*, Kingdom of Saudi Arabia, at http://vision2030.gov.sa/sites/default/files/NTP_En.pdf
25. "GCC recognises new Syrian opposition bloc", *Al-Jazeera*, 13 November 2012, at http://www.aljazeera.com/news/middleeast/2012/11/2012111217553953450 4.html.

26. "Force Assad out: Kingdom", *Arab News*, 14 February 2016, at http://www.arabnews.com/saudi-arabia/news/880396.
27. "Final Statement of the Conference of Syrian Revolution and Opposition Forces Riyadh, 10 December 2015", Ministry of Foreign Affairs, Kingdom of Saudi Arabia (MoFA, KSA), 14 December 2015, at http://www.mofa.gov.sa/sites/mofaen/ServicesAndInformation/ImportantIssues/Pages/ArticleID20151214143757814.aspx
28. In an op-ed in *The New York Times* in January 2016, Saudi Foreign Minister Adel al-Juberi underlined Saudi reservations about the deal, saying, "Superficially, Iran may appear to have changed. We acknowledge Iran's initial actions regarding the agreement to suspend its program to develop a nuclear weapon. Certainly, we know that a large segment of the Iranian population wants greater openness internally and better relations with neighbouring countries and the world. But the government does not." See also: Adel Bin Ahmed al-Jubeir, "Can Iran Change?", *The New York Times*, 19 January 2016, at https://www.nytimes.com/2016/01/19/opinion/saudi-arabia-can-iran-change.html?_r=1.
29. "Gulf Allies 'Back Iran Nuclear Deal' after US Security Guarantees", *BBC News*, 3 August 2015, at http://www.bbc.com/news/world-middle-east-33758939.
30. Ibid.
31. "Xi wraps up historic visit to Saudi Arabia, steps up energy cooperation", *Xinhua*, 21 January 2016, at http://news.xinhuanet.com/english/2016-01/21/c_135029295_2.htm,
32. Rashid Hassan, "Saudi Arabia, China to boost cooperation in fighting terror", *Arab News*, 7 November 2016, at http://www.arabnews.com/node/1007606/saudi-arabia
33. "Saudi, Chinese Special Forces Conclude their Joint Exercise", *Asharq Al Awsat*, 23 October 2016, at http://english.aawsat.com/theaawsat/world-news/saudi-chinese-special-forces-conclude-joint-exercise
34. "Delhi Declaration, Signed by King Abdullah bin Abdulaziz Al Saud of the Kingdom of Saudi Arabia and Prime Minister Dr. Manmohan Singh", Ministry of External Affairs, Government of India, 27 January 2006, http://mea.gov.in/bilateral-documents.htm?dtl/5969/Delhi+Declaration+Signed+ by+ King+Abdullah+bin+Abdulaziz+Al+Saud+of+the+ Kingdom+of+Saudi+ Arabia+ and+Prime+ Minister+Dr+Manmohan+Singh+of+India.
35. "Riyadh Declaration: A New Era of Strategic Partnership", Ministry of External Affairs, Government of India, 1 March 2010, at http://mea.gov.in/bilateral-documents.htm?dtl/3700/Riyadh+Declaration+A+New+Era+of+ Strategic + Partnership.
36. Indrani Bagchi, "India is our strategic partner, Pak historic ally: Saudi mantri", *Times of India*, 10 March 2016, at http://timesofindia.indiatimes.com/india/India-is-our-strategic-partner-Pak-historic-ally-Saudi-mantri/articleshow/51335386.cms.
37. "Sovereign Wealth Fund Rankings: Largest Sovereign Wealth Funds by Assets under Management", Sovereign Wealth Fund Institute (SWFI), at http://www.swfinstitute.org/sovereign-wealth-fund-rankings/
38. Department of Industrial Policy & Promotion (DIPP), Ministry of Commerce and Industry, Government of India.
39. "Petroleum and Natural Gas Minister visits Riyadh, Saudi Arabia", Press

Information Bureau, Government of India, Ministry of Petroleum & Natural Gas, 15 April 2016, at http://pib.nic.in/newsite/PrintRelease.aspx?relid=138895

40. "India-Saudi Arabia Joint Statement during the visit of Prime Minister to Saudi Arabia", Ministry of External Affairs, Government of India, 3 April 2016, at http://www.mea.gov.in/bilateral-documents.htm?dtl/26595/IndiaSaudi+Arabia+Joint+ Statement+during+the+visit+of+Prime+Minister+to+Saudi+Arabia+April+03+2016
41. Mohammed al-Sulami, "Saudi Security Forces Dismantle 4 Terror Cells, Arrest 18", *Arab News*, 16 February 2017, at http://www.arabnews.com/node/1055206/saudi-arabia.
42. Sandeep Dikshit, "After Defence MoU: Saudi Arabia and India Eye Diverse Areas for Tie-ups", *The Hindu*, 1 March 2014, at http://www.thehindu.com/news/national/after-defence-mou-saudi-arabia-and-india-eye-diverse-areas-for-tieups/article5737390.ece.
43. "India-Saudi Arabia Joint Statement during the visit of Prime Minister to Saudi Arabia," Ministry of External Affairs, Government of India.
44. "India-Saudi Arabia Bilateral Relations", Ministry of External Affairs, Government of India, December 2016, at https://www.mea.gov.in/Portal/ForeignRelation/India-Saudi_Bilateral_Relations.pdf.
45. "Over 10,000 India Workers Facing 'Food Crisis' in Saudi Arabia (Roundup)", *The Times of India*, 31 July 2016, at http://timesofindia.indiatimes.com/city/delhi/Over-10000-Indian-workers-facing-food-crisis-in-Saudi-Arabia-Roundup/articleshow/53470464.cms.
46. "V. K. Singh Visits Saudi Arabia Again to Help Laid-off Workers", *The Indian Express*, 20 August 2016, at http://indianexpress.com/article/india/india-news-india/v-k-singh-visits-saudi-again-to-help-laid-off-workers-2986074/.
47. Mohammed Rasooldeen, "King's order: Resolve cases of Indian workers in Saudi Oger urgently", *Arab News*, 3 August 2016, at http://www.arabnews.com/node/964051/saudi-arabia
48. 'General Category Workers' are Indian nationals employed in Saudi Arabia through employment contracts, and do not include domestic workers.
49. For details of the agreement, see Ministry of External Affairs, Government of India, "Question No. 2428 Agreement for Protection of Indian Workers in Saudi Arabia", Parliament Q&A, 23 March 2017, at http://www.mea.gov.in/rajya-sabha.htm?dtl/28234/question+no2428+agreement+for+protection+of+indian+workers+in+ saudi+arabia

9

UAE

Md. Muddassir Quamar

Key Information

Political System: Federation of seven Emirates ruled by different families; **Ruling Family**: Dubai (al-Maktoum); Abu Dhabi (al-Nahyan); Sharjah (al-Qasimi); Ras al-Khaima (al-Qasimi); Ajman (al-Nuaimi); Fujaira (al-Sharqi); and Umm al-Qaiwan (al-Mu'alla); **President:** Khalifa bin Zayed al-Nahyan (since 3 November 2004); **Prime Minister and Vice President:** Mohammed bin Rashid al-Maktoum (since 11 February 2006); **National Day:** 2 December; **Parliament**: 40-member partially elected Federal National Council; **Last Parliamentary Election**: 3 October 2015; **Major group in parliament:** NA; **National Carrier:** Emirates (Dubai); Etihad Airways (Abu Dhabi).

Socio-Economic Indicators

Area: 83,600 sq km; **Population:** 5.92 million; **Native:** 19 per cent; **Expats:** 81 per cent; **Religious Groups:** Citizens (Sunni 85 per cent; Shia 15 per cent); Residents (Muslim 76 per cent; Christian 9 per cent; Hindu and Buddhist 10 per cent; and Other 5 per cent); **Youth:** 13.53 per cent; **Population growth rate:** 2.47 per cent; **Life expectancy at birth:** 77.5 years; **Major population groups**: Emirati 19 per cent; other Arabs and Iranians 23 per cent; South Asian 50 per cent; European and East Asian 8 per cent; **Literacy rate:** 93.8 per cent; **National Currency**: Emirati Dirham (AED); **GDP:** US$ 375 billion; **Foreign Trade:** US$ 562.9 billion; **Defence budget:** 5.5 per cent of GDP (2011); **Sovereign Wealth Fund:** US$ 792 billion; **External Debt**: US$ 220.4 billion;

Per capita income: US$ 67,700; **Oil reserves:** 98 billion bbl; **Gas reserves:** 6.091 trillion m^3; **HDI rank:** 41; **Infant Mortality Rate**: 10.3 deaths/1,000 live birth; **UN Education Index:** 0.673; **Gender Inequality Index:** 0.232; **Labour Force:** 5.242 million; **Unemployment rate**: 2.4 per cent (2001 est.); **Urban Population:** 85.5 per cent; **Rate of Urbanization:** 2.87 per cent; **Last National Census**: 2005.

India Related

Indian Cultural Centre: Abu Dhabi (Inaugurated in 2009); **Number of Indians:** 2.8 million; **Number of places of worship for Indians**: Two Temples; One Gurudwara; 35 Churches; **Indian Schools:** 60; **Indian Banks:** State Bank of India (1); Bank of Baroda (7); Union Bank of India (1); Punjab National Bank (1); IDBI Bank (1); ICICI Bank (1); Yes Bank (1); HDFC; Indian Overseas Bank; **Currency exchange rate:** 1 AED = INR 17.47 (May 2017); **Last visit to India by the ruler**: Crown Prince Muhammad bin Zayed, January 2017; **Last Indian Prime Minister to visit**: Narendra Modi, August 2015.

* * *

Indo-UAE relations have witnessed a significant momentum since the August 2015 visit of Prime Minister Narendra Modi to the Emirate. Though bilateral relations have been robust even earlier, Prime Minister Modi's visit and the subsequent strings of engagements, including the participation of the Crown Prince of Abu Dhabi Muhammed bin Zayed al-Nahyan as the chief guest for the Republic Day celebrations in January 2017, have added the missing spark needed to build a strategic partnership. The Comprehensive Strategic Partnership (CSP) that was signed during the January visit is a step in that direction. Both countries have a common view of maintaining peace and security in the Middle East and South Asia, and see each other as stabilising players in the respective regions. The UAE's economic stability, cultural adaptability, and strategic significance are attractive for India; and India's strategic, economic, and civilizational depths amidst growing global standing adds to its historical significance for the Gulf and the UAE. An important aspect of bilateral relations is the mutual commitment towards peace, multiculturalism, and economic possibilities.

Domestic Developments

Political stability, economic prosperity, and cosmopolitanism define the UAE which is a federation of seven Emirates—Abu Dhabi, Ajman, Dubai, Fujairah, Ras al-Khaimah, Sharjah and Umm al-Qaiwan—that united in 1971 after independence from Britain.[1] When popular protests engulfed the Arab world in 2011–12, the UAE also witnessed some demonstrations and petitions; however, the situation did not escalate as the government moved swiftly to placate the anger and acted decisively to arrest those considered troublemakers, especially with Islamists leanings. Additionally, the government focused on education and economy to alleviate concerns about youth unemployment, a common cause of protests in most Arab countries. In the political arena, the Electoral College for the Federal National Council (FNC) was expanded nearly 20 times to include 129,274 citizens for the September 2011 elections.

The FNC, a 40-member partially elected advisory body, provides an opportunity for Emirati citizens to participate in the political process; however, it has a limited role in decision making. Until 2006, it was a fully nominated body; reforms introduced the idea of having 50 per cent of the members elected through an Electoral College. Amidst regional unrest, elections being were held in September 2011 with an expanded Electoral College; but a low turnout of 27 per cent raised serious questions about the credibility of the electoral process. The third election to the FNC was held in October 2015 when the Electoral College was expanded to 224,279. The turnout improved to 35 per cent, with one woman and 19 men elected. In an important change, voters were allowed to vote for only one candidate in his/her Emirate—previously they had the option of voting for half the number of representatives from each Emirate. Since political parties are not allowed, all candidates ran as independents. The campaigns revolved around local issues of job creation, better housing, and the improvement of health services. On 18 November 2015, the 16th FNC was convened, with 20 nominated and 20 elected members, with 31 men and nine women. For the first time in Emirati history, a woman, Amal al-Qubaisi, was elected as chair of the FNC. First elected to the FNC in 2006, Qubaisi also became the first woman to chair an Arab parliament.[2]

Political reforms in the UAE have been slow, and despite some changes in the process for FNC elections, the country remains a constitutional monarchy with a presidential system. According to the 1971 Constitution, the President has to be elected by the Federal Supreme Council that comprises of the ruler of each Emirate; it also appoints a Council of Ministers headed by a Prime Minister. By convention, however, the rulers of Abu Dhabi and Dubai serve as President and Prime Minister respectively, with a government largely comprising of technocrats. Demands for change, the formation of a fully elected executive body, and legislative rights for the FNC have surfaced from time to time; but the ruling families have been lukewarm to such demands, and have rejected electoral democracy as being against the historical and social fabric of the Emirates.[3]

Activists demanding democratic reforms have been detained, and at times slapped, with seditious charges. Social media has provided some room for public debate; but after the Arab Spring, the government has become extremely sensitive to social media activism. In one such incident (in March 2017), a prominent human rights activist, Ahmed Mansoor, was arrested for spreading "sectarianism and hatred on social media."[4] The human rights record of the UAE has come in for serious criticism as voices of dissent have been stifled, and the government has taken strong measures against Islamist leaning activists. A 2014 Amnesty International report alleged that the UAE has jailed activists demanding greater accountability without trial.[5]

One of the reasons for such allegations is a zero-tolerance approach towards any form of Islamist activism. The UAE has emerged as a major player in the Gulf and the Middle East for being against Islamists, and for countering growing Iranian influence. Along with Saudi Arabia, it supported the removal of President Mohammed Morsi in Egypt, and provided aid to the Abdel Fattah el-Sisi to consolidate power. It has been a major component of the Islamic military coalition formed by Saudi Arabia to fight terror in the region. In an important move, it actively participated in the Saudi-led war in Yemen to restore the government headed by President Abdrabbuh Mansur Hadi that was dislodged by the Houthi rebels, who have been provided moral and material support by Iran.

The situation in Yemen started to take a new shape when the Houthi rebels swiftly captured the capital city of Sana'a in late 2014, and declared the formation of a new government to replace the Hadi government in January 2015. With the failure of talks to restore the previous dispensation that Saudi Arabia and GCC support, Saudi Arabia launched *Operation Decisive Storm* in March 2015. Though the military intervention prevented the consolidation of Houthis, it has failed to restore the Hadi government, resulting in a deteriorating humanitarian situation with a huge loss of life and destruction. Both the UAE and Saudi Arabia have met with criticism, and have also lost a large number of soldiers due to Houthi counter attacks leading to serious repercussions at home. Resultantly, in June 2016, the UAE formally announced that it had achieved its goals in Yemen, and that its participation in the war was over. This was seen as a reaction to the killing of 45 Emirati soldiers in a Houthi launched missile attack on 5 September 2015 ... and mounting casualties.[6]

Due to the drop in oil prices, the GDP growth of the UAE has been sliding—from 4.6 per cent in 2014 down to 3.4 per cent in 2015—and is expected to come down further to 2.5 per cent during 2016-17.[7] Nevertheless, with investments in financial sector and growth in airline and tourism sectors, the UAE was able to tide over revenue losses from oil sector. It has also been able to achieve some success in diverting oil revenues to develop the non-oil sectors. The Emirati rulers have invested significantly in optimising oil production capacity, and are investing heavily in capacity building in renewable energy to be able to maximise oil exports.[8] With astute fiscal management and the proposal to implement VAT from 2018, the government aims to minimise dependence on oil exports.[9] It is also investing heavily in human resource development and creating a knowledge-based economy to adjust to changing market needs. Overall, the economic situation has started to recover from the recession and the adverse impact of falling oil prices.

Bilateral Relations

The Gulf countries figure prominently in Prime Minister Narendra Modi's diplomatic efforts to bring foreign investments in India and revitalise its economic growth. The Gulf has attracted the necessary attention with it economic potential and existing commercial and trade relations. Since coming to power in May 2014, Modi has invested diplomatic energy in revitalising Indo-Gulf relations. He visited the UAE (August 2015) as well as other countries along the Persian Gulf. With the UAE, the relations have hit a high point with Prime Minister Modi and Crown Prince al-Nahyan bonding personally; this resulted in India hosting the latter as chief guest for the Republic Day celebrations. Indeed, the Crown Prince visited New Delhi twice within a span of a year (February 2016 and January 2017).

Political Relations

Political engagements with the UAE have increased since the Bharatiya Janata party-led National Democratic Alliance (NDA) government came to power in May 2014. External Affairs Minister, Sushma Swaraj, visited the UAE in November 2014, paving the way for the first visit by an Indian prime minister since the May 1981 visit by Indira Gandhi. The historic visit by Prime Minister Modi in August 2015 changed the contours of bilateral relations as the two countries agreed to take the ties beyond trade and commerce, and elevate the Indo-UAE relations to a Comprehensive Strategic Partnership. The joint statement issued during the visit noted the need for a close strategic partnership, pointing that "[geographical] [p]roximity, history, cultural affinity, strong links between people, natural synergies, shared aspirations and common challenges create boundless potential for a natural strategic partnership between India and UAE."[10] The two leaders further confided that

> ...in the past, relations between the two governments have not kept pace with the exponential growth in relations between their people or the promise of this partnership. However, the need for a close strategic partnership between UAE and India has never been stronger or more urgent, and its prospects more rewarding, than in these uncertain times.[11]

The visit paved the way for a string of high level exchanges, with the heir to the Emirati throne visiting New Delhi in February 2016. The visit was significant as it provided momentum to reinvigorating political engagements, and underlined the need for enhancing economic ties and security cooperation. The joint statement issued during the visit underlined Indian efforts to improve ease of doing business, and measures taken to iron out problem areas for investment in the growing Indian market. It further noted the possibilities for Emirati investment in the manufacturing and infrastructure projects as well as the newly launched Digital India and Start up India programmes.[12] The two sides signed nine MoUs/agreements for cooperation in various areas, including cyber space and cyber security, renewable energy, and space research.[13]

The Crown Prince's visit was preceded by the visit of UAE Foreign Minister, Abdullah bin Zayed Al Nahyan, for the 11th Joint Commission Meeting held in September 2015, and a visit by India's Minister of State for External Affairs, V. K. Singh, for the High Level Task Force on Investment (HLTFI) in November. The February 2016 visit of the Crown Prince was followed by the first ever visit of an Indian Defence Minister to UAE in May 2016. During the visit of Manohar Parrikar, both sides pledged to "bolster security ties and explore the potential of trade in military equipment."[14]

Other visits from the Indian side include those of Finance Minister Arun Jaitley (November 2015), and Minister of State in-charge for petroleum and Natural Gas Dharmendra Pradhan (April 2016). The high point of political engagement came in January 2017 when the Crown Prince and Deputy Commander of the UAE Armed Forces returned to India as chief guest for the Republic Day celebrations. The visit reflected the consolidation of bilateral ties, and the significance the two sides attach to elevating the bilateral relations to the next level. The visit also signifies the importance India attaches to the UAE, and underlined the commitment between the two countries to enhance economic engagement through investment, and to deepen security cooperation to counter terror and combat radicalisation.[15]

The depth of strategic relations can be understood from the fact that the Emirati leadership was quick to condemn the Pathankot (January 2016)[16] and Uri (September 2016)[17] attacks. The joint statement issued during the January 2017 visit of the Crown Prince noted the problems India is facing due to cross-border and state sponsored terrorism.[18]

Economic Relations

India and the UAE share strong and robust economic relations that form the back bone of the bilateral ties. The UAE is India's third largest trading partner, the second largest export destination, and the fourth biggest source for imports. For the UAE, India is the second largest trading partner, the second largest export destination, and the third biggest source of imports. However, the volume of trade has declined from a high of US$ 75.4 billion in 2012–13 to US$ 49.7 billion in 2015–16 owing to low oil prices and an overall slowdown in global trade (see Table 9.1). Both countries are aware of the potential to increase bilateral trade. Hence, during Prime Minister Modi's visit to the UAE, they agreed to expand trade by 60 per cent in the next five years.[19] They also agreed to establish a US$ 75 billion UAE-India Infrastructure Investment Fund (UIIIF) to boost "investment in India's plans for rapid expansion of next generation infrastructure, especially in railways, ports, roads, airports, industrial corridors and parks."[20]

Both leaders also agreed to establish a joint India-UAE Business Forum (IUBF) that was jointly inaugurated by the Indian External Affairs Minister Sushma Swaraj and the UAE Foreign Minister Abdullah bin Zayed in September 2015. Speaking on the occasion, Emirati Minister of State, Reem al-Hashemi, said that bilateral trade has a potential to double within the next few years.[21] She also pointed out that, with 1,000 flights per week between the two countries, it is evident that people-to-people contacts are intense, commercial ties are robust, and the "leadership is committed to [taking] the bilateral relationship to a new level."[22]

Table 9.1: India-UAE Bilateral Trade (in US$ Million)

	2011–12	2012–13	2013–14	2014–15	201516
Exports	35,925.52	36,316.65	30,520.42	33,028.08	30,290.01
Imports	36,756.32	39,138.36	29,019.82	26,139.91	19,445.68
Total Trade	72,681.84	75,455.01	59,540.24	59,167.99	49,735.69
Share	9.14	9.54	7.79	7.80	7.73

Source: Adapted from Director General of Foreign Trade, New Delhi, at www.dgft.gov.in

Figure 9.1: India-UAE Bilateral Trade (in US$ Million)

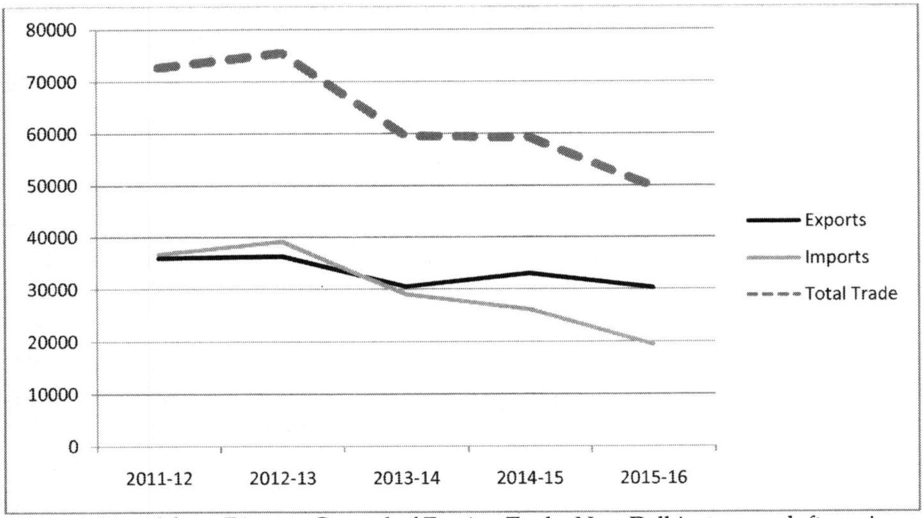

Source: Adapted from Director General of Foreign Trade, New Delhi, at www.dgft.gov.in

In 2015–16, India exported nearly US$ 30 billion worth of goods to the UAE and imported goods worth US$ 19 billion (see Table 9.1). The trade balance is in India's favour, and the bilateral trade basket is quite diversified with India exporting jewellery, heavy machinery, petroleum products, textiles, as well as food and dairy products, while importing crude oil, precious stones and pearls, plastic, iron, copper, aluminium, and animal products.[23] In October 2016, the second meeting of IUBF was held in Dubai, and was led by Minister of State for External Affairs, M. J. Akbar, from the Indian side. During his remarks, he said that India and UAE are keen to achieve the target of US$ 75 billion investments, and that the FDI inflow in India has witnessed an increase in the last two years.[24]

Energy

Despite India's efforts to diversify its energy basket, the UAE continues to play an important role in its energy security, and supplied nearly 8 per cent of its energy needs in 2015–16 (see Table 9. 2). It is India's fifth largest supplier of oil and gas; but as is evident from Table 9.2, oil contributes only 40 per cent of total imports, signifying the diversification in the goods that India imports from the UAE. The decline in the volume of energy trade between India and the UAE is mainly due to lower oil prices that had touched a high of US$ 140 per barrel in June 2014 but witnessed a sharp fall subsequently, to touch a bottom of US$ 30 per barrel in mid-2016. As of early 2017, it has consolidated to reach US$ 50 per barrel. While oil prices have stabilised, India is keen to improve its energy security, and the UAE has responded positively by agreeing to store oil in India's strategic storage facilities.

Table 9.2: Share of Oil in India's Imports from UAE (in US$ million)

Year	Oil Imports from UAE	Total Oil Imports	UAE Share in Total Oil Imports	Imports from UAE	Per cent of Oil in Imports from UAE
2011–12	15,102.54	172,753.92	8.74	36.756.32	40.79
2012–13	14,984.64	181,344.67	8.26	39,138.36	38.29
2013–14	13,263.35	181,382.59	7.31	29,019.82	45.70
2014–15	13,509.04	156,400.01	8.64	26,139.91	51.68
2015-16	7,912.80	96,953.06	8.16	19,445.68	40.69

Source: Adapted from Director General of Foreign Trade, New Delhi, at www.dgft.gov.in

Figure 9.2: Share of Oil in India's Imports from UAE

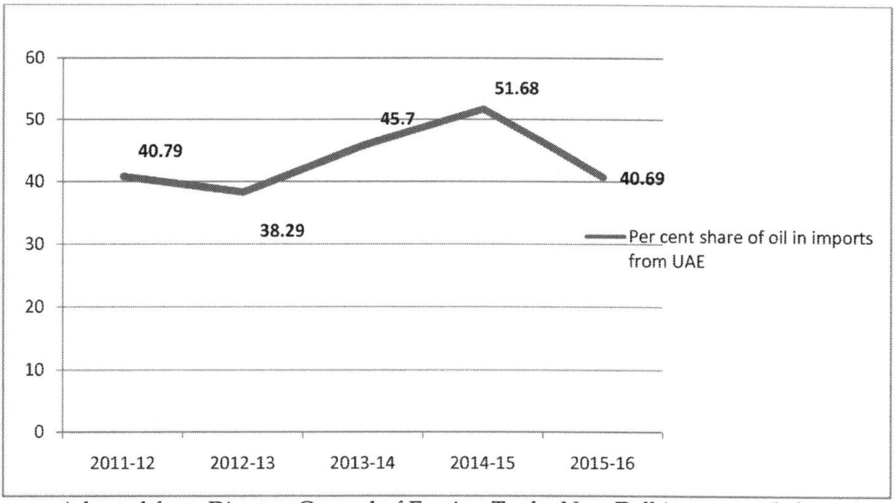

Source: Adapted from Director-General of Foreign Trade, New Delhi, at www.dgft.gov.in

Energy is an important component in bilateral trade relations, and the UAE supplies nearly 15 per cent of India's energy imports from the Persian Gulf that supplies nearly 60 per cent of India's total energy imports, and is a vital cog in its energy security (see Table 9.3). India imports less oil from the UAE than from other countries such as Saudi Arabia, Iraq and Iran; but there are immense possibilities to further enhance energy cooperation. During the visit of the Crown Prince in February 2016, India and UAE signed a strategic deal to store UAE's crude oil in India, of which two-thirds would be available to India for free.[25] It is part of India's quest to build "emergency underground storage of 36.87 million barrels of crude oil which can supply about 10 days of the country's average daily oil demand."[26] This is likely to significantly advance India-UAE energy ties. According to the deal, the Abu Dhabi National Oil Company (ADNOC) agreed to store about 6 million barrels of crude oil in India's maiden strategic storage facility at Mangalore. It will also lead to a significant increase in India's oil imports from the UAE. According to media reports, in 2017, India's total oil imports from UAE can reach up to 2.5 million tons against the 1.6 million tons in 2016.[27]

Table 9.3: India's Energy Imports from UAE (in US$ million)

	2011–12	2012-13	2013–14	2014–15	2015–16
Energy Imports from UAE	15,102.54	14,984.64	13,263.35	13,509.04	7,912.80
Total Energy Imports	172,753.92	181,344.67	181,382.59	156,400.01	96,953.06
Energy Imports from Persian Gulf	105,056.26	105,859.15	106,400.75	85,300.30	50,992.26
Share in Total Energy Imports (in per cent)	8.74	8.26	7.31	8.64	8.16
Share in Energy Imports from Persian Gulf (in per cent)	14.38	14.16	12.47	15.84	15.52

Source: Adapted from Director-General of Foreign Trade, New Delhi, at www.dgft.gov.in

Figure 9.3: Share of UAE in Energy Imports from Persian Gulf

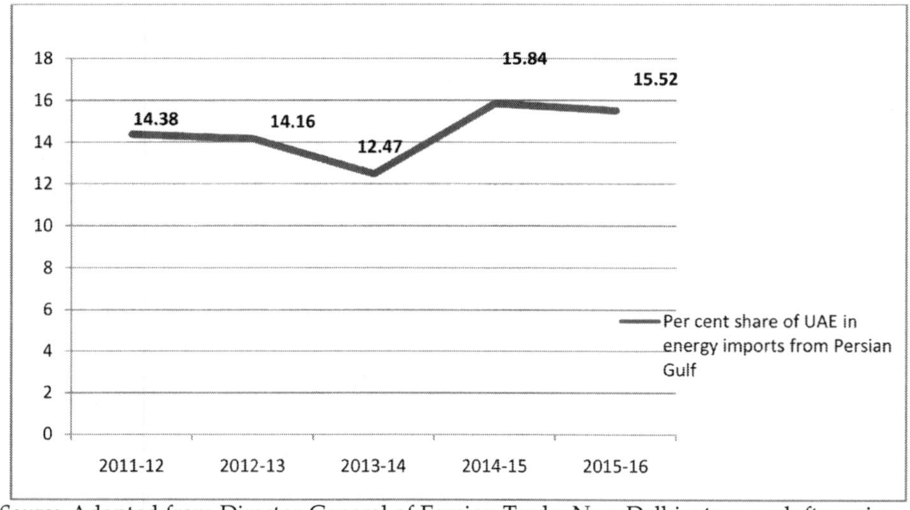

Source: Adapted from Director-General of Foreign Trade, New Delhi, at www.dgft.gov.in

Investment

As India looks to enhance FDI inflows and inject capital in the manufacturing and infrastructure sectors, the UAE acquires a key position. During the visit of Prime Minister Modi, the two sides agreed to establish a US$ 75 billion

UAE-India Infrastructure Investment Fund. The India-UAE HLTFI has held several meetings since September 2015 to discuss and finalise the modalities of the investment fund. According to media reports, the final agreement on the US$ 75 billion fund was to be signed during the visit of the Crown Prince in January 2017, but was delayed due to uncertainties on modalities to utilize the funds on India's part. However, it is expected to be signed in the coming months.[28] Notwithstanding the delay, both countries are committed to bringing more FDIs in India. Indeed, India has been taking steps to iron out problems faced by foreign investors due to bureaucratic bottlenecks, multiple clearances, time span for investment realisation, and corruption. In his remarks during the IUBF in October 2016, Minister of State for External Affairs, M. J. Akbar, said that India is committed to action oriented policy measures to alter the vicious circle of red tape that slows down FDIs and discourages foreign investors.[29]

In the past five years, India has witnessed an overall increase in FDI inflows, and the UAE has emerged as one of the leading sources. The overall FDI inflow has grown by 36 per cent to reach US$ 40 billion in 2015–16. Between April 2000 and September 2016, India received a cumulative investment of US$ 4.3 billion from the UAE, thus becoming the 10th largest source for FDIs in India.[30] Moreover, there has been a three-fold increase in FDI inflow from the UAE: from US$ 350 million in 2013–14 to US$ 1 billion in 2015–16, thus being the fifth largest investment source for India during the period.[31] In a media interview, the Indian Ambassador to the UAE, Navdeep Singh Suri said, "We hope that we can encourage some of the top companies in the UAE to either undertake investments or expand their investments in India, in real estate or petrochemicals." He was expressing the sentiments of the Indian government that is keen on investment from the Gulf States on its key development projects.[32]

While India is keen to attract foreign investment, especially from the UAE, Indian businesses too have invested in various sectors in the UAE. They have established a strong Indian footprint in the Emirati market. More than 800 leading Indian companies have opened their businesses in the Jebel Ali Free Zone (JAFZA), and many Indian business houses have a strong presence in Dubai and Abu Dhabi. Further opportunities are opening up as the UAE is looking to diversify its economy, strengthen its financial and service sectors, and establish the Emirates as a global tourism and sports hub.

Defence Cooperation

India and the UAE have bolstered their security and defence cooperation in recent years. Areas such as preventing terror finance, combating terrorism, counter radicalisation, intelligence sharing, and cyber security have emerged as priorities given the tumultuous situation in the Middle East, and the threat from terrorism and radicalisation. Regional security and international terrorism have emerged as mutual concerns. Thus, during the visit of the Crown Prince in January 2017, the two sides "agreed to coordinate efforts to counter radicalisation."[33] Given the threats emanating from regional turmoil, sectarian tensions, and global terrorism, India views the UAE as a partner in maintaining peace and stability in the Middle East and South Asia. India has been grappling with problem of online radicalisation, and even though it has not acquired humungous proportions yet, the need for preventing this phenomenon cannot be underestimated. Given the domestic fault lines, security and intelligence cooperation with Gulf countries is important to combat terrorism and to counter radicalisation.

Additionally, India and the UAE are keen to enhance defence cooperation to ensure maritime security and neutralise terrorist threats. A key development in this context was the visit of Defence Minister Manohar Parrikar to the UAE in May 2016 to discuss the strengthening of military-to-military ties, and to explore the possibilities for joint defence manufacturing and selling Indian military equipment to the UAE.[34] Military ties are growing and the two armies, navies, and air force have been engaging in joint exercises. In February 2016, the two sides agreed to boost cooperation in the defence sector through joint training and exercises.[35] In May-June 2016, a ten-day joint air combat exercise was held between the two air forces.[36] Indian Naval ships have regularly visited the Gulf coast and making port call in Abu Dhabi. Maritime security is also an important area, and both sides agreed to "enhance cooperation to strengthen maritime security in the Gulf and the Indian Ocean region," which "is vital for the security and prosperity of both countries."[37] India also announced that it is willing to extend assistance to the UAE to achieve its Mars Mission in 2020.[38]

Cultural Relations

India has deep cultural relations with countries in the Gulf. Indians have a special affinity with the UAE due to its cosmopolitan culture and diversity. In fact, cultural affinity plays an important role in the flourishing of the bilateral ties. India sees the Emirates as a diverse and multicultural place that allows religious freedom. Dubai has a Gurudwara and a Hindu temple and, during the visit of Prime Minister Modi, the ruling family of Abu Dhabi donated land for building a Hindu temple, and the foundation-laying ceremony was attended by the Prime Minister.[39] Indian festivals such as Diwali are widely celebrated by the vast Indian community in the UAE.[40]

Indian cuisine, cinema as well as art and literature are popular in the UAE, not only among expatriates but also among the Emiratis.

In addition, the Indian embassy in Abu Dhabi organises cultural activities while also encouraging and assisting Indian cultural associations in organising such activities to promote Indian culture. For example, the Indian Embassy hosted a Bhangra group in May 2016 and organised the first International Day of Yoga on 21 June 2015. Indian dance and song troupes regularly perform in Dubai and other Emirati cities, while art and painting exhibitions are also organised. The large Indian community of approximately 2.8 million has been a source of promotion of Indian culture, food habits, and even languages that strengthen bonds between India and the UAE. According to the Organisation of Economic Cooperation and Development (OECD) report, India-UAE is world's second largest migration corridor, with 2.8 million Indians migrating to UAE between 1995 and 2015.[41] Moreover, India as the world's highest recipient of remittances[42] receives almost 50 per cent of its total remittances from the GCC countries; and, among the GCC the highest amount—nearly 38 per cent—comes from the UAE.[43]

Domestic and unskilled Indians workers sometimes face adverse situations, and it is often difficult for them to find redress for their concerns. There have been instances when unskilled workers have faced exploitation due to the sponsorship system or *kafala*. India has been raising the issue at various forums with the UAE government that has taken measures to streamline local laws and create awareness about rights of workers. During his visit, Prime Minister Modi interacted with Indian workers, visited their camps, and stressed that the government would raise their issues at appropriate forums. The two government are working together to evolve transparent and open processes for recruitment and grievance redressal to avoid the exploitation of workers.[44]

Challenges

While the problem of missing political contacts has been addressed in the last two years, the challenge is to deliver on the promises. Undoubtedly, both India and UAE want to elevate their relationship to a strategic partnership, and have developed close security contacts. They also wish to develop their defence cooperation to the level of close military contact, exchange of personnel for training and research, and joint defence manufacturing. To achieve these objectives, India would require a persistent approach and follow up on issues that have been discussed and promised. It would also have to tread a fine line in keeping away from regional tensions to avoid derailing bilateral ties.

Another important area where Indo-UAE relations hold huge potential is investment. India is yet to finalise the US$ 75 billion investment fund deal that was first announced in August 2015. It could not be signed during the January 2017 visit of the Crown Prince of Abu Dhabi as India had not yet finalised the modalities. The UAE's Ambassador to India, Ahmed al-Banna, is reported to have said, "the ball is in the court of [the] Indian side to finalize the governance" for setting up the infrastructure investment fund and that the UAE side is "ready for it."[45] This is a classic example of the infamous slow and inefficient Indian follow up on important policy projects that have, in the past, cost it the inflow of foreign investment. While the UAE is keen to finalise the deal and kick-start investment in key projects, it is important that the Indian side streamlines the processes needed to attract these investments.

To ensure the continuous flow of investment from the UAE and other Gulf countries, India would not only require tying up the loose ends and streamlining structural problems but would also need to ensure that foreign investors are not caught in court cases due to third party corruption. In the past, this has prevented Emirati investors from investing in India because of the problems faced by Etisalat and Etihad in implementing projects.[46] Similarly, India would also need to ensure that efficient and skilled human resources are available, as the Gulf investors can bring financial resources but lack technical expertise. On the other hand, Indian business too have faced hurdles in investing in the UAE market due to the lack of clarity in commercial regulations, complicated local laws, and the lack of transparency in labour laws that prevent the full realisation of the potential for Indian investment. Bilateral trade has witnessed a slide, and India would have to look for non-energy sectors to deliver on the promise of increasing trade by 60 per cent in the next five years. Problems faced by migrant workers due to labour laws favouring local employees also need to be addressed in appropriate forums.

Conclusion

India has good relations with all the countries in the Gulf. However, its relationship with the UAE is unique, and indeed most encouraging. This is because of the significant commonalities and complementarities, and similarity in their world views. As India seeks to enhance its engagements with the Middle East and attract investments, improve trade, and develop close defence cooperation, it finds a willing partner in the UAE. The Emirates has emerged as a regional business and financial hub, and if India wishes to harness the potential for trade and commerce in the Middle East, excellent relations with the UAE are indispensable. At the same time, in the fight against global terrorism and countering radicalism, the UAE (along with other countries in the Gulf) is an important partner for India. Indo-UAE relations have gained the required momentum in the last two years with enhanced political engagement, the promise for growth in commercial relations and defence cooperation are also poised to move in a strategic direction.

NOTES

1. Ras al-Khaimah joined later in 1972.
2. Ayesha Al Khoori and Haneen Dajani, "Dr Amal Al Qubaisi becomes Region's First Female Leader of a National Assembly", *The National*, 18 November 2015, at http://www.thenational.ae/uae/dr-amal-al-qubaisi-becomes-regions-first-female-leader-of-a-national-assembly.
3. Anwar Gargash, "Amid challenges, UAE policies engage gradual reforms", *The National*, 26 August 2012, at http://www.thenational.ae/thenationalconversation/comment/amid-challenges-uae-policies-engage-gradual-reforms
4. "UAE Arrests Prominent Activist for Incitement – State News", *Reuters*, 21 March 2017, at http://in.reuters.com/article/emirates-activist-idINKBN16S0O4
5. "There is no Freedom Here: Silencing Dissent in the United Arab Emirates (UAE)," Amnesty International, 17 November 2014, http://www.amnestyusa.org/sites/default/files/mde_250182014.pdf
6. "Scores of Gulf Troops Killed in Yemen Conflict", *Al-Jazeera*, 5 September 2015, at http://www.aljazeera.com/news/2015/09/uae-emirati-soldiers-killed-yemen-150904101726433.html
7. "United Arab Emirates Economic Outlook: Spring 2016", MENA Economic Monitor Report: Spring 2016, The World Bank, at http://pubdocs.worldbank.org/en/141211460471550773/UAE-MEM-eng.pdf.
8. "United Arab Emirates to Invest $163bn in Renewables", *BBC News*, 10 January 2017, at http://www.bbc.com/news/world-middle-east-38575244
9. Babu Das Augustine, "UAE to Implement 5 per cent VAT from January 2018", *Gulf News*, 24 February 2016, at http://gulfnews.com/news/uae/government/uae-to-implement-5-per-cent-vat-from-january-2018-1.1678703
10. "Joint Statement between the United Arab Emirates and the Republic of India", Ministry of External Affairs, Government of India [MEA, GoI], 17 August 2015, at http://www.mea.gov.in/bilateral-documents.htm?dtl/25733/Joint_Statement_between_the_United_Arab_Emirates_and_the_Republic_of_India
11. Ibid.
12. "India-UAE Joint Statement during the State Visit of Crown Prince of Abu Dhabi", MEA, GoI, 12 February 2016, at http://www.mea.gov.in/bilateral-documents.htm?dtl/26349/India_UAE_Joint_Statement_during_the_State_ Visit_of_ Crown _Prince_of_Abu_Dhabi
13. Ibid.
14. Samanth Subramanian, "UAE and India set to Forge Closer Trade and Military Relations", *The National*, 17 May 2016, at http://www.thenational.ae/world/south-asia/uae-and-india-set-to-forge-closer-trade-and-military-ties.

15. Meena Singh Roy and Md. Muddassir Quamar, "India-UAE Relations: New Dimension to Strategic Partnership", *Issue Brief*, 17 February 2017, at http://www.idsa.in/system/files/issuebrief/ib_india-uae-relations_msroy_170217.pdf
16. "UAE Condemns Indian Air Force Base Terror Attack", *Khaleej Times*, 6 January 2016, at http://www.khaleejtimes.com/nation/government/uae-condemns-indian-air-force-base-terror-attack.
17. UAE Condemns Terror Attack on Indian Army Base", *Khaleej Times*, "18 September 2016, at http://www.khaleejtimes.com/20160918/3713/no-title.cc
18. Roy and Quamar, "India-UAE Relations", op. cit.
19. MEA, GoI, "Joint Statement...", 17 August 2015.
20. Ibid.
21. "India, UAE Set Up Joint Business Council", *Gulf News*, 4 September 2015, at http://gulfnews.com/business/economy/india-uae-set-up-joint-business-council-1.1578273
22. Ibid.
23. Director General for Foreign Trade, Ministry of Commerce and Industry, Government of India, "Export-Import Data Bank", at www.dgft.gov.in.
24. "Remarks by M. J. Akbar, Minister of State for External Affairs at India-UAE Business Forum, Dubai (October 20, 2016)", Ministry of External Affairs, Government of India, 20 October 2016, at http://mea.gov.in/Speeches; see also, Statements.htm?dtl/27519/Remarks_by_M_J_Akbar_Minister_of_State_for_External_ Affairs_at_IndiaUAE_Business_Forum_Dubai_October_20_2016.
25. "Store Our Oil and Take 2/3rd for Free: UAE's Offer to India", *Hindustan Times*, 11 February 2016, at http://www.hindustantimes.com/business/store-our-oil-and-take-2-3rd-for-free-uae-s-offer-to-india/story-fiSZwbJh6abWWM3Nfp EveI.html
26. "India-UAE Strategic Oil Reserve Deal: 10 Things to Know", *The Times of India*, 26 January 2017, at http://timesofindia.indiatimes.com/business/india-business/india-uae-strategic-oil-reserves-deal-10-things-to-know/listshow/56793334.cms.
27. Ibid.
28. Archis Mohan, "UAE Says Ball in India's Court to Set up $75 billion Investment Fund", *Business Standard*, 24 January 2017, at http://www.business-standard.com/article/economy-policy/uae-says-ball-in-india-s-court-to-set-up-75-billion-investment-fund-117012301042_1.html
29. "Remarks by M. J. Akbar...", MEA, GoI, 20 October 2016 op. cit.
30. "Factsheet on Foreign Direct Investment", Department of Industrial Policy and Promotion, Ministry of Commerce and Industry, Government of India [DIPP, GoI], April 2000 to September 2016, at http://dipp.nic.in/English/Publications/FDI_Statistics/2016/FDI_FactSheet_April_Sep_2016.pdf
31. Ibid.
32. "India, UAE Set to Upgrade Ties to Comprehensive Strategic Partnership", *The Economic Times*, January 13, 2017, at http://economictimes.indiatimes.com/news/defence/india-uae-set-to-upgrade-ties-to-comprehensive-strategic-partnership/articleshow/56525965.cms
33. "India-UAE Joint Statement during State Visit of Crown Prince of Abu Dhabi to India (January 24-26, 2017)", MEA, GoI, 26 January 2017, at https://www.mea.gov.in/bilateral-documents.htm?dtl/27969/India__UAE_Joint_Statement_during_State_visit_of_Crown_Prince_of_Abu_Dhabi_to_India_January_2426_2017

34. Sushant Singh, "Parrikar's UAE Visit to Focus on Widening Defence Relationship, Supply of Military Equipment", *Indian Express*, 16 May 2016, at http://indianexpress.com/article/india/india-news-india/parrikars-uae-visit-to-focus-on-widening-defence-relationship-supply-of-military-equipment/
35. "India-UAE Joint Statement...", MEA, GoI, 12 February 2016 op. cit.
36. "IAF Participation in Ex Desert Eagle – II at UAE", Press Information Bureau, Government of India, Ministry of Defence, 27 May 2016, http://pib.nic.in/newsite/PrintRelease.aspx?relid=145749
37. "India-UAE Joint Statement...", MEA, GoI, 12 February 2016 op. cit.
38. "Government Approves MoU between ISRO and the UAE Space Agency", *The Economic Times*, 25 May 2016, http://economictimes.indiatimes.com/news/economy/policy/government-approves-mou-between-isro-and-the-uae-space-agency/articleshow/52434197.cms
39. "UAE Allots Land for Temple on PM Narendra Modi's Visit", *The Economic Times*, 16 August 2015, http://economictimes.indiatimes.com/news/politics-and-nation/uae-allots-land-for-temple-on-pm-narendra-modis-visit/articleshow/48505434.cms
40. Sajila Saseendran, "Diwali in UAE is almost like in India, say Expats", *Gulf News*, 29 October 2016, http://gulfnews.com/news/uae/society/diwali-in-uae-is-almost-like-in-india-say-expats-1.1920570
41. Parag Deulgaonkar, "India-UAE Ranked World's Second Largest Migration Corridor in 2015, Says OECD", *Arabianbusiness.com*, 17 January 2017, http://www.arabianbusiness.com/india-uae-ranked-world-s-second-largest-migration-corridor-in-2015-says-oecd—659681.html
42. "Migration and Development Brief 27", The World Bank, April 2017, http://pubdocs.worldbank.org/en/992371492706371662/MigrationandDevelopmentBrief27.pdf
43. Rebecca Bundhun, "India Suffers Steep Decline in Remittances from GCC Nations", *The National*, 22 May 2016, http://www.thenational.ae/business/economy/india-suffers-steep-decline-in-remittances-from-gcc-nations
44. Anwar Ahmad, "Tighter Employment Rules for Indian Workers in UAE to Curb Crooked Job Agents", *The National*, 7 June 2015, http://www.thenational.ae/uae/tighter-employment-rules-for-indian-workers-in-uae-to-curb-crooked-job-agents.
45. Archis Mohan, "UAE Says Ball in India's Court..." op. cit.
46. While Etisalat eventually left the India market, the Etihad-Jet partnership materialised, and is currently running successfully.

10

YEMEN

Dipanwita Chakravortty

Key Information

Ruling Group/Party: General People's Congress (since 27 April 1993) and Ansar Allah (Houthi movement since 22 January 2015); **President:** Abdrabbuh Mansur Hadi (since 25 February 2012); Mohammed Ali al-Houthi, President of the Revolutionary Committee (since 22 January 2015); **Prime Minister:** Ahmad Obaid Bin Daghir (since 3 April 2016); **National Day:** 22 May; **Parliament**: 111-member nominated Shura Council and 301-member elected House of Representatives; **Last Parliamentary Election**: 27 April 2003; **Major group in parliament**: General People's Congress**; National Carrier:** Yemen Airlines.

Socio-Economic Indicators

Area: 527,968 sq km; **Population:** 27.29 million; **Native:** NA; **Expats:** NA; **Religious Groups:** Muslim 99.1 per cent (Sunni 65 per cent; Shia 35 per cent); Others (Jewish, Bahai, Hindu and Christian) 0.9 per cent; **Youth:** 21.16 per cent; **Population growth rate:** 2.37 per cent; **Life expectancy at birth:** 65.5 years; **Major population groups**: Predominantly Yemeni Arabs; some Afro-Arabs, South Asian, and European; **Literacy rate:** 70.1 per cent; **National Currency**: Yemeni Rial (YER); **GDP:** US$ 31.33 billion; **Foreign Trade:** US$ 127.924 million; **Defence budget:** 4.02 per cent of GDP (2012); **Foreign Reserve:** US$ 639.6 million; **External Debt**: US$ 7.661 billion; **Per capita income:** US$ 2,500; **Oil reserves:** 3 billion bbl; **Gas reserves:** 478.5

billion m^3; **HDI rank:** 160; **Infant Mortality Rate**: 47.4 deaths/1,000 live birth; **UN Education Index:** 0.339; **Gender Inequality Index:** 0.744; **Labour Force:** 7.47 million; **Unemployment rate**: 27 per cent (2014 est.); **Urban Population:** 34.6 per cent; **Rate of Urbanization:** 4.03 per cent; **Last National Census**: 2004.

India Related

Indian Cultural Centre: NA; **Number of Indians:** less than 500; **Number of places of worship for Indians**: A number of Old Hindu Temples in Aden; **Indian Schools:** One; **Indian Banks:** None; **Currency exchange rate:** 1 YER = INR 0.27 (Feb 2017); **Last visit to India by the ruler**: President Ali Abdullah Saleh, March 1999; **Last Indian Prime Minister to visit**: None since 1947.

* * *

Despite having strong historical relations with Yemen, India has not looked at the country with any specific policy or particular interest. Yemen has been relegated as a non-essential component in India's Middle East policy. The past decade has witnessed a lack of substantial bilateral interactions, the steady cancellation of notable investments in Yemen, lack of diversification in trade, and a gradual scaling down of cultural relations. This has been largely attributed to the recurrence of violence in the embattled country. Since 2011, India scaled down its exchanges with Yemen like many other countries, and bilateral trade reached the lowest point in the past five years. Diplomatic relations came to a halt in April 2015, when the Indian embassy in Sana'a was shifted to Djibouti after the successful evacuation of a large number of Indian migrants in Yemen.

Domestic Developments

The winds of political change hit the shores of Yemen in early 2011 when most of the Arab world was fighting with a new wave of popular dissent which became commonly referred to as the Arab Spring. On 3 February 2011, over 20,000 people came on the streets of Sana'a to protest against the rising food prices, unemployment, corruption, and deteriorating economic conditions.[1] Due to the apathy shown by the government, the protests soon turned against President Ali Abdullah Saleh who was compelled to step down on 27 February 2012. To end the crisis, in April 2011, the Gulf Cooperation Council (GCC) proposed an initiative that sought a smooth transition of power from President Ali Abdullah Saleh to Vice President Abdrabbuh Mansur Hadi. According to the initiative, the new President Hadi and his government had two years to implement an inclusive national dialogue that would help in the drafting of a new constitution before fresh elections were held in 2014.[2]

The process of transition of power began in November 2011 when President Ali Abdullah Saleh signed the GCC initiative. However, this was soon followed by a series of uprising and protests that created a situation that swiftly deteriorated into a civil war. The Zaidi-Shia group known as the Houthis, who are concentrated in the north-western part of the country, protested against the transition government as well as the National Dialogue Conference (NDC) which was held from 18 March 2013 to 24 January 2014.[3] At the same time, they were running a parallel government in three important provinces in Northern Yemen, namely Sada'a, Jawf, and Hajjah.[4] They not only had access to military bases but also to the Red Sea through Port Midi through which they carried out independent trade in weapons and petroleum. Flushed with money and weapons, they became crucial partners in the NDC process. However, during the process, the Houthis constantly rejected various proposals by the Hadi government, especially on the question of a Federal State.[5] Soon after the draft of NDC was finalised on 21 January 2014, the Houthis backed out of the process, and denounced all the outcomes. The Houthi spokesperson argued that the NDC had not changed the terms or composition of the current government and security institutions which allowed space for the traditional elite to carve a constitution favourable to their needs and demands.[6]

By August 2014, the Houthis came out in large numbers to protest against the Hadi government and compelled Prime Minister Mohammed Basindawa to resign; they also captured various state institutions simultaneously. They lay a siege on the President's office, forcing him to resign and, on 25 March 2015, Hadi fled to Saudi Arabia. On 21 September, the Houthi rebels captured Sana'a,[7] along with key government buildings and other institutions. On 6 February 2015, a Houthi representative announced from the Presidential Palace that the group had formally taken control of Yemen, and also stated that the House of Representative was dissolved and a presidential council would soon be formed to lead Yemen for the next two years.[8] The UN, which mediated the NDC, refused to acknowledge the announcement; the GCC also condemned the coup.

In retaliation to the coup, on 26 March 2015, Saudi Arabia along with other GCC countries launched a military campaign against Yemen which continued into 2017. The number of civilian deaths cannot be verified; but estimates put the number around 10,500 deaths by air-strikes, and around 3,000 due to collateral damage.[9] The extent of damage to the infrastructure and the economy cannot be quantified. Despite the complete devastation, the Houthis have managed to continue their fight against the coalition comprising of ten Islamic or Muslim majority countries, and maintain their strong hold. Saudi Arabia seems determined to continue its military campaign until it succeeds in re-installing the Hadi government in Sana'a, despite the increasing casualties and the brewing humanitarian crisis.[10] How long the conflict will continue depends on Saudi Arabia as well as on the amount of resources the GCC countries are willing to put into this operation in the current light of fluctuating oil-prices.

Reignited by the unrest in the north, the Southern Movement renewed calls for independence. On 14 October 2014, thousands of people demonstrated in Aden in support of secession and self-determination, and called on the Yemeni government and all military personnel stationed in the south to withdraw by 30 March 2015.[11] Over the following weeks, pro-independence rallies continued. In December 2014, several government buildings in Aden were taken over by the members of the Southern Movement. In the ensuing chaos, Al-Qaeda in the Arabian Peninsula (AQAP) escalated its terrorist attacks in the country, targeting Houthis and government institutions.[12]

In this backdrop, the AQAP managed to expand territories under its control in the southern part of country, and created a mini-state. Even though its leader, Nasir al-Wuhayshi, was killed in an American drone strike on 12 June 2015, the organisation continued to flourish under its new leader, Qasim al-Raymi. In April 2016, a senior Yemeni government official said in an interview that the war against the Houthis

> ... had provided a suitable environment for the ... expansion of al Qaeda. The withdrawal of government army units from their bases in the south, allowed al Qaeda to acquire very large quantities of sophisticated and advanced weapons, including shoulder-fired missiles and armed vehicles.[13]

In early April 2015, a week after *Operation Decisive Storm* headed by Saudi Arabia was announced, most of the Yemeni forces withdrew from the southern provinces, including Mukalla (one of the main sea-ports in the Gulf of Aden), and moved towards the North. The city was left defenceless, which allowed AQAP fighters to capture government buildings and release around 150 of their comrades from prison. They were supported by tribal leaders who aided them by looting army bases in a bid to claim independence from the North. The entire area became awash with advanced weaponry which was given by the US to the Yemeni government to fight the AQAP in the south.[14] They also looted the branch of Mukalla's main bank of an estimated US$ 100 million.[15]

With this swollen war loot, the AQAP established a quasi-state with Mukalla as its capital. The city of Mukalla was important to the AQAP as it provided easy access to sea-trade as well as strong defence. The AQAP abolished taxes for local residents, established Sharia courts,[16] and gained control over the several ports in Mukalla and Ash Shihr where it began to impose tax and custom tariffs on ships and traders. It started operating speedboats controlled by RPG-wielding fighters to impose levies on ship traffic, and earned an estimated amount of US$ 2 million every day on these port taxes.[17] The AQAP also began to run a black market for fuel smuggling. Most of the oil infrastructure came under the control of tribal leaders who were in alliance with the AQAP. According to a Reuters report, "six white oil tanks between Mukalla and Ash Shihr are linked by pipeline to the Masila oilfields which are estimated to hold more than 80 per cent of Yemen's total reserves."[18] This complete control over the oil pipelines prompted major international companies, like PetroMasila, Nexen Energy and Total, to shut down production and exports.

Apart from running an economic empire, the AQAP projected itself as a benevolent ruling organisation. It also refused to pledge allegiance to the Islamic State unlike other Al-Qaeda affiliates as it wanted to portray itself as different from the ISIS. The group routinely posts pictures of its members maintaining and repairing bridges, paving streets, delivering medicines, building hospitals, etc. in Hadramout and other cities under its control.[19]

Thus, since 2014, persistent violence, increased calls for secession, the breakdown of economic infrastructure, and the rise of two power centres in North and South Yemen—controlled by Houthis and AQAP, respectively—have led to a political impasse. As the domestic conflict continues unabated, the political viability of a unified Yemen becomes slimmer. Domestic developments have forced foreign policy and international relations to take a step back. In this light, the bilateral relations between India and Yemen have been seriously affected.

Bilateral Relations

India and Yemen share historical ties that can be dated back to the Roman Empire, and have been involved in trading through sea routes. Yemeni traders came to India to sell horses and weapons in exchange for spices. On the other hand, Indian merchants found Aden as the gateway to the Middle East and Europe.

In 1839, Aden became part of the British Empire, and was administered by the Bombay Presidency. Several families from Aden came and settled in India for economic purposes, most of them in southern India under the aegis of the Nizam of Hyderabad, and decided to stay back even after the independence of India.[20] On the other hand, many Indians belonging to the Bohra, Kachchi, and Khoja communities migrated to Aden during the late 19th century, and gradually became Yemeni citizens.

When India got independence several merchant families, especially from Gujarat, migrated to Yemen as it offered economic opportunities for investment as well as for trade. The strait of Bab-al-Mandab became an important passage for trade, connecting India to the rest of the Middle East and Europe. Once oil was discovered in South Yemen in the late 1950s, Aden became a global port because of increased economic activity. The oil trade sparked growth in all sectors of the economy, especially in infrastructure and trade. Many Indians migrated as labourers to the newly discovered oil port of Aden. Even after the independence of South Yemen, many Indians decided to stay back.

India was one of the first countries to establish diplomatic ties with the Yemen Arab Republic (YAR) in 1962, and People's Democratic Republic of Yemen (PDRY) in 1967. In 1990, YAR and PDRY merged to become the Republic of Yemen. Following the unification, a civil war started which came to an end in 1994 when the Republic of Yemen was finally consolidated. India recognised the newly unified Yemen and set up diplomatic ties.

Political Relations

India has always shared a cordial relation with Aden. However, this swiftly deteriorated since 2011 when the Arab Uprising hit the shores of Yemen, leading to the forced exit of President Ali Abdullah Saleh in February 2012. Constant violence in the streets, political tussles, rise of armed groups, and breakdown of law and order led to the collapse of the entire governmental structure of Yemen. By the beginning of 2015, like many other countries, India had scaled down its bilateral exchanges as they "were deeply concerned about the worsening political and security situation in Yemen."[21] In a statement, the Ministry of External Affairs (MEA) spokesperson said that, "India urges all parties to seek resolution through consensus and dialogue." It also stated that India, "as a longstanding friend of Yemen with close historical and people-to-people linkages, has been extending all possible bilateral assistance to Yemen."[22]

It is important to note that, during 2012–14, India restricted its support to Yemen only through international forums like Friends of Yemen. Bilaterally, it maintained silence over the transitional process, and reiterated its generic policy of "supporting dialogue between political partners and orchestrating peaceful measures to benefit the citizens of the state."[23] Unlike China or other regional leaders like the UK, India did not provide any bilateral aid to the transitional government headed by President Hadi; nor did it support or disapprove of any political partners in the ongoing turmoil in Yemen.[24] India maintained a "studied silence"[25] over the entire period of transition as well as during the swift spiral of civil war that gripped Yemen by the latter half of 2014. This act of diplomacy was the saving grace for India to successfully carry out *Operation Rahat* that is discussed later in the chapter.

Nonetheless, the worsening conditions prompted India to issue three travel advisories—on 21 January, 19 March, and 7 April 2015—to Indian citizens living in Yemen to leave the country as soon as possible, and to avoid travel to the same.[26] By the time the second advisory was issued, the situation on the ground had substantially worsened. More than 5,000 Indian citizens who did not heed the warnings were trapped.[27] There was constant aerial bombardment by the Saudi-led alliance which blocked all road traffic, and destroyed buildings, especially hospitals. Several hundred people who were trapped there became involuntary human shields for the Houthis; shops and markets were closed, and there was a constant fear of being attacked.

In this situation, the Indian embassy was inundated by requests for evacuation as well as for the issuance of emergency exit visas. On 26 March 2015, a control room was set up to handle these requests; but the ground reality slowly became more chaotic.[28] The Arab coalition, headed by Royal Saudi Air Force, attacked Yemen, and declared the airspace over the latter as a no-fly zone on 27 March. It became imperative for New Delhi to chalk out an evacuation plan for its citizens before the situation worsened. *Operation Rahat* was initiated on 30 March 2015, when the government ordered the evacuation of all its nationals from the strife-torn country.[29]

The Indian Navy diverted *INS Sumitra*, one of the newest Offshore Patrol Vessels which was on routine visit in the Gulf of Aden, for the task of evacuating Indians from the Port of Aden. On 31 March, 349 Indians were evacuated and transported to Djibouti. They were the first batch of Indians rescued by the navy from Yemen.[30] Two passenger ships, namely *MV Kavaratti* and *MV Corals* which usually ply between Kochi and the Lakshadweep Islands, were also diverted to Yemen. The guided missile destroyer *INS Mumbai* and guided-missile frigate *INS Tarkash* also sailed to meet the passengers' ships and escort them to Djibouti. This was necessary as the waters of the Gulf of Aden have been prone to pirate attacks since 2008.[31]

Meanwhile, several port cities, including the Port of Aden, were being constantly bombarded by shelling and aerial attacks. Permission for entry of any ships into the harbour was not being given by the local authorities. Small local boats were used to evacuate the waiting passengers to the naval ships.[32] Ports like Hodeidah, Ash Shih'r, and many more were covered in rotation by these ships. The sea evacuation ended on 11 April 2015, and 1,783 Indians and 1,291 foreigners were rescued by *INS Sumitra, INS Mumbai* and *INS Tarkash* (see Table 10.1).[33] Passenger ships *MV Kavaratti* and *MV Corals* helped to evacuate 475 passengers, including 73 Indians, 337 Bangladeshis, and 65 Yemeni citizens of Indian origin.[34]

Table 10.1: No. of People evacuated from Yemen during *Operation Rahat*

Date	Evacuation Port	Ship	Reached at Djibouti	No. of Indians	No. of Foreigners	Total
31 March	Aden	Sumitra	01 April	349	-	349
02 April	Al Hodeidah	Sumitra	03 April	306	11	317
04 April	Aden	Mumbai	04 April	265	176	441
05 April	Ash Shihr	Sumitra	05 April	182	21	203
06 April	Al Hodeidah	Mumbai	06 April	463	11	474
07 April	Al Hodeidah	Tarkash	08 April	54	20	74
09 April	Al Hodeidah	Sumitra	10 April	46	303	349
10 April	Aden	Tarkash	11 April	42	422	464
15 April	Al Hodeidah	Sumitra	16 April	76	327	403
				1,783	1,291	3,074

Source: Adapted from Indian Navy, at https://www.indiannavy.nic.in/content/ships-return-heros-welcome

Figure 10.1: No. of People evacuated by *MV Kavaratti* and *MV Corals* from Yemen during *Operation Rahat*

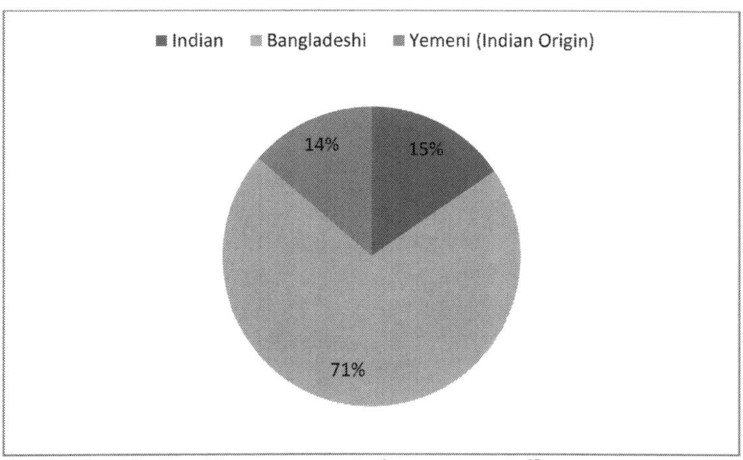

Source: Adapted from Indian Navy, at www.indiannavy.nic.in[35]

The Indian Air Force and Air India came together to begin the evacuation. Led by Ambassador Amrit Lugun, Indian diplomats in Sana'a and the MEA managed to negotiate "window-periods" when Saudi-led bombings temporarily ceased so as to allow the landing of Indian aircraft for evacuation.[36] India's High Commission in Sana'a managed to coordinate all the staff members in the Sana'a airport to accept Air India Airbus A321 and the Air Force's C-17 Globemaster planes to operate for nearly four days. On 3 April, Air India was allowed to fly to Yemen, and immediately two Airbus aircraft were deployed along with two C-17 Globemaster planes which had a capacity of 600 passengers.[37] Speaking on the situation, Minister of State for External Affairs, General V. K. Singh said that the

> The Saudis gave us permission to fly for only two and a half hours in a day. The situation in Sana'a was so chaotic that it was difficult to land two planes, segregate passengers for Kochi and Mumbai, check their papers, get them on board, and fly them back within the stipulated 150 minutes.[38]

Approximately 2,900 people were evacuated by air through 18 special flights out of Sana'a; the air evacuation ended on 8 April.

In the end, 6,688 people—of which 4,741 were Indians and 1,947 foreigners—were evacuated (see Figure 10.2). India assisted nationals of Pakistan, the US, the UK, Australia, Bangladesh, Bahrain, Canada, Cuba, Djibouti, Egypt, El Salvador, Ethiopia, France, Greece, Germany, Hungary, Indonesia, Iran, Iraq, Ireland, Italy, Jordan, Kenya, Kyrgyzstan, Lebanon, Maldives, Morocco, Myanmar, Mexico, Moldova, Nepal, New Zealand, Philippines, Romania, Russia, Somalia, Sweden, Sri Lanka, Sudan, Spain, Switzerland, Syria, Tanzania, Uzbekistan, the UAE, Uganda, Ukraine and Yemen.[39] The Indians evacuated from Yemen were from 27 states, and the maximum of 2,527 belonged to Kerala; of the rest, 427 hailed from Tamil Nadu, 368 from Uttar Pradesh, 293 from Maharashtra, 219 from Bihar, 195 from West Bengal, and 180 from Telangana/Andhra Pradesh besides others (see Table 10.2).[40]

V. K. Singh, a former Indian Army chief, travelled to both Djibouti and Sana'a to oversee the operations. He was the first Indian Minister of State to visit Yemen, and his visit came after 17 years of the last high profile visit which was in October 1999 when Vice President Krishan Kant went to Yemen. Although Singh's visit to Sana'a was not a political one, it still marked a high-profile interaction between the two countries. He coordinated various aspects of the Operation. The Embassy of India was shifted to Djibouti on 15 April 2015, when the evacuation was completed. Since then, there is no Indian diplomatic presence in Yemen.[42]

Figure 10.2: No. of People Rescued by Different Modes of Evacuation during *Operation Rahat*

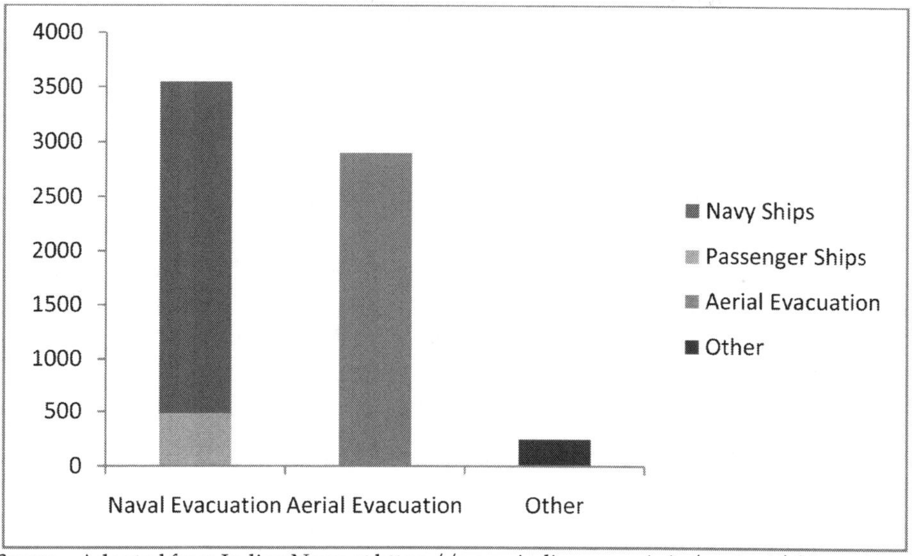

Source: Adapted from Indian Navy, at https://www.indiannavy.nic.in/content/ships-return-heros-welcome

Table 10.2: No. of Indians from each state evacuated from Yemen during *Operation Rahat*

States	No. of People Evacuated
Assam	3
Andaman and Nicobar	1
Bihar	219
Gujarat	115
Goa	30
Himachal Pradesh	5
Haryana	5
Jharkhand	20
Jammu and Kashmir	1
Karnataka	123
Kerala	2,527
Maharashtra	293
Manipur	3
Madhya Pradesh	47
Nagaland	2
Delhi NCR	23
Odisha	31
Puducherry	1
Punjab	31
Rajasthan	60
Tamil Nadu	427
Telangana/Andhra Pradesh	180
Tripura	1
Uttar Pradesh	368
Uttarakhand	30
West Bengal	195

Source: Adapted from Ministry of External Affairs, www.mea.gov.in[41]

Operation Rahat was successful primarily due to two reasons: one, India continued to maintain diplomatic silence over the whole transition-coup-civil war phase, and did not alienate any prospective power/stake holder. Secondly, the centuries old bonhomie between the people of both countries had created a generally good impression about Indians which allowed the government to manoeuvre the operation successfully.

Another facet of the Operation—one that has been least discussed in the media— was the rehabilitation programmes. Several state governments, including Kerala and Tamil Nadu, announced relief packages for the evacuees from Yemen.[43] They were given priority under various existing state and central government schemes for financial assistance as well as rehabilitation aid like free medical treatment. Although these efforts were noteworthy, the impact of the same was felt by only a few.

At the same time, approximately 200 Indian citizens who were registered in the Embassy refused to be evacuated. According to Anil Wadhwa, Secretary (East) in the External Affairs Ministry, "the main difficulty is that some people don't want to go." There are many reasons for this, such as being married to locals, some nurses not wanting to leave as their wages had not been paid, or labour contractors who had taken their money.[44] Apart from registered Indian migrants, there are a substantial number of illegal Indian migrants in Yemen, with estimates varying from 4,000 to 5,000.[45]

There is no information about the exact number of Indians (legal as well as illegal immigrants) who chose to stay back. While a section (including nurses and menial workers) stayed back due to lack of income in India, a few others were stuck because of losing their travel documents since their sponsors had fled the country due to the war, while others who had settled in Yemen for several years decided to face all eventualities. However, three major categories had specific reasons for not returning to India. First were Indian nurses, especially from Kerala, who had paid a huge amount of money to various recruitment agencies to get jobs in the Gulf (including Yemen) and, in the process, had heavy debts to repay. As the evacuation was taking place in the beginning of the month, they had not received their salaries. Thus, they refused to leave the hospital compound with unpaid salaries as huge debts were waiting for them back home.[46] Secondly, a large number of Bohra Muslims—a community known for intermarriage between India and Yemen—decided to stay back. Since most Bohras are usually involved in community businesses (like grocery shops), most of them decided to stay back to safeguard their properties and businesses. Farida Hizam, an Indian Bohra Muslim woman who married a Yemeni Bohra Muslim man, said that her husband decided to stay back in Yemen as "a lot of empty houses, both in Aden and the capital, are being looted after their owners run [away] for safety, so my husband wants to stay in our house."[47] Lastly, several workers who had studied from Yemeni universities under the Indo-Yemen Cultural Exchange programme refused to return as their degrees were not recognised by the Indian government, and were thus not in a position to get well-paid jobs in India. Many of them were doctors who had passed out of Hadramaut Medical College, and were working in various hospitals across Yemen.[48] While some of these issues were highlighted in the national media, many other such stories remain ignored and out of the spotlight.

Within a few months of the evacuation, many Indians started to return to Yemen. While some went back because their companies had started to operate again, others decided to return due to a bleak future in India. Various shipping firms and private companies began to operate by the end of 2015 when the Port of Aden was secured by forces loyal to Hadi. This resulted in many Indians returning to re-join their official positions.[49] Many nurses have also returned to their jobs. As there are no direct travel connections between India and Yemen, most of them travel to Jordan, and then catch a connecting flight to Sana'a through Yemen's national airline which operates three times a week to help commute sick Yemeni citizens to Jordanian hospitals.[50] Another popular travel route is through Djibouti, an island country just an hour away from Yemen through the sea. Both Jordan and Djibouti offer visas on arrival to Indian citizens, and thus it has become easier for immigrants to travel to Yemen even without a functioning Indian mission in the Yemeni capital.

As the situation in Yemen has not improved, Indians are still being caught in the cross fire. External Affairs Minister Sushma Swaraj tweeted (17 August 2016), "Some of those evacuated, returned to Yemen...We do not have our Embassy there. It is a war-torn situation. We are not in a position to evacuate people from Yemen at this stage."[51]

Economic Relations

The economy of Yemen is highly dependent on the production of oil and natural gas, with the country's oil exports accounting for around 90 per cent of its export revenues. Although, it accounts for only 0.2 per cent share of the Middle Eastern reserves, it still has large oil fields that have not been explored or brought into production. At present, there are 87 blocks out of which only 12 produce oil to break even the cost of production.[52] Apart from oil production and exports, Yemen also lies strategically near the Bab al-Mandab Strait which is an international energy choke point.

Due to the ongoing instability, oil production has steadily declined in Yemen. In 2008, the production was at 316,000 barrels per day (bpd) which declined to 127,000 bpd in 2014 and to 44,000 bpd in 2015.[53] Since 2014, most of the production has been controlled by the AQAP and the Houthis who sell the oil barrels in the black market, and use the finances to run their parallel government in the divided country. Foreign firms operating in Yemen were compelled to abandon operations and evacuate their staff. Nearly all hydrocarbon production in Yemen has been closed down. Pipelines and port facilities have been attacked and disrupted repeatedly, leading to enormous losses in the energy trading sector. The Aden refinery was shut down in April 2015, and was subsequently attacked in July. Yemen liquid natural gas plant was shut down since April 2015.[54]

The lack of data and the halting of nearly all energy sector activity does not allow for a complete understanding of the recent economic structure of Yemen. By mid-2016, there were reports of the resumption of oil production and exports from the Masila oilfields that were closed for 16 months. The Oil Minister, Saif al-Sharif,[55] reportedly stated that Yemen sold 3 million barrels of crude to the commodities trader Glencore.[56]

Table 10.3: India-Yemen Bilateral Trade (in US$ Million)

	2011–12	2012–13	2013–14	2014–15	2015–16
India's Exports to Yemen	730.62	1,477.27	1,306.99	992.13	399.79
India's Imports from Yemen	970.72	958.92	782.18	540.68	6.88
Total bilateral Trade	1,701.34	2,436.19	2,089.17	1,532.82	406.67
Share of Yemen in India's total trade	0.21	0.31	0.27	0.20	0.06

Source: Adapted from Director General of Foreign Trade, at http://dgft.gov.in

Figure 10.3: India-Yemen Bilateral Trade (in US$ Million)

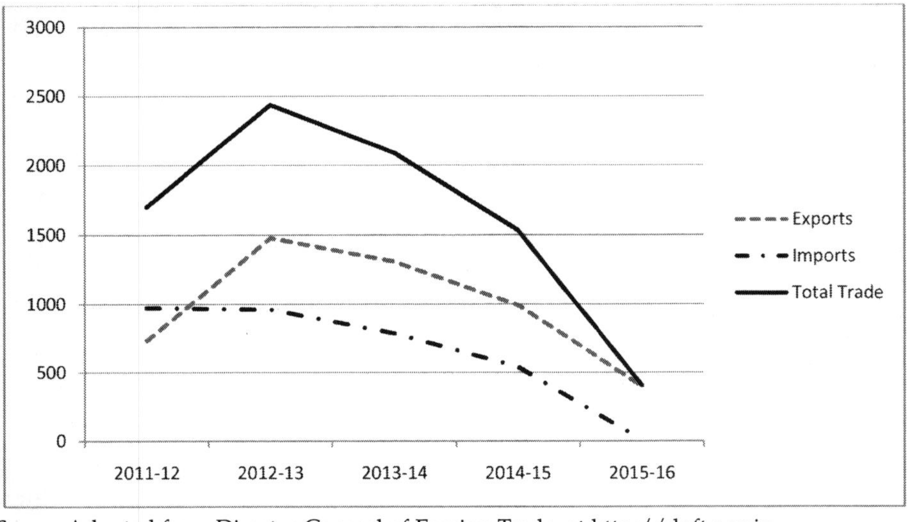

Source: Adapted from Director General of Foreign Trade, at http://dgft.gov.in

Table 10.4: Share of Oil in India's Imports from Yemen (in US$ million)

Year	Oil Imports from Yemen	Total Oil Imports	Yemen's Share in Total Oil Imports	Imports from Yemen	Per cent of Oil in Imports from Yemen
2011-12	955.26	172,753.92	0.55	970.72	98.11
2012-13	942.00	181,344.67	0.52	958.92	98.24
2013-14	762.62	181,382.59	0.42	782.18	97.50
2014-15	516.68	156,400.01	0.33	540.68	95.56
2015-16	0.01	96,953.06	0.00	6.88	0.15

Source: Adapted from Director General of Foreign Trade, at www.dgft.gov.in.

Figure 10.4: Share of Oil in India's Imports from Yemen (in US$ million)

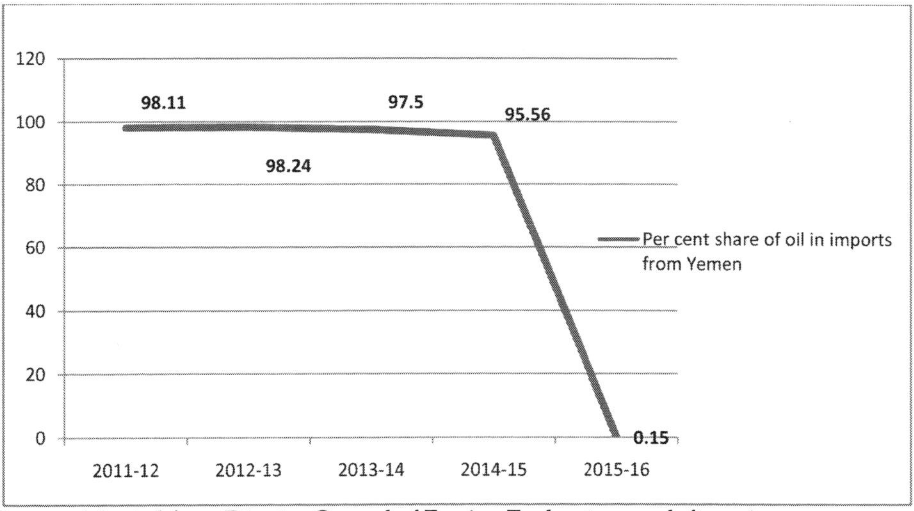

Source: Adapted from Director General of Foreign Trade, at www.dgft.gov.in.

Table 10.5: India's Energy Imports from Yemen

	2011–12	2012–13	2013–14	2014–15	2015–16
India's Energy Imports from Yemen	955.26	942.00	762.62	516.68	0.01
India's Total Energy Imports	172,753.92	181,344.67	181,382.59	156,400.01	96,953.06
Total Energy Imports from Persian Gulf	105,056.26	105,859.15	106,400.75	85,300.30	50,992.26
Share in Total Energy Imports (in per cent)	0.55	0.52	0.42	0.33	0.00
Share in Energy Imports from Persian Gulf (in per cent)	0.91	0.89	0.72	0.61	0.00

Source: Adapted from Director General of Foreign Trade, at www.dgft.gov.in

Figure 10.5: Share of Yemen in Energy Imports from Persian Gulf

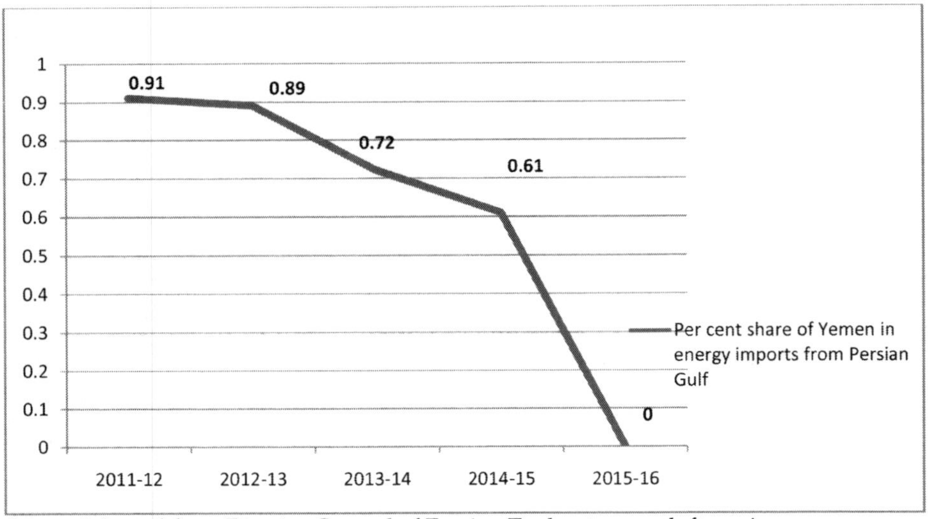

Source: Adapted from Director General of Foreign Trade, at www.dgft.gov.in

Due to the political turbulence in Yemen, economic relations with India have also faltered. Bilateral trade recorded a steep fall from the previous year, with imports from Yemen reducing to the lowest in the past five years. In 2013–14, India's imports were US$ 782.18 million which declined to US$ 540.68 million in 2014–15, and finally dwindled to US$ 6.88 million in 2015–16. India's exports too reduced from 2013–14 when they stood at US$ 1.47 billion to US$ 399.79 in 2015–16 (see Table 10.3). The decrease in imports and exports from 2013–14 to 2015–16 is 99.1 per cent and 69.4 per cent, respectively. The combined downfall of both imports and exports led to a further falling of Yemen's share in India's total trade, from 0.27 per cent in 2013–14 to 0.06 per cent in 2015–16.

This fall in the volume of trade can be attributed not only to the political turmoil in Yemen but also to the lack of diversification. Hydrocarbon remains the main item in India's imports from Yemen. This is so despite the collapse of several pipelines and the reduction of oil production. Until 2014–15, more than 95 per cent of India's imports from Yemen were oil-related. The recent turmoil has resulted in the constant downscaling of imports from Yemen. In 2013–14, oil imports from Yemen were US$ 762.63 million which fell down to 0.01 per cent in 2015–16 (see Tables 10.4 and 10.5). On the other hand, India largely exports rice, grains, and other consumable items to Yemen which are in constant demand in the country. The raging war has led to an impasse in the trading sector as most ports have closed their activities, except for Port of Aden and Hadramaut which have intermittently allowed ships to dock for trading purposes.[57] Media reports regarding the sinking of an Indian cargo ship heading towards Yemen near Oman (27 August 2016) reveal that consumer items, including food and medicines, are still being traded despite the lack of diplomatic relations or other political ties.[58]

Cultural Relations

Even though India "shares a historic relation with age old ties"[59] with Yemen, politico-cultural relations in the past five years have been limited to institutional exchanges rather than people-to-people contact. The number of tourists from Yemen to India has reduced sharply since 2010. There has also been a decrease in the number of students arriving from Yemen. Several communities, like the Bohra community in India, have continued to maintain religious and social ties with their brethren in Yemen. Presently, there are approximately 300,000 people of Yemeni origin residing in India, of which 150,000 reside in Andhra Pradesh and Telangana. On the other hand, there are approximately 100,000 people of Indian origin who are Yemeni citizens, and reside near Aden and Hadramaut.[60] The close cultural ties between the people can be observed through various common customs and expressions. Several families of Yemeni origin from Hyderabad have married their children in Yemen, and vice versa.

The strong cultural tie was one of the reasons of the success of *Operation Rahat*. Despite the ongoing turmoil and the absolute breakdown of the political structure in the country, local Yemenites helped Indian migrants and their brethren to reach ports of evacuation safely. The Houthis and other armed groups gave passage to Indian citizens through curfew areas.[61] Several Indian origin Yemenis, especially members of the Bohra community, played an important role in acting as 'middle-men' between the Indian diplomatic set-up and the various political outfits in Sana'a and Aden.[62] They were able to negotiate a window of opportunity for evacuation, and convince the local authorities to provide exit papers for several hundred Indians.[63] The close traditional ties have kept the bilateral relation still functioning despite the breakdown of political and economic relations.

Conclusion

India has continued to maintain diplomatic silence over the turmoil in Yemen. This political tactic has given it enough space to maintain cordial relations with all parties involved in the conflict. This allowed for the successful evacuation of its citizens by its army in April 2015. India was one of the very few countries which was permitted to do so. However, the same 'silence' has also back-fired in India's stand on terrorism in the international arena. Until date, India has not issued any statement against the terror activities of AQAP. On 7 September 2014, AQAP released a statement praising the establishment of Al-Qaeda in the Indian Subcontinent (AQIS) and, since then, has repeatedly urged Indian Muslims to join its ranks.[64] Despite this, India has continued to remain officially silent.

The bilateral relations between India and Yemen have been on the wane since 2011. Economic ties, political relations, and social bonds have diminished in the past two years. With the continuance of the Saudi-led intervention in Yemen, the prospect of improving these ties in the near future look bleak. Since the closing of the Indian embassy in Sana'a, there have been no political visits, exchanges, or meetings. Trade too has suffered drastically, with India's imports from Yemen witnessing a sharp drop while oil imports have completely halted. The only saving grace in this desolate relation has been the continuance of people-to-people contact through existing bonds. The future of Yemen looks uncertain; so does the bilateral relation between India and Yemen.

NOTES

1. Lina Sinjab, "Yemen protests: 20,000 call for President Saleh to go," *BBC News*, 3 February 2011, at http://www.bbc.com/news/world-middle-east-12353479.
2. United Nations Security Council Report, March 2012, at http://www.securitycouncilreport.org/monthly-forecast/2012-03/lookup_c_glKWLeMTIsG_b_7996437.php
3. Jeremy M. Sharp, "Yemen: Background and US Relations", *Congressional Research Service*, 11 February 2015, at https://www.fas.org/sgp/crs/mideast/RL34170.pdf.
4. "Houthis Control Sa'ada, Help Appoint Governor", *National Yemen*, 29 March 2011, at http://nationalyemen.com/2011/03/29/houthis-control-sa%E2%80%99ada-help-appoint-governor/; see also, "Houthis Close to Control Hajjah Governorate, Amid Expectations of Expansion of Control over Large Parts of Northern Yemen", *Islam Times*, 9 November 2011, at http://www.islamtimes.org/en/doc/news/112627/.
5. Yara Bayoumy, "Yemen's Federal Plan a bold idea, but many hurdles remain', *Reuters*, 23 February, at http://www.reuters.com/article/us-yemen-politics-analysis-idUSBREA1M05720140223; see also, Alexandra Lewis, "Yemen's Creation of Federal Republic leaves major grievances unresolved," *World Politics Review*, 18 February 2014, at http://www.worldpoliticsreview.com/articles/13571/yemen-s-creation-of-federal-republic-leaves-major-grievances-unresolved
6. Laura Kasinof, "How the Houthis did it', *Foreign Policy*, 23 January 2015, at http://foreignpolicy.com/2015/01/23/how-the-houthis-did-it-yemen-hadi-arab-spring/.
7. Jeremy M. Sharp, "Yemen: Background and US Relations", op. cit.
8. Hussain Al-Bukhaiti, "From Failure to Success: How the Houthis saved the Arab Spring", *Yemen Times*, 18 February 2015, at http://www.yementimes.com/en/1861/opinion/4909/From-failure-to-success-How-the-Houthis-saved-the-Arab-

Spring.htm; see also, Gregory D. Johnsen, "Meet the group that now rules Yemen," *Buzzfeed News*, 6 February 2015, at https://www.buzzfeed.com/gregorydjohnsen/meet-the-group-that-now-rules-yemen?utm_term=.mtA4wPjXa#.jvNVMDQgj

9. "Yemen conflict: At least 10,000 killed, says UN," *BBC News*, 17 January 2017, at http://www.bbc.com/news/world-middle-east-38646066
10. Ranjit Gupta, "Yemen: Why the current strife will continue," *Spotlight West Asia*, IPCS 4860, 6 April 2015.
11. Laura Kasinof, "Yemen: From the Arab Spring to a Leaderless Nation,' *Defence One*, 26 January 2015, at http://www.defenseone.com/threats/2015/01/yemen-arab-spring-leaderless-nation/103692/
12. AQAP was formed in January 2009 when two distinct branches of Al-Qaeda came together to form a single militant organisation. The antecedents of this insurgent group can be traced back to the 1990s when hundreds of mujahedeen returned from Afghanistan after years of fighting the Soviets. Due to the collapse of Soviet Russia and the changing geo-political landscape, these former mujahedeen were not allowed to resettle in their own countries, like Saudi Arabia and Iraq, and were instead repatriated to Yemen by the then Yemeni ruler, Ali Abdullah Saleh, who welcomed them. These militants settled in South Yemen and started to form rudimentary terror outfits; most of them were led by Osama Bin Laden who had also settled in Yemen. Soon after its formation in 2009, they carried out various terror attacks which prompted the US to pressurise the Yemeni government to launch an offensive against them. However, the tides of the Arab Spring in 2011 changed the fortunes of AQAP.
13. Yara Bayoumy, Noah Browning, and Mohammad Ghobari, "How Saudi Arabia's war in Yemen has made al Qaeda stronger – and richer," *Reuters*, 8 April 2016, at http://www.reuters.com/investigates/special-report/yemen-aqap/
14. Brian Bennett, Laura King, "Al Qaeda in Yemen using chaos of war to carve out terrorism haven", *Los Angeles Times*, 17 April 2015, at http://www.latimes.com/world/middleeast/la-fg-us-alqaeda-20150418-story.html
15. Yara Bayoumy, Noah Browning, and Mohammad Ghobari, "How Saudi Arabia's war in Yemen has made al Qaeda stronger – and richer," op. cit.
16. Katherine Zimmerman, "AQAP expanding behind Yemen's frontlines," *Critical Threats*, 17 February 2016, at https://www.criticalthreats.org/analysis/aqap-expanding-behind-yemens-frontlines
17. Yara Bayoumy, Noah Browning, and Mohammad Ghobari, "How Saudi Arabia's war in Yemen has made al Qaeda stronger – and richer," op. cit.
18. Ibid.
19. "Profile: Al Qaeda in the Arabian Peninsula", *BBC News*, 16 June 2015, at http://www.bbc.com/news/world-middle-east-11483095
20. "India-Yemen Relations", Ministry of External Affairs, Government of India, February 2013, at http://www.mea.gov.in/Portal/ForeignRelation/Yemen_brief_for_ MEA_s_website.pdf
21. "India concerned about worsening situation in Yemen", *The Hindu*, 14 February 2015, at http://www.thehindu.com/news/national/india-concerned-about-worsening-situation-in-yemen/article6895493.ece
22. "India deeply concerned over Yemen situation, favours dialogue", *Indian Express*, 14 February 2015, at http://indianexpress.com/article/india/india-others/india-

deeply-concerned-over-yemen-situation-favours-dialogue/

23. "India-Yemen Relation," Ministry of External Affairs, Government of India, January 2016, at https://www.mea.gov.in/Portal/ForeignRelation/Yemen_Jan_2016_english.pdf
24. China has been extremely vocal regarding its support for the Hadi government and its rejection of the Houthi coup. For details, see "China throws its weight behind Hadi government in Yemen", *Gulf News*, 3 December 2016, at http://gulfnews.com/news/gulf/yemen/china-throws-its-weight-behind-hadi-government-in-yemen-1.1939156. See also, Robert Cusack, "China 'does not approve' of new Houthi government," *The New Arab*, 4 December 2016, at https://www.alaraby.co.uk/english/news/2016/12/4/china-does-not-approve-of-new-houthi-government
25. P. R. Kumaraswamy, *Reading the Silence: India and the Arab Spring*, Jerusalem: The Leonard Davis Institute for International Relations, The Hebrew University of Jerusalem, 2012. The term "studied silence" was used to describe India's reaction towards the Arab Spring, which for many was a sign of indifference to popular sentiments. For the author, it was a preference "for stable and internally viable political states in the region" (p. 3).
26. "Travel Advisory for Indian Nationals travelling to Yemen," 1 April 2015, Ministry of External Affairs, Government of India, at http://www.mea.gov.in/press-releases.htm?dtl/26588/Travel+Advisory+ for+Indian+Nationals+travelling+to+Yemen
27. Sahil Makkar, "The dramatic evacuation of Indians from Yemen", *Business Standard*, 18 April 2015, at http://www.business-standard.com/article/beyond-business/out-of-yemen-115041701186_1.html
28. "Closure of Control Room in Ministry of External Affairs", Ministry of External Affairs, Government of India, 21 April 2015, at http://www.mea.gov.in/press-releases.htm?dtl/25084/Closure+of+Control+Room+in+Ministry+of+External+Affairs
29. Sahil Makkar, "The dramatic evacuation of Indians from Yemen", op. cit.
30. "Op 'Rahat' in Yemen : Navy rescues stranded Indians", Indian Navy, at https://www.indiannavy.nic.in/content/op-rahat-yemen-navy-rescues-stranded-indians
31. Ibid.
32. "OP 'Rahat' Update", Indian Navy, at https://www.indiannavy.nic.in/content/op-rahat-update
33. "IN Ships Return to Hero's Welcome", Indian Navy, at https://www.indiannavy.nic.in/content/ships-return-heros-welcome
34. "*MV Kavaratti* and *MV Corals* Arrive at Kochi", Indian Navy, at https://www.indiannavy.nic.in/content/mv-kavaratti-and-mv-corals-arrive-kochi
35. Ibid.
36. Sahil Makkar, "The dramatic evacuation of Indians from Yemen", op. cit.
37. Suhasini Haider, "Air India gets nod to fly into Sana'a", *The Hindu*, 3 April 2015, at http://www.thehindu.com/news/national/yemen-indians-rescue-air-india-gets-nod-to-fly-into-sanaa/article7064202.ece
38. Sahil Makkar, "The dramatic evacuation of Indians from Yemen," op. cit.
39. "Suo-Moto Statement by Minister of External Affairs and Overseas Indian Affairs in Rajya Sabha on "Recent Developments in the Republic of Yemen and Efforts

Made for Safe Evacuation of Indian Nationals from There", Ministry of External Affairs, Government of India, 27 April 2015, at http://www.mea.gov.in/Speeches-Statements.htm?dtl/25129/SuoMoto_Statement_by_Minister_of_External_ Affairs _and_Overseas_Indian_Affairs_in_Rajya_Sabha_on_Recent_ Developments_ in_ the_Republic_of_Yemen_and_Effor
40. Ibid.
41. Ibid.
42. Ibid.
43. "Jobs for Indian Returning from Yemen", 23 April 2015, Government of India, Rajya Sabha, Unstarred Question no. 27, at http://www.mea.gov.in/rajya-sabha.htm?dtl/25104/Q_NO27_JOBS_FOR_INDIAN_ RETURNING_ FROM _ YEMEN
44. "200 Indians refuse to leave Yemen as rescue ends," *Gulf Times*, 10 April 2015, at http://www.gulf-times.com/story/434419/200-Indians-refuse-to-leave-Yemen-as-rescue-ends
45. Renuka Phadnis, "Yemen crisis: brother of stranded engineer blames Indian government", *The Hindu*, 30 March 2015, at http://www.thehindu.com/news/cities/bangalore/yemen-crisis-brother-of-stranded-engineer-blames-indian-government/article7046760.ece
46. Minister of State for External Affairs, General V. K. Singh said in an interview that, "Our people who were working there were very happy, except that when the situation went bad they thought it is better that we get evacuated. Otherwise there were a lot of people, for example a bunch of nurses I spoke to said that they are not happy going back. So it was a shock ... You are trying to evacuate somebody back home and they are saying I am not happy to go back home. When I asked them why, they said we have a very good job here and we are only going back because our parents are crying at home and asking us to come. They wanted to stay back and I am quite sure by now, they must be already back in Yemen. "A lot of people have gone back." For details, see "V.K. Singh lauds Bohra community's role in 'Operation Rahat'", *The Times of India*, 9 October 2015, at http://timesofindia. indiatimes.com/india/VK-Singh-lauds-Bohra-communitys-role-in-Operation-Rahat/articleshow/49285386.cms. See also, "From death-trap to debt-trap: Indian nurses returning from Yemen in a s pot", *Tehelka*, 18 April 2015, at http://www.tehelka.com/2015/04/from-death-trap-to-debt-trap-indian-nurses-returning-from-yemen-in-a-spot/
47. "India's Bohra Muslims are back safely from Yemen but have many reasons to still be anxious", *The Scroll*, 9 April 2015, at https://scroll.in/article/719205/indias-bohra-muslims-are-back-safely-from-yemen-but-have-many-reasons-to-still-be-anxious
48. "Forced to return from war-torn Yemen, 2 Indian medical aspirants stare at bleak future", *Narada News*, 15 October 2016, http://naradanews.com/2016/10/two-indian-girls-on-the-verge-of-losing-their-career/
49. "Despite ongoing crisis, many Indians returning to Yemen in search of jobs", *The Indian Express*, 10 September 2015, at http://indianexpress.com/article/india/india-others/despite-ongoing-crisis-many-indians-returning-to-yemen-in-search-of-jobs/
50. Ibid.
51. "Evacuation of Indians from Yemen not possible now, says Sushma", *Hindustan*

Times, 17 August 2016, at http://www.hindustantimes.com/india-news/evacuation-of-indians-from-yemen-not-possible-now-says-sushma/story-HOcLqS392jCj7grZDMI6qJ.html

52. "Yemen: International Energy Data and Analysis", US Energy Information Administration (USEIA), 24 September 2015, at https://www.eia.gov/beta/international/analysis_includes/countries_long/Yemen/yemen.pdf
53. Ibid.
54. "Yemen: International Energy Data and Analysis", USEIA, 30 September 2015, at https://www.eia.gov/beta/international/analysis.cfm?iso=YEM;for further details, see, "Oil Sector Recovery in Yemen Urgently Needed," *Yemen Socio-Economic Update*, Ministry of Planning and International Co-operation, Government of Yemen, Issue 14, May 2016. http://reliefweb.int/sites/reliefweb.int/files/resources/yseu14_english_final_1.pdf
55. Minister Sharif is part of the government in exile headed by President Hadi, and is located currently at Aden.
56. "Exiled Yemen government sells crude to Glencore–agency", *Reuters*, 27 July 2016, at http://www.reuters.com/article/yemen-oil-idUSL8N1AD5HX
57. "Fighting erupts over control of Yemen's Aden port," Al Jazeera, 4 January 2016, at http://www.aljazeera.com/news/2016/01/fighting-erupts-control-yemen-aden-port-160103135753845.html
58. "Indian ship heading for Yemen sinks off Oman", *Al-Arabiya*, 28 August 2016, at http://english.alarabiya.net/en/News/middle-east/2016/08/28/Indian-ship-heading-for-Yemen-sinks-off-Oman-.html
59. "India-Yemen: Rich history of intense contacts", Embassy of India in Sana'a, Republic of Yemen, at http://eoisanaa.org/india-yemen-rich-history-of-intense-contacts/
60. "India-Yemen Relations", op. cit.
61. In a *BBC* Video titled 'The Rush to Flee Yemen's Capital' dated 8 April 2015, during 1:53-2:00 seconds, there is a video grab of Houthi rebels smiling with Indian citizens during the evacuation. The video can be accessed at: http://www.bbc.com/news/world-middle-east-32216712
62. Sahil Makkar, "The dramatic evacuation of Indians from Yemen," op. cit.
63. Prime Minister Narendra Modi called King Salman of Saudi Arabia to permit Air India to land in Sana'a for a few hours to complete the evacuation; the nitty-gritty of local clearances and permissions for exit were done by the local communities in Yemen, especially the Bohra community. For further details, read: "VK Singh lauds Bohra community's role in 'Operation Rahat'," *The Times of India*, op. cit.
64. "AQAP Endorses AQIS, Considers it "Vanguard" of Muslims in the East," 7 September 2014, at https://scholarship.tricolib.brynmawr.edu/bitstream/handle/10066/17007/AQP20140907.pdf?sequence=4&isAllowed=y.

11

THE GCC

Poonam Khatana

The changing dynamics of domestic and regional politics in the Middle East ensured continued turbulence during 2015 and 2016. The GCC monarchies remained embroiled in firefighting issues, ranging from economic troubles due to lower oil prices, Saudi-led military intervention in Yemen, the ISIS threat, and growing Iranian regional influence. The six-member GCC—comprising Bahrain, Kuwait, Oman, Qatar, Saudi Arabia, and the United Arab Emirates—shares important economic, cultural, and strategic relations with India since its formation in 1981. The GCC countries fulfil the majority of India's oil and gas requirements. India's interests in the regional organization have deepened due to significant trade and investment relations along with increasing expatriate presence. Hence, peace and stability in the region acquires greater significance for India.

Developments within the GCC

Iran is the common cord that most members of the GCC consider responsible for the instability prevailing throughout the Middle East. Hence, the GCC has demanded assurances from the US with regard to countering Iranian regional influence while welcoming the Iranian nuclear deal negotiated between Iran and P5+1.[1]

The civil war in Yemen, which transformed into a proxy war between Saudi Arabia and Iran, has played an important role in shaping the regional dynamics. In 2015, the Foreign Ministers of the GCC countries attended a meeting in Riyadh to discuss the military operation in Yemen. Justifying the military operation, Qatar's Foreign Minister Khalid al-Attiyah stated that "The Decisive Storm operation[2] showed the GCC's historical responsibility towards Yemen".[3] Oman is the only GCC country which refused to join the Saudi-led military operation in Yemen. The reason behind its posture can be explained by two factors. First, by doing this, Oman showed that it is independent from the Saudi sphere of geopolitical influence. The second reason was to pursue a diplomatic solution to this conflict in the international arena. Omani Minister of State for Foreign Minister Yusuf bin Alawi stated that "Oman is a nation of peace. We cannot work on peace efforts at the same time we would be part of a military campaign."[4] Oman also placed an initiative before Saudi Arabia and Iran for achieving a peaceful resolution to the Yemen crisis.

Meanwhile, being a close ally, the UAE supported Saudi military intervention. Yemen plays a crucial role in the UAE's geostrategic matrix due to Bab-el-Mandab, the narrow strait which unties Yemen from the Horn of Africa that forms link between the Red Sea and the Gulf of Aden. All GCC countries are dependent on this strait for trade with Europe and North America. Thus, establishing peace and stability in Yemen is of vital interest to the UAE.[5] For the last few years, there has been a constant issue with regard to the membership of Yemen into the GCC. The GCC countries have not been enthusiastic even though they were keen to include Jordan and Morocco in the regional bloc. Hence, the Arabian Peninsula has been politically divided due to the exclusion of Yemen from the GCC.[6]

The 36th annual GCC summit took place in Riyadh on 9 December 2015 which saw a broad consensus on a variety of political, social, and economic issues such as combating extremism, security cooperation, support for a political solution to crises in Yemen and Syria, and firm support for the Palestinian cause.[7] Additionally, economic integration and issues of environment protection were also given importance. Moreover, steps with regard to simplifying customs procedures of entry and exit points among GCC members were also discussed during the Summit.

The year 2015 marked a watershed in the politics of GCC countries since the UAE allowed Israel to open a diplomatic mission—accredited to the International Renewable Energy Agency (IRENA)—on 27 November 2015. It gained extensive international attention since the UAE has officially repudiated any moves to recognise the existence of Israel.[8] It has been followed by engagements with other GCC countries—like clandestine dialogues with Saudi Arabia on the containment of Iran and efforts to revive unofficial diplomatic ties with Israel by Qatar. The GCC's declining concern about Palestine and suggestions of Saudi desire to import sophisticated

Israeli military technology can explain this expansion of the Israel-GCC security cooperation.[9] This informal cooperation can shape the current geopolitical power balance in the Middle East.

In January 2016, the execution of the Shia cleric Nimr al-Nimr in Saudi Arabia prompted protests in Iran which led to the severing of diplomatic relations between Saudi Arabia and Iran. In the same month, Bahrain and Sudan followed suit while the UAE downgraded its relations with Tehran, and recalled its envoy.[10] Earlier, due to tensions over the death of more than 500 Iranian pilgrims in the stampede during the Hajj in 2015, Iran took a decision not to send pilgrims in 2016.[11]

On 26 May 2016, with regard to the Syrian crisis, the meeting was held in Moscow between GCC foreign ministers and their Russian counterpart, Sergey Lavrov, towards renewing political efforts to end the civil war.[12] Meanwhile, the GCC countries faced severe international criticisms for their negligence towards mitigating the Syrian refugee crisis. Since most of the Gulf economies are heavily dependent on foreign labours, demographics were considered an important factor in determining the indifferent attitude of the GCC countries towards Syrian refugees. The influx of refugees was seen as a major threat to the already-volatile demographic base.[13] However, Saudi Arabia and Qatar have donated about US$ 900 million while the UAE has provided US$ 530 million in humanitarian aid to Syrian refuges in Jordan and elsewhere since 2012.[14]

The 37th annual GCC summit was held in Manama, Bahrain on 7 December 2016.[15] The promotion of GCC unity and economic integration among the GCC member states was one of the important points of discussion. Though the countries condemned all forms and manifestations of terrorism, their prime focus was on stopping terror-financing. Some developments with regard to extending strategic partnerships with Jordan and Morocco towards forging closer relations were also discussed.[16] However, Kuwait's Emir Sheikh Sabah al-Ahmad highlighted the weak economy of the GCC as a result of falling oil prices, and suggested the need for GCC states to "continuously consult and coordinate"[17] with each other due to global changes. The highlight of the summit was to establish a new strategic alliance between the GCC and the United Kingdom (UK), with Prime Minister Theresa May attending the summit as a special guest.[18]

India and the GCC

As a collective entity, the importance of GCC for India lies in its energy security, the volume of trade, and the large presence of Indian expatriates. Due to lower oil prices and international slowdown, trade figures witnessed a more than 30 per cent decline between 2013 and 2016 (see Table 11.3). As a result, India's trade deficit with the GCC has fallen from US$ 46 billion to US$ 14 billion in last three years.[19] The drop in oil prices also impacted remittances from the region, leading to a 2.2 per cent fall, which occurred for the first time in last six years. In 2014–15, remittances to India from the GCC amounted to US$ 36.7 billion, and dropped slightly to US$ 35.9 billion in 2015–16.[20] According to the World Bank, if oil prices stay low for a prolonged period, or undergo unforeseen drops, remittances from GCC to India could fall further in the future.[21] It is important to note that GCC countries are the biggest source, contributing about 60 per cent of total remittances received by India in 2015–16 which contributed nearly 3.3 per cent to its GDP. Thus, remittances help develop an organic link between India and the GCC countries.[22]

Despite the slowdown in the GCC market, the migration of Indian workers continued. Under the ECR category, more than 675,000 Indian workers chose to migrate to the GCC countries in search of work in 2015. The maximum of 306,000 (39 per cent) preferred Saudi Arabia while about 225,000 (29 per cent) migrated to the UAE. Even Qatar and Oman attracted 59,000 (7.5 per cent) and 85,000 (11 per cent) Indian workers (see Table 11.1)

Table 11.1: Workers Migrating from India, 2015 (ECR Category)

Country	Numbers migrated	Share (in per cent)
Saudi Arabia	306,000	39.18
UAE	225,000	28.80
Qatar	59,000	7.55
Oman	85,000	10.88
Malaysia	21,000	2.68
Others	85,000	10.88
Total	781,000	

Source: Ministry of External Affairs, Government of India (MEA), *Annual Report 2015–16*, p.210

Figure 11.1: Workers emigrating from India, 2015 (ECR Category)

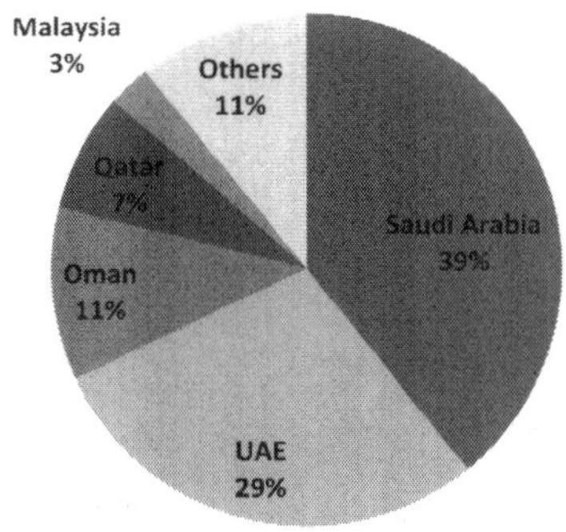

Source: Adapted from Ministry of External Affairs, Government of India (MEA), *Annual Report 2015–16*, p.210

According to India's Ministry of External Affairs, as of December 2016, nearly 8.49 million Overseas Indians lived in the GCC countries.[23] Saudi Arabia and UAE top the list by accounting for 35 per cent and 33 per cent respectively. While Bahrain has the lowest—with only 3.7 per cent—Kuwait, Oman, and Qatar account for 10.87 per cent, 9.37 per cent and 7.06 per cent respectively (see Table 11.2 below).

Table 11.2: Population of Overseas Indians in GCC countries (December 2016)

Country	Non-Resident Indians (NRIs)	Persons of Indian Origin (PIOs)	Overseas Indians	Share (in per cent)
Bahrain	312,918	3,257	316,175	3.72
Kuwait	921,666	1,594	923,260	10.87
Oman	795,082	919	796,001	9.37
Qatar	600,000	Nil	600,000	7.06
Saudi Arabia	3,001,018	3,567	3,004,585	35.37
UAE	2,800,000	3,751	2,803,751	33.01
Total	8,430,684	13,088	8,492,754	100

Source: Population of Overseas Indian, December 2016, Ministry of External Affairs (MEA), Government of India.

Trade and commerce continue to be a mainstay of Indo-GCC relations. In 2015–16, India's exports to the GCC stood at US$ 41.71 billion.[24] The merchandise of exports to each GCC country is different: for example, petroleum products and cereals dominate exports to Saudi Arabia and Oman while gems and jewellery, petroleum products, apparel and garments dominate Indian exports to the UAE. India exports cereals to Kuwait, metals (such as iron and steel) to Bahrain, and ship and floating structure industry to Qatar.[25] During 2015–16, the bilateral trade between India and the GCC amounted to US$ 97.46 billion, witnessing a decline of US$ 36.24 billion—that is, nearly 27 per cent since 2014–15 when it was US$ 133.7 billion.[26] For 2015–16, UAE and Saudi Arabia were the prime contributors in the bilateral trade, amounting to approximately US$ 50 billion and US$ 27 billion, respectively. Bahrain, with approximately US$ 1 billion, attained the last spot in bilateral trade; Kuwait, Oman, and Qatar accounted for approximately US$ 6.2 billion, US$ 3.8 billion, and US$ 9.9 billion, respectively. The GCC's share in India's total trade consisted of 15.15 per cent during 2015–16, which was a decline of nearly 2 per cent compared to 2014–15 (see Table 11.3 below).

Table 11.3: India-GCC Bilateral Trade (in US$ million)

Country	2011–12	2012–13	2013–14	2014–15	2015–16
Bahrain	1,345.97	1,268.13	1,202.60	919.23	1,011.04
Kuwait	17,621.05	17,649.21	18,214.69	14,580.85	6,217.20
Oman	4,668.08	4,609.21	5,763.45	4,131.69	3,865.50
Qatar	13,724.30	16,380.26	16,677.04	15,659.69	9,924.20
Saudi Arabia	37,501.00	43,783.89	48,622.60	39,268.98	26,715.56
UAE	72,681.84	75,455.01	59,540.24	59,167.99	49,735.69
Total Trade with GCC	147,542.24	159,145.71	150,020.62	133,728.43	97,469.19
India's Total Trade	795,283.41	791,137.33	764,605.09	758,371.89	643,296.75
Share in Total Trade	18.32	20.12	19.62	17.63	15.15

Source: Adapted from Director-General of Foreign Trade, New Delhi, at www.dgft.gov.in

Figure 11.2: India-GCC Bilateral Trade (in US$ million)

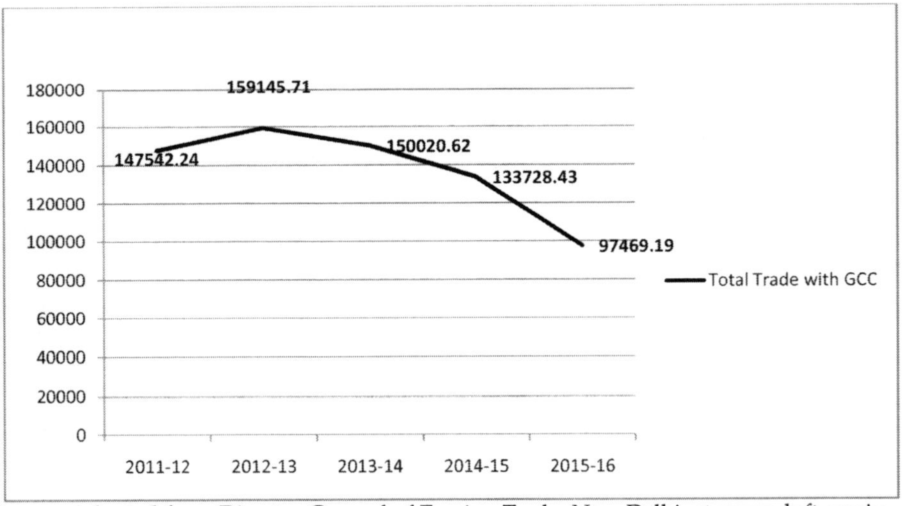

Source: Adapted from Director-General of Foreign Trade, New Delhi, at www.dgft.gov.in

India and GCC have continued to remain engaged in enhancing and expanding trade and commercial relations as well as tapping potential bilateral investments. The 4th GCC-India Industrial Forum (previously known as GCC-India Industrial Conference),[27] with the theme "Opportunities and Challenges", was held at the King Abdullah Economic City, Jeddah on 18–19 November 2015. Closer economic ties—including a free trade zone and partnerships in different areas such as healthcare, agriculture, energy, and information technology—were important matters of discussion. In this Forum, Saudi Arabia's Commerce and Industry Minister Tawfiq al-Rabiah underlined the deep rooted relationship shared by India and the GCC countries, and added: "Our ties are based on trust, friendship, mutual interests and cultural and trade exchanges. India has had a close connection with Arab and Islamic culture".[28]

The relationship between India and the GCC has witnessed significant improvement but remain anchored in energy, trade, and Indian expatriates. The growing flight connectivity between India and the GCC countries due to increasing economic interaction and the presence of Indians signifies growing people-to-people contacts.[29] Moreover, apart from considering India an economic power, it is also perceived as an important placatory power that can play a crucial role in establishing peace and stability in the region. India is exploring mutually beneficial relations with GCC countries in the economic and security fields. For its domestic investment and infrastructural development, India perceives the sovereign wealth funds (SWFs) of GCC countries as a potential source. Moreover, "Food-energy security" is also considered another significant area of cooperation between India and the GCC countries, since they import 80 per cent of rice and 60 per cent of other food commodities from India.[30]

Political contacts with the GCC have also remained robust, with the 9th annual India-GCC political dialogues held on the sidelines of the 70th United Nations General Assembly (UNGA) in New York (30 September 2015) in which External Affair Minister Sushma Swaraj identified the GCC countries as "an extended part of our neighbourhood".[31] The finalisation of the India-GCC Free Trade Agreement as well as the operationalisation of the India-GCC Framework Agreement as early as possible, were two important matters raised by her. Moreover, she also invited the GCC countries to participate in the 'Make in India' campaign.[32] The string of bilateral visits and meetings between India and the GCC countries during 2015–16 witnessed a thriving liaison stretching across the region to India.

India is heavily dependent on the GCC countries to fulfil its energy needs, and imports about 60 per cent of oil and gas from the GCC countries. In 2015–16, India's total energy imports amounted to about US$ 96.95 billion in which import from the GCC accounted for approximately US$ 35.77 billion and this was US$ 27.54 billion less than the previous year. During 2015–16, nearly 36 per cent of total energy imports came from the GCC countries, which is approximately 4 per cent less than the previous two years. Even the GCC share in energy imports from the Persian Gulf to India declined by 4 per cent, and reached to 70 per cent in 2015–16 (see Table 11.4).

Table 11.4: India's Energy Imports from GCC (in US $Million)

	2011–12	2012–13	2013–14	2014–15	2015–16
India's Total Energy Imports	172,753.92	181,344.67	181,382.59	156,400.01	96,953.06
Energy Imports from GCC	73,510.80	76,034.70	78,630.85	63,314.27	35,771.49
Total Imports from Persian Gulf	105,056.26	105,859.15	106,400.75	85,300.30	50,992.26
GCC Share in Total Imports (in per cent)	42.55	41.93	43.35	40.48	36.90
GCC Share in Imports from Persian Gulf(in per cent)	69.97	71.83	73.90	74.23	70.15

Source: Adapted from Director-General of Foreign Trade, New Delhi, at www.dgft.gov.in

Figure 11.3: India's Energy Imports from GCC

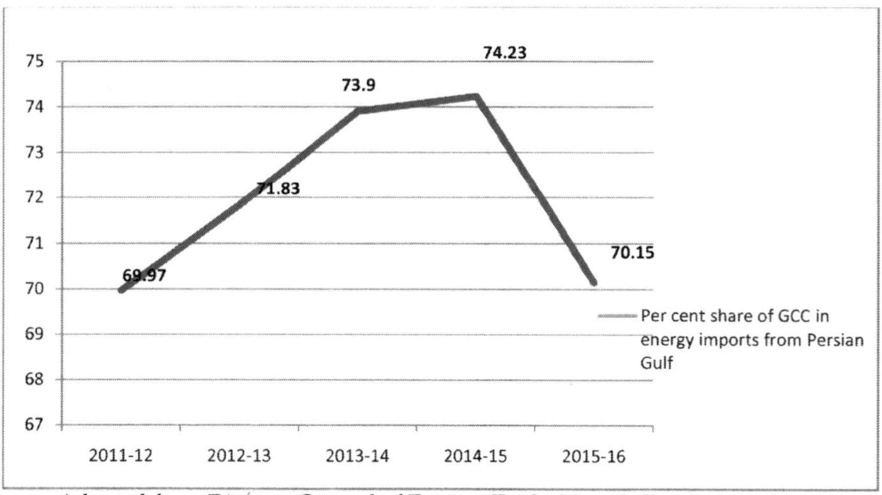

Source: Adapted from Director-General of Foreign Trade, New Delhi, www.dgft.gov.in

The Indian government is aware of the importance of establishing strategic partnerships with the GCC countries. Prime Minister Narendra Modi's emphasis is not just on 'Looking East' but also 'Linking West'. During his visit to Saudi Arabia in April 2016,[33] both countries agreed to establish a deeper partnership by focusing on investments and joint ventures in petrochemical complexes as well as in areas of research and development (R&D). Both also agreed to enhance cooperation in strengthening maritime security. By conducting joint exercises with GCC navies and increasing its visits to GCC ports, the Indian Navy has tried to establish a closer and institutionalized relationship with GCC countries.

UAE alone contributed 80 per cent of GCC FDI flow to India.[34] Indeed, FDI inflows from UAE to India witnessed the highest growth in 2015–16 which doubled to US$ 1 billion as compared to the previous year.[35] In addition to Saudi Arabia and UAE, Qatar is equally important to India since it is the largest supplier of LNG that accounted approximately for 65 per cent of India's total imports in 2015–16.[36]

Besides energy and trade relations, areas such as deterring piracy, preventing the trafficking of narcotics and weapons, and protecting sea lines of communication are important for India-GCC cooperation. On 24 January 2016, the First Ministerial Meeting of the Arab-India Cooperation Forum was held in Manama, Bahrain, and a 'Manama Declaration' was released.[37] India's External Affairs Minister Sushma Swaraj who led the Indian delegation emphasized cooperation in fighting against terrorism. In her opinion, this will be a "turning point" in Indian-Arab ties.[38]

Conclusion

Economic interdependence defines the relationship between India and the GCC. Trade and commerce as well as Indian migrant workers contribute huge remittances to the Indian economy every year. Moreover, both countries see a huge potential in the area of the investment, and wish to expand cooperation therein. However, involvement in major economic projects in the GCC region as well as further investment by the GCC in areas such as education (especially higher education), health care, agriculture, Information and Technology, and research and development (R&D) would shape their relationship more successfully. Even education exchange programmes, including regular interaction between students, scholars, and academicians, would help to create a platform for the cross fertilisation of ideas and thoughts regarding issues crucial to both India and the GCC. Like the UAE—the country which is contributing the highest FDI to India—measures should be taken to increase FDI from other GCC countries. Since the GCC fulfils more than half of its energy requirement, India's primary focus should be on the diversification of the requirement along with the efforts to opt for renewable sources of energy. Investment in energy infrastructure is also an important area of cooperation.

Some challenges include the issue of the protection of the rights of Indian expatriates present in the GCC countries. Moreover, in recent years particularly, the great challenge lies in balancing GCC and Iran which has become important for India. While there is no dearth of opportunities when it comes to investing in India, the complicated bureaucratic procedures make this task most difficult. As a result, investors look for other countries having less complex rules. Thus, India should also take some steps in this particular direction to encourage investors from the GCC countries. In addition to all these, the establishment of an inclusive institutional mechanism for strategic dialogue is of vital importance.

2015–16 has proved to be tumultuous for the Middle East region in general and the GCC in particular because of the crisis in Yemen as well as a weakening of economies resulting from falling oil prices. The relationship between India and the GCC need not be confined to economic relations; it can also play an important role in the peace and stability of the region. This would also provide safeguards to Indians living in the GCC countries. Due to falling oil prices, bilateral trade figures witnessed a drop. However, other areas of cooperation—like investment, business, information technology (IT), telecommunication, pharmaceuticals, healthcare, tourism, and infrastructure—have witnessed constant improvement. India is looking towards opting for renewable energy sources and the GCC countries are also seeking to diversify their economies. A combination of Indian human resources and GCC capital would provide both sides with additional platforms for the exploration of more areas of cooperation.

NOTES

1. Ismaeel Naar, "US-GCC talks aimed to reassure over Iran nuclear deal", *Al-Arabiya*, 3 August 2015, at https://english.alarabiya.net/en/perspective/analysis/2015/08/04/Analysis-U-S-GCC-talks-on-Iran-much-more-on-fixing-new-realities-.html.
2. Ghassan Shabaneh, "Operation Decisive Storm: Objectives and Hurdles", *Al-Jazeera*, 14 April 2015, http://studies.aljazeera.net/en/reports/2015/04/2015412115549719521.html
3. "GCC foreign ministers in Riyadh to discuss Yemen crisis", 30 April 2015, at http://www.thenational.ae/world/gcc-foreign-ministers-in-riyadh-to-discuss-yemen-crisis
4. Giorgio Cafiero, "Oman breaks from GCC on Yemen conflict", *Al-Monitor*, 7 May, 2015, at http://www.al-monitor.com/pulse/originals/2015/05/oman-response-yemen-conflict.html#ixzz4bbec6TP3
5. Daniel Wagner and Giorgio Cafiero, "The UAE's High Stakes in Yemen", *The Huffington Post*, at http://www.huffingtonpost.com/daniel-wagner/the-uaes-high-stakes-in-y_b_8170042.html
6. Farea Al-Muslimi, "A History of Missed Opportunities: Yemen and the GCC", 5 January 2016, at http://carnegie-mec.org/diwan/62405
7. "36th GCC Summit Final Communiqué", *Gulf News*, 10 December 2015, at http://gulfnews.com/news/gulf/saudi-arabia/36th-gcc-summit-final-comminque-1.1635378
8. Samuel Ramani, "Israel Is Strengthening Its Ties With The Gulf Monarchies", *The Huffington Post*, at http://www.huffingtonpost.com/samuel-ramani/why-israel-is-strengthening_b_11946660.html
9. Ibid.
10. Aarti Nagraj, "US seeks to pacify GCC states about Iran nuclear deal", *Gulf*

Business, 24 January 2016, at http://gulfbusiness.com/us-seeks-to-pacify-gcc-states-about-iran-nuclear-deal/.

11. Aresu Eqbali et al., "Iran Cancels Participation in Hajj Pilgrimage", *The Wall Street Journal*, 30 May 2016, at https://www.wsj.com/articles/iran-cancels-participation-in-hajj-pilgrimage-1464514941
12. "Syria civil war tops Russia-Arab Gulf meeting agenda", *Al-Jazeera*, 26 May 2016, at http://www.aljazeera.com/news/2016/05/syria-civil-war-tops-agenda-russia-gcc-meeting-160526085707690.html
13. Felice Friedson and Joshua A. Holmes, "As Europe Faces Syrian refugee Crisis, Gulf States Slammed for not taking in Arab Brethren" , *The Jerusalem Post*, 10 February 2016, at http://www.jpost.com/Middle-East/Analysis-Gulf-states-face-bad-rap-on-Syrian-refugee-issue-444448
14. Luay Al-Khatteeb, "The Gulf states should do more for Syrian refugees", The Brookings Institution, 30 September 2015, at https://www.brookings.edu/blog/markaz/2015/09/30/the-gulf-states-should-do-more-for-syrian-refugees/
15. "37th GCC Summit issues final communiqué", *Arab News*, 8 December 2016, at http://www.arabnews.com/node/1021001/saudi-arabia
16. Ibid.
17. Zainab Kharfati, "GCC 'faces challenges' as summit begins", *Al-Arabiya*, 6 December 2016, at https://english.alarabiya.net/en/News/middle-east/2016/12/06/GCC-union-will-be-the-primary-topic-of-37th-summit-in-Manama-.html
18. "Joint declaration at GCC summit raises hopes and expectations", *The National*, 11 December, 2016, at http://www.thenational.ae/opinion/comment/joint-declaration-at-gcc-summit-raises-hopes-and-expectations
19. "Indian merchandise exports to 6 GCC nations down 19% in 2015-16", *The Hindu*, 23 May 2016, at http://www.thehindubusinessline.com/economy/indian-merchandise-exports-to-6-gcc-nations-down-19-in-201516/article8636579.ece
20. Ibid.
21. Rebecca Bundhun, "India suffers steep decline in remittances from GCC nations", *The National*, 22 May 2016, at http://www.thenational.ae/business/economy/india-suffers-steep-decline-in-remittances-from-gcc-nations
22. "Personal Remittances, Received (% of GDP)", The World Bank, 2016, http://data.worldbank.org/indicator/BX.TRF.PWKR.DT.GD.ZS?name_desc=false.
23. The exact number of India expatriates in GCC countries is 8,492,754. See, "Population of Overseas Indians", Ministry of External Affairs, Government of India, December 2016, at http://mea.gov.in/images/attach/NRIs-and-PIOs_1.pdf.
24. "India-GCC Relations", Embassy of India, Riyadh, 26 May 2016, at http://www.indianembassy.org.sa/Content.aspx?ID=890
25. "Indian merchandise exports to 6 GCC nations down 19% in 2015-16", *The Hindu*, op. cit.
26. "India-GCC Relations", Embassy of India, Riyadh. op. cit.
27. "Brochure: Opportunities and Challenges", 4th GCC-India Industrial Forum, 18–19 November 2015, King Abdullah Economic City, Jeddah, Kingdom of Saudi Arabia, at http://gccindiaforum.in/Document/Gulf_Brochure.pdf
28. Siraj, Wahab, "GCC and India discuss closer trade ties at Rabigh", *Arab News*, 19 November 2015, at http://www.arabnews.com/economy/ news/837501
29. Hassan Rashid, "GCC relations with India changing dynamics beyond traditional

links", *Arab News*, 26 January 2015, at http://www.arabnews.com/saudi-arabia/news/694851.

30. Girijesh Pant, "Reconstructing India-GCC Relation in the Context of Arab Uprising", in Meena Singh Roy (ed.), *Emerging Trend in West Asia: Regional and Global Implications*, New Delhi: Pentagon Press, 2014, pp. 257–279.
31. "Swaraj pushes for India-GCC Free Trade Agreement", *The Hindu*, 1 October 2015, at http://www.thehindu.com/news/national/swaraj-pushes-for-indiagulf-cooperation-council-free-trade agreement/article7710985.ece
32. Ibid.
33. "India-Saudi Arabia Joint Statement during the visit of Prime Minister to Saudi Arabia (3 April 2016)", 3 April 2016, Ministry of External Affairs, Government of India, at http://www.mea.gov.in/bilateral-documents.htm?dtl/26595/IndiaSaudi+Arabia+Joint+Statement+during+the+visit+of+Prime+Minister+to+Saudi+Arabia+April+03+2016.
34. "UAE has 80% of GCC investment in India", Emirates 24/7, 10 February 2016, http://www.emirates247.com/business/uae-has-80-of-gcc-investment-in-india-2016-02-10-1.620519.
35. Jyotindra Dubey , "FDI inflow from UAE to India more than doubled to $ 1 bn", *Hindustan Times*, 31 Aug 2016, at http://www.hindustantimes.com/business-news/fdi-inflow-from-uae-to-india-more-than-doubled-to-1-bn/story-yqK8y7zHF7Ghp9ap9CuNdL.html
36. Zikrur Rahman, "Modi's Qatar visit to Bridge the Remaining Gulf with GCC", *The Pioneer*, 4 June 2016, at http://www.dailypioneer.com/columnists/oped/modis-qatar-visit-to-bridge-the-remaining-gulf-with-gcc.html
37. "Manama Declaration of the First Ministerial Meeting of the Arab-India Cooperation Forum (January 24, 2016)", Ministry of External Affairs, Government of India, 24 January 2016, at http://www.mea.gov.in/outoging-visitdetail.htm?26292/Manama+Declaration+of+the+First+Ministerial+Meeting+ of+the+ArabIndia+Cooperation+Forum+January+24+2016
38. "India Arab League Vow to Check Terror, Funding Sources", *The Hindu*, 25 January 2016, at http://www.thehindu.com/todays-paper/tp-national/India-Arab-League-vow-to-check-terror-funding-sources/article14019174.ece.

12

CHINA

Swati Arun

Commenting on President Xi Jinping's first visit to the Middle East in January 2016, Li Shaoxian, the deputy head of China's Institute of Contemporary International Relations, said, "China is the only great nation without imperial interests or demands in the Middle East."[1] However, this statement runs in the face of the gradual shift in China's policy towards the Middle East, especially after the Arab Spring. It has slowly and gradually abandoned its erstwhile foreign policy dictum of "keeping a low profile" and "avoiding leadership" in dealing with threats to national interest. It has, in fact, initiated several multilateral economic projects and mediated between conflicting states, and slowly abandoned its "non-interventionist" policy. China imports about half of its oil requirements from the Middle East and, in the current state of regional instability, it risks loss of business by maintaining its distance from regional politics. The looming uncertainty after the Arab Spring has worked as a catalyst for China to change its strategy, for now the relations cannot be completely void of political influence.

As the US gradually lessens its engagements in the region, many Arab states are worried about the vacuum and are Looking East, especially towards China. China's economic forays into the region have created opportunities to expand investments and allow the Gulf economies to tide over problems in times of crisis. China has managed to carve a huge share of the Middle Eastern market, and includes the region in its One Belt One

Road (OBOR)[2] initiative, thus countering instability by boosting the economy. However, while China tries to tackle conflicts with the economic carrot, it might prove to be a heavy liability because of the convoluted and complex problems facing the region. From using diplomacy to engaging with disputing parties and providing aid to rebuild the region, China has started to also establish military relationships with defence sales and joint exercises—all signifying its growing interests and stakes in the region.

Chinese policy towards the Persian Gulf started to take a new shape under Deng Xiaoping, and with Soviet disintegration and the end of the Cold War, Beijing intensified its commercial forays into the Gulf. It simultaneously built strategic links with countries like Iran, and in the words of John Calabrese, no longer remained "a marginal player". Neither did the Gulf remained "peripheral" to China's strategic interests.[3] It continued to build further commercial and political ties with other countries in the Gulf, including Saudi Arabia and the UAE; at the same time, it began building strategic commercial links in Iraq after 2005. Despite the regional turmoil and instability since the Arab Spring, Chinese involvement in the Gulf has remained strong, and is marked by major commercial stakes. Though it has preferred to remain militarily uninvolved, it has built strategic relations with major stakeholders in the region, including non-state actors.

In the last two years, Beijing has intensified its diplomatic and political engagements with Gulf countries as well as strengthened its security and counter-terror links. However, trade and commerce remain the most important aspect of Chinese forays into the Gulf. So far, India—which has significant stakes in the Gulf—has not faced any serious problem due to Chinese involvement; but it will have to watch developments closely and carve out its policies accordingly.

Politics and Diplomacy

In the on-going crisis in Yemen, China found itself in a tough spot between Iran and Saudi Arabia, its top trading partners and oil suppliers. It presented two sets of challenges—one, to its economy, namely, potential loss of trade, threat to investment projects, and disruption in oil supply; and two, fear of the spread of extremism in the already restive Xinjiang region.[4] However, in the last two years, China has juggled successfully between the two regional adversaries and remained neutral in the Yemen crisis, calling for political resolutions rather than military ones. In doing so, it did not accuse any party, Iran or Saudi Arabia, for disrupting the peace. It upheld Yemen's right to sovereignty and independence while maintaining relations with both

Iran-supported Houthi militia as well as the Saudi-supported government of Abdrabbuh Mansur Hadi.[5] After President Hadi and his government resigned in January 2015, Saudi Arabia started air strikes on Yemen against the Houthi rebels, thereby fuelling the crisis.

Reflective of the uncertainty, in March 2015, the Chinese navy evacuated its citizens and nationals belonging to other countries from Yemen. It was the first naval mission where China helped another country with evacuations. In April, in response to the Yemen crisis, President Xi Jinping cancelled his first official visit to Saudi Arabia, Moreover, China stepped up efforts to defuse tensions between Riyadh and Tehran. In April 2015, in a telephonic conversation with King Salman, Xi expressed China's concerns over the Yemeni crisis, and suggested resolving the conflict through political negotiation.[6] In December 2016, China expressed concerns after the armed Houthis and their political allies formed a government. It reiterated that it does "not support any side in Yemen taking any unilateral action that complicates the situation."[7]

In December, Beijing hosted a delegation from the Yemeni Houthi Ansarullah movement for talks to discuss the conflict and how it could reach an acceptable resolution.[8] The Houthi government is rejected by all international parties, except Iran. The Chinese position, though not entirely neutral or without preferences, was one of declared "non-intervention" in any matters that might lead it into taking a stand—as in Iraq. During Xi Jinping's visit to Riyadh in 2016, China affirmed its support for Yemen's government against the Houthi rebels.[9]

Sino-Iranian relations have been good; but the Chinese refusal to allow Iran's entry in the Shanghai Cooperation Organization (SCO) as a full member reflects its indecision regarding what role it wants Iran to play in its Middle East policy.[10] Another argument could be that it did not want to give the SCO an anti-US character due to Iranian membership, even though the latter is an Observer since June 2005.[11] Probably in an attempt to avoid picking favourites, President Xi Jinping during his visit to the region (January 2016) elevated China's relations with both Riyadh and Tehran into 'strategic partnership[s]'.[12]

China's strategy to mitigate the Yemen crisis involved heavy investment, boosting trade, and strong diplomatic ties with the region. In the past, China showed extreme enthusiasm to engage with the Gulf countries through the China-Arab States Cooperation Forum (CASCF) which was established in 2004. At the 6th Ministerial Conference in 2014, President Xi proposed a "1+2+3" pattern of cooperation—energy as the core, then infrastructure plus trade and investment facilitation as two wings. Additionally, three areas of high tech cooperation—nuclear energy, space satellites, and other new energy initiatives—were included.[13] Keeping up with the expectations, in the past two years, China has pledged substantial investment in the Gulf, and signed several MoUs. During his January 2016 visit to Cairo, President Xi Jinping announced aid of US$ 55 billion to the Arab League.[14]

China has been active in trying to pacify Iran and Saudi Arabia, especially after the January 2016 Saudi execution of Nimr al-Nimr, a popular Shia dissenting cleric from the restive Eastern Province. Xi Jinping promptly dispatched his Deputy Foreign Minister, Zhang Ming, to both Tehran and Riyadh, urging both the sides to remain calm. Consequently, Xi Jinping also rearranged his travel itinerary by adding an unplanned stop in Tehran, thereby replacing his planned visit to the UAE. Thus, the Chinese President became the first foreign leader to visit Iran after the lifting of the sanctions following the signing of the Joint Comprehensive Plan of Action in July 2015.[15] China wants to present itself as a as a reliable great power from whom countries along the Persian Gulf can seek political and diplomatic support.

Trade and Commerce

The Persian Gulf region has 55 per cent of the world's proven crude oil reserves and 41 per cent of known natural gas reserves.[16] China is one of the largest consumers of energy, and is the leading importer of Gulf oil and gas. By 2035, China is projected to become the largest oil importer as demand is speculated to rise from the current 6 million barrels per day (bpd) to 13 million bpd.[17] The Paris-based International Energy Agency (IEA) has speculated that, by 2035, Chinese imports from the Gulf region would be doubled. Likewise, other estimates suggest that 90 per cent of Middle Eastern oil would go to Asia, given the decline in American imports due to fracking, hydraulic fracturing, and shale gas.[18] Meanwhile, China is reportedly targeting to enhance its strategic oil reserves from the current 37 days to 100 days by 2020.[19]

Chinese relations with the Gulf States have largely been associated with business. In the last decade itself, its trade with the Gulf increased 600 per cent to US$ 230 billion in 2014.[20] It imported 6.2 million barrels/per day (bpd) of crude oil in 2014, and half of it or 3 million bpd came from the Gulf.[21] With the slump in oil prices, the Gulf countries reached out for foreign investment in infrastructure, energy, oil drilling, and heavy industry. With its active commercial diplomacy, China emerged as the leading investor and business partner, signed several agreements, and pledged investment for infrastructure development with an eye on the OBOR initiative.[22] China has significant bilateral trade with individual Gulf states; however, the collective trade with nine Persian Gulf countries amounted to US$ 260 billion in 2014 but dropped to US$ 193 billion in 2015 (see Table 12.1).

Among the Gulf States, Saudi Arabia is China's largest trade partner and, in 2015, it imported goods worth US$ 21.16 billion and exported goods worth US$ 30.02 billion, with the trade balance remaining in China's favour. Similarly, in 2014, Chinese imports from the Kingdom stood at US$ 20.57 billion and its exports at US$ 48.5 billion, amounting to nearly 14 per cent of China's total international trade.[23] It has also signed agreements to establish joint ventures with big Saudi companies. For example, in October 2015, Saudi Basic Industries Corporation (SABIC), the world's largest petrochemical company, planned more than three joint venture projects in China.[24]

During Xi Jinping's Gulf visit in January 2016, China announced a common investment fund worth US$ 20 billion for the UAE and Qatar. An additional US$ 10 billion was promised as commercial loans to boost cooperation in the energy sector with the Gulf States, while a further US$ 10 billion was offered as preferential loans to stimulate investments.[25] President Xi Jinping and King Salman signed 14 agreements and MoUs during Xi's visit. China promised to invest US$ 2.43 billion to build a nuclear manufacturing equipment industrial cluster, first scheduled to be online in 2022, and then 15 more by 2032.[26] It was also agreed that the joint venture between Saudi's Aramco and China's Petroleum and Chemical Corporation (Sinopec) would undergo a US$ 1–1.5 billion expansion.[27] Even though Saudi Arabia is an American ally, its relations with China have soared in the past decade, oil being the key factor.[28]

Beijing's relations with the UAE have also soared in the economic domain as both are more focused on high-tech joint ventures in construction and renewable energy.[29] It is estimated that 60 per cent of total Chinese trade to Europe and Africa passes through the UAE.[30] This dependence raises its stakes in regional security. China accounts for 10 per cent of the total Emirati non-oil trade, and an estimated 300,000 Chinese nationals live in the UAE, in addition to 4,200 Chinese companies, 356 trade agencies, and more than 2,500 Chinese trade labels registered therein.[31] The UAE continues to be the largest Middle East market for Chinese products and, in 2014, it overtook India as UAE's largest non-oil trade partner.[32]

Table 12.1: China-Gulf Trade (US$ million)

	2012			2013			2014			2015		
	Total	Export	Imports	Total	Export	Import	Total	Export	Import	Total	Export	Import
Bahrain	1,550.81	1,202.78	348.03	1,544.11	1,238.93	305.18	1,415.75	1,231.78	183.96	1,123.39	1,011.85	111.54
Iran	36,465.84	11,597.45	24,868.39	39,426.51	14,036.65	25,389.86	51,842.34	24,338.49	27,503.85	33,827.55	17,770.11	16,057.45
Iraq	17,567.59	4,911.82	12,655.77	24,878.85	6,894.09	17,984.76	28,505.08	7,743.84	20,761.24	20,583.86	7,909.23	12,674.63
Kuwait	12,556.99	2,089.18	10,467.81	12,262.15	2,675.51	9,586.64	13,433.69	3,428.72	10,004.96	11,269.74	3,772.67	7,497.07
Oman	18,787.02	1,811.58	16,975.44	22,941.46	1,900.84	21,040.61	25,861.24	2,065.38	23,795.86	17,163.81	2,116.39	15,047.42
Qatar	8,483.20	1,205.10	727,810	10,174.26	171,091	846,335	10,590.74	2.254.01	8,336.73	6,890.01	2,275.64	4,614.37
Saudi Arabia	73,314.22	18,452.35	54,861.87	72,190.53	18,739.81	53,450.71	69,083.27	20.575.24	48,508.03	51,633.98	21,612.93	30,021.05
UAE	40,420.29	29,568.32	10,851.97	46,234.82	33,411.30	12,823.53	54,797.86	39,034.51	15,763.36	48,534.20	37,020.16	11,514.03
Yemen	5,559.15	1,955.10	3,604.06	5,200.12	2,138.82	3,061.30	5,134.17	2,201.31	2,932.85	2,328.11	1,429.97	898.14
Total	214,705.11	72,793.68	862,443.34	234,852.81	252,126.95	989,977.59	260,664.14	80,067.11	157,790.84	193,354.65	94,918.95	98,436

Source: National Bureau of Statistics of China, *China Statistical Yearbook*, at http://www.stats.gov.cn

Figure 12.1: China-Gulf Trade, 2012–15 (US$ million)

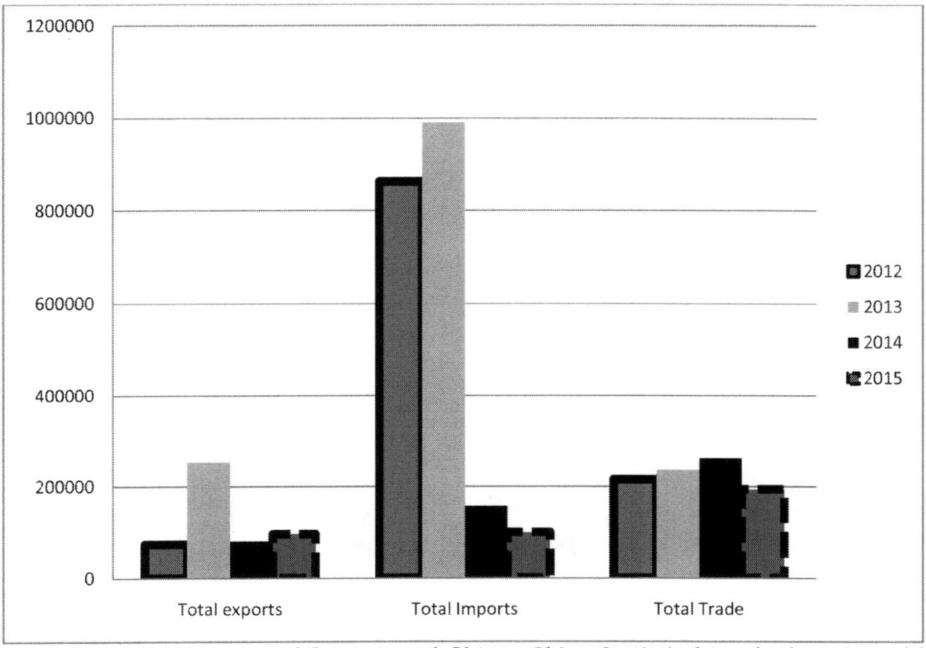

Source: National Bureau of Statistics of China, *China Statistical Yearbook*, at http://www.stats.gov.cn

China's relations with Iran withstood the hardships of sanctions.[33] In 2015, the bilateral trade stood at US$ 33.82 billion. China exported goods worth US$ 16.74 billion and imported products worth US$ 17.77 billion (see Table 12.1). Of the Chinese imports, non-oil commodities were worth US$ 9.15 billion while of its total exports to Iran non-oil goods comprised US$ 12.56 billion.[34] China's support to Iran throughout the nuclear impasse and sanctions as well as its continued trade was acknowledged by President Hassan Rouhani who said, "China has always stood by the side of the Iranian nation during hard days."[35] During Xi Jinping's January 2016 visit to Tehran, Supreme Leader Ayatollah Ali Khamenei acknowledged the friendship and understanding between the two states, and said, "The Islamic Republic will never forget China's cooperation during the sanctions era."[36] After the sanctions were lifted, competitive Chinese companies which were not allowed to trade with Iran earlier—because of having US partners—could invest in Iran, and the process has already been started with several agreements signed during Xi's visit.[37]

There were expectations that Iran would be inducted as a member of SCO which would boost its foreign trade. At the SCO summit in Ufa in July

2015, Iran's Deputy Foreign Minister, Ebrahim Rahimpour said, "We will get a chance to develop active trade ties with all the SCO member countries after the sanctions against Iran are removed". He said that, current annual trade volumes between Iran and the SCO states stood at about US$ 90 billion.[38] However, in June 2016, China refused Iran's membership in the SCO, despite assurance from President Xi Jinping during his January visit. Commenting on the situation, Foreign Minister Wang Yi said that the current focus was on the full membership of Pakistan and India in the SCO.[39]

Despite the setback, cooperation between the two states was soaring. President Xi Jinping told his Iranian counterpart Hassan Rouhani (during the latter's visit to China in September 2015) that, "China will prioritize its energy and financial cooperation with Iran."[40] During their meeting in Tehran (2 January 2016), both sides signed a 25 year economic, political, and military cooperation pact, as also 17 agreements ranging from oil drilling to nuclear energy, infrastructure projects facilitating Iran in the larger OBOR project. Rouhani predicted that the bilateral deals would boost bilateral trade tenfold—to US$ 600 billion annually in the next decade.[41]

A memorandum of understanding (MoU) for the expansion of industrial, mineral, and investment cooperation was also signed during the visit. According to Iran's SHATA news agency, the memorandum focuses on bilateral cooperation and investment in the construction of passenger trains as well as in the manufacturing of trucks, trailers, and auto parts. The MoU also proposed the transfer of technical know-how for the production of drilling rigs as well as investment in all areas related to the copper industry, chemical fertilizers, glass fibre, lead, etc. The memorandum covers 20 projects which would be implemented through finance or joint investment.[42] Throughout the meeting, the focus remained on infrastructure. "Connectivity is the artery of the thousand-mile land and maritime silk roads. To build connectivity with Middle East countries, China should start with transportation infrastructure," said Zhang Shuyu, a researcher with the University of International Business and Economics.[43]

China has expanded its presence in Iraq by committing to several commercial and developmental projects. In December 2015, Iraqi Prime Minister, Haidar al-Abadi, visited Beijing to increase Chinese investment to "rebuild the country." The Iraqi leader and his Chinese counterpart, Li Keqiang, signed five agreements, pledged to establish a long-term energy partnership, and increase energy cooperation, including oilfield projects and refinery construction.[44] Li Keqiang said that, "Iraq is an important partner of China in the region", and that China was willing to increase cooperation in areas of oil exploitation and refinery construction.[45] The joint statement mentioned that China pledged to channel

> more investment to the energy sector and higher cooperation between government and undertakings in the areas of crude oil trade, oil-gas exploration and development, oilfield engineering service and technology, construction of storage and transportation facilities, chemical refining engineering and energy equipment [and that it wishes to] help Iraq improve its production capacity of cement, steel, flat glass and engineering machinery.[46]

Vice Minister Zhang Ming said that both parties reached the consensus to use China-made equipment to support oil-gas explorations. Additionally, Prime Minister Li and Prime Minister Abadi signed a MoU on the promotion of "Silk Road Economic Belt" and "21st Century Maritime Silk Road."

Iraq's oilfields are among the largest in the Middle East and are open to foreign investments; China is its top foreign investor. However, most of Iraq's oil is drilled by international oil companies under the Kurdistan Regional Government (KRG). China has established direct links with the KRG and opened a Consulate in Irbil in December 2014.

China has good economic and trade relations with other GCC countries as well. These include Kuwait, Qatar, Bahrain, and Oman. In March 2016, Kuwait's crude oil export to China hit 409,000 bpd—a 30 per cent rise from 2015. China-Kuwait trade has been steady and, in 2015, the total trade stood at US$ 11.2 billion—a minor drop from the US$ 13.4 billion the previous year, mainly attributed to falling oil prices. With Qatar, bilateral trade stood at US$ 4.8 billion (QR17.5 billion) in 2016—down from US$ 5.9 billion (QR21.5 billion) in 2015. Qatar's major imports are iron and steel; flat rolled iron; bars, angles, and shapes of steel; aluminium plates, sheets and strips; copper tubes and pipe fittings; and railway or tramway track construction heavy tools and equipment, among other products.[47]

Qatari exports to China include liquefied natural gas; minerals, fuels, petroleum oil and petroleum products; plastics and its products; and miscellaneous petrochemical products. Like many other states, Qatar set in motion policies to attract more trade from China in Yuan. In 2015, Qatar launched the MENA (Middle East and North Africa) region's first Renminbi centre, "[w]hich has helped attract more trade transactions in the Chinese currency".[48] The Industrial and Commercial Bank of China's (ICBC), located in the Qatar Financial Centre, is the clearing bank for the centre. Since its inauguration in June 2015, the total currency transaction was approximately US$ 60 billion or 419 billion Chinese Yuan. Likewise, China's FDI in Qatar rose 77.5 per cent in 2016.[49]

With Bahrain, Chinese trade were less compared to other GCC countries, with a total trade of US$ 1.1 billion in 2015 (see Table 12.1). Oman is an important economic partner and, in March 2016, Oman hosted the 8th China-Oman Joint Committee of Economic and Trade in Muscat. The two sides discussed investment opportunities in Oman, and applauded the progress in bilateral relations.[50] On 23 May 2016, an agreement was reached between Oman's government and Chinese investors to develop a new US$ 10.7 billion industrial city near the port of Duqm by 2022.[51] This project is expected to help Oman strengthen its construction sector. According to media reports, in total about "35 projects will be undertaken, including the construction of an oil refinery capable of processing 235,000 bpd, a petrochemical complex, a concrete plant, a steel smelter, a glass factory, an aluminium plant, and a solar factory to produce panels and batteries."[52] China and Oman have also been discussing the Omani participation in the OBOR that would help the economic development of Oman.[53]

China was the top importer of Omani exports in 2015, with 50 per cent of the total exports[54] and retained the top position in importing crude oil from Oman. It purchased 180.99 million barrels from Oman in the first nine months of 2016 or 74.97 per cent of Oman's total export of 241.41 million barrels.[55] In 2015, China imported 237.56 million barrels, out of a total 308.14 million barrels exported by Oman. China is also the top export and import destination of Yemen, carving out a share of 39 per cent and 15 per cent respectively, in 2015.[56]

Defence and Security

While China faces internal problems—especially with some extremist groups like the East Turkestan Islamic Movement (ETIM)[57]—an alarming wave of Uyghurs from the disturbed Xinjiang region have been joining the ISIS in large numbers. In 2014, the ISIS leader Abu Bakr al-Baghdadi said that China was on a par with states such as Israel, India, and the United States as an "oppressor" of Muslims.[58] This announcement was followed by the group's execution of a Chinese citizen, Fan Jinghui, in Iraq in November 2015. There were also reports of about 300 Chinese Muslims fighting alongside ISIS.[59] This has become an obvious threat facing China's strategic engagements and economic ambitions in the region.

In the wake of the Paris attacks in November 2015, in the summit meeting of Asia Pacific Economic Cooperation (APEC) held in Pasay in November 2015, Chinese President Xi called terrorism "the common enemy of all human beings."[60] Foreign Minister Wang Yi said, "China is also a victim of terrorism, and cracking down on ETIM should become an important part of the international fight against terrorism."[61] In December 2015, China adopted its first counter-terrorism law.[62]

During his visit to the Gulf countries in January 2016, Xi Jinping pledged to expand security cooperation and oppose terrorism. The *People's Liberation Army Daily* reported (17 October 2016) that China held its first anti-terror exercise with Saudi Arabia to combat terrorism and non-traditional security threats.[63] In the same month, China voiced its support for Iraq to retake Mosul from ISIS. However, in February 2016, Foreign Minister Wang Yi said that, "China will not take part in any coalition fighting 'Terrorist groups' in the Middle East, but will do its fair share in its own way and is already helping Iraq."[64] In other words, it would be counterproductive for China to align itself with any one side while the future still remained uncertain. Since it maintains ties with all parties to protect its investments and citizens in the region, it is perhaps best for it to remain neutral.[65]

Further, Sino-Saudi counter-terrorism cooperation witnessed some movement when, in November 2016, Meng Jianzhu (special envoy of the Chinese President) met King Salman and signed a five year plan for security cooperation. The plans included counter-terrorism cooperation and joint military exercises.[66] In October 2016, both countries conducted their first joint anti-terrorism drill near Chongqing. The *People's Liberation Army Daily* reported that, "[t]his joint anti-terrorism training is directed at raising the two militaries' ability to combat terrorism and non-traditional security threats."[67]

China has made agreements with Saudi Arabia, the UAE, and Iraq for the sale of CH (Cai Hong, or Rainbow-4), a medium-altitude, long endurance, armed drone. Reportedly, Saudi Arabia and the UAE are employing it in their fight against Yemen's Houthi rebels, and Iraq against ISIS forces.[68] Good relations with China have led to the sharing of military technology with the UAE. For example, when the US refused to sell armed drones to the Emirates, China offered a cheap duplicate in the Predator or the Wing Long which, reportedly, the UAE used during the Yemen crisis.[69] On the nuclear front, post-sanctions Iran became free to engage in civil nuclear agreements which would benefit China. In 2016, the head of Iran's Atomic Energy Commission, Ali Akbar Salehi, announced that Tehran planned to accept help from China for the construction of two nuclear power plants. Furthermore, Ali Akbar Salehi (the head of the Atomic Energy Organization of Iran) and Xu Dazhe (the head of China's Atomic Energy Authority) agreed on "cooperation for [the] reconfiguration of the Arak nuclear facility, along with nuclear cooperation in economic, research and industrial areas."[70]

The growing military partnership between China and the Gulf also underscores China's intentions. In the last two years, the UAE, Iraq, Iran, and Saudi Arabia have made several visits to China to secure military partnerships, and China has signed MoUs with Iran, Iraq, and Saudi Arabia to further establish "military to military relations."[71] In this regard, though OBOR is solely intended to maximize business and regional economic cooperation among all actors, it is highly likely to extend its reach beyond economics. Commenting on the developing relations between the two countries, Senior Colonel Zhang Ge, Defence Attaché of the Chinese Embassy in Kuwait said, "military to military cooperation are on the right track and we are confident for more bilateral events in [the] future."[72]

China, the Gulf and India

The OBOR came out as an important component of Chinese foreign policy for the year 2015–16. This was signified by a year around promotion occurring both within and outside the country. Two major debates have come out of its new relationship with the Middle East promoted extensively through OBOR: one, China is free riding on the security provided by the US; and two, China only has economic interests. The former argument is largely provided by Western observers, while Middle Eastern thinkers subscribe to the latter. It is possible to conclude that, keeping in mind the pattern wherein China leverages its massive economic strength vis-à-vis smaller powers (like Philippines), it would utilize the same leverage in the Middle East. However, the question that arises is: towards what end? Certainly, China needs to bring its economy back to normal, as economic growth is directly linked to the legitimacy and power of the Communist Party of China (CCP). However, should the Middle East be complacent or oblivious to the impending consequences of such asymmetrical relations with China?

India has been a close partner of the Middle East; but with growing Chinese power in the Gulf, India requires to take a more proactive stand. For one, Chinese interests might only be business at present; but this could change and, in the long run, China accumulating soft power in the Gulf could diminish India's position. The "new normal" state of affairs between the US and China suggests a struggle between a global power and a rising power, and the dissatisfied power would try (has been trying) to change the rules of the international order to a preferred end. Against this backdrop, a classic case of a security dilemma sets in: India should not have to deal with an overpowering China in its second tier neighbourhood merely because weaker powers in the Middle East would be unable to defy Chinese rules changing the international order. This would not bode well with India.

In another case of leveraging economic interdependence in a conflict situation, China might use such a power to control energy transfer to India, hampering its growth and capability. However, for now, China sits in a favourable position in the Middle East, and India needs to catch up. An accurate estimate of Chinese 'power' in the Middle East can only be asserted after a successful implementation and functioning of the OBOR vision.

Moreover, the region is under stress over the US withdrawal. Though China oscillates between non-intervention and the protection of self-interest, it categorically denies any interest in tackling conflict and regional issues as a main participant, and prefers to stay an invisible mitigator—as in 2015 and 2016 when it mediated between Iran and Saudi Arabia. In yet another attempt to defy the intentions of world leadership, in his speech to the Arab League, Xi Jinping said China has not been seeking proxies and would not try to fill any vacuum left. However, while OBOR will provide commercial benefits to the region, it would also require China to get involved in matters of both security and politics, to maintain regional stability for the sake of its investments and personnel. And if anything, the Communist Party of China (CCP) cares more for financial sustainability and security.

NOTES

1. Alice Su, "'Let's not talk politics': China builds Middle East ties through business", *Al-Jazeera* America, 20 February 2016, at http://america.aljazeera.com/articles/2016/2/20/china-middle-east-business-politics.html.
2. Laurence Brahm, "The New Silk Road will Link China with the Middle East," *Business Insider*, 6 June 2016, at http://www.businessinsider.com/new-silk-road-to-link-china-and-middle-east-2016-6?IR=T.
3. John Calabrese, "China and the Persian Gulf: Energy and Security", *Middle East Journal*, 1998, Vol. 52, No.3, pp. 351–366.
4. Claude Arpi, "The Xinjiang Takeover: China's Master-Stroke," *The Pioneer*, 20 April 2017, at http://www.dailypioneer.com/columnists/edit/the-xinjiang-takeover-chinas-master-stroke.html.
5. Shannon Tiezzi, "The Elephant in the Room during Xi's Trip to Saudi Arabia: Iran", *The Diplomat*, 21 January 2016, http://thediplomat.com/2016/01/the-elephant-in-the-room-during-xis-trip-to-saudi-arabia-iran/
6. Owen Mathews, 'China: Iran's new Best friend', *Newsweek*, 2 December 2016, at http://www.newsweek.com/2016/02/12/china-irans-hassan-rouhani-xi-jinping-421614.html
7. "China expresses concerns as Yemen's Houthi form government", *Reuters*, 2 December, 2016, http://in.reuters.com/article/yemen-security-china-idINKBN13S01L
8. "Features of China's Policies in Yemen War", *Middle East Observer*, 3 December 2016, at https://www.middleeastobserver.org/2016/12/03/features-of-chinas-policies-in-the-war-in-yemen/

9. "China backs Yemeni government says Xi from Riyadh", *The New Arab*, 20 January 2016, at https://www.alaraby.co.uk/english/news/2016/1/20/china-backs-yemeni-government-says-xi-from-riyadh
10. "China Refuses Iran's Membership in the Shanghai Cooperation Organisation despite Russia's Insistence", Rudaw, 24 June 2016, http://www.rudaw.net/english/middleeast/iran/24062016.
11. Kevjn Lim, "Iran's Shanghai Dream," *Foreign Affairs*, 25 July 2016, at https://www.foreignaffairs.com/articles/china/2016-07-25/irans-shanghai-dream.
12. "President Xi Jinping Arrives in Riyadh for State Visit to Saudi Arabia," Ministry of Foreign Affairs, People's Republic of China [FMPRC], Press Release, 20 January 2016, at http://www.fmprc.gov.cn/mfa_eng/topics_665678/xjpdstajyljxgsfw/t1333529.shtml; see also, "Xi Jinping Arrives in Tehran for State Visit to Iran", FMPRC, Press Release, 23 January 2016, at http://www.fmprc.gov.cn/mfa_eng/topics_665678/xjpdstajyljxgsfw/t1335158.shtml.
13. "Arab Policy Paper", *Xinhua*, 13 January 2016, at http://news.xinhuanet.com/english/china/2016-01/13/c_135006619.html
14. Gal Luft, "China's Grand Strategy for the Middle East", *Foreign Policy*, 26 January 2016, at http://foreignpolicy.com/2016/01/26/chinas-new-middle-east-grand-strategy-iran-saudi-arabia-oil-xi-jinping/
15. Thomas Erdbrink, "China Deepens its Footprint in Iran after Lifting of Sanctions", *The New York Times*, 24 January 2016, at https://www.nytimes.com/2016/01/25/world/middleeast/china-deepens-its-footprint-in-iran-after-lifting-of-sanctions.html.
16. *International Energy Outlook, 2016*, US Energy Information Administration, May 2016, https://www.eia.gov/outlooks/ieo/pdf/0484(2016).pdf.
17. "China FDI to Qatar up 77.5% in 2016, says trade official", *Gulf Times*, 3 April 2017, at http://www.gulf-times.com/story/543003/China-FDI-to-Qatar-up-77-5-in-2016-says-trade-offi
18. "The Great Well of China," 18 June 2015, *The Economist*, at http://www.economist.com/news/middle-east-and-africa/21654655-oil-bringing-china-and-arab-world-closer-economically-politics-will.
19. Meng Meng and Chen Aizhu, "China Goes Underground to Expand its Strategic Oil Reserves," *Reuters*, 6 January 2016, at http://www.reuters.com/article/us-china-oil-reserves-idUSKBN0UK2NO20160106.
20. "The Great Well of China", *The Economist*, op.cit.
21. Mirek Dusek and Maroun Kairouz, "Is China pivoting towards the Middle East?", *World Economic Forum*, 4 April 2017, at https://www.weforum.org/agenda/2017/04/is-china-pivoting-towards-the-middle-east/.
22. Christopher Fix, "China's New Silk Road a Fast Lane for Trade", *Barron's*, 10 December 2015, at http://www.barrons.com/articles/chinas-new-silk-road-a-fast-lane-for-trade-1449649589.
23. "Saudi Arabia", The Observatory of Economic Complexity, at http://atlas.media.mit.edu/en/profile/country/sau/
24. Deema Almashabi, "Saudi Arabia's Sabic Plans More Than Three Ventures in China", Bloomberg, 18 October 2015, at https://www.bloomberg.com/news/articles/2015-10-18/saudi-arabia-s-sabic-plans-more-than-three-ventures-in-china
25. "China to invest $55 billion in Middle East infrastructure", *Out-Law.com*, 27 January 2016, at https://www.out-law.com/en/articles/2016/january/china-to-

invest-55-billion-in-middle-east-infrastructure/
26. John J. Xenakis, "World View: China Signs Nuclear Deals with Saudi Arabia and Iran", Breitbart, 23 January 2016, at http://www.breitbart.com/national-security/2016/01/23/23-jan-16-world-view-china-signs-nuclear-deals-with-saudi-arabia-and-iran/
27. Ibid.
28. Wang Jin, "China and Saudi Arabia: A New Alliance?", *The Diplomat*, 2 September 2016, at http://thediplomat.com/2016/09/china-and-saudi-arabia-a-new-alliance/; see also, Daniel Wagner and Giorgio Cafiero, "Is the U.S. Losing Saudi Arabia to China?", *Huffington Post*, at http://www.huffingtonpost.com/daniel-wagner/is-the-us-losing-saudi-ar_b_4176729.html.
29. LeAnne Graves, "Chinese Investment to Spur Middle East Renewable Energy Ambitions," *The National*, 6 December 2015, at http://www.thenational.ae/business/energy/chinese-investment-to-spur-middle-east-renewable-energy-ambitions
30. Courtney Trenwith, "China-UAE Trade: Enter the Dragon", *arabianbusiness.com*, 10 March 2013, at http://www.arabianbusiness.com/china-uae-trade-enter-dragon-492242.html.
31. Christina Lin, "UAE's Increasing Role in China's Security Calculus", *Asia Times*, 29 March 2017, at http://www.atimes.com/uaes-increasing-role-chinas-security-calculus/.
32. "China Overtakes India as Dubai's Largest Trade Partner", *Gulf News*, 23 March 2015, http://gulfnews.com/business/economy/china-overtakes-india-as-dubai-s-largest-trade-partner-1.1478108.
33. Srikanth Kondapalli, "China and the Iranian Nuclear Issue: Converting Challenges into Opportunities", *Contemporary Review of the Middle* East, 2016, vol. 3, no. 1, pp. 63-76.
34. Tehran Chamber of Commerce, Industries, Mines and Agriculture [TCCIMA], "Iran, China to develop trade, transport ties", 5 January 2016, htttp://www.tccim.ir/english/newsfullstory.aspx?nid=6400&sword=china
35. *Mail Online*, "China Seeks 'New Chapter' with Iran after Sanctions End", 23 January 2016, http://www.dailymail.co.uk/wires/ap/article-3413245/China-seeks-new-chapter-Iran-sanctions-lifted.html.
36. Michael Singh, "China's Middle East Tour", *Foreign Affairs*, 24 January 2016 at http://www.washingtoninstitute.org/policy-analysis/view/chinas-middle-east-tour
37. "New side of Iran-China trade", *TCCIMA*, 31 August 2015, at http://www.tccim.ir/english/newsfullstory.aspx?nid=6243&sword=china
38. "Iran, SCO to Develop Trade Ties after Sanctions' Lift: Official", *TCCIMA*, 12 July 2015, at http://www.tccim.ir/english/newsfullstory.aspx?nid=6175&sword=china
39. "China refuses Iran's membership in the Shanghai Cooperation Organization despite Russia's insistence", *Rudaw*, 24 June 2016, http://www.rudaw.net/english/middleeast/iran/24062016
40. Ben Blanchard and Michael Perry, "China's Xi Says to Prioritize Energy Cooperation with Iran," *Reuters*, 29 September 2015, at http://www.reuters.com/article/us-china-iran-idUSKCN0RT0B920150929
41. "Belt & Road Initiative shores up China-Mideast cooperation", *Xinhuanet*, 23

January 2016, http://news.xinhuanet.com/english/2016-01/23/c_135038752.htm

42. "Iran, China sign MoU to boost industrial, mineral and investment cooperation", Ministry of Industry, Mine and Trade, Islamic Republic of Iran, 23 January 2016, at http://en.mimt.gov.ir/news/301881-Iran-China-sign-MoU-boost-industrial-mineral-and-investment-cooperation.html?t=News
43. "News Analysis: Belt & Road Initiative shores up China-Mideast cooperation", *Xinhuanet*, 23 January 2016, at http://news.xinhuanet.com/english/2016-01/23/c_135038752.htm
44. "China, Iraq ink economic, military agreements during Abadi visit", *The BRICS Post*, 23 December 2015, at http://thebricspost.com/china-iraq-ink-economic-military-agreements-during-abadi-visit/#.WQHHqFOGORs
45. "China, Iraq sign memo to promote energy partnership", The State Council, People's Republic of China, 23 December 2015, at http://english.gov.cn/premier/news/2015/12/23/content_281475259135066.htm
46. "China, Iraq sign memo to promote energy partnership", *Xinhuanet*, 22 December 2015, http://news.xinhuanet.com/english/2015-12/22/c_134942270.htm
47. "China FDI to Qatar up 77.5% in 2016, says trade official", *Gulf Times*, 3 April 2017, at http://www.gulf-times.com/story/543003/China-FDI-to-Qatar-up-77-5-in-2016-says-trade-offi
48. Ibid.
49. "China FDI to Qatar up 77.5% in 2016, Says Trade Official", China Invests Overseas, 5 April 2017, at http://www.china-invests.net/20170405/43566.aspx.
50. "8th Meeting of China-Oman Joint Committee of Economics and Trade Held in Muscat", Ministry of Commerce, People's Republic of China, 25 March 2016, at http://qiankeming2.mofcom.gov.cn/article/activity/201603/20160301285909.shtml
51. "Built on a total area of about 1172 hectares Usufruct agreement for China-Omani industrial park in Duqm signed", Duqm Special Economic Zone Authority, 24 May 2016, at http://www.duqm.gov.om/sezad/media/news/built-on-a-total-area-of-about-1172-hectares-usufruct-agreement-for-china-omani-industrial-park-in-duqm-signed
52. "China's investment in $10.7bn in Oman to provide building boost", *The National*, 20 August 2016, at http://www.thenational.ae/business/property/chinas-investment-in-107bn-city-in-oman-to-provide-building-boost
53. "Wang Yong Visits Oman", MFA, PRC, 23 May 2016, at http://www.fmprc.gov.cn/mfa_eng/zxxx_662805/t1366321.shtml
54. "With 50 per cent share, China top importer of Omani goods", *Times of Oman*, 10 July 2016, http://timesofoman.com/article/87673/Oman/Government/With-50-per-cent-share-China-top-importer-of-Omani-goods
55. "China retains top position in importing Oman Crude", *Times of Oman*, 24 October 2016, at https://www.pressreader.com/oman/times-of-oman/20161024/281779923663575
56. "Yemen", The Observatory of Economic Complexity, at http://atlas.media.mit.edu/en/profile/country/yem/
57. "Why is there Tension between China and the Uighurs?", *BBC News*, 26 September 2014, at http://www.bbc.com/news/world-asia-china-26414014.
58. Michael Clarke, "How China Uses Fear of Terrorism to Justify Increased State Power", *CNN*, 9 June 2016, at http://edition.cnn.com/2016/06/08/asia/china-

xinjiang-terrorism-clarke/.

59. "About 300 Chinese fighting alongside ISIS", *The Gulf Today*, 16 December 2014, at http://gulftoday.ae/portal/9f9208b2-0e36-47a7-959d-cc413e9a9184.aspx
60. "APEC Economic Leaders Call for Increased International Cooperation against Terrorism", *Xinhuanet*, 19 November 2015, at http://news.xinhuanet.com/english/2015-11/19/c_134834292.htm.
61. "China says global war on terror should also target Uighur militants", *Reuters*, 16 November 2015, at http://www.reuters.com/article/france-shooting-china-idUSKCN0T506M20151116
62. "China adopts first counter-terrorism law in history", *Xinhuanet*, 27 December 2015, at http://news.xinhuanet.com/english/2015-12/27/c_134956054.htm
63. "China holds first anti-terror drills with Saudi Arabia", *Reuters*, 27 October 2016, at http://www.reuters.com/article/us-china-saudi-security-idUSKCN12R0FD
64. "China rules out joining anti-terrorism coalitions, says helping Iraq", *Reuters*, 12 February 2016, at http://www.reuters.com/article/us-mideast-crisis-china-idUSKCN0VL1SV
65. Mordechai Chaziza, "China's Middle East Policy: The ISIS Factor", Middle East Policy Council, at http://www.mepc.org/chinas-middle-east-policy-isis-factor.
66. Samuel Ramani, "China and Saudi Arabia's Burgeoning Defence Ties", *The Diplomat*, 16 November 2016, at http://thediplomat.com/2016/11/china-and-saudi-arabias-burgeoning-defense-ties/
67. "China holds first anti-terror drills with Saudi Arabia", *Reuters*, 27 October 2016, at http://www.reuters.com/article/us-china-saudi-security-idUSKCN12R0FD
68. "China is Top Combat Aerial Drone Supplier to Muslim Military Powers", *China Topix*, 7 December 2016, at http://www.chinatopix.com/articles/107623/20161207/china-top-combat-aerial-drone-supplier-muslim-military-powers.htm
69. Michael Cruickshank, "Chinese drones: Cheap, lethal and flying in the Middle East", *Middle East Eye*, 7 April 2016; at http://www.middleeasteye.net/news/china-drones-1492124367
70. Debalina Ghosal, "China Pivots to the Middle East and Iran", *Yale Global Online*, 7 July 2016, at http://yaleglobal.yale.edu/content/china-pivots-middle-east-and-iran
71. "China, Iraq establish strategic partnership", *China Mail*, 22 December 2015, at http://eng.chinamil.com.cn/news-channels/today-headlines/2015-12/22/content_6827379.htm
72. "Kuwait-Chinese military relations developing: Official", *Kuwait Times*, 2 August 2016, http://news.kuwaittimes.net/pdf/2016/aug/02/p02.pdf.

13

PAKISTAN

Divya Malhotra

Pakistan-Gulf relations lie at the interface of emotions, interests, and ideology. Since its birth in 1947, Pakistan has looked towards the Maghreb (West) for support. The Persian Gulf region has held specific significance in Pakistan's foreign policy calculus as well as in the psyche of common Pakistanis. Once the Viceroy of India decided to grant independent status to Pakistan, the Saudi King was the first head of state to felicitate Mohammed Ali Jinnah, the first Governor General of Pakistan; and Iran extended an equally warm response. Geographically, Pakistan has the advantage of being at the crossroads of West, South, and Central Asia, and of being surrounded by Iran, Afghanistan, China, and India. Its coastline along the Arabian Sea brings it into close contact with the countries along the Persian Gulf. Its ideological and geographical intimacy with the Gulf has eventually translated into strong economic, political, military as well as cultural ties.

Historically, Islam was the main point of confluence between Pakistan and its Gulf neighbourhood. Saudi Arabia's support in wars with India won it a special spot and, by the fact of geography, its Shia neighbour Iran also cultivated close ties. The Shah offered support to Islamabad during its wars with India. However, the strategic strength of India vis-à-vis Pakistan became pronounced with the latter's continued failures, particularly its territorial loss in the 1971 war. Moreover, Islamabad's tilt towards the Arab world also made Tehran uncomfortable. Nonetheless, its self-projection as the "personification of Islam" was used by Pakistan to forge easy friendships with all the littoral states of the Gulf.[1] Even though Pakistan has mostly adopted a neutral stance towards regional conflicts, it could never remain unaffected by the regional turmoil. Therefore, at times, it has assumed the role of a moderating agent.[2] On the whole, the six-member Gulf Co-operation Council (GCC) states, along with Iran and Iraq, have been a significant component of its strategic calculus and its vital stakes in the region. Over time, the Persian Gulf has sustained its significance in Pakistan's foreign policy blueprint.

In 2014, Pakistan's Gulf equation was dominated by the Saudi factor. Since the election of Nawaz Sharif as Prime Minister in June 2013, there has been sustained activism in the bilateral relations between Pakistan and the Gulf countries. An important development was the Saudi success in diluting Pakistan's non-partisan stance on the Syria issue. A Joint statement issued by both the parties in February 2014 regarding the "formation of an interim governing body to replace the Bashar al Assad regime" testifies to the claim.[3] On the other hand, Iran took a back seat in Pakistan's priorities due to sanction-related restrictions and pressure from Washington. The change of stance on the Syria issue further punctured relations with Tehran. In parallel, Islamabad continued to engage with leaderships in other Gulf countries. On the whole, the Nawaz Sharif government managed to forge close political, economic, and military equations with its extended neighbourhood in the Middle East as their interests converged on multiple levels, while relations with Iran went downhill.

This essay explores the areas of convergence as well as contradictions between Pakistan and the Persian Gulf countries in 2015 and 2016. A special emphasis would be on its cautious engagement with its Shia neighbour Iran, and how it calibrated its ties between two mutually hostile countries—Saudi Arabia and Iran. Bilateral ties would be discussed in the contexts of diplomatic engagement, defence cooperation, economic synergy, and migrant dynamics.

Diplomatic Engagement and Political Equations

The last two years—that is, 2015 and 2016—can be labelled as years of shaky diplomacy for Pakistan, with the Joint Comprehensive Plan of Action (JCPOA) bringing Iran back into the international arena, and the Yemen crisis causing diplomatic tremors. As Saudi-Iran relations soured over Yemen and other issues, Pakistan found itself amidst a geopolitical conundrum. While it managed to balance its position towards securing its economic interests, its "vague and ambiguous" stance attracted derision from Saudi Arabia and its allies.[4] Thus, its decision to detach and distance itself from the regional conflict strained and soured its relations with some of the Gulf monarchies despite the number of official visits exchanged. Saudi Arabia and Pakistan displayed active diplomatic engagement with maximum state visits, while war-torn Iraq did not see any official engagements.

Saudi Arabia

Saudi Arabia and Pakistan have shared a historically strong bond, guided by interests as well as religious-cultural affinities. During the period under review, their political and security leaderships came together many times. However, this delicate alliance was put to test in 2015 when Riyadh asked for Islamabad's aid in *Operation Decisive Storm* against the Houthis rebellion, a Shia politico-religious movement in which other Arab states, including Egypt, Morocco, Jordan, Sudan, Kuwait, the UAE, Qatar, and Bahrain, took part.[5] The political leadership of Pakistan did not succumb to Riyadh's pressures, and chose not to get embroiled militarily. In a smart political move, this position was legitimised through a unanimous resolution adopted in the special joint session of parliament held on 10 April 2015 that called on the government to "maintain neutrality in the Yemen conflict so as to be able to play a proactive diplomatic role to end the crisis"; and at the same time, the *Majlis-e-Shura* (Parliament) expressed "unequivocal support for the Kingdom of Saudi Arabia, and affirms (this) in case of any violation of its territorial integrity."[6]

Most scholars and observers have seen this development as a balancing act, wherein Pakistan tried to strike a fine balance between the two regional rivals, thereby preventing a further polarisation of the region. Nevertheless, this development can also be looked at from an internal security angle, suggesting that Pakistan did not want to open a third front. Its military has been at war with religious extremists to contain home grown terrorism.[7] On the Afghan border, up to 30,000 military personnel have been engaged in *Operation Zarb-e-Azb* since 2014 to eliminate foreign and indigenous militants hiding in the North Waziristan province.[8] Moreover, its border issues with India on the east also demand military engagement. Under such circumstances, supporting the Saudi-led military operation in Yemen would have put serious pressure upon the Pakistani military, thereby jeopardizing its operations on the two fronts.

The only advantage Pakistan could have gained by way of denying military assistance to the Saudis is a possible role of mediator to dissolve tensions. It was the only non-Arab Islamic nation that could potentially engineer a face-saving solution to achieve a cease-fire and de-escalate the Yemen war.[9] Nonetheless, the lines of communication remained open between the two countries and there were continued interactions, evident in high-level visits (see Table 13.1).

Iran

Interests overpower emotions in diplomacy, and the case of Iran testifies the claim. Iran-Pakistan relations had been stalled as a consequence of the US-led sanctions imposed on Iran in 2012. However, there has been a reversal since the signs of sanction-removal surfaced in 2015. Finally, as the JCPOA came into effect in October 2015 and sanctions were lifted in January 2016, Pakistan hurried to reconcile its stalled relations. Ever since, there has been a notable upsurge in Pakistan's political contacts with Iran. Cautious engagement under sanctions and many calculative rendezvous after sanctions-lift has been Pakistan's mantra while devising its relations with Iran.

With signs of nuclear negotiations becoming clearer, trade and investment emerged as the dominant themes of deliberations in 2015. There was Foreign Minister level interaction in April 2015 when Iranian Javad Zarif visited Pakistan. The main objective of this visit was to discuss Pakistan's position on the calculative Yemen issue, and enhance economic ties between the two countries; but there was little headway on the security front.[10] Pak-Iran diplomacy slowly gained momentum; this was evident in the visit of its Commerce Minister, Khurram Dastagir Khan, to Tehran in April 2015 for the seventh Pakistan-Iran Joint Trade Committee meeting, and the subsequent meeting of the Pak-Iran Joint Working Group and Technical Committee on Trade in August 2015 to frame a five-year strategic plan for bolstering bilateral trade.

The dawn of 2016 saw Pakistan's shuttle diplomacy between Saudi Arabia and Iran. After visiting Riyadh, Prime Minister Nawaz Sharif stopped over to meet Iranian Defence Minister to pacify tensions brewing between the two Gulf neighbours. In response to global developments, Pakistan opened a new chapter of ties in the post-sanction era by lifting sanctions against Iran in accordance with the UNSC Resolution 2231 in February 2016.[11] In March, Iranian President Hassan Rouhani visited Pakistan (the first Iranian head of state to visit Pakistan in 14 years)[12] and discussed issues relating to border management, and pushed for greater cooperation in energy and investment business. This visit was also significant in the light of Pakistan's refusal to join the Saudi led military alliance in Yemen.

During President Rouhani's second visit in September 2016, Iran's willingness to get aboard the China Pakistan Economic Corridor (CPEC) was highlighted. This could be seen as its strategy for reaching out to newer markets and enhancing its economic footprint.[13] Iran is the only Persian Gulf country with which Pakistan shares a border, and has border issues regarding illegal trade and clashes. In 2016, Pakistani authorities started building a gate at the country's border with Iran—at Taftan in Baluchistan's Chagai district.[14] The stalled Iran-Pakistan gas pipeline is yet another important and unresolved bilateral issue. Even though Prime Minister Nawaz Sharif had taken up the matter with Iranian President during his visit to Tehran in 2014, no tangible progress was made. While Iran has completed the work on the pipeline on its side of the border, Pakistan has only offered rhetorical support to this project by announcing a new deadline (2018) for the completion of the project.[15]

The UAE

Relations between the Pakistan and the UAE reached a new low when the Emirati Minister of State for Foreign Affairs warned Pakistan of having to pay a "heavy price for taking an ambiguous stand,"[16] which was perceived to be de facto equivalent of siding with Iran over the Yemen conflict. Since then, there has been no significant progress in the relations between the two on the diplomatic front. The attack on the Deputy Prime Minister and Interior Minister of the UAE while travelling in the Guchak area of the Panjgur district of Baluchistan (on a Houbara Bustard hunting expedition in December 2016) worsened the relations further. The frostiness that has crept into UAE-Pak relations has been labelled as the prime reason for the UAE's growing proximity with Pakistan's adversaries, including India. No radical shift is expected in the UAE-Pak ties even as the UAE has been steadily increasing bilateral ties with other South Asian economies. However, the two countries have continued to deepen the economic engagement. This can be gauged from the fact that the UAE came second only to China in terms of Foreign Direct Investment in 2016, with an investment of US$ 111 million in Pakistan's economy.[17] Moreover, the strong diaspora linkages between the two countries would always act as a buffer while mending their relations.

Bahrain

Prime Minister Nawaz Sharif undertook a two-day visit to Bahrain in January 2015 to discuss potential areas of economic cooperation and increasing bilateral trade which then stood at US$ 200 million.[18] The meeting culminated in the signing of several MoUs in sectors ranging from arts, culture, education, and business.[19] The signing of the agreement to declare the capital cities of Islamabad and Manama as the twin cities also signalled diplomatic warmth and optimism. In July 2016, in a goodwill gesture,

Bahrain granted the Royal Pardon to 82 Pakistani inmates due to the special efforts made by Ambassador Javed Malik.[20] However, Islamabad received a major jolt in October when Bahrain extended support for the Indian position on the Kashmir issue by questioning Pakistan's portrayal of Kashmiri militants as freedom fighters.[21] This was an exceptional diplomatic gain for India from a member of the Organisation of Islamic Cooperation (OIC) that has traditionally backed Islamabad. Nonetheless, the year ended on a positive note, with deliberations between Pakistan's Foreign Affairs Advisor Sartaj Aziz and Bahrain's Foreign Minister Khalid al-Khalifa during the Manama Security Dialogue in December.[22] Thus, diplomatically, the relations remained sound despite sporadic hiccups.

Qatar and Kuwait

Qatar engaged in bilateral talks with Pakistan regarding energy, investment, trade, defence and manpower in March 2015.[23] Qatar also showed interest in co-financing the Neelum-Jhelum hydropower project, and supported the proposed Free Trade Agreement (FTA) between Pakistan and the GCC. However, these promises could not translate into action.[24] The signing of US$ 1 billion LNG gas supply deal and several other MoUs in the field of health, media, education, and research during Nawaz Sharif's visit to Qatar in February 2016 also garnered attention.[25]

Kuwait and Pakistan had two major bilateral exchanges in the two years. On the side lines of the 42nd OIC Council of Foreign Ministers (CFM) meeting in Kuwait City in May 2015, Pakistan's Foreign Affairs Advisor, Sartaj Aziz, met with Khalid al-Sabah, Deputy Prime Minister and Minister of Foreign Affairs of Kuwait to discuss visa and investment related issues.[26] On a similar format, the second round of political consultations was held in Kuwait in the summer of 2016, with representatives of Ministry Foreign of Affairs from both the sides.[27]

Iraq and Oman

Islamabad's engagement with Iraq during these two years was characterised by diplomatic silence. Iraq garnered some media attention when the report regarding 100 Pakistanis, who travelled to Iraq and Syria to join the Islamic State (IS), surfaced in January 2016.[28] Relations with Oman got a boost in September 2016, when Pakistani Foreign Affairs Advisor, Sartaj Aziz, visited Muscat to augment bilateral cooperation.[29]

Defence Dialogue and Cooperation

The Pakistan army is highly revered among the Persian Gulf nations who look towards the former to train their military personnel and upgrade their warfare architecture. In March 2015, the Pak-Saudi joint exercise *Samsam-5* was conducted in Taif, involving the participation of 292 Pakistani troops.[30] In December 2015, the navies of Pakistan and Bahrain conducted a series of bilateral exercises, *Shaheen Al Jazeera*; these have been conducted regularly since 1997 at Karachi and Manama alternatively. The exercises are aimed at enhancing counter terrorism and maritime security. In February-March 2016, Pakistan participated in the *North Thunder* joint military exercise conducted by Saudi Arabia in Taif, along with 20 other Muslim nations.[31] The political and diplomatic fissures over Yemen did not prevent Saudi Arabia from conducting joint military exercises with Pakistan. This is reminiscent of the cordial bond shared by the two nations.[32] Thereafter, in August 2016, Israel, the UAE, and Pakistan participated in the joint military exercise at Nellis Air Force base in Nevada in the US.[33] This gained media attention because Pakistan and UAE do not have diplomatic relations with Israel. This exercise raised a controversy in Islamabad,[34] but the issue faded sooner than expected.

As the diplomatic impasse between sanction-hit Iran and Pakistan started loosening, both conducted a joint naval exercise in the strategic waters of the Strait of Hormuz in April 2016; in September, the Iranian Navy's 43rd flotilla docked at Karachi port for a joint drill.[35] In December, Pakistan and Oman conducted the joint naval exercise *Thamar al Tayyab* at Karachi Port, which was the eighth in the series.[36] These exercises with Saudi Arabia, Bahrain, UAE, and Iran were aimed at enhancing operational and tactical coordination and understanding between the militaries of the participating countries.

Besides these exercises, military-specific ministerial visits are also indicative of the level of defence diplomacy. There was active and continued interaction between the militaries of the respective countries (see Table 13.1). In January 2015, Prime Minister Nawaz Sharif and the Chief of the Air Staff, Rafique Butt, paid two separate visits to the Bahrain Defence Forces' Headquarters in Manama to discuss issues relating to military cooperation.[37] In February and March, the Army Chiefs of UAE and Pakistan came together to discuss military capabilities and cooperative framework. In April, a high level defence delegation from Islamabad went to Riyadh to hold talks with the Saudi Defence Minister Khawaja Asif, and in June, the Commander of the Kuwait navy met Pakistan's Naval Chief and Air Chief to deliberate over maritime security issues. While the first half of the year witnessed high-level defence interactions, the latter half of the year witnessed two separate visits by the Qatar Army Chief in August to discuss maritime threats in the

Indian Ocean, and Commander of the Kuwait Air Force (December 2015) to deliberate over security issues.

Table 13.1: Number of Defence visits to Pakistan in 2015 and 2016

Country	Visits in 2015	Visits in 2016
Bahrain	2	0
UAE	2	0
Saudi Arabia	1	3
Kuwait	2	0
Qatar	1	2
Iraq	0	1

Source: Adapted from *Pakistan Watch*, Middle East Institute, New Delhi. http://www.mei.org.in/front/search/search.php

Note: Defence visits include visits by Defence Ministers or senior officials from the Ministry of Defence. The ministries and media sources do not cover all the visits, and thus the actual number may be more than the numbers identified here.

Figure 13.1: Number of Defence visits

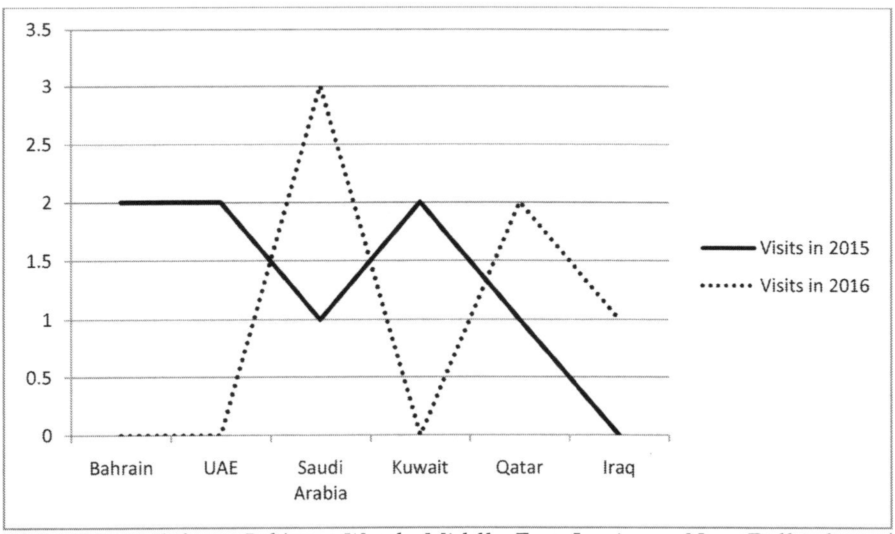

Source: Adapted from *Pakistan Watch*, Middle East Institute, New Delhi. http://www.mei.org.in/front/search/search.php

The year 2016 was relatively dull in defence diplomacy and dialogues (see Table 13.1). In March, the Pakistani Federal Minister for Defence Production, Tanveer Hussain, held a meeting with Iraqi Defence Minister Khalid al-Obeidi in Baghdad to offer military and security cooperation in the revamping of the Iraqi Security Forces. In April, the Chief of Air Staff, Sohail Aman, discussed air force training related issues with both his Saudi counterpart Ahmed Alshaa'lan and Defence Minister Prince Muhammad bin Salman al-Saud during his visit to Royal Saudi Air Operations Centre. In November, the Commander of the Royal Saudi Air Force, Saleh al-Otaibi, visited Joint Staff Headquarters in Rawalpindi to discuss bilateral matters relating to military cooperation with Rashad Mahmood, Chairman of Pakistan's Joint Chiefs of Staff Committee.

Doha and Islamabad inked two defence related dialogues: first, in June when an important defence production agreement entitled Pakistan Aeronautical Complex (PAC) to supply Super Mushshak Aircraft to the Qatar Air Force; second, in October, when Mamnoon Hussain's visit to Doha reaffirmed interests of both sides in furthering defence cooperation.[38]

While Saudi Arabia ranks high on the defence cooperation parameter, it is essential to study the other side of the defence equation, and highlight what Islamabad offers to its Gulf neighbours. Almost fifty per cent of arms and ammunition exports from the Pakistan Ordnance Factory (POF)—a unit under Ministry of Defence Production—goes to the GCC countries.[39] In 2016, Saudi Arabia emerged as the largest importer of Pakistani arms and ammunition,[40] and there have been signs that the UAE could be the next export destination for made-in-Pakistan weaponry.[41]

As 2015 was drawing to a close, Saudi Arabia floated the idea of an inter-regional mechanism to combat terrorism, particularly the Islamic State of Iraq and Syria (ISIS). The Saudi proposal to form a NATO-like military alliance—called the Islamic Military Alliance (IMA)—attracted immense global attention.[42] The coalition included Egypt, UAE, Qatar, Malaysia, Turkey, Pakistan, and several African nations. Iran, along with the two ISIS front lines countries, Syria and Iraq, were excluded.[43] The composition of the alliance suggests that it is part of the Saudi doctrine aimed to build a Sunni coalition for countering Iran-led Shia influence in the region. Reports have re-confirmed that, at the end of the joint military exercise (including 21 Muslim nations) held in the northern part of the Kingdom in March 2016, Saudi Arabia reasserted its ideas and designated Islamabad to chalk out the framework.[44] Since the inception of the idea in December 2015, the reactions of Pakistani officials regarding their inclusion in the alliance seemed to signal that they were not consulted before on this issue, and that it was an impromptu decision made by the Saudis.[45]

Moreover, in January 2016, Foreign Affairs Advisor, Sartaj Aziz assured the international community that, despite joining the Islamic military alliance, Pakistan would refrain from direct military engagement in Saudi Arabia or any other country.[46] However, in April, it played its counter-balancing stroke and agreed to extend all possible help, including the deployment of troops if the territorial integrity of Saudi Arabia came under threat.[47] Thus, Islamabad's reaction was slow and measured. Interestingly, Saudi Arabia's assumption of Pakistan's blind support was not new, as Riyadh had earlier also nominated it as part of its military alliances against Yemen without prior consultation and consent, and hoisted its flag at the alliance's media centre.[48] However, Pakistan's refusal to side with Saudi Arabia—in congruence with its policy of not deploying its troops outside the country's borders except for UN peacekeeping missions—created a rift between the two Sunni allies.[49] Riyadh's decision to posit Islamabad at the centre of the alliance cannot be discounted as a mere coincidence. Playing the Pakistan card was indeed a calculative strategy to sideline Iran. With former Army Chief, Raheel Sharif, becoming the face of the Iran-less alliance,[50] it would be interesting to gauge how the decision impacts Islamabad's relations with its Shia neighbour.

While the alliance may silence Western claims of the inaction of the Muslim world regarding the problem of terrorism, in some quarters it is believed that this coalition was labelled as a "new adventure" for Prince Mohammed bin Salman in order to disperse attention from the failures of the Yemen coalition.[51] The action plan still remains ambiguous. Since the Saudis are occupied in Yemen, there has been no significant development on this front, and their counter-terrorism mark sheet still remains blank.

Economic Synergy

The trade equation between Pakistan and the Persian Gulf countries has been uneven and skewed in favour of the latter. A basic assessment of the situation can be done based on changes in balance of trade. Trade balance improves owing to two circumstances: fall in imports or rise in exports, and it is important to analyse which of the two factors lead to the change in trade account. A comparison of trade balance in 2014–15 and 2015–16 (see Table 13.2, Table 13.3 and Table 13.4) signals that while bilateral trade remained largely unfavourable for Pakistan, it still managed to reduce its trade deficit marginally with four countries: the UAE, Saudi Arabia, Oman, and Kuwait. It registered a fall in imports from these four countries in 2014–15 and 2015–16, accompanied by a drop in exports to first three. The fall in imports was greater than the drop in exports, thereby indicating a slight fall in overall deficit figures.

Nonetheless, imports continued to exceed the exports, and deficit prevailed. The only country with which it raised its exports was Kuwait. This led to a marginal deficit correction, but the rise in exports was not enough to offset a trade deficit. Iraq was the only country which recorded a trade surplus in both years. However, the quantum of surplus went downwards in 2015, registering a fall of 37 per cent in the surplus account due to overall drop in bilateral trade—that is, export as well as imports.

The Pakistan-Bahrain trade equation shifted from the deficit to the surplus category on account of a steep fall (75 per cent) in imports from Bahrain, accompanied by a slight drop in exports (15 per cent) from Pakistan. More detailed analysis reveals that Islamabad reduced its fuel imports from Bahrain from US$ 80 million to US$ 7.78 million—a sharp fall of 90 per cent. Since the drop in imports from Bahrain exceeded the drop in exports to Bahrain, a surplus situation was achieved.[52] With regard to Iran and Qatar, its trade deficit rose on account of a steep rise in its imports. In the case of Iran, there was a steep rise in imports of fuel which increased from US$ 58 million in 2014 to US$ 118 million in 2015.[53] Similarly with Qatar, there was sharp rise in fuel imports from US$ 0.8 million in 2014 to US$ 153 million in 2015.[54]

Table 13.2: Pakistan's Trade Composition (2014–15)

Country	Exports (US$ million)	Imports (US$ million)	Trade Balance 2014-15 (US$ million)
UAE	1.324	7.077	–5.753
Saudi Arabia	0.509	4.417	–3.907
Oman	0.185	1.133	–0.947
Kuwait	0.097	2.954	–2.856
Iran	0.043	0.185	–0.142
Qatar	0.074	0.180	–0.106
Bahrain	0.082	0.111	–0.029
Iraq	0.047	0.016	+0.030

Source: Adapted from World Bank, at http://wits.worldbank.org/

Table 13.3: Pakistan's Trade Balance (2015–16)

Country	Trade Balance (US$ million)	Exports (US$ million)	Imports (US$ million)
UAE	–4,835	0.899	5.734
Saudi Arabia	–2,575	0.431	3.006
Oman	–443	0.170	0.614
Kuwait	–1,612	0.100	1.712
Iran	–228	0.032	0.260
Qatar	–255	0.063	0.319
Bahrain	+40	0.069	0.028
Iraq	+19	0.031	0.011

Source: World Bank, at http://wits.worldbank.org/.

Table 13.4: Pakistan's Trade Balance with Persian Gulf nations

Country	Trade Balance 2014–15 (US$ million)	Trade Balance 2015–16 (US$ million)
UAE	–5.753	–4.835
Saudi Arabia	–3.907	–2.575
Oman	–0.947	–0.443
Kuwait	–2.856	–1.612
Iran	–0.142	–0.228
Qatar	–0.106	–0.255
Bahrain	–0.029	+0.040
Iraq	+0.030	+0.019

Source: Adapted from World Bank, at http://wits.worldbank.org/

In 2015, Pakistan's top five import partners included the UAE (second) and Saudi Arabia (third) from which it imported 13 per cent and six per cent of their total annual imports respectively, while none of the Persian Gulf nations were among the top five buyers of its domestically produced goods.[55] Thus, Pakistan's dependence on the Persian Gulf nations becomes evident in this unbalanced transactional relation.

Interestingly, the diplomatic coldness over the Yemen issue did not impede economic engagement between the UAE and Pakistan which had the maximum trade exchange in 2015.[56] The spill-over effects of the political impasse were not visible in trade which remained rather immune and unaffected. Equally important is the nature of the dependence, as is reflected clearly in Table 13.5 and Table 13.6. The trade profile of Persian Gulf countries clearly signals that petroleum related products dominate the export-side (Bahrain being the only exception) while rice dominates the import-side of the trade equation (Iran being the only exception). Thus, the Persian Gulf continued to cater to Pakistan's energy needs and also offered a market for its primary goods.

Table 13.5: Composition of Exports from the Persian Gulf to Pakistan (2015) (in US$ million)

Country	Main Item of export	Value (share in per cent)	Total Exports to Pakistan
UAE	Crude Petroleum	2,900 (56)	5,380
Saudi Arabia	Refined Petroleum	1,460 (48)	3,010
Kuwait	Refined Petroleum	1,290 (79)	1,630
Oman	Refined Petroleum	458 (80)	575
Qatar	Petroleum Gas	152 (45)	340
Bahrain	Scrap Iron	7.8 (22)	36.4
Iran	Petroleum Gas	5.0 (21)	242
Iraq	Petroleum Gas	4.12 (19)	10.7

Source: Observatory of Economic Complexity, at http://atlas.media.mit.edu/en/visualize/tree_map/hs92/export/irq/pak/show/2015/

Figure 13.2: Imports from Persian Gulf to Pakistan (2015)

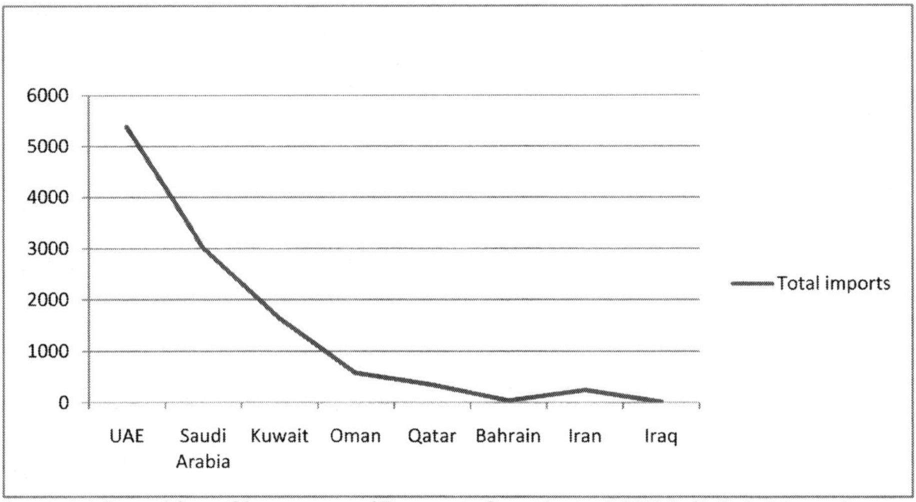

Source: Adapted from Observatory of Economic Complexity, MIT Media Lab. Massachusetts, 2015, at http://atlas.media.mit.edu/en/visualize/tree_map/hs92/export/irq/pak/show/2015/

Table 13.6: Composition of Pakistani Exports to Persian Gulf (2015) (in US$ million)

Country	Main Item of export	Value (share in per cent)	Total Imports to Pakistan
UAE	Rice	135 (15)	899
Saudi Arabia	Rice	85.6 (16)	551
Kuwait	Bovine Meat	39.8 (20)	201
Oman	Rice	116 (54)	215
Qatar	Rice	26 (27)	160
Bahrain	Rice	16.6 (17)	98.5
Iran	Paper	19.7 (61)	32.3
Iraq	Tents and Sails	7.27 (23)	31.3

Source: Observatory of Economic Complexity, at http://atlas.media.mit.edu/en/visualize/tree_map/hs92/import/irq/pak/show/2015/

Labour Dynamics

The labour factor has traditionally been pivotal to Pakistan-Gulf relations, and latter's contribution in the form of remittances elevates it in Islamabad's strategic calculus. The Gulf region absorbs huge manpower from Pakistan, and this labour migration culminates in a huge inflow of foreign exchange. Saudi Arabia has traditionally been the largest source of remittance flows and, in 2015 and 2016, retained its position, followed by the UAE and other

Figure 13.3: Pakistani Exports to Persian Gulf (2015)

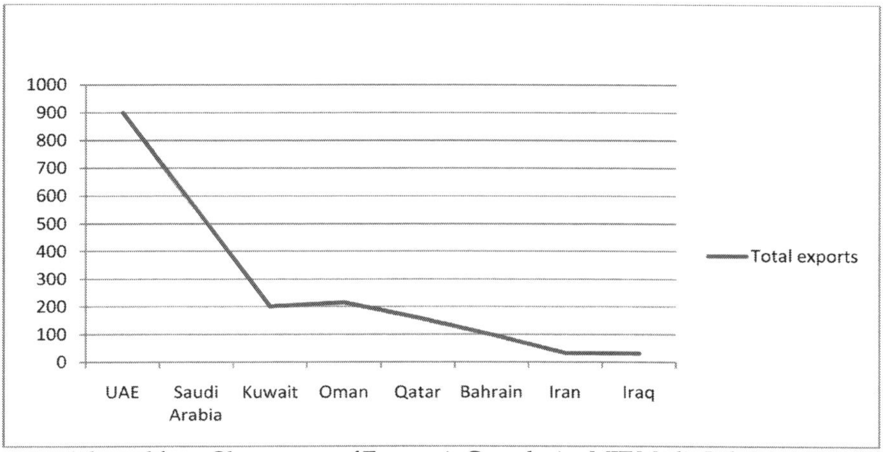

Source: Adapted from Observatory of Economic Complexity, MIT Media Lab. Massachusetts. 2015, at http://atlas.media.mit.edu/en/visualize/tree_map/hs92/import/irq/pak/show/2015/

GCC nations.[57] The trend is evident from Table 13.7 and Figure 13.1. The statistics present a positive picture in quantitative terms as there has been an increase in foreign remittances in 2015–16. According to the State Bank of Pakistan estimates, the total remittance inflow showed an upward trend, marginally increasing from US$ 15.23 billion in 2015 to US$ 16.04 billion in 2016 (see Table 13.7). More detailed statistics—as seen in Table 13.7—clearly indicate an annual rise in remittance inflows from all GCC countries. Among other GCC nations, Kuwait was the largest contributor of remittances in 2015—at US$ 617 million while Oman topped the chart in 2016 with US$ 670 million (see Table 13.7).

Table 13.7: Annual Flow of Remittances to Pakistan (in US$ million)

Country	2015	2016
Saudi Arabia	4,565	4,837
UAE	3,409	3,549
Kuwait	617	621
Qatar	285	309
Oman	561	670
Bahrain	308	372
Total from GCC	9,745 (63.9 %)	10,358 (64.5 %)
Total	15,235	16,044

Source: Adapter from State Bank of Pakistan, http://www.sbp.org.pk/ecodata/Homeremit.pdf.

Note: State Bank of Pakistan (SBP) report includes 2016 data from July 2016 to March 2017. SBP does not give separate data for Iran and Iraq.

Figure 13.4: Remittance inflow to Pakistan (in US$ million)

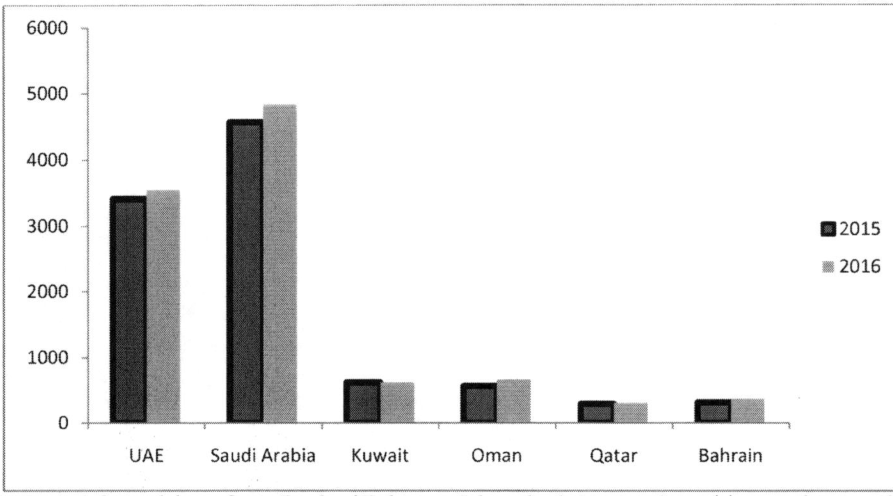

Source: Adapted from State Bank of Pakistan. Islamabad. 2016, at http://www.sbp.org.pk/ecodata/Homeremit.pdf

The importance of remittances in the economy of Pakistan can be gauged from the fact that it contributed 6.79 per cent to its total US$ 270.96 billion GDP in 2014–15.[58] While overall numbers (as stated above) reflect a rise in remittances, the slump in crude oil prices worldwide during 2015–16 led to internal economic contraction in oil-centric economies of the Persian Gulf. This domestic disequilibrium also pushed down the demand for labour, resulting in payment issues, massive layoffs, and contraction in volume of remittances. A mid-year comparative analysis of remittance flow (see Table 13.8) demonstrates reduced remittance flows between July 2015 and July 2016, a period which registered a steep fall in crude oil prices.

Table 13.8: Mid-year Review of Remittances

Country	Remittances (July 2015) Million US$	Remittances (July 2016) Million US$
Saudi Arabia	474.42	378
UAE	367.51	293.72
Other GCC states	197.86	169.61

Source: PK Revenues, at http://www.pkrevenue.com/finance/workers-remittances-fall-sharply-in-july-2016/

The case of the Saad construction company, which abandoned its expatriate employees due to financial bankruptcy, had a negative multiplier effect and discouraged many prospective immigrants to look towards the

Gulf for a better life.[59] In August 2016, Syed Rashidi, Minister for Overseas Pakistanis and Human Resource Development, paid a five-day visit to Saudi Arabia to resolve salary and work-related issues facing Pakistani immigrants in camps in Riyadh, Jeddah, Taif, etc.[60] While the Saudi government was ready to assist the stranded labour by arranging for a free return to their home country, there was dual resistance to this plan: first, the immigrants were hesitant to leave Saudi Arabia without monetary compensation since it would worsen their financial condition and render them unemployed in their home country; second, the return of the expatriates would burden the domestic economy by adding to unemployment numbers. However, no immediate solution could be found and, in September 2016, thousands of unpaid workers were sent back.[61] The employees were on a state contract with the construction giant; but that did not stop the Saudi government from deporting them without settling their arrears.

Of over eight million Pakistanis settled overseas, 3.9 million are based in Arab countries along the Gulf, with the majority (2.1 million) concentrated in Saudi Arabia.[62] They have been earning their livelihood by working in these countries. However, such incidents have cast a shadow upon the reliability of these countries in recruiting Pakistani labour on a long term basis. Lower visa applications for Gulf States are indicative of a negative economic environment.[63] Fluctuating oil prices have exposed the fragility of the oil-centric economic system as well as the risk of overdependence on such economies.

Retrospective View

An assessment of relations in 2015 and 2016 indicate that Pakistan-Persian Gulf relations exhibited an over-all positive trajectory, with minor hiccups. In 2015 and 2016, Riyadh stood highest on the radar of diplomacy and defence cooperation, and Iraq scored the lowest on the diplomacy scorecard. The UAE, Bahrain, Kuwait, and Qatar cultivated close economic relations despite differences over Yemen, and the GCC's foreign exchange contribution to state coffers was significant. After the success of P5+1 and the Iran nuclear deal, Islamabad also strengthened its connection with Tehran, which had been stalled due to sanctions. In 2017, progress on the Iran-Pakistan gas pipeline and Iran's interest to get aboard CPEC would remain relevant issues. However, history testifies that such economic interests and gains are set aside whenever they cast a shadow over defence and security concerns. Economic factors are less likely to affect Islamabad's foreign policy posturing as any loss in investment from the Persian Gulf can be counterbalanced by Foreign Direct Investment (FDI) from China. An evaluation of defence diplomacy signalled that there was close cooperation with the militaries of all the GCC states.

The lifting of international sanctions on Iran, the Saudi-led military intervention in Yemen, the ensuing rift with the UAE, and the inclusion of Pakistan in the Sunni Islamic Military Alliance were some testing moments in the country's Persian Gulf relationship. Certainly, the most interesting and audacious foreign policy move was Pakistan's neutral response to Yemen. With its delicate balancing act and measured diplomacy, Islamabad managed to retain its relationships with its next-door neighbour Iran as well as its Sunni ally—Saudi Arabia. However, this gamble may prove costly in the long term as the Saudi Arabia-led alliance is nowhere near victory in Yemen, with media reports suggesting high casualties amongst the coalition forces due to constant missile attacks by the Houthis. Thus, in the case of Saudi failure in Yemen, Pakistan would have to share the blame for showing a cold shoulder to Riyadh.

Conclusion

Historically, Pakistan had been an important factor in India's relations with the Middle East, especially towards the Gulf countries. This was as much because of Pakistan's ability to invoke pan-Islamic brotherhood as to India's own ineptitude at delinking its Middle East policy from Pakistan. Post-Cold War geopolitical changes forced India not only to introduce economic reforms but recalibrate its foreign policy, and gradually to de-hyphenate Pakistan from its Gulf policy. With growing interdependence and economic incentives, Pakistan no longer dominates India's bilateral relations with Persian Gulf countries. This has further started to move in a direction that makes Pakistan isolated even from its traditional friends; moreover, due to growing concerns about it sheltering wanted criminals and sponsoring terrorism in South Asia, this isolation has been aggravated. Though India does not have any direct interest in Gulf-Pakistan relations, growing concerns about Pakistan's sponsoring terror can adversely affect its relations with the otherwise 'brotherly' Gulf countries.

NOTES

1. Shirin Tahir-Kheli, "India, Pakistan, and the Persian Gulf", *Asian Affairs*, 10(3), pp. 32–36, at https://www.jstor.org/stable/30172979?seq=1#page_scan_tab_contents
2. Nadim Qamar, "Pakistan and the Persian Gulf", U.S. Army War College (Pennsylvania), 25 April 1991, at http://www.dtic.mil/dtic/tr/fulltext/u2/a236931.pdf

3. Kamran Yousaf, "Ouster of Assad regime: Riyadh wins Islamabad's support on Syria", *The Express Tribune*, 18 February 2014, at https://tribune.com.pk/story/673146/ouster-of-assad-regime-riyadh-wins-islamabads-support-on-syria/
4. "UAE minister warns Pakistan of 'heavy price for ambiguous stand' on Yemen", *Dawn*, 15 April 2015, at https://www.dawn.com/news/1175284
5. "Operation Decisive Storm: Reshuffling Regional Order", Position Paper, *Al-Jazeera Centre for Studies*, 6 April 2015, at http://studies.aljazeera.net/mritems/Documents/2015/4/7/20154783015689734Operation%20Decisive%20Storm.pdf
6. "Full text of Pakistan resolution on Yemen", *Dawn*, 13 April 2015, at https://www.dawn.com/news/1175696/full-text-of-pakistan-resolution-on-yemen
7. Subhash Kapila, "Pakistan Heartland Struck by Indigenous Terrorist Strikes", *South Asia Analysis Group*, 27 February 2017, at http://www.southasia analysis.org/node/2125
8. Annyssa Bellal, *The War Report: Armed Conflict in 2014*, Oxford: Oxford University Press, 2015.
9. Bruce Riedel, "Why Pakistan Said No to King Salman", *U.S. News*, 14 April 2015, at https://www.usnews.com/news/articles/2015/04/14/why-pakistan-said-no-to-king-salman.
10. "Javad Zarif Visits Pakistan", *The Nation*, 10 April 2015, at http://nation.com.pk/editorials/10-Apr-2015/javad-zarif-visits-pakistan
11. Divya Malhotra, *Pakistan Watch*, No. 64, Middle East Institute New Delhi, March 2016, at http://www.mei.org.in/documentsettings/pdf/1149_pdf.pdf.
12. Monish Gulati, "The Pakistan Factor in India-Iran Ties", *South Asia Monitor*, 23 May 2016, at http://southasiamonitor.org/detail.php?type=sl&nid=17156.
13. Syed Sammer Abbas, " 'Iran wants to be part of CPEC', says Rouhani", *Dawn*, 22 September 2016, at https://www.dawn.com/news/1285404
14. "Pakistan-Gate Construction at Iran Border in final Stage", *Times of Islamabad*, 15 August 2016, at https://timesofislamabad.com/pakistan-gate-construction-at-iran-border-in-final-stage/2016/08/15/
15. "Iran-Pakistan gas pipeline to complete by 2018", *Press TV*, 12 June 2016, at http://www.presstv.com/Detail/2016/06/12/470044/Iran-Pakistan-gas-project
16. Tilak Devasher, "Pakistan and the Saudi-Iran Face-Off", Vivekananda International Foundation, 3 February 2016, at http://www.vifindia.org/article/2016/february/03/pakistan-and-the-saudi-iran-face-off; and *The News*, "UAE minister terms statement on Pakistan 'personal opinion'". 11 May 2015, at https://www.thenews.com.pk/latest/4269-uae-minister-terms-statement-on-pakistan-personal-opinion
17. M. Aftab, "UAE, Saudi Arabia lead FDI revival in Pakistan", *Khaleej Times*, 21 March 2016, at http://www.khaleejtimes.com/international/pakistan/uae-saudi-arabia-lead-fdi-revival-in-pakistan
18. M. Haider, "PM Nawaz leaves for Bahrain on two-day visit", *Dawn*, 7 January 2015, at https://www.dawn.com/news/1155471
19. "Pakistan, Bahrain sign several agreements, MoUs", *The Express Tribune*, 7 January 2015, at https://tribune.com.pk/story/818031/pakistan-bahrain-ties-rooted-in-shared-history-pm/
20. "Bahrain grants 'Royal Pardon' to 82 Pakistani inmates", *Daily Times*, 4 July 2016, at http://dailytimes.com.pk/pakistan/04-Jul-16/bahrain-grants-royal-pardon-to-82-pakistani-inmates

21. "Bahrain support for India on Kashmir", *The Telegraph*, 26 October 2016, at https://www.telegraphindia.com/1161026/jsp/nation/story_115682.jsp
22. "Pakistan, Bahrain Pledge to Boost Trade Ties", *Radio Pakistan*, 11 December 2016, at http://www.radio.gov.pk/11-Dec-2016/pakistan-bahrain-pledge-to-boost-trade-ties
23. "Emir of Qatar arrives in Islamabad on two-day visit", *The News*, 23 March 2015, at https://www.thenews.com.pk/latest/2653-emir-of-qatar-arrives-in-islamabad-on-two-day-visit
24. "PM Nawaz seeks Qatari investment", Board of Investment, Government of Pakistan, 24 March 2015, at http://boi.gov.pk/ViewNews.aspx?NID=355; and "Royal visit: PM Nawaz seeks Qatari investment", *The Express Tribune,* 24 March 2015, https://tribune.com.pk/story/858021/royal-visit-pm-nawaz-seeks-qatari-investment/
25. I. Haider, "Pakistan, Qatar sign $1 billion annual LNG supply deal", *Dawn,* 11 February 2016, at https://www.dawn.com/news/1238619
26. "Adviser's Meeting with Deputy Prime Minister and Minister of Foreign Affairs of the State of Kuwait", Embassy of Pakistan, Doha, Qatar; Government of Pakistan, *Press Release,* 27 May 2015, at http://www.mofa.gov.pk/qatar/pr-details.php?prID =2823
27. "Pakistan, Kuwait Agree to Enhance Exchange of Businessmen's Visits", *Radio Pakistan,* May 31 2016, at http://www.radio.gov.pk/31-May-2016/pakistan-kuwait-agree-to-enhance-exchange-of-businessmen-s-visits
28. "Around 100 Pakistanis left for Syria, Iraq to join Da'ish: Punjab Law Minister", *The Express Tribune,* 4 January 2016, at https://tribune.com.pk/story/1021663/around-100-pakistanis-left-for-syria-iraq-to-join-daish-punjab-law-minister/
29. "Sartaj Aziz meets Pakistani community in Oman", Associated Press of Pakistan, 3 September 2016, at https://www.app.com.pk/sartaj-aziz-meets-pakistani-community-in-oman/
30. Paulami Sanyal, *Pakistan Watch*, No. 53, Middle East Institute New Delhi, April 2015, at http://www.mei.org.in/documentsettings/pdf/1000_pdf.pdf.
31. Loulla-Mae Eleftheriou-Smith, "Saudi Arabia launches 'North Thunder' military drill with troops from 20 nations", *Independent,* 15 February 2016, at http://www.independent.co.uk/news/world/middle-east/saudi-arabia-launches-north-thunder-military-drill-with-troops-from-20-nations-a6874771.html
32. "Army chief witnesses Saudi-Pak joint training exercise near Jhelum", *Dawn,* 30 October 2015, at https://www.dawn.com/news/1216402
33. Gili Cohen, "Israel Air Force to Participate in U.S. Drill alongside Pakistani, U.A.E. Jets", *Ha'aretz,* 3 August 2016, at http://www.haaretz.com/israel-news/.premium-1.734899 ,
34. "Pakistan's joint military drills with Israel raise controversy", *Press TV,* 4 September 2016, at http://www.presstv.ir/DetailFr/2016/09/04/483057/Pakistan-joint-military-drills-Israel-raise-controversy
35. "Iran, Pakistan hold joint naval drills", *Al-Masdar News (AMN)*, 2 October 2016, at https://www.almasdarnews.com/article/iran-pakistan-hold-joint-naval-drills/.
36. "Omani ships dock at Karachi for joint naval exercise", *Economic Times,* 13 December 2016, at http://economictimes.indiatimes.com/news/defence/omani-ships-dock-at-karachi-for-joint-exercise/articleshow/55960517.cms

37. Paulami Sanyal, *Pakistan Watch*, No. 51, Middle East Institute New Delhi, February 2015, at http://www.mei.org.in/documentsettings/pdf/986_pdf.pdf.
38. "Mamnoon lauds defence ties with Qatar", *The Express Tribune*, 24 October 2016, at https://tribune.com.pk/story/1207843/new-heights-mamnoon-lauds-defence-ties-qatar/.
39. "Gulf countries import half of Pakistan Ordnance Factories arms supplies", *Al-Arabiya*, 28 February 2017, https://english.alarabiya.net/en/perspective/features/2017/02/28/Gulf-countries-import-half-of-Pakistan-Ordnance-Factories-arms-supplies.html.
40. Bilal Khan, "Saudi Arabia is Pakistan's largest arms importer; POF reveals new rifle program", *Quwa*, 7 May 2016, http://quwa.org/2016/05/07/saudi-arabia-pakistans-largest-arms-importer-pof-reveals-new-rifle-program/.
41. Mateen Haider, "Saudi Arabia largest importer of Pakistani arms", *Dawn*, 6 May 2016, https://www.dawn.com/news/1256712
42. Karen DeYoung, ,"Saudi Arabia launches 'Islamic military alliance' to combat terrorism", *The Washington Post*, 15 December 2015, https://www.washingtonpost. com/world/national-security/saudi-arabia-launches-islamic-military-alliance-to-combat-terrorism/2015/12/15/ad568a1c-a361-11e5-9c4e-be37f66848bb_ story.html?utm_term=.0766f389e16d
43. Islamic military alliance when it was formed on 15 December 2015 included 34 countries, namely, Bahrain, Bangladesh, Benin, Chad, Comoros, Cote d'Ivoire, Djibouti, Egypt, Gabon, Guinea, Jordan, Kuwait, Lebanon, Libya, Malaysia, Maldives, Mali, Mauritania, Morocco, Niger, Nigeria, Pakistan, Palestine, Qatar, Saudi Arabia, Senegal, Sierra Leone, Somalia, Sudan ,Togo, Tunisia, Turkey, the UAE, Yemen.
44. Caroline Mortimer, "Saudi Arabia 'planning Nato-like military alliance of Muslim states", *Independent*, 15 March 2016, http://www.independent.co.uk/news/world/middle-east/saudi-arabia-proposes-nato-like-military-alliance-of-muslim-states-reports-say-a6933056.html
45. Baqir Sajjad Syed, "Pakistan surprised by its inclusion in 34-nation military alliance", *Dawn*, 16 December 2015, https://www.dawn.com/news/1226723
46. Mateen Haider, "Pakistan will not send ground troops as part of Saudi-led military alliance: Aziz", *DAWN*, 13 January 2016, https://www.dawn.com/news/1232480
47. Kamran Yousaf and Abdul Manan, "Yemen imbroglio: Pakistan mulls limited mission for Saudi security", 1 April 2015, at https://tribune.com.pk/story/862216/yemen-imbroglio-pakistan-mulls-limited-mission-for-saudi-security/
48. "Pakistan unaware of inclusion in Saudi Arabia led 34-nation military bloc", *Economic Times*, 16 December 2015, at http://economictimes.indiatimes.com/news/defence/pakistan-unaware-of-inclusion-in-saudi-arabia-led-34-nation-military-bloc/articleshow/50201781.cms
49. Kamran Yousaf and Abdul Manan, "Yemen", op. cit.
50. Fahad Chaudhry, " 'Raheel Sharif leading Saudi alliance will bring unity to Muslim world': Nasser Janjua", *Dawn*, 27 March 2017, at https://www.dawn.com/news/1323144/raheel-sharif-leading-saudi-alliance-will-bring-unity-to-muslim-world-nasser-janjua
51. Ramy Aziz, "The Purpose of Saudi Arabia's Islamic Military Coalition", *Policy Analysis*, The Washington Institute, 4 February 2016, at http://www.washington

institute.org/policy-analysis/view/the-purpose-of-saudi-arabias-islamic-military-coalition.

52. "Product Imports by Pakistan from Bahrain 2015", World Integrated Trade Solution (WITS), at http://wits.worldbank.org/CountryProfile/en/Country/PAK/Year/2015/TradeFlow/Import/Partner/BHR/Product/all-groups.
53. "Product Imports by Pakistan from Iran, Islamic Republic, 2014", World Integrated Trade Solution (WITS), at http://wits.worldbank.org/CountryProfile/en/Country/PAK/Year/2014/TradeFlow/Import/Partner/IRN/Product/all-groups
54. "Product Imports by Pakistan from Qatar 2015", World Integrated Trade Solution (WITS), at http://wits.worldbank.org/CountryProfile/en/Country/PAK/Year/2015/TradeFlow/Import/Partner/QAT/Product/all-groups
55. "Pakistan", The Observatory of Economic Complexity (OEC), at http://atlas.media.mit.edu/en/profile/country/pak/#Exports
56. "Pakistan exports, imports and trade balance By Country 2015", World Integrated Trade Solution (WITS), at http://wits.worldbank.org/CountryProfile/en/Country/PAK/Year/2015/TradeFlow/EXPIMP/Partner/by-country
57. Alam Kazim, "Saudi Arabia remains largest source of remittances for Pakistan", *The Express Tribune*, 16 July 2016, at https://tribune.com.pk/story/1142758/saudi-arabia-remains-largest-source-remittances/
58. International Monetary Fund, World Economic Outlook Database, 2015, at https://www.imf.org/external/pubs/ft/weo/2015/02/weodata/index.aspx.
59. "Issue of Pakistani workers in Dhammam being pursued: FO", *The News International*, 27 June 2016, at https://www.thenews.com.pk/print/130962-Issue-of-Pakistani-workers-in-Dammam-being-pursued-FO
60. Divya Malhotra, *Pakistan Watch*, No. 70, Middle East Institute New Delhi, September 2016, at http://www.mei.org.in/documentsettings/pdf/1210_pdf.pdf.
61. "Unpaid Pakistani Workers to Fly Home", *Arab News*, 28 September 2016, http://www.arabnews.com/node/990761/saudi-arabia
62. Tahir, "Number of Overseas Pakistanis – Latest Statistics", *Paki Mag*, 8 October 2015, http://www.pakimag.com/politics/number-of-overseas-pakistanis-latest-statistics.html. The statistics do not include Iraq.
63. Sohail Khattakand Taimur Khan, "As oil price falls, job opportunities dry up for Pakistanis in Saudi Arabia", *The National*, 24 August 2016, http://www.thenational.ae/world/south-asia/as-oil-price-falls-job-opportunities-dry-up-for-pakistanis-in-saudi-arabia

14

THE UNITED STATES

Md. Muddassir Quamar

Since the outbreak of popular uprising in the Arab world, commonly referred to as the Arab Spring (December 2010), the US has been facing difficult policy choices due to the fast changing internal and regional situations in the Middle East. The Obama Administration (2009–17) took time to assess the situation, and responded by gently nudging long-serving Arab rulers to respect the people's demands.[1] Many in the region rued the US reluctance to come to the rescue of close allies, such as Hosni Mubarak of Egypt.[2] Two factors were largely responsible for the hands-off response of the Obama Administration: first, the administration was concerned about the US being seen as overtly supportive of repressive regimes vis-à-vis a democratic upsurge;[3] secondly, the overbearing economic costs of external interventions amidst economic sluggishness after the 2008 recession loomed large in the perceptions of the Administration over the possibility of any interventions in Egypt or Syria.[4] President Obama was elected in November 2008 because of his promises of economic recovery and withdrawal from Iraq and Afghanistan; however, the Arab Spring and its fallouts made it difficult for him to fulfil these commitments.

Despite the reluctance, the US could not completely keep away from the regional crises. It was drawn back into Iraq due to the emergence of the Islamic State in Iraq and Syria (ISIS). It intervened in Libya through NATO and later regretted it, blaming the European countries of pushing it into an avoidable war;[5] it was also drawn into the Syrian theatre due to the spill over effect from Iraq. It could not avoid the war in Yemen because of its commitment to fight Al-Qaeda and because of Saudi insistence on a military confrontation with Houthis militias. But President Obama's reluctance to open another war front in Iran largely contributed to finding a negotiated solution to the latter's controversial nuclear programme. A deal—the Joint Comprehensive Plan of Action (JCPOA)—was reached in July 2015, and has been in force since January 2016.

The final two years of Obama administration had to endure difficult policy choices in the Persian Gulf and the Middle East. They were marked by waning American appetite for involvement in regional affairs.[6] This allowed regional (Iran) and extra-regional players (Russia and China) to weigh in their options, and expand their involvement.[7] Hence, Iran expanded its influence in Iraq, Syria, Yemen, while Russia—sensing an opportunity—intervened in Syria on behalf of the Assad regime. China too has been expanding its economic influence in the Persian Gulf and the Middle East. The Trump Administration (which took office in January 2017) has not signalled a clear direction in its Middle East policy, and has remained unpredictable. It would be important to see if it chooses to continue with the withdrawal symptoms shown by the Obama Administration or whether it re-invigorates its involvement in regional affairs. Early signs show that it might choose the latter.

This essay maps out US policy choices in the Gulf in the final two years of the Obama Administration within the context of the changing regional situation, and its impact on India's engagements with the Gulf. The most important aspects of this are the US policy towards Iran, declining American appetite for involvement in regional affairs, and rising Saudi-Iranian tensions and their impacts on India. Simultaneously, the essay also reflects on how US foreign policy choices can affect India's relations with the Persian Gulf which it considers its 'extended neighbourhood' and where it has vital stakes emanating from its energy security needs and considerable expatriate population.

The US and the Persian Gulf

Since end of the Second World War, especially after the East of Suez policy of Great Britain in 1968, the US has been significantly involved in the geopolitics of the Persian Gulf and maintains good relations with all regional countries—except Iran, with which it had a major fallout since the Islamic revolution in 1979. The US also has considerable military presence in the region, with bases in Bahrain, Qatar, Kuwait, and the UAE. The Fifth Fleet of the US Navy is based in Bahrain; it also maintains small military contingents in Oman, UAE, and Kuwait. Qatar's Al-Udeid Airbase serves as the forward headquarters of CENTCOM, and was instrumental in the US-led invasion of Iraq.[8] Until 2003, the US had maintained a military base in Saudi Arabia that was withdrawn due to increasing public resentment against US military presence.[9] However, both the countries continue to maintain strong military ties.[10] Saudi Arabia was instrumental in the American 'war on terror' operations in Yemen in 2009–10 which were aimed at eliminating the Al-Qaeda in the Arabian Peninsula (AQAP). The US also has strong military ties with Oman where it had maintained an air base until 2004. In addition, the US maintains a military presence in Iraq; this is so despite the withdrawal of combat forces in 2011 and was due to the rise of ISIS as well as growing threat perceptions. The US has redeployed nearly 5,000 forces in Iraq as of December 2016, a majority of whom are military advisors and trainers.[11]

Though the US involvement in the region goes back to the Second World War and the Cold War period, in recent times, the fallout of the invasion of Iraq in March 2003 and the Arab Spring protests have been major causes for continued US entanglement in regional politics. The rise of the ISIS has been the most significant development that forced the Obama Administration, determined to withdraw US forces from Iraq,[12] to bring back its forces. On top of it, the antagonistic relations with Tehran loomed large in regional politics, and Iran's controversial nuclear programme kept the US preoccupied for over a decade. The US has also been significantly involved in the 'war on terror' in Yemen. Ever since the Saudi-led forces launched military operations in March 2015 to confront the rise of the Houthi militias, it has provided air support, supplied equipment, and even deployed a small contingent of special ground forces to support Saudi-led coalition operations in Yemen.[13] Thus, if one looks at US involvement in the Gulf in 2015–16, three issues come to the fore: the fight against ISIS, the Iranian nuclear deal, and the ongoing conflict in Yemen.

Fighting the Islamic State

The two most important events responsible for the rise of ISIS have been the US-led invasion of Iraq in 2003 and the outbreak of civil war in Syria in 2011. The US attack led to the collapse and breakdown of central authority in Iraq, and fuelled sectarian civil strife.[14] This eventually resulted in the consolidation of Sunni insurgent groups into an umbrella organisation—the Mujahideen Shura Council—in 2006, which later evolved into the Islamic State of Iraq (ISI).[15] After the 2011 protests and disturbances in Syria, the ISI sensed an opportunity, and expanded its operations inside Syria. By mid-March 2013, it made significant territorial gains, and declared the formation of the *al-Dawlah al-Islamiyah fi al-Iraq wa al-Sham* (the Islamic State in Iraq and the Levant (ISIL), also known as ISIS, or by the Arabic acronym *Daesh*) that was eventually declared to be a global caliphate (*al-Dawlah al-Islamiyah*) in June 2014 by its leader, Abu Bakr al-Baghdadi.[16]

The US has been involved in fighting the ISIS through a broad coalition of regional and international forces. It has undertaken a number of combat operations against the ISIS in Iraq and Syria since 2013.[17] But largely, US policy has focussed on capacity building and training for the Iraqi military and the Kurdish fighters. According to official US sources, more than two-thirds of the US forces in Iraq are involved in advisory and training roles for the Iraqi Security Forces and the Kurdish Peshmerga forces; the rest are involved in intelligence gathering and supporting roles.[18] The two important operations that have attracted most of American attention have been the ongoing battle for retaking the cities of Mosul in Iraq (since October 2016) and Raqqa in Syria (since November 2016) from ISIS control. Both cities have served as operational and administrative headquarters for running the Islamic State.

By late 2016, a coalition of Iraqi Security Forces, Kurdish Peshmerga, and Iran-backed a Shia militia—the Popular Mobilisation Forces (PMF) supported by the US and other international forces—made significant advances to retake Mosul, and liberated several towns and villages from the ISIS control.[19] The progress, however, has been slow and blemished with heavy casualties due to densely populated areas and the urban warfare tactics used by the ISIS.[20] The war in Iraq has caused huge civilian casualties accentuating a humanitarian crisis, and has led to a massive displacement of Iraqi civilians who have been forced to take refuge in neighbouring countries, or seek asylum in Europe.[21] Indeed, the flow of refugees from Iraq and Syria has created a refugee crisis in Europe, leading to an increase in larger anti-immigration sentiments in many European countries.[22]

Though the US has been committed to fighting the ISIS, it has not waged a full-fledged 'war on terror' as it did against the Al-Qaeda in Afghanistan in the aftermath of the 11 September 2001 attacks. It has been reluctance to intervene in Syria even after the 2013 chemical attacks that the Administration had previously termed as a 'red line'. This has indicated that the US is averse to waging another war in the Middle East. In other words, whilst committed to fighting the ISIS, the Obama administration was wary of scaling up military engagement in Iraq and Syria primarily due to economics cost as well as the loss of personnel, both of which became major domestic debates.[23] Under these circumstances, Washington preferred to undertake minimalistic responsibility, and argued that its regional and European allies should do more to fight these wars, and not remain as "free-riders."[24]

The Iranian Nuclear Deal

One of the most important foreign policy achievements of the Obama Administration has been the signing of the Iranian nuclear deal. The negotiations on this issue began in 2006; it took almost a decade and several rounds of negotiations to reach a deal that would ease nuclear-related economic sanctions on Iran, and would curtail both its nuclear enrichment activities as well as its uranium stockpile.[25] Serious negotiations could begin between Iran and the P5+1 (Five permanent members of the UNSC—US, Russia, China, the UK and France—and Germany) only after the coming to power of President Hasan Rouhani in Iran in 2013, and the Joint Plan of Action (JPOA) was signed in November that year. Negotiations continued over Iran fulfilling its commitments made in the JPOA and the lifting of some sanctions, eventually leading to the signing of the final deal (JCPOA) in July 2015.

The deal is important because it has created hopes for a peaceful solution to the Iranian nuclear programme. However, it also has major geopolitical implications. For one, it indicates a change in US policy towards Iran, and paves the way for ending the near global isolation of Iran. On the other hand, it has serious ramifications for regional politics, with the GCC countries led by Saudi Arabia and the UAE as well as Israel becoming uneasy over growing Iranian regional influence and its ambitions to eventually secure a nuclear arsenal. Thus, the Gulf monarchies have upped the rhetoric against Iran, and have accused Tehran of meddling in the internal affairs of Arab countries such as Lebanon, Bahrain, Yemen, Iraq, and Syria. This has created serious tensions as Iran has adopted a muscular policy to extend its regional influence which is deeply resented by Saudi Arabia that has its own ambitions. For its part, Israel sees Iran as the most potent security threat.[26]

Saudi Arabia, along with other GCC countries, is wary of the US shifting its regional policy and accommodating Iranian regional ambitions.[27] Though they have been reassured that the nuclear deal only pertains to the Iranian nuclear programme and does not indicate a major change in US policy, this has been deeply resented by Saudi Arabia. The new Saudi leadership since January 2015 has adopted a more aggressive stance in its foreign policy projections.[28] On the other hand, Israel has been wary of Iran eventually acquiring nuclear weapons which can threaten its national more so security because of Iranian support for the Palestinian cause. The Obama Administration had reassured Israel of its commitments towards preventing Iran from acquiring a nuclear arsenal as well as towards the security of the Israeli state.[29] The US and Israel also signed a defence aid agreement worth US$ 38 billion for ten years in September 2016.

The election of Donald Trump has raised concerns about the scrapping of the Iranian nuclear deal by the US. Trump had spoken against the deal during his campaign, and had pledged to scrap it if elected.[30] However, analysts have argued that it will be difficult for the US to unilaterally withdraw from the deal as it is a multilateral deal, and has been approved by the United Nations.[31] Nevertheless, questions over the nuclear deal remain and, as has been argued by Samuel Rajiv (in another essay in this volume), domestic dynamics in the US as well as in Iran pose challenges to its smooth implementation. Indeed, the signing of JCPOA has removed one contentious issue, even if temporarily, from US foreign policy challenges.

The Yemen War

The situation in Yemen started to unravel with intensified protests in 2011 that gradually deteriorated into an armed conflict and the erosion of the central authority. A deal brokered by the GCC, and backed by the UN and the US led to the transition of power in February 2012. A UNSC backed as well as a US and Saudi supported National Dialogue then ensued to transform the political system, with a focus on finding a consensus for political order and power sharing. After months of negotiations and numerous conferences, the process culminated with an agreement in January 2014.[32] However, the planned political transition failed due to differences between stakeholders in the implementation of the agreement.[33] One of the major problems was the refusal of the Ansarullah, a Houthi militia, to agree to the political process because it accused the government of Abdrabbuh Mansur Hadi of scuttling the rights of the Zaidi Shias. The group then launched an armed offensive, and eventually took over the capital Sana'a in September 2014. He declared the dismissal of the Hadi government and the formation of a new transition government led by the Houthi movement in January 2015.[34]

In March 2015, Saudi Arabia along with a number of GCC and other Arab countries launched a military operation to restore the Hadi government and alter the advances made by the Houthi militia that they believe has been supported by Iran.[35] The Saudi-led coalition has, however, found it difficult to seriously push back the Houthi gains. The mounting civilian casualties and the worsening humanitarian crisis has earned the coalition serious international criticism for accentuating the war in Yemen. In the meanwhile, Former President Ali Abdullah Saleh has joined hands with the Houthi movement, thus strengthening the fight against Yemeni forces. The Houthis have been able to maintain their stronghold in north Yemen that has traditionally been a Zaidi stronghold.

Since the beginning of the Saudi-led military operation in March 2015, the US has provided air support, intelligence inputs, and military equipment. It supports a political resolution based on the UNSC resolution 2216 adopted in April 2015 that calls for the restoration of the Hadi government. It also imposes an arms embargo on the Houthi movement and demands that they withdraw their militia from Sana'a and other cities.[36] Nonetheless, US policy has come under severe criticism for supporting a Saudi-led war that has not achieved much ground success; indeed it has worsened the humanitarian crisis in Yemen. According to a report by the Congressional Research Service, "[d]uring the last year of the Obama Administration, US policy towards the conflict in Yemen shifted toward a more nuanced approach after initially emphasizing strong support for the Saudi-led coalition's campaign and the restoration of Hadi's presidency."[37] Sensing a convoluted conflict, the Obama Administration called for a political solution but did not completely abandon support for the Saudi-led coalition's operations because of the fear of Yemen falling into Iranian influence as well as growing advances made by the AQAP.

Changes in US Gulf Policy under President Obama

During the Cold War, oil and regional security were the main drivers of US policy in the Gulf, with Saudi Arabia and Iran its 'twin pillars' to contain Soviet influence in the Persian Gulf.[38] The dynamics changed after the 1979 Islamic revolution which forced the US to adopt the policy of 'dual containment' to counter both Iranian and Iraqi threats to its interests.[39] With the changed dynamics, Saudi Arabia emerged as the most important ally for the US in the Gulf, and the relationship between the two countries included strong business and defence ties. Saudi Arabia is one of the most important markets for the US military industry, and Saudi businesses have invested significantly in the US market. At the same time, oil continues to be a major source for strong bilateral relations despite numerous divergences cropping up in recent years, especially due to the shale gas revolution.[40]

The US policy in the Gulf underwent some changes under the Obama Administration which was most importantly reflected in the scaling down of the military intervention in Iraq, rapprochement with Iran, and tensions with Saudi Arabia. In a nutshell, the US showed signs of fatigue and the waning interests for involvement in regional affairs of the Gulf. This was most clearly spelled out in an interview President Barack Obama gave to *The Atlantic* towards the end of his term. When asked about his decision not to intervene in Syria despite early warnings of chemical weapons being the "red line", President Obama said,

> The perception was that my credibility was at stake, that America's credibility was at stake. And so, for me to push the pause button at that moment, I knew, would cost me politically. And the fact that I was about to pull back from the immediate pressures and think through in my own mind what was in America's interest, not only with respect to Syria but also with respect to our democracy, was as tough a decision as I've made—and I believe ultimately it was the right decision to make.[41]

On the issue of Saudi-Iran tensions, he observed,

> The competition between the Saudis and the Iranians—which has helped to feed proxy wars and chaos in Syria and Iraq and Yemen—requires us to say to our friends as well as to the Iranians that they need to find an effective way to share the neighbourhood and institute some sort of cold peace.[42]

These statements were accompanied by significant actions on the ground: the completion of military withdrawal from Iraq in December 2011; the insistence on finding a negotiated settlement with Iran to resolve the controversial nuclear programme; tensions with Saudi Arabia over inaction on the fall of Hosni Mubarak (in Egypt); limited intervention in Syria; and secondary involvement in Yemen. All these showed that the Obama Administration was inclined towards scaling down its involvements in the Gulf and Middle East.

These changes did not decisively alter the Gulf policy of the US and indeed, it continues to remain the only security guarantor in the region which is vital for global energy security. Thus, security in the Persian Gulf remains a cornerstone of US policy, and Saudi Arabia as well as the other GCC countries remains the most important US allies in maintaining this security. Even though many have seen the Iranian nuclear deal as a rapprochement between the US and Iran, with the potential for far reaching changes in regional geopolitics and alliances,[43] the election of Donald Trump has again changed the dynamics. Though he has remained unpredictable so far, President Trump has indicated that the US might go back to its pre-Obama policy of strong relations with Saudi Arabia and Israel and pronounced hostility towards Iran.

Implications for India

India has vital stakes in the Persian Gulf region because of energy security and the safety of its large expatriate population. With the US being the sole security provider and arbiter in regional affairs, Indian interests are intertwined with US policy. Indian interests and stakes would be affected by any policy changes by the US, especially if it substantially scales down its involvement or revamps its engagements. This had become a major issue of discussion during the Obama presidency which had, as noted above, indicated scaling down its involvement in the Middle East. However, things are looking different with the new administration; but its contours would depend on future developments and whether the new administration chooses to continue with the Obama policy, or reverse it. Irrespective of its direction, the US will remain the sole security guarantor in the Persian Gulf for the foreseeable future. India will have to watch out for any major policy shifts and changes.

The most important aspect of the US factor in India's engagements with the Persian Gulf is its relations with Iran. The Iran-US-India triangle has been a centre of speculation for a long time and, on occasion, has caused tension in Indo-Iranian relations. The US pressures have caused India to take an antagonistic position regarding the Iranian nuclear programme, including its voting pattern in the International Atomic Energy Agency (IAEA) since 2005,[44] and its virtual abandoning of the Iran-Pakistan-India (IPI) gas pipeline.[45] Furthermore, India had to considerably scale down its oil purchases from Iran due to US and international sanctions on the Iranian oil industry.[46] This became a major issue in early 2015 when the negotiations on Iranian nuclear deal were going on, and were in the concluding stages. In March 2015, the US included three Indian petroleum companies—Oil and Natural Gas Corporation (ONGC), Indian Oil Corporation (IOC), and Oil India Ltd (OIL)—in the list of companies trading with Iranian oil companies, and warned them of sanctions.[47]

The three firms were exploring for oil and gas in the Farsi offshore block in Iran between November 2013 and December 2014, and had proposed to invest US$ 5.5 billion after discovering 21.68 trillion cubic foot natural gas. However, they failed to sign a contract with the Iranian government, possibly due to US sanctions.[48] As an impact of the pressure from the US, India stopped importing oil from Iran for the month of March in 2015. This was to "keep the fiscal-year figure in line with sanctions limits."[49] Despite the temporary halt, the US continued to apply pressure on India. However, this did not deter India's plan to go ahead with the signing of the Chabahar port development agreement in May 2015. New Delhi even expressed readiness to fend off more US pressure. The US Ambassador to India, Richard Verma, cautioned India against "rushing in" with further investments, and went on to say, "there was need to maintain the international solidarity that has brought this hard fought diplomatic victory, but we are not over the finish line yet."[50] Thus, the US factor was responsible for the delay in signing the Chabahar deal.

Simultaneously, there were some concerns raised by some US lawmakers as to what India "would do with money owed to Teheran in unpaid bills if the deal fell." The amount was estimated at US$ 8.8 billion since 2012 which was meant for the purchase of crude oil.[51] India faced difficulty in paying US$ 6.5 billion to Iran for oil transactions, and the problem was aggravated due to the reluctance of European banks to process the payments.[52] Though US pressure has eased with the signing of the nuclear deal, the payment row with Iran has not yet been resolved. The issue was discussed during Prime Minister Modi's visit to Iran in May 2016 and the subsequent high level engagements between the two countries. It has been suggested that part of the payments would be made through investments in the Iranian economy.[53]

Apart from Iran, India has remained largely immune to any changes in the US policy regarding the Gulf, and has benefitted from the security and stability ensured by the US military presence. In fact, countries like China and India have often been dubbed as the beneficiaries of US military presence since they can extend their business and economic interests in the Gulf without having to align their strategic interests with those of the US.[54] China has come in for more criticism; there has been a significant concern in the US regarding Chinese economic forays in the region and its long term implication for the US and its interests. India will have to be prudent and alert regarding new developments and geopolitical games in the region, and choose its steps carefully to protect its interests. The most important question for India in the Gulf as far as the US factor is concerned would be to respond to calls for greater engagement, especially in the wake of both waning US involvement as well as growing Chinese incursions in the region.

Conclusion

Despite showing withdrawal symptoms under President Obama, the US remains the pre-eminent power in the Persian Gulf. It is the only country with a large military presence, strong security and defence alliances, and considerable political influence in the region. By signing the nuclear deal with Iran, and by maintaining minimal involvement in the Yemen war, the Obama Administration showed inclinations towards a change in policy but not a paradigm shift. In fact, the new Trump Administration has shown a tendency of maintaining the existing arrangement of close alliance with Saudi Arabia and other GCC countries to contain growing Iranian influence. This would be easier said than done because of the forays of new powers—

China and Russia—in the Gulf and the Middle East. For India, the situation has been favourable so far, and it has benefitted because of the security structure provided by the US. However, with the changing geopolitical environment, it would have to weigh its options and choose a path that would ensure the maintenance of peace and stability in the region.

NOTES

1. "Remarks by the President on the Middle East and North Africa", Office of the Press Secretary, The White House, 19 May 2011, at https://obamawhitehouse.archives.gov/the-press-office/2011/05/19/remarks-president-middle-east-and-north-africa.
2. David E. Sanger and Eric Schmitt, "U.S.-Saudi Tensions Intensify with Mideast Turmoil", *The New York Times*, 14 March 2011, at http://www.nytimes.com/2011/03/15/world/middleeast/15saudi.html.
3. "Remarks by the President", The White House, op. cit.
4. Yoel Guzansky, "The End of American Era in the Middle East?" *Strategic Assessment*, January 2013, Vol. 15, No. 4, pp. 25–36.
5. President Obama in his interview to *The Atlantic* magazine termed the Libyan intervention as the 'worst mistake' of his presidency. See also, Dominic Tierney, "The Legacy of Obama's 'Worst Mistake'", *The Atlantic*, 15 April 2016, at https://www.theatlantic.com/international/archive/2016/04/obamas-worst-mistake-libya/478461/.
6. Ibid. See also: Yaroslav Trofimov, "America's fading Footprint in the Middle East," *The Wall Street Journal*, 9 October 2015, at https://www.wsj.com/articles/americas-fading-footprint-in-the-middle-east-1444411954.
7. Ilan Goldenberg and Julie Smith, "U.S.-Russia Competition in the Middle East is Back," *Foreign* Policy, 7 March 2017, at http://foreignpolicy.com/2017/03/07/u-s-russia-competition-in-the-middle-east-is-back/; see also, Geoffrey Aronson, "China's Vision of the Middle East," *Al-Jazeera*, 21 January 2016, at http://www.aljazeera.com/indepth/opinion/2016/01/china-vision-middle-east-160121052018955.html.
8. Bret Baier, "U.S. Moving Central Command Units to Qatar", *Fox News*, 11 September 2002, at http://www.foxnews.com/story/2002/09/11/us-moving-central-command-units-to-qatar.html.
9. Anthony H. Cordesman, *Saudi Arabia Enters Twenty-first Century: The Military and International Security Dimensions*, Washington, DC: CSIS, 2003, pp. 35–39.
10. "US-Saudi Relations", Backgrounder, Council on Foreign Relations, 12 May 2017, at https://www.cfr.org/backgrounder/us-saudi-relations.
11. Christopher M. Blanchard and Carla E. Humud, "The Islamic State and U.S. Policy", *Congressional Research Service Report*, No. R43612, 2 February 2017, at https://fas.org/sgp/crs/mideast/R43612.pdf.
12. In fact, by December 2011, the US had completely withdrawn its combat forces from Iraq, and only 150 US personnel remained for securing the US embassy compound. See, Tim Arango and Michael S. Schmidt, "Last Convoy of American Troops Leaves Iraq," *The New York Times*, 18 December 2011.
13. Thomos Gibbons-Neff and Missy Ryan, "U.S. Forces now on the Ground

Supporting Combat Operations in Yemen, Pentagon Says," *The Washington Post*, 6 May 2016, at https://www.washingtonpost.com/news/checkpoint/wp/2016/05/06/u-s-forces-now-on-the-ground-supporting-combat-operations-in-yemen-pentagon-says/?utm_term=.3be22b90e4f6.

14. "Tony Blair admits 2003 Iraq Invasion led to Rise of ISIS, Apologises for Mistake", *The Indian Express*, 25 October 2015, at http://indianexpress.com/article/world/world-news/2003-iraq-invasion-played-role-in-rise-of-islamic-state-former-britain-pm-tony-blair/. See also, Ishan Tharoor, "Iraq's Crisis: Don't Forget the 2003 U.S. Invasion," *The Washington Post*, 16 June 2014; and Raymond Hinnebusch, "American Invasion of Iraq: Causes and Consequences," *Perceptions*, 2007, the Vol. 12, No. 1, pp. 9–27.
15. For a detailed reading about the evolution and functioning of the ISIS, see Fawaz A. Gerges, *ISIS: A History*, Oxford and Princeton: Princeton University Press, 2016; and Patrick B. Johnson et al., *Foundations of the Islamic State: Management, Money, and Terror in Iraq*, Santa Monica, California: RAND Corporation, 2016.
16. Hannah Strange, "Islamic State Leader Abu Bakr al-Baghdadi Addresses Muslims in Mosul", *The Telegraph*, 5 July 2014, at http://www.telegraph.co.uk/news/worldnews/middleeast/iraq/10948480/Islamic-State-leader-Abu-Bakr-al-Baghdadi-addresses-Muslims-in-Mosul.html.
17. Blanchard and Humud, "The Islamic State and US Policy", op.cit.
18. Ibid.
19. "Battle for Mosul: The Story So Far", *BBC News*, 17 May 2017, http://www.bbc.com/news/world-middle-east-37702442.
20. Jane Arraf, "As ISIS Strategy Evolves, Mosul Battle Gets Tougher on Iraqi Forces", National Public Radio, 24 December 2016, at http://www.npr.org/2016/12/24/506817288/as-isis-strategy-evolves-mosul-battle-gets-tougher-on-iraqi-forces.
21. "Another Year of Relentless Violence in Iraq", Iraq Body Count, 2016, at https://www.iraqbodycount.org/analysis/numbers/2016/.
22. "Europe's Rising Far Right: A Guide to Most Prominent Parties", *The New York Times*, 4 December 2016, at https://www.nytimes.com/interactive/2016/world/europe/europe-far-right-political-parties-listy.html?_r=0.
23. Greg Jaffe and Missy Ryan, "In White House's Iraq Debate, Military Brass Pushed for Doing Less", *The Washington Post*, 13 June 2015, at https://www.washingtonpost.com/world/national-security/in-white-houses-iraq-debate-military-brass-pushed-for-doing-less/2015/06/13/8db17e30-1138-11e5-9726-49d6fa26a8c6_story.html?utm_term=.251468c5b218.
24. Jeffrey Goldberg, "The Obama Doctrine: The U.S. President Talks through his Hardest Decisions about America's Role in the World," *The Atlantic*, April 2016, at https://www.theatlantic.com/magazine/archive/2016/04/the-obama-doctrine/471525/.
25. For full text of the JCPOA see, "Joint Comprehensive Plan of Action", Vienna, 14 US Department of State, July 2015, at https://www.state.gov/documents/organization/245317.pdf.
26. For an assessment of challenges facing Israel in a changing regional situation, see Itamar Rabinovich, "Israel and the Changing Middle East", *Middle East Memo*, No. 34, Brookings, January 2015, at https://www.brookings.edu/wp-content/uploads/2016/06/Israel-Rabinovich-01292015-1.pdf. See also, Chuck Freilich, "The United States, Israel, and Iran: Defusing an 'Existential' Threat," *Arms*

Control Today, 3 November 2008, at https://www.armscontrol.org/print/3407.

27. "Why Saudi Arabia and Israel Oppose Iran Nuclear Deal", *Al-Jazeera*, 14 April 2015, at http://www.aljazeera.com/news/2015/04/saudi-arabia-israel-oppose-iran-nuclear-deal-150401061906177.html.
28. Nwaf Obaid, "The Salman Doctrine: The Saudi Reply to Obama's Weakness", *The National Interest*, 30 March 2016, http://nationalinterest.org/feature/the-salman-doctrine-the-saudi-reply-obamas-weakness-15623.
29. Jim Zanotti, "Israel: Background and U.S. Relations in Brief", Congressional Research Service Report, No. R44245, 17 May 2017, at https://fas.org/sgp/crs/mideast/R44245.pdf.
30. Jay Solomon, "Trump Faces Battle to Undo Iran Nuclear Deal", *The Wall Street Journal*, 11 November 2016, at https://www.wsj.com/articles/trump-faces-battle-to-undo-iran-nuclear-deal-1478860207.
31. Sabrina Siddiqui, "Why Republican Promises to Scrap Iran Nuclear Deal May Not be Met", *The Guardian*, 21 July 2015, at https://www.theguardian.com/world/2015/jul/21/iran-nuclear-deal-why-republican-promises-scrap-may-not-be-met.
32. "Yemen's National Dialogue Conference Concludes with Agreement", *BBC News*, 21 January 2014, at http://www.bbc.com/news/world-middle-east-25835721.
33. Farea al-Muslimi, "Why Yemen's Political Transition Failed", *Carnegie Diwan*, 16 April 2015, at http://carnegie-mec.org/diwan/59803.
34. "Yemen's Houthis Form Government in Setback to Peace Process," *Reuters*, 28 November 2016, at http://www.reuters.com/article/us-yemen-security-government-idUSKBN13N1ZQ.
35. The issue of Iranian support to the Houthi movement has remained contentious, and though evidence of Iran providing small weaponry and low scale training to the group have been found, its involvement in Yemen is certainly lesser in comparison to that in Syria, Iraq, Lebanon, or even in the Palestinian conflict. See, Martin Reardo, "Saudi Arabia, Iran and the 'Great Game' in Yemen", *Al-Jazeera*, 25 March 2015, at http://www.aljazeera.com/indepth/opinion/2014/09/saudi-arabia-iran-great-game-ye-201492984846324440.html.
36. "Security Council Demands End to Yemen Violence, Adopting Resolution 2216 (2015), with Russian Federation Abstaining", United Nations, 14 April 2015, at https://www.un.org/press/en/2015/sc11859.doc.htm.
37. Jeremy M. Sharp, "Yemen: Civil War and Regional Intervention", Congressional Research Service Report, No. R43960, 21 March 2017, at https://fas.org/sgp/crs/mideast/R43960.pdf, p. 13.
38. Hussein Sirriyeh, *US Policy in the Gulf, 1968-1977: Aftermath of British Withdrawal*, London: Ithaca Press, 1984.
39. Alex Edwards, *'Dual Containment' Policy in the Persian Gulf: The USA, Iran, and Iraq, 1991-2000*, New York: Palgrave Macmillan, 2014.
40. "US-Saudi Relations", Council on Foreign Relations, op. cit.
41. "'The Obama Doctrine': The Atlantic's Exclusive Report on the U.S. President's Hardest Foreign Policy Decisions", *The Atlantic*, 10 March 2016, https://www.theatlantic.com/press-releases/archive/2016/03/the-obama-doctrine-the-atlantics-exclusive-report-on-presidents-hardest-foreign-policy-decisions/473151/
42. Ibid.
43. For example, see: Mahmood Monshipouri and Manochehr Dorraj, "U.S.-Iran

Relations after the Nuclear Deal", *Georgetown Journal of International Affairs*, 7 November 2016, http://journal.georgetown.edu/u-s-iran-relations-after-the-nuclear-deal/. See also, Shivshankar Menon, "The Iran Nuclear Deal Changes the Regional Game But is Good News for India", *The Wire*, 16 July 2015, at https://thewire.in/6500/the-iran-nuclear-deal-changes-the-regional-game-but-is-good-news-for-india/.

44. Siddharth Varadarajan, "India's Anti-Iran Votes were Coerced, says Former U.S. Official", *The Hindu*, 16 February 2007, at http://www.thehindu.com/todays-paper/tp-national/Indias-anti-Iran-votes-were-coerced-says-former-U.S.-official/article14721223.ece.
45. Meenakshi Iyer, "Pipeline Pressures", *Hindustan Times*, 29 April 2006, at http://www.hindustantimes.com/india/pipeline-pressures/story-wXjxqtRgHK26UctiydANNL.html.
46. Nidhi Verma, "India's 2015 Iran Oil Imports Fall by a Quarter – Trade", *Reuters*, 7 January 2016, at http://in.reuters.com/article/india-iran-oil-import-idINKBN0UL0NV20160107.
47. "IOC, ONGC, OIL among 5 companies named by US administration for Iran ties", *The Times of India*, 8 March 2015, at http://timesofindia.indiatimes.com/business/india-business/IOC-ONGC-OIL-among-5-companies-named-by-US-administration-for-Iran-ties/articleshow/46491009.cms
48. Ibid.
49. "India skips Iran oil imports for first time under US pressure", *The Economic Times*, 31 March 2015, at http://economictimes.indiatimes.com/news/industry/energy/oil-gas/india-skips-iran-oil-imports-for-first-time-under-us-pressure/articleshow/46756988.cms
50. Dinakar Peri, "US sounds caution as India inks port deal with Iran", *The Hindu*, 7 May 2015, at http://www.thehindu.com/news/national/us-sounds-caution-as-india-inks-port-deal-with-iran/article7178309.ece
51. Yashwant Raj, "India dragged into US debate on Iran", *Hindustan Times*, 22 August 2015, at http://www.hindustantimes.com/world/india-dragged-into-us-debate-on-iran/story-cxdI2Kr5Ruu3Nbyhgf4AhN.html
52. Suhasini Haidar, "U.S. sanctions still block Iran payments", *The Hindu*, 16 May 2016, at http://www.thehindu.com/news/national/U.S.-sanctions-still-block-Iran-payments/article14321178.ece
53. "India ready to clear $6.5 billion of Iran's oil dues", *The Indian Express*, 1 May 2016, at http://indianexpress.com/article/india/india-news-india/india-ready-to-clear-usd-6-5-billion-of-irans-oil-dues-2779243/
54. For example, see; Theodore Karasik, "The GCC's New Affair with China", *MEI Policy Focus* 2016, 6 February 2016, at http://www.mei.edu/sites/default/files/publications/Karasik_GCCChina_PF6.pdf. See also, Lee Hudson Teslik, "China-Gulf Economic Relations", CFR Backgrounder, 2 June 2008, at https://www.cfr.org/backgrounder/china-gulf-economic-relations.

15

RUSSIA

Meena Singh Roy and Rajorshi Roy

Russia has been an active player in the Middle East, especially since its September 2015 military intervention in Syria which signalled its re-emergence as a key player in the geo-politics of the region. Its subsequent diplomatic initiative to resolve the Syrian crisis, arguably, reflects the recalibration of Kremlin's policy towards a region from where it had largely withdrawn since the beginning of the 1990s. This withdrawal had resulted in Moscow focussing primarily on its detente with the West while preserving its interests in its 'near abroad', and developing a new strategy towards the Asia-Pacific. As such, a volatile region in its close proximity largely remained on the periphery of its priorities. Notably, Russia's linkages with the Middle East go back to the Ottoman Empire, apart from the region being a major theatre of Cold War rivalry.

In this light, Russia's recent initiatives have seen it navigate a complex web of regional and extra-regional interests. This is particularly relevant given the perception of a disengaging US even though President Donald Trump's May 2017 visit to the region appears to have allayed that image. It has, nevertheless, seen Moscow attempt to channel a solution to the Syrian conundrum, deepen its cooperation with Iran, step up ties with Israel, Egypt and Iraq, formulate a working relationship with the Gulf Cooperation Countries (GCC), and restore ties with Turkey.[1] The outcomes, interspersed with the proverbial ebb and flow of ties, appear to be a work in progress. This includes setting up de-conflicting zones in Syria, establishing coordination with the US to tackle terrorism in light of American strikes on

Syria's chemical weapons, repairing ties with Turkey post the downing of a SU-24 fighter jet, coordinating OPEC production cuts with Saudi Arabia, and selling a stake in Rosneft to Qatar.

This essay examines various aspects of Russia's engagement with the Middle East during 2015–16, and the prospects of its ability to stay relevant in the region. It argues that geo-politics, given Russia's confrontation with the West, and President Vladimir Putin's effort to project Russia as an assertive power in the region and beyond, appears to be a key driving force in Moscow's renewed engagement. However, a number of other strategic calculations also seem to be at play. These include a broad mix of political, security, and economic interests. Its political interests are driven by promoting Moscow's vision of "shaping a fair and sustainable world order." This has been identified as a priority in its foreign policy concept of 2016.

> The Russian Federation's foreign policy is aimed at creating a stable and sustainable system of international relations based on the generally accepted norms of international law and principles of equal rights, mutual respect and non-interference in domestic affairs of States, so as to ensure solid and equal security for each and every member of the global community.[2]

More importantly, avoiding international isolation is a part of its political interest to expand its relations with the countries in the Middle East. Its economic interests are managing the impact of economic sanctions by promoting its trade ties, protecting the interest of Russian energy companies, finally, securing its strategic space in the region, and fighting radical Islamist groups which pose a security threat back home.

Renewed Engagement

Since the end of the Cold War, Russian foreign policy has primarily oscillated between the *Atlanticists* and the *Eurasianists*—that is, the outreach towards the West and Eurasia, respectively.[3] In this light, the priority accorded to the Middle East, often referred to as part of Russia's 'near east' (*blizhnii vostok*), remained much lower in the pecking order.[4] The 2008,[5] 2013,[6] and 2016 foreign policy doctrines enumerated the need to

> ...make a meaningful contribution to stabilizing the situation in the Middle East and North Africa, support collective efforts aimed at neutralizing threats that emanate from international terrorist groups, and promote political and diplomatic settlement of conflicts in regional States.[7]

A careful analysis reveals Russian footprints in the region being much below the cherished goals. Therefore, its military intervention in Syria likely marks a turning point in its engagement with the Middle East.

On Syria, Russia's position was articulated in its 2016 foreign policy concept, which noted that Moscow

> ...stands for a political settlement in the Syrian Arab Republic and the possibility for the people of Syria to determine their future based on the Geneva communiqué of 30 June 2012, statements by the International Syria Support Group and relevant UN Security Council resolutions.[8]

This policy faces many challenges due to the complex set of problems in the Persian Gulf region, mainly the growing confrontation between Iran and Saudi Arabia.

To further expand its relations with the countries in the Middle East and North Africa, Russia has been making use of the ministerial meeting of the Russian-Arab Cooperation Forum, and has continued its engagement through the strategic dialogue with the Cooperation Council for the Arab States of the Gulf. In addition, Moscow has taken full advantage of its observer status in the Organisation of Islamic Cooperation (OIC) to promote its cooperation with the larger Islamic world. In the last two years, Russia continued to maintain good relations with Israel while supporting the Palestinians. Explaining its stand on the Israel-Palestinian conflict, its foreign policy concept noted,

> As a permanent member of the UN Security Council and member of the Middle East Quartet of international mediators, Russia will further strive to achieve a comprehensive, fair and lasting resolution of the Israel-Palestinian conflict in all its aspects consistent with international law.[9]

Russia's Middle East strategy encompasses five important elements. First, it wants to re-establish its image as a decisive and assertive power to reclaim its role and protect its core interests. Second, it does not welcome regime change by military intervention, learning its lesson, particularly, after the fall of Saddam Hussain and Muammar Qaddafi in Iraq and Libya respectively that not only destabilised the region but had a negative impact on Russia's economic and strategic interests. As a result, Moscow came out in support of the Assad regime in Syria to prevent its interests being jeopardised by a change of regime. Third, during President Putin's second term (2012 onward), Moscow took full advantage of President Barrack Obama's policies to increase its footprint. This perception about US disengagement provided Russia the space for a greater acceptability of a Russian role in the Middle East. Fourth, Moscow in this period of re-engagement with the region pursued a much more pragmatic policy as compared to its ideological pursuit of the past. Finally, Putin's focus was towards building ties with Middle Eastern countries to help manage Russia's isolation, pursue economic interests, develop ties with countries where it has market advantages, cooperate in the areas of oil and gas, nuclear energy, and gain access for Russian arms sales. To achieve these goals, Russia enhanced its engagement with a host of countries, including Iran, UAE, Saudi Arabia, Israel, Egypt, Algeria, Tunisia, Morocco and Jordan.

Moscow's re-engagement with the Middle East can be examined by analysing its four major drivers: geo-politics, Islamic State and terrorism, economic partnership, and military footprint.

Geo-politics

In many ways, the genesis of this realignment appears to be Russia's confrontation with the West. This has compelled Moscow to overcome its diplomatic isolation by attempting to re-establish itself as a pillar of global diplomacy. The confrontation stems from its fundamental differences with the US regarding Russia's place and position in global affairs. It can be argued that the Ukrainian crisis was the culmination of core differences between Russia and the West over Moscow's status as an equal partner. The Western economic sanctions, the continuing NATO expansion eastwards, and the installation of missile defences in Russia's borderlands have reinforced Kremlin's suspicions about the US-led strategy to contain it in its own neighbourhood.

These developments appear to have influenced Moscow's attempts to create a more representative world order that would safeguard its core interests. This is particularly relevant, given the asymmetrical and unequal competition between Russia and the West.[10] As a result, strengthening ties with countries that follow an independent policy has become a key pillar of its foreign policy.[11] Therefore, in numerous ways, the existing standoff is about the need to preserve or establish a new world order depending upon which side of the US-Russia divide one is on.

As such, Russia's outreach to the Middle East can be seen through the lens of the prevailing geo-political landscape that the Kremlin finds itself in. By creating facts on the ground, Russia has been able to establish a foothold in the regional landscape. Having done so, the resolution of the Syrian conundrum will be a litmus test of its projected image of being an indispensable actor in resolving key conflicts. As mentioned earlier, here Russia is exposed to many challenges. At one level, retaining Iran within Moscow's sphere of influence is extremely crucial; at other level, it is equally important for Russia to have close cooperation with the GCC states to secure its interest in the energy market and other economic factors. The growing Iran-Russia cooperation does not auger well in the event of increasing Saudi-Iran confrontation. In fact, this undermines Moscow's diplomatic effort to settle the Syrian conundrum by making the Saudis less inclined to talk to the Russians. Thus, the growing Shia-Sunni rift in the region, and Russia's close engagement with Tehran raises the risk for Kremlin to be viewed as unfriendly towards the Sunni world, which Moscow cannot afford to jeopardise given the fact that more than 15 million Russian Muslim population is Sunni.

Since the beginning of the civil war in Syria and subsequent to Kremlin's military intervention, Russia has been depicted by the Salafi groups as the new Crusader. The radical Sunni Islamists have called for Jihad against Moscow. The downing of Russian aircraft in Egypt on 31 October 2015 was one such example of retaliation by Islamists against Moscow's air strikes in Syria. Aware of these regional complexities, Moscow has carefully navigated the Middle East by maintaining balanced engagement with all the regional states. In January 2016, it offered to play the role of a mediator between Iran and Saudi Arabia, but without much success due to lack of Saudi trust as they view Russia as a close partner of Iran. Russia's involvement in Libya could be viewed as a return to that country to compensate its losses (fall of Qaddafi resulted in losses amounting to some US$ 20 billion) in the past, and create leverage of influence on the West. Moscow has substantially increased its involvement in the Libyan civil war by having active consultation with General Khalifa Haftar, a commander of main military factions in the civil war, to supplying arms with help from Egypt. From the Russian perspective, this gives it another geo-political lever to make it more relevant in the region as compared to the West. By supporting General Haftar, Moscow is also trying to create a pro-Russian group in the future Libyan regime.

Moreover, despite its good relations with Israel, there is disconnect between Russia's aims in the Middle East and Israel's objectives. Some senior Israeli officials are of the view that Russia's position on Iran and Hezbollah and its support to Bashar al-Assad were in contrast to Israel's positions. They feel "Russia thinks and acts as a superpower, and as such it often ignores Israeli interests when it doesn't coincide with the Russian interest."[12]

Despite these differences, both Israel and Russia take their relations seriously. After Russia's military involvement in Syria, both governments have kept communication channels open to avoid any kind of accidental confrontation. Prime Minister Benjamin Netanyahu paid three visits to Russia during 2016.

The Islamic State and Terrorism

Terrorism and religious extremism emanating from the Middle East remain a major cause of concern for Russia. It has been estimated that between 5,000 to 7,000 fighters from Russia and the post-Soviet countries had joined the Islamic State of Syria and Iraq (ISIS).[13] A number of extremist groups, particularly in the Muslim dominated Northern Caucasus region, had pledged allegiance to the ISIS. The April 2017 St. Petersburg bombing is, in many ways, a reflection of the spread of radical ideology in Russia.[14] Moreover, the danger of ISIS fighters returning home to carry out terror strikes remains a distinct possibility.

In this light, approximately 12–15 per cent or about 16 to 20 million of Russia's population is Muslim.[15] The Russian Federation comprises of several predominantly Muslim republics, including Chechnya and Dagestan in the North Caucasus to Tatarstan and Bashkortostan in the Volga River Basin. Moreover, a large number of Central Asian migrants, who are predominantly Muslim, reside in Russia. There exist many fault lines that range from economic slowdown and inter-ethnic discords to lack of assimilation and weakness of state structures that make several Russian regions fertile ground for breeding ISIS ideology. According to a Russian expert, "Radical ideology is spreading across Russia; and since [the] 1990s, terrorism is a constant threat all over the country, particularly in the major cities."[16]

Meanwhile, Russia also faces the risk of a spill over of terrorism and instability from Central Asia and Afghanistan. The violent Islamic Movement of Uzbekistan (IMU) has not only pledged allegiance to the ISIS but also sought to regain a foothold in northern Afghanistan—an area that lies in close proximity to Central Asia. Other organisations like the Hizb ut-Tahrir remain active in the region. One cannot rule out the Central Asian radicals in Syria and Iraq and their compatriots in the Af-Pak region coordinating their militant activities against CARs. In fact, an ISIS map of 2014 highlights the group's plans to expand its territories in regions that were under the historical Arab Caliphates from the seventh to the thirteenth centuries.[17] The post-Soviet space was part of those Caliphates. Therefore, given the centrality of extremist ideology in these emerging scenarios, tackling the ISIS at its source has been an important driver of Russia's Middle East policy.

In April 2015, Foreign Minister Sergei Lavrov noted that Russia is arming Iraq and Syria to help them fight the Islamic State which poses a serious threat to his own country.

> [The] Islamic State is our main enemy at the moment. If only because hundreds of Russian citizens, hundreds of Europeans, hundreds of Americans fight alongside IS...they are already coming back...and to enjoy themselves could stage vile acts at home.[18]

Russia's main concern in Syria has been that the fall of the Assad regime can result in spreading greater instability in the entire region and send radical Islamists to Russia and Central Asia. Moscow's military operations in Syria are driven by two factors: first, to keep the Assad regime in power in order to secure Russian strategic interests in Syria. It wants to retain its strategic assets, mainly its presence in the Tartus naval base and the Khmeimim airbase in Syria. Russian leadership wanted to prevent the repeat of Libya and Iraq in Syria, as this could be inimical to its strategic interests. Second, the spread of radical Islamists groups to Russia and Central Asia pose a serious security threat, and hence the expanding influence of the ISIS and terrorism are viewed as significant challenges by the Russian leadership.

Economic Partnerships

Since 2014, the Russian economy has faced the dual whammy of western sanctions and lower oil prices that have exposed its inherent structural deficiencies. As a result, economic growth shrunk in excess of 4.5 per cent in 2015.[19] More importantly, real disposable income has fallen by 12.3 per cent, leading to an increase in poverty and unemployment levels.[20] Several regions, particularly the monotowns, suffer from unsustainable levels of mounting debt. With protests breaking out in several parts of Russia, there has emerged a perception that the social contract between the state and the people—of promoting economic growth in lieu of political stability—could unravel in the future. This can have an impact on the presidential elections due in 2018. Consequently, seeking investments and newer markets that can tide over the ongoing crisis appear to be a vital pillar of Russia's Middle East strategy. This involves a broad spectrum of military, hydrocarbon, agriculture, and nuclear sectors.

In one of the biggest deals in the post-Soviet era, the Russian state holding company Rosneftgaz signed a deal with the Qatar Investment Authority (QIA) in December 2016 to sell 19.5 per cent stake (worth US$ 11.37 billion) in Rosneft, considered as the crown jewel of the Russian hydrocarbon sector.[21] It represents one-fifth of Rosneft's privatisation portfolio.[22] In the past, QIA had bought a US$ 500 million stake in V.T.B bank and a 25 per cent stake in St. Petersburg's Pulkovo airport.[23] Meanwhile, in January 2017, it was reported that QIA is likely to sign a US$ 2 billion deal with the Russian Direct Investment Fund to invest in Russia's new oil extraction projects.[24] This assumes significance, given the compelling rationale for Russia to invest in new oil fields since a majority of its existing projects have crossed their peak production.

Equally important for Russia is Iran with whom it has signed a number of economic deals during President Hassan Rouhani's visit to Moscow in March 2017.[25] Highlighting their roadmap for cooperation in trade and industry, the economic agreements covered diverse sectors ranging from infrastructure development to information and communication technology, oil and gas, agriculture, tourism, power generation, and a free trade zone with the Eurasian Economic Union. It was pointed out that their bilateral trade increased by a whopping 70 per cent in 2016.[26]

Despite Iran being a potential rival in the gas market, Moscow has preferred cooperation to confrontation. This approach is rooted in the fact that the authorities do not see Iran replacing Russia in the gas market in the next decade. Moscow has been trying to buy some stakes in the energy projects of Iran and, during the Baku Summit in August 2016, Putin and Rouhani called for closer cooperation and management in the oil and gas sphere, particularly for the joint development of the Caspian hydrocarbon resources and shared use of the existing pipeline infrastructure. A plan to supply natural via Azerbaijan to the northern provinces of Iran in exchange gas for Iranian liquefied natural gas that Russia companies will receive in the Persian Gulf was formulated.[27] Despite Russian leadership's support and desire to promote its involvement in Iran's gas sector, until March 2017 there was not much progress on this.[28]

On the nuclear front, Russia has sought to build reactors in Iran, Jordan, Turkey and Egypt.[29] In the hydrocarbon sector, Russian companies have invested in Iraq while Russia has sought to build the Turkish stream pipeline that will transport gas to Europe via Turkey, thereby bypassing Ukraine and substituting for the South stream pipeline blocked by Bulgaria. Russia has also sought to coordinate OPEC production cuts with Saudi Arabia in the hope of stabilising oil prices.

A close look at Russia's economic partnership with the Middle East during 2015–16 reflects a low level of trade as compared to that with OECD and the EU. However, the region still holds great significance and, in some cases, key importance for select Russian industries, including oil and gas, petrochemical, military industrial complex, space, and agriculture. In 2015, Russia's overall trade with the Middle East amounted to US$ 37 billion, which is 7 per cent share in its overall trade of about US$ 526.5 billion. Similarly, in 2016, Russia's overall trade with the Middle East amounted to US$ 28.6 billion, accounting for 6 per cent share in Russia's overall trade (approx. US$ 468 billion).[30] Russia's major trading partners have been OECD and the EU (as is evident in Tables 15. 1 and 15. 2). In the Middle East, Turkey, Israel, Egypt, Iran, Iraq, and the UAE have been its key trading partners. Israel and the UAE import around 16 per cent of precious stones and metals from Russia, and the Middle East is also a major importer of its grains. By 2016, Egypt, Israel, and Saudi Arabia were the largest importers of Russian wheat, barley, and rye.[31]

More importantly, Russia's trade with its major ally, Syria, declined from US$ 312 million in 2015 to US$ 193 million in 2016. Similarly, Russia's trade with Saudi Arabia dropped to US$ 492 million in 2016 from US$ 926 million in 2015. However, its trade saw an upward trend in case of Kuwait and Oman. Surprisingly, Russia's trade with Bahrain increased from US$ 12.193 million in 2015 to US$ 53.6 million in 2016 (Table 15.1).

Table 15.1: Russia's Trade with Middle East in 2015 and 2016 (in US$ million)

Country	Exports (2015)	Imports (2015)	Total Trade (2015)	Exports (2016)	Imports (2016)	Total Trade (2016)
Bahrain	4.32	7.87	12.193	47	6.6	53.6
Israel	1,539	806	2,345	1,466	720	2,186
Jordan	240.5	19	259.5	156.5	18	174.5
Iraq	1,807	0.12	1,807.12	917	0	917
Iran	1,016	268	1,284	1,881	303	2,184
Yemen	208	0.17	208.17	156	0.17	156.17
Qatar	13.7	24.5	38.2	17	34.5	51.5
Kuwait	406	0.083	406.08	480	0.12	480.12
Lebanon	632	8	640	528.5	11	539.5
UAE	1,081	164.5	1,245.5	971	273	1,208
Oman	104	2.5	106.5	118	2.5	120.5
Saudi Arabia	771	155	926	351	141	492
Palestine	2.9	0.5	3.4	1.7	0.6	2.3
Syria	307	5	312	182	11	193
Turkey	19,287	4,059	23,346	13,582	2,161	15,743
Egypt	3,676	414	4,090	3,784	374	4,158

Source: Russia Federal Customs Service: Customs Statistics of Foreign Trade http://stat.customs.ru/apex/f?p=201:7:1678029183890439::NO

Table 15.2: Russia's Trade with Other Regions (in US$ billion)

Region	Trade in 2015	Trade in 2016
CIS	66	57.27
OECD	312	262.65
EU	236	200
APEC	147	140
Germany	45	40.7
China	63.5	66
Netherlands	44	32

Source: Russia Federal Customs Service: Customs Statistics of Foreign Trade http://stat.customs.ru/apex/f?p=201:7:1678029183890439::NO

Military Footprint

Increasing its military footprint has been one of the key features of Russia's engagement with the Middle East in 2015-16. Russia's military intervention in Syria, its first beyond its immediate neighbourhood since the end of the Cold War—highlights the significant transformation of its armed forces. Not only has it send a message of a mobile and reliable force but also helped create facts on the ground, thereby helping establish a firm foothold in the region. Riding the wave of its military modernisation programme, the intervention has, arguably, also been a projection of the qualitative shift in the capabilities of its military hardware to potential buyers. This has held it in good stead in negotiating new weapons deals with the regional countries.

It is important to note that, in the past, Russia has been one of the largest arms exporters in the world. More importantly, in the present context, the arms manufacturing industry has a sound economic significance for the sanctions-crippled Russian economy. The industry provides about 20 per cent of all manufacturing jobs in the country, and employs around three million people. Thus, to deal with its critical economic situation, President Putin has ensured that the arms manufacturing industry is not only export-oriented but serves state defence orders, making it one of the drivers of the Russian economy.[32] According to the senior editor of *Russia Direct*, Alexey Khlebnikov, Russia wants to restore its Soviet-era position in the arms market, which drastically declined with the collapse of the USSR.[33] Since the Middle East has been a major arms importing region, Russia wants to avail every opportunity to increase its share. A senior defence analyst, Ben Moores, has said that the Middle East is the biggest regional market, offering opportunities worth US$ 110 billion in the coming decade.[34] Russia sold an estimated US$ 14–15 billion worth of weapons globally in 2016. Africa accounts for US$ 21 billion of outstanding contracts, with a vast majority signed with Algeria and Egypt.[35] The Middle East accounted for 36 per cent of Russia's overall arms exports in 2015.[36]

While the politico-economic benefits of Russia's arms transfers are well documented, what is often ignored is the 'rouble dividend' that Russia earns through exports. The additional income can cushion the economic crisis from getting worse. Moreover, an accompanying benefit of the military operation in Syria is that it allows Russia to test new weapons in conditions that are far from ideal.[37] It also tests the preparedness and ability of its personnel to stage a campaign far from its periphery.

Since 2016, Russia has signed deals with Iran, apart from agreements with Iraq, Egypt, Syria, and Algeria.[38] The full resumption of the arms trade with Iran became a key event of 2016. Moscow and Tehran finally managed to put behind all the ill feeling over Russia's previous decision of not supplying S-300PMU-1 SAM systems, and Russia delivered four S-300PMU-2 batteries worth US$ 1 billion. This was the first large arms delivery to Iran after the signing of the nuclear agreement between Tehran and the six international mediators. Speaking about the future of Russia-Iran military cooperation, Alaeddin Boroujerdi, the Iranian Chairman for the Committee for Foreign Policy and National Security, was quoted as stating, "The cooperation between Russia and Iran carries on, our armed forces continue to buy MI-17 helicopters from the Russian Federation, we also got the S-300 from Russia."[39] There are more than 50 Russian-made helicopters in Iran today, the most popular being the MI-17. Iran is also interested in Russia's Bastion mobile coastal defence missile system, equipped with supersonic Yakhont anti-ship missiles—Russia's latest S-400 Triumph anti-aircraft missile system developed by Almaz-Antey—Russian fighter jets as well as other arms and equipment.[40] Both countries have been negotiating the supply of a large number of weapons and hardware. During his visit to Tehran in November 2016, the head of the defence and security committee of the Russian upper house of parliament, Viktor Ozerov, confirmed negotiations with Iran worth US$ 10 billion. He said that the negotiations included T-90 tanks, artillery systems, and various aircraft. However, this was not just a one time delivery; rather it was a number of deliveries over the forthcoming years. It was clarified that until 2020, arms deliveries will only be made with the consent of the UN Security Council.[41]

The other important country in the region for Russia has been Iraq. Russia supplied four Su-25 attack aircraft, 10 Mi-28NE attack helicopters, Mi-35 helicopters, and an unknown number of Panstir-S1 gun-missile AA systems. Russia took full advantage of the American disengagement with Egypt to increase its arms exports. The US suspended its military aid to

Cairo for about two years after the 2013 military coup in that country. Under these circumstances, the Egyptian regime wanted to modernise its military arsenal by acquiring ammunition from Russia, and diversifying its military supplies to ensure regime security. Cairo also got financial aid from the UAE and Saudi Arabia, which allowed the Egyptian military regime to boost its military acquisitions. Russia transferred three repaired Mi-8 helicopter units, one S-300VM air defence system, and the R-32—a Project 12421 missile boat armed with the Moskit anti-ship missile system—to Egypt.[42]

Algeria is one of the biggest customers of Russian arms—about 14 per cent of its total export share. However, the bilateral agenda is rather modest.[43] Algeria signed a contract for the new Su-32 (Su-34) tactical bomber, took delivery of the first eight Su-30MKI (A) planes under a 2015 contract; received three Mi-26T2 heavy helicopters; and an unknown number of Panstir-S1 gun-missile AA systems. In fact, it became one of the largest importers of Russian tanks in 2016, having taken delivery of approximately 100 T-90SA units.[44] According to SIPRI estimates, Algeria has been the third largest recipient of Russian Arms during 2007–16. Moscow has not been very successful as an arms supplier to the UAE and Saudi Arabia, where the US and other European powers have been the traditional suppliers. However, Jordan bought four of the heavy Mi-26T2 helicopter models, and Turkey placed an order for a single SBJ tactical bombers.[45]

A major theatre of Moscow's military operation, Syria received a broad range of ground weapons systems, and 10 upgraded Su-24M2 tactical bombers. Due to the situation in the country, Syria has mainly received ammunition and spare parts; but major arms have not been delivered since 2013.[46] Some of the geo-political gains of the military intervention in Syria by Russia are: firstly, a demonstration of Moscow's capability to stand by its ally Assad, and prevent regime change by force as had happened in case of Libya and Iraq; second, it helped Russia come out of isolation to which it was subjected after the annexation of Crimea and intervention in Eastern Ukraine. By February 2016, it was becoming clear that, without support from Russia, it would be difficult to find any solution to the Syrian crisis. Third, this situation also helped Putin's effort to re-establish Moscow's image as a great power and exhibit its military power; and four, Russia acquired a major airbase in Hmeinim in Syria. The use of SAM-400's gave Russia control of a considerable amount of airspace in the Middle East region. In addition, Moscow also expanded its naval facility in the Syrian part of Tartus adding several floating docks and warehouses, thus making it a full-fledged naval base protected by the SAM-300 anti-aircraft systems. Finally, Russian intervention resulted in reinforcing its relations with Iran.

Although Russian military intervention did strengthen the hands of Assad regime with some success on the ground, but it is understandable that Moscow does not have enough economic and military wherewithal to bring Syria back under full control by force. Russian and other experts are of the opinion that Moscow is overstretching its role which would be difficult to sustain. In a recent article, Fyodor Lukyanov said that, for Russia, "The risk of overstretching itself becomes more than just a risk. The intention to compensate for the lack of capabilities with the determination to use military force may be effective only to a certain extent".[47] In this context, Robert O. Freedman acknowledged the gains of Russian intervention in Syria by stating that,

> ...the decisive Russian military intervention in Syria has demonstrated, at least so far, that far from being a quagmire, Russian military intervention in Syria has had a major effect, strengthening both [the] military and political position of the Assad regime.[48]

At the same time, he emphasised that it would not be possible for Moscow to sustain its position because it does not have "financial position to sustain being a superpower", and that its success in Syria was made possible by the failure of the US to take serious military action at an appropriate time.

Thus, Moscow is looking for a settlement through a national dialogue between the regime and the opposition. This, in Moscow's view, is the most viable option in the current situation. However, Russia is looking for a settlement favourable to its interests. This would include the territorial integrity of Syria, protecting the existing government apparatus, and the formation of a united anti-IS coalition. How the situation will unfold in Syria in the future, is not very clear despite Assad regaining control of territories from the ISIS. It is also not very clear how US-Russia cooperation will be shaped under the Trump Administration.

Implications for India

A combination of political and economic complementarities at the regional and global levels has enabled India and countries in the Middle East to consolidate their age-old ties. India cannot but be affected by new developments in the region. The ongoing political transformation in the region as well as the realisation of India's rise in stature as an emerging regional power has necessitated a fresh look at this geo-strategically important region.

India and Russia may have different goals to pursue based on their national interests; but instability and growing extremism in the Middle East negatively impacts both India and Russia. Both countries want to mitigate the negative impact of extremist groups like the Islamic State and Al-Qaeda. New Delhi, Moscow, and Tehran are working very closely in developing connectivity through the International North South Corridor (INSTC). [49]

Conclusion

During 2015–16, Russia pursued a much more active engagement with the Middle East and North African countries, thereby increasing its political and military footprints. It was also able to transform its active role into actual influence. However, it is important to note that, in many ways, this was made possible due to the Obama Administration's reluctance to play a more active role in the region. This got reflected particularly in Syria, Egypt, Israel, and Turkey. As a result, Syria, Iran, UAE, Saudi Arabia, Israel, Egypt, Algeria, Tunisia, Morocco, and Jordan became the major vectors of Russia's renewed focus to enhance its diplomatic engagement. The regional perception about Russia in the Middle East also changed because of its greater involvement and active role in the Syrian Civil War in a situation where the US was viewed to be withdrawing from the region. However, how far Russia's resurgence in the Middle East will go remains to be seen. Some Russian experts, like Alexey Khlebnikov, are of the view that Moscow's key goal in the region is to counter-balance US influence without any desire to take over their role. He has said, "Russian leadership clearly understands that the country does not have the capacity to do so...."[50]

Russia's long term engagement with the region is likely to be tested by the perception of Moscow punching above its weight on the Middle Eastern stage. This flows from the prevailing domestic economic crisis, and the lack of global competitiveness of the Russian economy. Thus, the presence of several competing regional and extra-regional interests will be a key test of Russian diplomacy to stay relevant in the current geo-political minefield of the Middle East.

NOTES

1. Dmitri Trenin, "Russia in the Middle East: Moscow's Objectives, priorities and Policy Drivers", Carnegie Moscow Center, at http://carnegieendowment.org/files/03-25-16_Trenin_Middle_East_Moscow_clean.pdf
2. "Foreign Policy Concept of the Russian Federation", Ministry of Foreign Affairs of the Russian Federation, 30 November 2016, at http://www.mid.ru/en/foreign_policy/official_documents/-/asset_publisher/CptICkB6BZ29/content/id/2542248
3. Bobo Lo, "Russia and the New World Order", Chatham House, 2015, p. 232.
4. Ibid.

5. "The Foreign Policy Concept of the Russian Federation", President of Russia, 12 January, 2008, at http://en.kremlin.ru/supplement/4116
6. "Concept of the Foreign Policy of the Russian Federation", Ministry of Foreign Affairs of the Russian Federation, 18 February, 2013, at http://www.mid.ru/en/foreign_policy/official_documents/-/asset_publisher/CptICkB6BZ29/content/id/122186
7. "Foreign Policy Concept of the Russian Federation", Ministry of Foreign Affairs of the Russian Federation, 30 November, 2016, at http://www.mid.ru/en/foreign_policy/official_documents/-/asset_publisher/CptICkB6BZ29/content/id/2542248
8. Ibid.
9. Ibid.
10. Dmitri Trenin, "The Ukraine Crisis and the Resumption of Great-Power Rivalry", Carnegie Moscow Center, 9 July, 2014, at http://carnegie.ru/2014/07/09/ukraine-crisis-and-resumption-of-great-power-rivalry-pub-56113
11. Ibid.
12. Sergei Karpukhin, "Russia Has Long-term Ambitions In the Middle East: Israeli Official", *Reuters*, 15 November, 2016, at http://www.huffingtonpost.com/entry/russias-long-term-middle-east-ambitions_us_582b58b1e4b0e39c1fa68898
13. "Putin: 7,000 people from ex-Soviet republics estimated to fight alongside ISIS", *RT*¸ 16 October 2015, at https://www.rt.com/news/318826-putin-isis-soviet-republics-fighters/
14. "8 people detained in connection with St. Petersburg Metro bombing – official", *RT*, 7 April, 2017, at https://www.rt.com/news/383752-eight-detained-petersburg-metro-bombing/
15. "Why some Russian women embraced Islam", Russia Beyond the Headlines, 26 January, 2016, at https://www.rbth.com/politics_and_society/society/2016/01/26/why-some-russian-women-embraced-islam_562247
16. Dmitri Trenin, "Russia in the Middle East: Moscow's Objectives, priorities and Policy Drivers", op. cit.
17. "Central Asia at Danger: the Islamic State Will Not Halt at the Caspian Sea", *The Times of Central Asia*, 25 August, 2014, at http://www.timesca.com/news/6339-central-asia-at-danger-the-islamic-state-will-not-halt-at-the-caspian-sea
18. "'Russia arms Iraq, Syria to help combat Islamic State' Lavrov", *Reuters*, 22 April 2015, at http://www.reuters.com/article/us-mideast-crisis-russia-lavrov-idUSKBN0ND1GL20150422
19. " 12,3% " [The real income of Russians decreased by 12.3% in two years]," Itar-Tass, 20 December, 2016, at http://tass.ru/obschestvo/3889149
20. Ibid
21. "Russia signs Rosneft deal with Qatar, Glencore", *Reuters*, 11 December 2016, at http://www.reuters.com/article/us-russia-rosneft-privatisation-idUSKBN13Z0QB
22. Theodore Karasik, "Why is Qatar Investing so much in Russia?", Middle East Institute, 8 March 2017, http://www.mei.edu/content/article/why-qatar-investing-so-much-russia
23. Ibid
24. "Qatar sovereign wealth fund plans another $2bn Russian investment", *Financial Times*, 25 January 2017, https://www.ft.com/content/86c658e8-401d-3582-815e-

3e7dc4861c0d?mhq5j=e2

25. Julia Sveshnikova, "Was Rouhani's visit to Russia actually successful?", *Al-Monitor*, 5 April 2017, at http://www.al-monitor.com/pulse/originals/2017/04/iran-russia-rouhani-putin-visit-moscow-success.html
26. Ibid.
27. "Новый газовый картель: Россия, Иран, Азербайджан" (New Gas Cartel: Russia, Iran and Azerbaijan), *Pravda*, 9 August 2016, at https://www.pravda.ru/economics/materials/gas/09-08-2016/1309352-iran-0/
28. Alexei Topalov, "Россия замахнулась на иранские недра" (Russia threatens Iran's interests), *Gazeta*, 14 March 2017, at https://www.gazeta.ru/business/2017/03/13/10574165.shtml,
29. Ibid.
30. Russia Federal Customs Service: Customs Statistics of Foreign Trade, at http://stat.customs.ru/apex/f?p=201:7:1678029183890439::NO
31. Ibid.
32. "New Russian arms deals could shake up Mideast market", *Al-Monitor*, 25 August 2015, at http://www.al-monitor.com/pulse/originals/2015/08/russian-arms-supply-middle-east.html#ixzz4lxwa1Xn4
33. Stasa Salacanin, "Weapons Sales: The Key to Russia's Middle East agenda", *The New Arab*, 13 March, 2017, at https://www.alaraby.co.uk/english/indepth/2017/3/13/weapons-sales-the-key-to-russias-middle-east-agenda
34. "Saudi Arabia outpaces India to become top defence importer", *Reuters*, 8 March 2015, at http://in.reuters.com/article/defence-supplies-saudi-idINKBN0M40FC20150308
35. Andrey Frolov, "Russian Arms Trade in 2016", *Moscow Defence Brief*, No 3(59), 2017, at http://mdb.cast.ru/mdb/1-2017/item2/article1/
36. Ibid.
37. Ruslan Pukhov, "A Proving Ground of the Future," *Russia in Global Affairs*, 30 March, 2016, at http://eng.globalaffairs.ru/number/A-Proving-Ground-of-the-Future-18075
38. "Воздушно-коммерческие силы [Demand of Russian weapons after Syria]," *Kommersant*, 28 March, 2016, at http://www.kommersant.ru/doc/2932551
39. "Russia, Iran plan $10bn arms supply to Tehran", *RT*, 14 November, 2016, at https://www.rt.com/news/366871-russia-iran-weapons-delivery/
40. Ibid.
41. Ibid.
42. Andrey Frolov, "Russian Arms Trade in 2016", op. cit.
43. "New Russian arms deals could shake up Mideast market", *Al-Monitor*, 25 August 2015 at http://www.al-monitor.com/pulse/originals/2015/08/russian-arms-supply-middle-east.html#ixzz4lxwa1Xn4
44. Andrey Frolov, "Russian Arms Trade in 2016", op. cit.
45. Ibid.
46. Ibid.
47. Fyodor Lukyanov, "A Failed New World Order and Beyond: Russian View", *Strategic Analysis*, Special Issue: Russia in Global Affairs, Vol. 40(6), November-December 2016, pp 478.
48. Robert Freedman, "Russian Foreign Policy in the Middle East 2015–16: Pushing on an Open Door", *Johnson's Russia List*, 3 November 2016, at http://

russialist.org/russian-foreign-policy-in-the-middle-east-2015-2016-pushing-on-an-open-door/

49. For details see: Meena Singh Roy, "International North-South Transport Corridor: Re-energising India's Gateway to Eurasia", IDSA Issue Brief, 18 August 2015; see also, "Modi's Visit to Iran: Will it provide a New Momentum to Bilateral Relations?" IDSA Issue Brief, 16 May 2016; and "The Trajectory of India-Russia Ties: High Expectations and Current Realities", *Indian Foreign Affairs Journal*, Vol. 11, No. 4, October-December 2016, pp. 322–331.

50. Stasa, Salacanin, "Weapons Sales: The Key to Russia's Middle East agenda", *The New Arab*, 13 March, 2017, at https://www.alaraby.co.uk/english/indepth/2017/3/13/weapons-sales-the-key-to-russias-middle-east-agenda

16

THE IRAN NUCLEAR DEAL

S. Samuel C. Rajiv

The Joint Comprehensive Plan of Action (JCPOA) of 14 July 2015 was achieved after tortuous negotiations between Iran and the P5+1 interlocutors: China, France, Russia, the United Kingdom, the United States, and Germany. The negotiations process began in 2006 in the aftermath of the Iranian nuclear issue being referred to the United Nations Security Council (UNSC) in February of that year. The protagonists met in Vienna, Istanbul, Moscow, among other places, over the course of a decade.

The process gained traction after the coming to power of President Hassan Rouhani in 2013. He was elected on the back of difficult economic conditions facing Iran as a result of stringent multi-lateral (primarily the UN) and unilateral (the US and European Union [EU]) sanctions. The UN sanctions primarily related to travel bans and asset freezes of entities and individuals associated with Iran's nuclear programme while the US and EU sanctions targeted Iran's primary source of foreign exchange, its oil exports, and cut off Iran's links to the global financial system by denying access to SWIFT. Nations importing Iranian oil (primarily China, India, Japan, South Korea, and Turkey after July 2012 when the EU ban on import of Iranian oil kicked in), had to severely curtail their quantities.

President Rouhani came to power promising to provide a government of "prudence and moderation". This was in contrast to the previous government headed by Mahmoud Ahmadinejad (2005–13), which had vitiated the low levels of political trust between Iran and its interlocutors through belligerent rhetoric. Despite passing stringent sanction measures targeting Iran's oil exports and threatening penalties for engaging in business with the Central Bank of Iran (CBI), the Barack Obama administration's 'dual track' strategy held out the prospects of a negotiated settlement, if Iran was willing to "constructively engage" with its interlocutors.

The Joint Plan of Action (JPOA) was eventually agreed on 24 November 2013. Iran agreed to a set of confidence building measures (CBMs) to assuage the concerns of its interlocutors. These included measures like not enriching uranium beyond 5 per cent and not making any additions to its nuclear infrastructure at Natanz and Fordow, among others. The P5+1, on their part, agreed not to impose any additional sanction measures, and to allow Iran access to some portion of its money held in the bank accounts of oil-importing countries. The JPOA began to be implemented from January 2014. It was extended twice (in July 2014 and November 2014) as the parties jostled to come to an agreement on the final terms of the nuclear deal. During the time period that the JPOA was in force (January 2014–July 2015), Iran was able to access nearly US$ 12 billion of its oil money.[1]

The Lausanne Framework was agreed on 2 April 2015, after 14 rounds of talks and 18 months of negotiations (in the aftermath of the JPOA) on the finer aspects of the obligations and responsibilities that each side would assume under the terms of a final deal. Contingent on an International Atomic Energy Agency (IAEA)-verified implementation of certain key nuclear-related steps, Iran's interlocutors agreed to terminate/cease the application of key sanctions measures. There was some contention as to the sequencing of the steps each side would take in the immediate aftermath of the Framework, namely, the link between the nature of sanctions relief and Iran's nuclear commitments. These, however, were eventually resolved as the JCPOA was agreed upon.

This essay begins by highlighting some of the key features of the JCPOA, and then focuses attention on the key challenges to the deal emanating from domestic political dynamics in the US and Iran. The next section delineates the regional dynamics after the signing of the JCPOA. The increased US military support to its allies ranging from Israel to Saudi Arabia as well as the publicized nature of the interactions involving Saudi Arabia and the UAE with Israel are highlighted. The chapter closes with an examination of the implications and consequences for India as a result of the developments in the aftermath of the JCPOA.

The Key Features

The JCPOA began to be implemented from 16 January 2016 (Implementation Day). This was after the IAEA verified Iran's implementation of key nuclear-related measures, including being satisfied with its explanations regarding the possible military dimensions (PMD) of its nuclear activities. These PMD concerns were prominently flagged in the November 2011 report of the IAEA Director General (DG) to the Board of Governors (BOG).[2] Some of the key nuclear-related measures that Iran agreed to as part of the JCPOA included the reduction in its stockpile of uranium hexa fluoride (UF_6) (to 300 kilograms), reduction in the number of centrifuges (to 5060 IR-1 centrifuges for 10 years), the calandria of the Arak reactor being made inoperable by filling it with concrete, among other measures.[3] Iran had over 8,700 kilograms of UF_6 and over 15,000 IR-1 centrifuges at Natanz, out of which more than 9,000 were operating as of May 2015. Another 2,700 IR-1 centrifuges at Fordow were not in operation since the JPOA began to be implemented. Iran's commitments as part of the JCPOA were, therefore, significant reductions in its nuclear infrastructure.

Iran began to provisionally implement the IAEA Additional Protocol (AP) from Implementation Day. The AP is a key IAEA transparency measure that Iran had stopped implementing voluntarily in February 2006 in the immediate aftermath of its UNSC referral. It was implementing it provisionally from December 2003 to February 2006. Iran would ratify the AP eight years after 'Adoption Day', or when the IAEA reaches the 'Broader Conclusion' that all of Iran's nuclear activities are for peaceful purposes. Adoption Day was 18 October 2015—90 days after the UNSC passed Resolution 2231, endorsing the JCPOA. Eight years after Adoption Day would be the JCPOA Transition Day while 10 years after Adoption Day would be the Termination Day, when the provisions of the JCPOA would no longer be valid. However, Iran would continue to be bound by some key commitments for a period of 15 years which, among others, include not engaging in R&D on uranium or plutonium metal machining, and not enriching UF_6 beyond 3.67 per cent.

These CBMs that Iran agreed to are significant given that the IAEA DG in his quarterly reports to the BOG over the years had repeatedly flagged the "lack of confidence" regarding the peaceful nature of Iran's nuclear programme. This was despite repeatedly acknowledging that all of Iran's nuclear material was accounted for. It is pertinent to note that Iran's refusal to implement the AP was among one of the key issues of contention with its interlocutors and the IAEA in the preceding years. Iran held that the provisions of its comprehensive safeguards agreement (CSA) with the IAEA (which entered into force on 15 May 1974) were enough to address any concerns emanating from its nuclear programme. The IAEA, on its part, held that the AP was an essential tool to address concerns given Iran's refusal to allow access to military sites like Parchin, where the IAEA contended experiments involving nuclear material might have taken place.[4]

The transparency measures contained in the JCPOA are far more stringent than those even required by the AP, or those currently being implemented by other members of the Nuclear Non-Proliferation treaty (NPT). The JCPOA, for instance, ensures the 'long-term' presence of IAEA inspectors; daily access to IAEA inspectors to Natanz for 15 years (which, incidentally, would be the only location for all of Iran's nuclear-enrichment related activities); the surveillance of centrifuge rotors for 20 years; the surveillance of uranium ore concentrate production for 25 years, among others. In the case of a dispute, the IAEA requests for access to facilities or locations; a Joint Commission established pursuant to the JCPOA (made up of representatives of the P5+1 and the EU Foreign Policy Chief, who would look at the IAEA requests and come to a decision—with no quorum required for the majority decision); and the entire process not taking more than three weeks from the initial IAEA request.

In return for these nuclear-related commitments, the P5+1 agreed to provide relief relating to sanctions that were imposed in response to Iran's nuclear concerns. All UNSC sanctions were terminated in the aftermath of Resolution 2231. Restrictions on Iran's oil exports were removed, as were restrictions on the provision of insurance services on ships carrying Iranian oil, restrictions on the quantum of foreign investments in Iran's energy infrastructure, among a host of other relief measures. Iran was also reconnected to SWIFT from February 2016.

Challenges to JCPOA Implementation

Since January 2016, the JCPOA is being implemented smoothly, with the IAEA certifying Iranian compliance.[5] However, domestic constituencies in the US and Iran opposed to the nuclear agreement have continued to vent their opposition to the JCPOA.

Domestic Dynamics in the US

The most serious challenge to the JCPOA came with the inauguration of Donald Trump's Presidency in January 2017. Throughout his campaign, Trump criticized the Iran nuclear agreement as a 'bad deal' that he would repeal once he came to power.[6] President Trump and his officials have criticized Iran's ballistic missile tests as being against the terms of the JCPOA. In the immediate aftermath of Iran testing a ballistic missile on 29 January 2017, the Trump Administration imposed sanctions on 25 individuals and entities connected to the ballistic missile programme as well as to the Iranian

Revolutionary Guard Corps-Qods Force (IRGC-QF). The Trump administration also announced that an inter-agency review of the nature of the sanctions relief granted to Iran was being conducted, despite acknowledging that Iran was keeping up with its JCPOA commitments.

Earlier, in September 2015, the US Senate had narrowly failed to pass a disapproval resolution on the JCPOA, when backed by four Democratic Senators, 54 Republican Senators failed to come up with the necessary 60 votes for such a resolution to be approved. The Republican-controlled US Senate (54 as against 44 Democrats and two Independents) and the House of Representatives (246 Republicans as against 187 Democrats) though are considering bills that seek to further tighten the pressure on Iran. For instance, the 'No US Financing for Iran Act' was passed in the House of Representatives in a highly partisan vote (243–174) on 17 November 2016. It has since been referred to the Senate Committee on Banking, Housing, and Urban Affairs. The Act seeks to prevent US financial institutions from financing the sale of American passenger planes to Iran.

However, despite such measures, Iranian airline companies are pursuing mega deals with American aircraft manufacturers, like Boeing. Iran Air, for instance, inked a deal for 80 passenger planes worth more than US$ 16 billion with Boeing, just ahead of Trump's inauguration in December 2016. Another airline, Aseman, inked a US$ 3 billion deal in early April 2017 for 30 737 MAX aircraft, with deliveries set to begin in the 2019–22 timeframe.[7] Boeing is pursuing these deals with the full permission of the US government. Thus, this does indicate that even if President Trump wants to pressurize Iran on its ballistic missile and alleged terrorism-related activities among others, the Administration might not be willing to take any negative action that would harm the US economy and job prospects.

The Iran Sanctions Act (ISA) was renewed by the US Congress in December 2016, with Iran alleging that the move was in violation of the JCPOA. The ISA was an important part of the US sanctions architecture, with critical legislations—like the 2010 Comprehensive Iran Sanctions and Divestment Act (CISADA), for instance—threatening one or more ISA sanctions for violating its provisions. Any business transactions with the sanctioned entities prior to the JCPOA would have attracted CISADA provisions which threatened ISA sanctions (like preventing access to US EXIM Bank loans; the denial of US export licenses; a ban on US government procurement contracts; among others) against entities investing above a certain limit in Iran's energy infrastructure. It was CISADA which, in fact, extended the ISA from 2011 till 31 December 2016.

The JCPOA provides relief from such CISADA sanctions provisions, given that Iranian entities that were under nuclear-related sanctions on the Commerce Department sanctions list have been de-listed. However, some US Congressmen argued that it was essential to have an 'active' ISA in place in case sanctions may have to be re-imposed on Iran for any future violations, and that the sanctions architecture provided by the ISA would cater to the so-called 'snap back' provision of the JCPOA.[8] It is pertinent to note, however, that the 'snap-back' of sanctions in the JCPOA specifically refers to the re-imposition of UNSC sanctions and not of unilateral sanctions.[9]

President Trump's Executive Order (late January 2017) banning citizens from Iran (apart from Iraq, Libya, Somalia, Sudan, Syria, and Yemen) from entering the US for a period of 90 days led to considerable criticism for targeting Muslim-majority countries. Iranian Foreign Minister Javed Zarif stated that President Trump's 'Muslim ban' was a "great gift to extremists".[10] On its part, the Trump Administration insisted that these restrictions did not constitute a 'Muslim ban' but were meant to implement the US Refugee Admissions Programme (USRAP), and pointed out that the countries short-listed were designated as "countries of concern" for travel purposes by the Department of Homeland Security (DHS), and that Iran, Iraq, Sudan, and Syria were designated by the preceding Obama Administration while Libya, Somalia, and Sudan were added in 2016.

While the order was challenged in courts, in March 2017 the Administration removed Iraq from the list, insisting that Iraq merited a "different treatment" given the "close cooperative relationship" between the US and Iraq, and the US commitment to combat the Islamic State in Iraq and Syria (ISIS).[11] On Iran, however, the Administration insisted that Tehran did not cooperate with the US on counter-terrorism efforts, and highlighted that it has been designated as a "state sponsor of terrorism" since 1984. It further charged that Iran continues to support groups like the Al-Qaeda, Hezbollah, and Hamas.[12]

Domestic Dynamics in Iran

On 13 October 2015, the Iranian Majlis passed a law allowing for the implementation of the JCPOA, with 161 members voting in favour, 59 members voting against, and 13 abstentions.[13] However, domestic opposition in Iran to the JCPOA has continued due to a combination of ideological factors, and the inability of the benefits accruing from the deal actually impacting the economy which was not doing well on account of sanctions pressure. Iran did gain access to over US$ 100 billion of its currency reserves held in foreign banks in the aftermath of JCPOA Implementation Day.

However, analysts noted that more than half of the money was owed to debtors, like China.[14]

Iran's oil exports reached pre-sanctions levels of 4 million barrels per day (bpd) by October 2016.[15] When the CBI's second quarter figures for 2016/17 were released in January 2017, it was however, at about 3 per cent.[16] While these were encouraging figures, given that Iran's GDP was a negative 6 per cent when President Rouhani took over in August 2013, it was less than the 4 per cent in the first quarter of 2016. Meanwhile, foreign investments in Iran's oil industry have not been forthcoming despite the coming into being of new production contracts, the Iran Petroleum Contracts (IPC), in August 2016. The IPC require a foreign company to tie up with a domestic company to pursue oil exploration. Further, the time period within which the foreign companies could recoup their investments was extended to at least 20 years from the time-period of about five years for the earlier 'buy-back' model of contracts.

Reports in April 2017 indicate that the implementation of the IPC policy is facing hurdles, and that the policy framework is being reviewed by the Supreme National Security Council.[17] Iran would have to overcome such bottlenecks quickly as it is in need of massive investments to develop the over 50 hydro-carbon fields and 18 exploration blocks.[18] In remarks made on 10 May 2017, the Deputy Head of the National Iranian Oil Company (NIOC) stated that Iran was looking at more than US$ 80 billion of foreign investments over the course of the next two years to develop its hydro-carbon resources.[19]

The Supreme Leader Ayatollah Ali Khamenei has on numerous occasions reiterated that the Islamic Republic would continue its ideological opposition to American policies in the region. In a letter to President Rouhani on the occasion of the Implementation Day of the JCPOA in January 2016, Khamenei warned the government not to 'neglect' the "treachery and [the possible] breach of promise by arrogant states, the US in particular."[20] In remarks made in early August 2016, Khamenei charged that "six months have passed since the signing of the JCPOA, [but] no evident and tangible effect has been seen with regard to the livelihood state of [the Iranian] people."[21] When the US House of Representatives agreed to extend the ISA in late November 2016 for another 10 years, Khamenei charged that the move was against the JCPOA, and warned that the nuclear deal "must not turn into leverage for [mounting] pressure on the Iranian nation and country."[22]

In his New Year's message on March 21, 2017, Khamenei again reiterated the need to develop the country's "economy of resistance", and declared the current year (2017–18) as the "Year of Economy of Resistance, Production and Job Creation."[23] The "Economy of Resistance" focusing on indigenous production and jobs has been regularly touted by the Supreme Leader as a key remedy to overcome the challenges of sanctions that Iran faced in the past decade. Declaring 2016–17 as the "Year of Economy of Resistance, Practical Steps and Action", Khamenei further criticized US military strikes on the Syrian air base in April 2017 as an "aggression" and the "violation of international law."[24] He also charged the Americans as being responsible for 'creating Daesh', and for continuing to strengthen it.

Regional Dynamics

Iran's regional rivals have been wary of the outcome of the nuclear negotiations as they believed that a nuclear deal would aid the increase of Iran's geo-political stature. Further, they were also worried that the JCPOA was the initial step that would eventually lead the US to accommodate Iranian concerns and priorities across regional trouble spots like Yemen and Syria. On its part, the Obama administration reassured its Gulf Cooperation Council (GCC) allies that the JCPOA was only about addressing Iranian nuclear concerns, and that there was no 'grand bargain' involved in the nuclear negotiations. It further reiterated that the US would continue to oppose Iran's actions that it held to be destabilising across the region.

Acting true to its assurances to its allies, the Obama Administration extended the "national emergency with respect to Iran" which was first imposed in 1995, and extended annually ever since, even after the JCPOA. While extending the designation on 13 January 2017, President Obama insisted that,

> ...irrespective of the JCPOA ... certain actions and policies of the Government of Iran continue to pose an unusual and extraordinary threat to the national security, foreign policy, and economy of the United States.[25]

Iran, along with Sudan and Syria, has continued to be designated as 'state sponsors of terrorism' by the US State Department.[26] The Trump Administration sanctioned the Tehran Prisons Organisation and its former head in May 2017 for human rights abuses, the first such human rights-related designations since December 2014.[27]

While the Obama and the Trump Administrations have kept up such pressure on Iran, another important effort has been to strengthen the military capabilities of the America's regional allies in order to assuage their concerns. Israel and the US signed the terms of a new 10 year defence cooperation agreement, worth US$ 38 billion, in September 2016. At the signing ceremony US National Security Advisor, Susan Rice highlighted that the Obama Administration provided military aid worth US$ 24 billion to Israel since 2009.[28] Israel became the first country to have the F-35 fighter aircraft, with five in service of the Israeli Air Force as on April 2017.

The US military help to other regional allies like Saudi Arabia has also been significant. The Obama Administration concluded arms sales agreements worth over US$ 58 billion to Riyadh between 2009 and 2015. In the aftermath of the JCPOA, some of the deals that the US concluded include those relating to Black hawk helicopters, Patriot Advanced Capability-3 (PAC-3) missile defence systems, main battle tanks and surface combatant ships.[29] The US has also been assisting the Saudi-led military operation in Yemen by refuelling aircraft, and supplying intelligence, among others, against Iranian proxies. Rising civilian death tolls due to indiscriminate Saudi bombings that began in March 2015 (on the cusp of the JCPOA), however, made the Obama Administration to stop the transfer of nearly US$ 400 million worth of munitions in December 2016.[30] As against this, reports noted that the Trump Administration was looking to provide more intelligence and surveillance support to ongoing and future Saudi military operations.[31]

In his presidential campaign, Donald Trump had vowed to put pressure on Riyadh to appropriately compensate the US for its security support which, according to him, ensured the survival of the Saudi regime. After taking over as President, Saudi Defence Minister, Deputy Crown Prince Mohammed bin Salman, was his first White House guest from the region.[32] President Trump's first overseas visit in May 2017 was also to Saudi Arabia, and from then on to Israel, the Vatican, Brussels, for the NATO Summit and the G-7 Summit in Sicily. Analysts noted that the Saudis were welcoming President Trump, ignoring his past statements and his temperament with an "eye on Iran."[33]

An interesting aspect of the regional dynamics in the run-up to the JCPOA and its aftermath has been the convergence of geo-political interests between the Arab Gulf states and Israel. On numerous occasions, Prime Minister Benjamin Netanyahu has highlighted the fact that Israel and the Arab states were on the same side of the strategic divide with respect to Iranian nuclear concerns. The former Saudi Ambassador to the US Anwar Eshki, and his Israeli interlocutor Dore Gold held unprecedented five rounds of talks focused on the Iran challenge since 2014.[34] While Saudi Arabia continues to be locked in a geo-political struggle for supremacy in regional hotspots like Yemen and Syria with Iran, the Saudi King Salman, during his first visit to the US in September 2015 in the aftermath of the JCPOA, welcomed the JCPOA. Israel, for its part, has continued to express scepticism of the ability of the JCPOA to effectively counter Iranian nuclear concerns, and has charged that the deal only postpones the inevitable nuclear arming of Tehran.[35]

Apart from such interactions with Saudi Arabia, Israel has taken part in multi-lateral military exercises featuring the air force of the United Arab Emirates (UAE) in the US and Greece. *Iniohos 2017* took place in Greece during 27 March – 6 April, with the air forces of the US and Italy being the other participants, apart from Israel and the UAE. Meanwhile, the *Red Flag* exercises in the US took place in August 2016, featuring the air forces of Israel, the UAE, Pakistan, and Spain. Such 'above-the-radar' military exercises involving countries with which Israel does not even have formal diplomatic relations like the UAE is, indeed, a significant example of interest alignment in the aftermath of the JCPOA.

Implications for India

As one of the biggest importers of Iranian oil, India was negatively affected by the secondary sanctions measures targeting Iran's oil exports. During 2009–16, India's energy imports more than halved in terms of both value and quantity (from over 14 per cent to less than 7 per cent).[36] Since the removal of restrictions in the aftermath of the JCPOA, India's oil imports registered a nearly 76 per cent increase in terms of value over the corresponding period in the previous year. From April 2016–February 2017, India's oil imports from Iran stood at US$ 7.85 billion, as against US$ 4.46 billion during 2015–16.[37] India's oil minister Dharmendra Pradhan told the Lok Sabha in November 2016 that Indian oil companies had paid about US$ 3.5 billion to the NIOC, and that about US$ 2.5 billion was yet to be paid.[38]

India's political engagement with Iran in the aftermath of the JCPOA hit a high gear with Prime Minister Narendra Modi visiting Tehran in May 2016. An important trilateral agreement involving Afghanistan regarding the development of the port of Chabahar was signed, and India agreed to develop and operate five berths at Chabahar for a period of five years. A railway line from Chabahar, whose construction India is funding would, upon completion, eventually take Indian goods to Afghanistan as well. Oil Minister Pradhan as well as External Affairs Minister Sushma Swaraj visited Iran in April 2016, with Pradhan's being the first visit by an Indian Oil Minister in over nine years. Transport Minister Nitin Gadkari visited Iran in May 2015, with discussions regarding Chabahar an important part of his itinerary. Iranian Foreign Minister Javed Zarif came to India in August 2015, in the immediate aftermath of the JCPOA.

While such high-level interactions are essential to take the relationship forward, the kidnapping of an Indian national and former naval officer Kulbushan Jadhav from Chabahar in March 2016 added a new dimension to the relationship. Pakistan has charged that Jadhav was engaged in destabilizing activities in its restive Baluchistan province from his base in Chabahar. India has rubbished the Pakistani allegations, has pointed to the glaring inconsistencies in its narrative, and is currently locked in a legal battle at the International Court of Justice to secure his release. Some reports suggest that Jadhav was kidnapped by a Sunni extremist group owing allegiance to the Al-Qaeda which had also targeted Iranian border guards in the past.[39]

However, analysts have expressed surprise at the 'silence' of Iran in the entire episode and its lack of investigative support.[40] The MEA spokesperson told reporters in April 2017 that Iran had not responded to India's request to carry out an investigation into the issue. Iranian analysts were cited as stating that Tehran was uncomfortable with India's growing security ties with GCC countries, like the UAE.[41] Crown Prince of Abu Dhabi Sheikh Mohamed bin Zayed Al Nahyan was the Chief Guest at the Republic Day parade in January 2017. Prime Minister Modi has also visited the UAE in August 2015 as well as Saudi Arabia and Qatar in May and June 2016, respectively. Such enhanced political interactions are an essential part of the government's 'Act West' policy in motion.[42] To view India's ties with these important countries in India's 'proximate neighbourhood' as a 'zero-sum' game is a gross misreading of India's massive stakes in the region, animated by energy imports and diaspora linkages.

Conclusion

No doubt India would be wary of the Trump Administration's increasing use of the sanctions card to punish Iran for issues like alleged human rights violations and ballistic missile tests. While most analysts believe that the administration would not unilaterally withdraw from the UNSC-recognised JCPOA, increasing sanctions pressure from the US adds enormously to the domestic political challenges of President Rouhani, who was re-elected in May 2017. It also confirms the worst fears about US motives, as repeatedly warned by Supreme Leader Khamenei. With Riyadh being the first stop of his first ever overseas tour, followed by Israel, President Trump has clearly advertised his regional strategic priorities. It remains to be seen if such gestures from their superpower patron, along with the massive military support highlighted earlier, would assuage America's Middle Eastern allies who are wary of an increase in Iran's regional standing as a result of the effective implementation of the JCPOA.

NOTES

1. "Guidance relating to the provision of certain temporary sanctions relief in order to implement the Joint Plan of Action reached on 24 November 2013, between the P5+1 and the Islamic Republic of Iran, as extended through 30 June 2015", US Treasury Department, at http://www.treasury.gov/resource-center/sanctions/Programs/Documents/guidance_ext_11252004.pdf
2. See "Implementation of the NPT Safeguards Agreement and relevant provisions of Security Council resolutions in the Islamic Republic of Iran", IAEA, GOV/2011/65, 8 November 2011, at https://www.iaea.org/sites/default/files/gov2011-65.pdf
3. See, United Nations Security Council, S/RES/2231 (2015), 20 July 2015, at http://www.un.org/en/ga/search/view_doc.asp?symbol=S/RES/2231 (2015). The text of the JCPOA is at Annex A of this resolution.
4. For an examination of the Iran-IAEA contentions, see S. Samuel C. Rajiv, "'Politicised Safeguards': Iran–IAEA Contentions, Drivers and Policy Implications'", *Strategic Analysis*, 38(5), pp. 688–702.
5. See, "Verification and monitoring in the Islamic Republic of Iran in light of United Nations Security Council resolution 2231 (2015)", IAEA, GOV/2017/10, 24 February 2017, at https://www.iaea.org/sites/default/files/gov2017-10.pdf
6. See for instance, Sarah Begley, "Read Donald trump's Speech to AIPAC", *TIME*, 22 March 2016, at http://time.com/4267058/donald-trump-aipac-speech-transcript/
7. Nasser Karimi and Jon Gambrell, "Boeing signs $3 billion deal to sell planes to Iran airline", *USA Today*, 4 April 2017, at https://www.usatoday.com/story/money/business/2017/04/04/boeing-co-says-signed-new-deal-iranian-airline/100013846/
8. Michael Bowman, "Iran Considers Renewal of US Sanctions a Violation of Nuclear Deal", *VOA News*, 2 December 2016, at http://www.voanews.com/a/congress-renews-united-states-sanctions-law-iran/3619509.html
9. See S/RES/2231(2015), pp. 19-20.
10. "History to record 'Muslim Ban' as great gift to extremists", *Mehr News*, 29 January 2017, at http://en.mehrnews.com/news/123091/History-to-record-Muslim-Ban-as-great-gift-to-extremists
11. See, "Executive Order Protecting the Nation from Foreign Terrorist Entry into the United States", The White House, Office of the Press Secretary, 6 March 2017, at https://www.whitehouse.gov/the-press-office/2017/03/06/executive-order-protecting-nation-foreign-terrorist-entry-united-states
12. Ibid.
13. "Guardian Council approves JCPOA amid stormy Majlis session", *Islamic Republic News Agency*, 16 October 2015, http://www.irna.ir/en/News/81801135/
14. Kenneth Katzman, "Iran sanctions", Congressional Research Service, 14 April 2017, pp. 56, at https://fas.org/sgp/crs/mideast/RS20871.pdf
15. "Zanganeh: Secondary Sources Put Iran Crude Output at 4mbd", SHANA (Petro Energy Information Network), 17 October 2016, at http://www.shana.ir/en/newsagency/271098/Zanganeh-Secondary-Sources-Put-Iran-Crude-Output-at-4mbd
16. "'Economic Trends' No. 85, summer 1395 (2016/2017) Released", Central Bank

of Iran, 30 January 2017, at http://www.cbi.ir/showitem/15703.aspx

17. "Iran security body reviewing new IPC oil contracts: Minister", *Reuters*, 9 April 2017, http://www.reuters.com/article/us-iran-energy-contracts-idUSKBN17B09Y
18. See, "Projects", National Iranian Oil Company, at http://www.nioc.ir/portal/home/?generaltext/165305/165402/165360/Projects (Accessed May 15, 2017).
19. "Iran to Sign $80bn Oil Deals in 2 Years", *Iran Business News*, 10 May 2017, at http://www.iran-bn.com/2017/05/10/iran-to-sign-80bn-oil-deals-in-2-years/
20. "The Leader thanks President Rouhani, his administration on successful nuclear talks", The Office of the Supreme Leader, 19 January 2016, at http://www.leader.ir/en/content/14050/Ayatollah-Khamenei-responds-to-President-Rouhani%E2%80%99s-letter-about-the-JCPOA.
21. "The Leader's Remarks in Meeting with People from Various Walks of Life", The Office of the Supreme Leader, 2 August 2016, at http://www.leader.ir/en/speech/16093/The-Leader%E2%80%99s-Remarks-in-Meeting-with-People-from-Various-Walks-of-Life.
22. "Ten-year Extension of Iran Sanctions Violation of JCPOA", The Office of the Supreme Leader, 23 November 2016, at http://www.leader.ir/en/content/16801/The-Leader%E2%80%99s-remarks-in-meeting-with-Basij-forces.
23. "New Year a time for creating more jobs, boosting production", The Office of the Supreme Leader, 20 March 2017, at http://www.leader.ir/en/content/17772/The-Leader%E2%80%99s-message-on-the-Iranian-New-Year
24. "US missile strikes on Syria a strategic mistake", 9 April 2017, at http://www.leader.ir/en/content/17935/Leader%E2%80%99s-remarks-on-the-US-strikes-against-Syria
25. "Notice: Continuation of the National Emergency With Respect to Iran", The White House, Office of the Press Secretary, 13 January 2017, at https://obamawhitehouse.archives.gov/the-press-office/2017/01/13/notice-continuation-national-emergency-respect-iran
26. "Country Reports on Terrorism 2015", US Department of State, at https://www.state.gov/j/ct/rls/crt/2015/index.htm
27. "Report Pursuant to the Comprehensive Iran Sanctions, Accountability, and Divestment Act of 2010 (CISADA), as Amended", US Department of State, 17 May 2017, at https://www.state.gov/e/eb/rls/othr/2017/270917.htm
28. Barak Ravid, "U.S., Israel Sign Historic 10-year, $38-billion Military Aid Deal", *Ha'aretz*, 14 September 2016, at http://www.haaretz.com/israel-news/1.742074
29. Christopher M. Blanchard, "Saudi Arabia: Background and US Relations", Congressional Research Service, 20 September 2016, pp. 33–34 , at https://fas.org/sgp/crs/mideast/RL33533.pdf,
30. Miren Gidda, "US considering more military assistance for Saudi Arabia in Yemen's Civil War", *Newsweek*, 20 April 2017, at http://www.newsweek.com/yemen-civil-war-us-saudi-arabia-airstrikes-houthi-rebels-587018
31. Ibid.
32. Josh Rogin, "Trump resets US-Saudi relations, in Saudi Arabia's favor", *The Washington Post*, 16 March 2017, at https://www.washingtonpost.com/news/josh-rogin/wp/2017/03/16/trump-resets-u-s-saudi-relations-in-saudi-arabias-favor/?utm_term=.ac060c15ddef
33. Martin Chulov, "Saudis eye Iran and ignore Trump's temperament as red carpet rolled out", *The Guardian*, 19 May 2017, at https://www.theguardian.com/world/

2017/may/19/saudi-arabia-trump-visit-us-relations

34. David A. Graham, "Israel and Saudi Arabia: Togetherish at Last?", *The Atlantic*, 5 June 2015, at https://www.theatlantic.com/international/archive/2015/06/israeli-saudi-relations/395015/
35. For an examination, see S. Samuel C. Rajiv, "Deep Disquiet: Israel and the Iran Nuclear Deal", *Contemporary Review of the Middle East*, March 2016, Vol. 3, No. 1, pp. 47–62.
36. See S. Samuel C. Rajiv, "Iran Sanctions and India: Navigating the Roadblocks", *IDSA Monograph Series*, July 2016, No. 52, pp. 56, at http://www.idsa.in/system/files/monograph/monograph52.pdf,
37. "Export Import Data Bank", Ministry of Commerce and Industry, Government of India, at www.commerce.nic.in
38. "Indian refineries owe over $2 bn oil dues to Iran: Dharmendra Pradhan", *Business Standard*, 21 November 2016, at http://www.business-standard.com/article/markets/indian-refineries-owe-over-2-bn-oil-dues-to-iran-dharmendra-pradhan-116112100543_1.html
39. Rahul Kanwal, "Revealed: 'Spy' Kulbhushan Yadav not caught but abducted by extremist Sunni group Jaishul Adil", *India Today*, 30 March 2016, at http://indiatoday.intoday.in/story/india-today-exclusive-extremist-sunni-group-jaishul-adil-kidnapped-indian-businessman/1/631151.html
40. Kallol Bhattacharjee, "Iran's silence on Jadhav baffling", *The Hindu*, 16 April 2017, at http://www.thehindu.com/news/national/irans-silence-on-jadhav-baffling/article18072438.ece
41. Ibid.
42. See S. Samuel C. Rajiv, "Modi's 'Act West' Policy in Motion", *SPMRF*, 15 March 2017, at http://www.spmrf.org/modis-act-west-policy-motion/

Policy Options

MEI Team

1. **Avoid regional entanglement:** India has friendly relations with all countries along the Persian Gulf, and has strategic interests due to energy security as well as the presence of over eight million expatriates. Given the regional complexities, it will have to avoid taking sides and eschew any suggestions of mediation or overt diplomatic outreach in resolving regional issues. The raging civil wars in Iraq opened up new avenues for engagement with the Kurdish regional government in the North, but the situation in Yemen requires distancing from all groups. At the regional level too, it should continue to engage with all sides without antagonizing any of the countries, and without taking sides in the flaring tensions.
2. **Admit regional rivalry for influence**: In recent years, the tensions between Iran and Saudi Arabia for regional influence hegemony—most visibly played out in Bahrain, Yemen, and within the GCC—have increased. While taking sides is not a sensible proposition, the Indian government will have to recognise that its ability to pursue fruitful bilateral relations will not only be compartmentalized but has to be managed skilfully.
3. **Recognise sectarianism**: A significant portion of violence and turmoil in the wider Middle East is the result of sectarianism and the unwillingness of various political groups to compromise on their narrow sectarian agenda. Adopting a contrary position of denial will be unsustainable.
4. **Face the ISIS challenge**: Even though the ISIS menace seems on the verge of collapse, it does not bring an end to the ideological problem of Salafi-jihadism, and the terror that ensues. The Indians attracted

towards the ISIS need to be managed, and even though the number is small, a few dozen radicalized returnees can create havoc in the already complex and fragile domestic communal situation.

5. **Managing the US**: The new Trump Administration has given indications of reviewing the scaled down engagements with the Persian Gulf and the Middle East. India would have to be quick in adapting to the changing circumstances, and avoid moral compass in judging US actions in the region, including in dealing with Iran.
6. **Security Engagement**: Without appearing to be intrusive, India should expand its military and security contacts with the Gulf region. The problems of sea piracy, the protection of sea lanes of communication, and terrorism should motivate India to engage with the Arab countries and Iran in furtherance of its interests.
7. **Strengthen trade**: Except for Bahrain, UAE and Yemen, India has high trade deficits with all the Persian Gulf countries. This imbalance is primarily due to the skewed nature of India's imports in favour oil and gas. In countries like Iraq, Kuwait, Qatar, Saudi Arabia, and Yemen, hydrocarbons account for more than 90 per cent of India's imports. India should capitalize on the diversification plans of countries.
8. **Enhance two-way investments**: Though investments are its prime agenda, the diplomatic outreach has not materialized due to bureaucratic bottlenecks and unattractive opportunities. India will have to ensure that investments are not entangled in domestic political and legal traps through transparency, efficiency, and professionalism.
9. **Abandon the obsession with China and Pakistan**: India needs to recognise and follow the politico-economic engagement and presence of China and Pakistan in the Persian Gulf; but it should avoid looking at the region primarily through these two countries lest its policy becomes reactive and counter-productive.
10. **Promote Persian Gulf studies**: The importance of the Persian Gulf and the wider Middle East is not reflected by the promotion of these areas in the country. While only a handful of institutions have some interest in the Persian Gulf, most think tanks are dominated by their obsession with South Asia. This level of ignorance about a region of considerable importance cannot be sustained for long.
11. **Evolve contingency plans**: Domestic unrest in the region following the outbreak of Arab Spring in 2011 forced India to organise the evacuation of its expatriate community from Egypt, Libya, and Yemen. The number of those brought home from these countries was

significant but manageable. However, the number of Indian workers in other Gulf countries are substantial (often more than half a million), and thus, the government would do well to develop and put in place a contingency plan which could become operational immediately, as and when required.

12. **Arabization of the labour force**: Oil-rich Arab countries are pursuing the indigenization of their workforce. The process has been slow and even uneven; but it poses a long-term threat to India. If India were to continue to send expatriate workers to the region, it would have to impart skills development and make its labour force competitive, regarding both skills and wages.

13. **Use right nomenclature**: There is a welcome trend in government circles to describe the region as the Middle East rather than the archaic West Asia. The Middle East is a term of self-identity for the region, and employing other nomenclature is both a sign of unfamiliarity with regional discourses and a sign of hegemony. One hopes that the same applies to other historical expression—that is, Persian Gulf. Like other geographic terms such as the Arabian Sea, the Indian Ocean, and the South China Sea, the expression 'Persian Gulf' does not denote Iranian ownership of the said waters, and there is no reason for India to settle for a prefix-less 'Gulf' to describe the Persian Gulf.

CONTRIBUTORS

P. R. Kumaraswamy teaches the contemporary Middle East at Jawaharlal Nehru University, New Delhi, and is the Honorary Director, Middle East Institute, New Delhi (www.mei.org.in)

Meena Singh Roy is a Research Fellow at the Institute for Defence Studies and Analyses IDSA), New Delhi.

Alvite Singh Ningthoujam is a Senior Research Associate at the Vivekananda International Foundation, New Delhi, and focuses on Middle Eastern security dynamics, international terrorism, and the Islamic State of Iraq and Syria (ISIS), in particular. His other research areas include Israel's arms exports, Indo-Israeli relations, and Indo-Iranian ties. He also served as a Fellow at the Begin-Sadat (BESA) Centre for Strategic Studies, Bar-Ilan University, Israel, 2010–11.

Dipanwita Chakravortty is a doctoral candidate at the Centre of West Asian Studies, Jawaharlal Nehru University, New Delhi. Her thesis is on "The Gender Debates in the Israel Defence Forces." She is a recipient of the Israeli Government Scholarship 2015–16 under which she was associated with the Ben-Gurion University as a Research Fellow in the Conflict Management and Resolution Program. She has written various articles/essays on India-Yemen relations, the conflict in Yemen, and Elections in the Middle East.

Divya Malhotra is a doctoral candidate at the Centre of West Asian Studies, School of International Studies, Jawaharlal Nehru University, New Delhi.

Hirak Jyoti Das is a doctoral candidate at the Centre of West Asian Studies, School of International Studies, Jawaharlal Nehru University, New Delhi.

Jatin Kumar is Research Assistant, Institute for Defence Studies and Analyses (IDSA), New Delhi, and is a doctoral candidate at the Centre of

West Asian Studies, School of International Studies, Jawaharlal Nehru University, New Delhi.

Manjari Singh is a SYLLF Fellow and a doctoral candidate at the Centre of West Asian Studies, School of International Studies, Jawaharlal Nehru University, New Delhi.

Md. Muddassir Quamar is Associate Fellow, Institute for Defence Studies and Analyses (IDSA), New Delhi.

Poonam Khatana is a doctoral candidate at Centre for West Asian Studies, School of International Studies, Jawaharlal Nehru University, New Delhi. Her thesis focuses on the economic and political implications of Syrian refugees in Lebanon.

Prasanta Kumar Pradhan is an Associate Fellow, Institute for Defence Studies and Analyses (IDSA), New Delhi.

Premanand Mishra is a doctoral candidate at the Centre for West Asian Studies, School of International Studies, Jawaharlal Nehru University, New Delhi. He has MA and M. Phil. Degrees from SIS, JNU. He has participated in many national and international conferences, and has previously worked as a journalist. His interest area is discourses on Islam.

Priyanka Mittal is a doctoral candidate at the Centre of West Asian Studies, School of International Studies, Jawaharlal Nehru University, New Delhi.

S. Samuel C. Rajiv is an Associate Fellow, Institute for Defence Studies and Analyses (IDSA), New Delhi and is concurrently pursuing his Ph.D. degree at Centre for West Asian Studies, School of International Studies, Jawaharlal Nehru University, New Delhi. His recent publications include monographs titled *Iran Sanctions and India: Navigating the Consequences* (IDSA, July 2016) and *Indian Responses to Israel's Gaza Operations* (BESA Centre, May 2016).

Swati Arun is a Research Assistant, Institute for Defence Studies and Analysis (IDSA), and doctoral candidate in the Centre for East Asian Studies, School of International Studies, Jawaharlal Nehru University. Prior to this, she worked with the Centre for Air Power Studies (CAPS). Her research interests include China-US relations, China's Foreign Policy, East Asian security, and international politics and strategy.

INDEX